STARVING FOR JUSTICE

RALPH ARMBRUSTER-SANDOVAL

STARVING FOR JUSTICE

*Hunger Strikes, Spectacular Speech, and
the Struggle for Dignity*

THE UNIVERSITY OF
ARIZONA PRESS
TUCSON

The University of Arizona Press
www.uapress.arizona.edu

ISBN-13: 978-0-8165-3258-2 (cloth)
ISBN-13: 978-0-8165-3793-8 (paper)

Cover design by Lori Lieber
Cover photograph: El Congreso de UCSB 1994 hunger strike, Naomi García and Edwin Lopez representing all hunger strikers collectively and their immediate demands for justice to a packed audience of children, parents, community members, media, allies, and onlookers from near and far, Campbell Hall, UC Santa Barbara, May 1994. Photo by Lisa Valencia Sherratt, El Congreso de UCSB alumnus and former historian.

Publication of this book is made possible in part by the proceeds of a permanent endowment created with the assistance of a Challenge Grant from the National Endowment for the Humanities, a federal agency.

Library of Congress Cataloging-in-Publication Data
Names: Armbruster-Sandoval, Ralph, 1968– author.
Title: Starving for justice : hunger strikes, spectacular speech, and the struggle for dignity / Ralph Armbruster-Sandoval.
Description: Tucson : The University of Arizona Press, 2017. | Includes bibliographical references and index.
Identifiers: LCCN 2016039010 | ISBN 9780816532582 (cloth : alk. paper)
Subjects: LCSH: Hunger strikes—California. | Student protesters—California. | Hispanic American college students—California. | University of California, Los Angeles—Student strike, 1993. | University of California, Santa Barbara—Student strike, 1994. | Stanford University—Student strike, 1994.
Classification: LCC HN79.C23 H8425 2017 | DDC 303.6/1—dc23 LC record available at https://lccn.loc.gov/2016039010

Printed in the United States of America
♾ This paper meets the requirements of ANSI/NISO Z39.48-1992 (Permanence of Paper).

Por El Congreso de UCSB y toda gente que está trabajando por un mundo justo, un mundo sin dolor, hambre, y pobreza.

To El Congreso de UCSB and all people working for a more just world, a world without pain, hunger, and poverty.

CONTENTS

ILLUSTRATIONS

ACKNOWLEDGMENTS

SOMETIMES THINGS TAKE LONGER THAN EXPECTED. Several months before I started working in the Chicana and Chicano Studies Department at the University of California, Santa Barbara (UCSB), some Chicana/o, Latina/o students asked me about the 1994 hunger strike on that campus. The interview took place inside El Centro Arnulfo Casillas, a historic "counter-space" that once housed the Chicano Studies Department, the Center for Chicano Studies, El Congreso, the Chicano Educational Opportunity Program (EOP), and the Colección Tloque Nahuaque. I remembered saying rather sheepishly that I didn't know too much about it. It was 1998 and I had spent the past five years exploring sweatshops and transnational labor-organizing campaigns that involved Central American and U.S. unions and nongovernment organizations. Despite my scholar-activist credentials, I felt embarrassed because the UCSB hunger strike—along with hunger strikes at the University of California, Los Angeles (UCLA); Stanford; UC Irvine; and the University of Boulder, Colorado—shattered the prevailing "post-racial" discourse that emerged after the social movements of the 1960s. In 1994, Rage Against the Machine released a powerful song called "Year of the Boomerang," based partially on Frantz Fanon's *Wretched of the Earth* (1961), a book that foresaw imperialism sowing the seeds of its own destruction. With Reagan and Bush pushing reactionary policies that undermined gains that people of color, women, queer people, and workers made in the 1960s and 1970s, a

Fanonian popular uprising emerged both here and abroad as the Zapatista National Liberation Army came out into the open on January 1, 1994, the very same day that the North American Free Trade Agreement (NAFTA) went into effect. This was the same year that Democratic president Bill Clinton introduced the draconian Operation Gatekeeper and California Republican governor Pete Wilson embraced what was initially called the Save Our State (SOS) ballot measure, which later became known as Proposition 187.

The 1980s and 1990s were not pleasant. In 1984, Time Zone, a short-lived musical group that paired hip-hop artist Afrika Bambaataa and punk rock star John Lydon (from the Sex Pistols), released their most popular single, titled "World Destruction." With Bambaataa repeatedly saying "speak about destruction" and Lydon sneering "the rich get richer, the poor are getting poorer," Time Zone clearly outlined neoliberalism's bankrupt promises. The military-industrial complex, the prison-industrial complex, racial and class polarization, and environmental degradation all presaged the band's apocalyptic message.

Because the "end times" were quite near, Bambaataa and Lydon urged and begged their listeners to "speak about destruction." In Chiapas, the "wretched of the earth" fought back with guns, while those on university campuses fought back with their bodies. In both cases, people spoke about destruction in the most spectacular fashion possible, making the invisible (injustice) visible. Through self-sacrifice and starvation, Chicana/o and Latina/o students partially transformed people's "hearts of stone" into "hearts of flesh," prompting them to support their demands for social change. While they didn't fully achieve all their demands, they did create long-lasting reforms, making their campuses more dignified and just.

The Chicana/o and Latina/o students that interviewed me back in 1998 were proudly affiliated with El Congreso, a militant social justice organization that emerged in the mid-1970s. Many Chicana/o and Latina/o students joined in the early 1990s because they were morally outraged about budget cuts, fee increases, exorbitant salaries for top UCSB officials, anti-immigrant politics, toxic pesticides that poisoned farm workers, deportations, a fragmented and weak Chicano Studies Department, and much, much more. Having exhausted all other options, they stopped eating for nine days. When the strike ended, UCSB's administrative leaders buckled, backing demands for more Chicano studies faculty. Had these students not taken such significant risks, I simply would not have been hired. Seen from this perspective, I felt obligated and compelled to document the 1994 UCSB hunger strike and other similar actions at UCLA and Stanford University. This book is the first one that has ever been published on these three strikes, but it certainly won't be the last. Future scholars will most certainly explore these actions from unique theoretical approaches and develop rapport with different participants. While I spoke with many people on all three campuses, some politely declined to be interviewed for this study.

Thankfully, most students and faculty were eager to share their stories and experiences. Naomi García and Edwin López, for example, spent countless hours with me, talking not only about the 1994 UCSB hunger strike but also the context and climate that sparked that action. Rodolfo Acuña, Salvador Barajas, J. Manuel Casas, Gladys de Necochea, Dick Flacks, Alma Flores, Marío T. García, Geoff Green, Abel Gutiérrez, Gabriel Gutiérrez, Tino Gutiérrez, Francisco Lomelí, Marisela Márquez, Mike Muñoz, Denise Segura, Benjamin Torres, Lisa Valencia Sherratt, André Vásquez, Michael Young, and Don Zimmerman also spoke with me about the UCSB hunger strike. Alma Flores, Naomi García, and Edwin López, moreover, shared with me their personal archives, which contained invaluable memos, newspaper articles, flyers, and other crucial materials. Lisa Valencia Sherratt also generously shared with me her collection of hunger strike photos. The pictures of second-year student and El Congreso member during the hunger strike, Valencia Sherratt, particularly the one on this book's front cover of Naomi García and Edwin López in wheelchairs, captured the spirit and sacrifices of *all* the students who were involved in the nine-day action. Lisa kindly donated these photos to the California Ethnic and Multicultural Archives, which is housed in the UCSB Library's Special Collections Department. Many thanks to long-time CEMA Director Salvador Guereña and CEMA Archival Processing Specialist Mari Khasmanyan for digitizing and scanning the pictures on the UCSB hunger strike for publication. I would especially like to thank Harold Salas-Kennedy, Pete Villareal, Ozzie Espinoza, Yolanda García, Lupe Navarro-García, and Yolanda Márquez for their tremendous assistance on this project. I have relied heavily on them over the years for insights about Chicano EOP and the wider Santa Barbara community.

Like Naomi García and Edwin López, Milo Alvarez was an absolutely critical voice for understanding the 1993 UCLA hunger strike. Alvarez spoke with me for hours, patiently answering multiple questions for clarification and expansion over email. He provided a substantive, clear-cut historical analysis of the unique moment that existed in the late 1980s and early 1990s that helped spark the UCLA hunger strike. Alvarez helped me see that the hunger strike was really the culmination of a three-year battle to create an independent Chicano Studies Department that really began in the late 1960s. I feel extremely fortunate that Santiago Bernal, Richard Chabrán, Bonnie Chávez, Leobardo Estrada, John Fernández, Blanca Gordo, Juan José Gutiérrez, Tom Hayden, Evelyn Hu-Dehart, Scott Kurashige, Reynaldo Macías, Jorge Mancíllas, Jackie Mendoza, Claudia Mitchell-Kernan, Cindy Montañez, Joaquín Ochoa, Vilma Ortiz, Raymond Paredes, Horacio Roque Ramírez, Andrea Rich, Daniel Solórzano, Ali Tabrizi, Michelle Téllez, Abel Valenzuela, Scott Waugh, and Charles Young all shared with me their reflections and memories about the UCLA hunger strike. I would be remiss if I didn't recognize and praise UCLA Chicano Studies Resource Center librarian Lizette Guerra. Having come across the CSRC's extensive holdings on the 1993 hunger strike, I was thrilled but overwhelmed given the university's expensive copying fees. Seeing how critical these documents, papers, and archival materials were, Guerra provided me with a healthy discount. Without this considerate gesture, this study may not have been completed. I should also thank *Los Angeles Times* archivist Ralph Drew for locating the May 12, 1993, Faculty Center photo of Michelle Téllez and the March 10, 1968, photo of César Chávez breaking his twenty-five day fast with Senator Robert F. Kennedy. Thanks, too, to Axel Koester for granting permission to use his photo of Rosa and Jorge Mancíllas and to the UCLA *Daily Bruin* for Cindy Montañez's photo.

I knew very little about the Stanford hunger strike until I spoke with Naomi García, who told me, "You should interview my childhood friend, Eva Silva. You know she was one of the hunger strikers and they were all women." Following her lead, I interviewed Silva several times in Salinas, where she and García grew up. Eva gently walked me through the historical background that helped spark this three-day strike, including Cecilia Burciaga's firing and inappropriate laughter during a showing of a short video documenting the effect of dangerous pesticides on farm workers. Having been inspired by César Chávez as a youngster, Silva stated that what he called for was "common sense," just as what she and her fellow Chicana hunger strikers were calling for constituted common sense, too. After speaking with Silva, I interviewed Stanford Chicana hunger striker Elvira Prieto, who shared with me a powerful unpublished paper she wrote about the strike while she was pursuing her master's degree at

Harvard University in the late 1990s. I finally talked with the other two hunger strikers, Tamara Alvarado and Julia González Luna, who spoke passionately about how their concerns went beyond creating a Chicano Studies Department. While they cared passionately about Chicano Studies, Alvarado and González Luna felt strongly that they could have achieved more; that is, had the strike not ended after three days, they might have been more successful in obtaining dignity for farm workers, Latinas/os living in East Palo Alto, and others struggling for a better life. These reflections, especially from González Luna, helped me better understand what all three hunger strikes were about—not Chicana/o studies per se, but dignity for all people struggling to be free. I am extremely thankful that not only did Alvarado, González Luna, Prieto, and Silva speak with me but so too did Cecilia Burciaga, Alberto Camarillo, Gerhard Casper, Luisa Fraga, Chris González Clarke, Gina Hernández Clarke, Jonathan Inda, Michael Jackson, James Leckie, Alma Medina, Miguel Mendoza, Ramón Saldívar, and Judy Tzu-Chun Wu. Condoleezza Rice, unfortunately, did not respond to numerous requests to be interviewed for this study. Finally, I am grateful for *Stanford Daily* Chief Operating Officer Kevin Zhang for scanning and preparing for publication several photos from the 1994 hunger strike. Thanks, too, to the *San Jose Mercury News* for granting permission to use Cecilia Burciaga's photo taken during the strike's first day.

Besides acknowledging the many students, faculty, and staff who generously talked with me about these hunger strikes, I would like to thank various people who read and made suggestions and criticisms of this manuscript—Ana Barba, Rosie Bermudez, Edna Bonacich, Alfredo Carlos, Dick Flacks, Diane Fujino, Erick Iniguez, and George Lipstiz. All errors, of course, are mine. Edna's contributions are especially noteworthy. Since graduating from UC Riverside in 1998, she has always provided me with substantive and speedy feedback, even though she is no longer my dissertation adviser. She is a true friend, mentor, comrade, and colleague. Thank you, Edna, for all your love and support for more than twenty years now.

As the narrative above indicates, many Congresistas are responsible for making sure this history was documented and recorded. I would like to thank Lucha Arevalo, Alfredo Carlos, Nicholas Centino, Paulina Cortez, Carmen Cuevas, Ana Rosa Rizo-Centino, John Delgado, Francisco Fuentes, Gisela Gaona, Andrea Garavito-Martínez, Adriana Gómez, Rigo Gutiérrez, Denise Jaramillo, Jessica Lozano, Alejandra Luna, Soralla Marquez, Elizabeth Montaño, Norma Orozco, Angela Portillo, Fernando Ramírez, Eduardo Ruiz, Gloria Sánchez,

Lorena Santos, Kathy Serrano, Saul Serrano, Veronica Serrano, Miguel Solis, Darcy Tilipapalotl, César Tinoco, Esther Trujillo, Veronica Valadez, Jennifer Viveros, and Eddie Zamora. I know that I have left out so many names here. Please forgive me for not providing a more exhaustive list. Over the years, I have been incredibly blessed to have known thousands of students, many of whom were politically active in many different organizations besides El Congreso here at UCSB. I must mention here Nayra Pacheco, Rosio Almaguer, Sophia Armen, Marisa Salinas, Sandy Escobedo, Melissa Vasquez, Charlene Wambui Macharia, Cervin Morris, Liz González, Desaray Rivas, Ariana Andrade, Abigail Salazar Rodríguez, Danielle Stevens, Dana Patterson, Jacqueline Partida, Lynn Becerra, Paola Villegas, Aurea Martínez, Jeffrey Chipix, Azucena Gutiérrez, Gloria Campos, Felipe Rodríguez Flores, Jenny Vasquez, Cindy Mata, Nicholas Pascal, Jorge Rosas, Theresa Christenson, Alex Razo, Ismael Huerta, Mario Galicia, Clarissa Kusel, Carol Barahona, Marícela Morales, Erika Matadamas, Nancy Alvarado, Vanessa Terán, Vanessa Tejada, Cecilia Castro, Emil Marmol, Jaret Ornelas, Tania Saenz, Rita Durate, Saul Zevada, Angelica Quirarte, Francisco Jasso, Juan Osuna, Lupe Hernández, Sal Soto, Alejandra Melgoza, and Rosalinda García.

I want to also extend warm appreciation to Kristen Buckles and all the staff at the University of Arizona Press for embracing this project with such enthusiasm and goodwill. I never imagined that my work would be supported like it has been, and I am forever grateful for the rigorous, critical, and positive feedback that I received from two anonymous reviewers. Thank you, Kristen, for your patience and walking me through the entire manuscript-submission process and for making excellent suggestions along the way.

Finally, I want to thank my family for all their love and constant support over the years. When my last book was published, Meg and I knew our family was going to get a little bit bigger. Sol Justicia was born in 2005 and Sky was born in 2007. Thank you, Sol and Sky, for your love, kindness, silliness, and willingness and patience while I finished writing this book. I have been away far too many weekends working on it. I'm truly sorry that I have missed out on so many things. I love you both more than you know. Thank you, Meg, for everything. We have been together since high school. You have seen and heard it all and yet you still stay with me. I read you both books and you provided excellent suggestions, especially about nutrition and fasting. All proceeds are yours, love. Thanks Mom, Dad, and Stephanie for your constant support and encouragement, and the same goes to Roberta and Michael. Julie and Barry Beard, my in-laws, always provided cookies, berry pie, and love. We sure do miss them, as we do Nicholas José Armbruster. I wish they were all here for the party we will have when the book is released. Thank you also to James, Sunshine, Tyler, Rick, Megan, Jeanna, Jasmine, Kylie, Braxton, Kenny, Scotty, Cindy, Jase, Penelope, and to all the Beard, Armbruster, and Sandoval families. And thank you to Radhule, Gary, Mark, John, Carren, and Stewart for helping me get across troubled waters. It's finally done—let's celebrate and go out and change the world. Sending you all *abrazos* and much, much love!

STARVING FOR JUSTICE

1

STARVING FOR JUSTICE

Hunger Strikes, Spectacular Speech, and the Struggle for Dignity

Hunger strikers believe that the voice of hunger has a power disproportion- ate to its source. Hunger can strengthen the weak, inspire the timid, bully the powerful. The voice of hunger can free the oppressed and right injustice. It can alter history. . . . Hunger strikes are about changing the world and shaming the world. Hunger strikers strip down to nothing and transform their nakedness. Their helplessness is their offering. Their show of weakness is their strength.
SHARMAN APT RUSSELL (2005)

What are words for when no one listens anymore?
What are words for when no one listens it's no use talking at all.
Do you hear me?
Do you care?
MISSING PERSONS, "WORDS" (1982)

INTRODUCTION

HIGH-RISK ACTIVISTS—PEOPLE who put their lives on the line nonvi- olently to create positive social change—have long intrigued scholars and the general public alike (Loveman 1998; McAdam 1986; Nepstad and Smith 1999; Taylor and Raeburn 1995). What sparks one to start moving— to actively oppose segregation, slavery, sweatshops, climate change, domes- tic violence, deportations, war, poverty, hunger, and so on? Having taken these initial steps, what prompts someone to take ever-increasing risks, mov- ing from innocuously signing online petitions and clicking "like" on Face- book to putting "one's body upon the gears and upon the wheels, upon the levers, upon all the apparatus," as University of California (UC), Berkeley, Free Speech Movement leader Mario Savio memorably stated fifty years ago

(Cohen 2009)?[1] What might lead a person to sacrifice their life, going days or even weeks without food, as many hunger strikers have done, or even light their bodies on fire with gasoline (Biggs 2005, 2013; Fierke 2013; Morrison Welsh 2008; Russell 2005; C. Ryan 1994; Scanlan, Stoll, and Lumm 2008)?

These questions lie at the heart of this book. In the late 1980s, I became increasingly politicized and radicalized through the Central American solidarity and sanctuary movements (Bibler-Coutin 1993; Chinchilla, Hamilton, and Loucky 2009; L. Churchill 2009; Nepstad 2004; Peace 2012; Perla Jr. 2008, 2009; C. Smith 1996; C. Weber 2006).[2] While attending classes as an undergraduate student at California State University (CSU), Long Beach, I worked with El Rescate, a nonprofit organization based in downtown Los Angeles that provided Salvadoran immigrants with legal counseling and other forms of assistance, as an unpaid intern documenting human rights abuses.[3] The Salvadoran civil war had been going on for nearly a decade; tens of thousands of people, including Archbishop Óscar Romero, had been killed.[4] The day before he was assassinated, Romero courageously stated, "I would like to make a special appeal to the men of the army. . . . No soldier is obliged to obey an order contrary to the law of God. . . . I implore you, I beg you, I order you in the name of God, stop the repression" (Brockman 2005: 241–42; Wright 2009: 130). His spectacular speech—his *hunger for justice*—inspired and infuriated many. The very next day, while celebrating Mass, he was shot and later died. The United Nations Truth Commission (1993) discovered that Salvadoran military officials were responsible for his death and the vast majority of those who were killed during the civil war.[5]

On December 2, 1980, nine months after Romero's assassination, four U.S. churchwomen—Jean Donovan, Dorothy Kazel, Maura Clarke, and Ita Ford—were all raped and killed in El Salvador (Carrigan 2005; Evans 2005; Noone 1995). One year later, more than nine hundred people, mostly women and children, were massacred in El Mozote, a small, largely evangelical Christian community that mostly supported the military government (Binford 1996; Danner 1993). Nearly eight years later, six Jesuit priests, their housekeeper, and her daughter were assassinated in San Salvador on the grounds of the University of Central America (UCA), a private, Catholic-based institution that favored nonviolent social transformation (Cerna and Ignoffo 2014; Lassalle-Klein 2014; Sobrino 1990, 2003; Whitfield 1994).

In *Convictions of the Soul: Religion, Culture, and Agency in the Central American Solidarity Movement*, sociologist Sharon Erickson Nepstad (2004) examines how these deaths and many more less-publicized ones generated tremendous moral outrage, especially among progressive Christians and Catholics in the United States. What made them even more horrifying was the shocking discovery that the Salvadoran military officers responsible for killing Romero, the churchwomen, the El Mozote villagers, and the Jesuits and their two female assistants were *all* trained at the United States Army School of the Americas (SOA) (Gill 2004).

Currently known as the Western Hemisphere Institute for Security Cooperation (WHINSEC), located at Fort Benning, Georgia, the SOA was initially based in Panama.[6] It was established in 1946 to maintain long-standing U.S. hegemony in Latin America (Galeano 1997; Gill 2004; LaFeber 1993). After the Cuban Revolution in 1959, the United States stepped up its efforts to contain "communism" by training more soldiers from Latin American countries at the SOA (LaFeber 1993). These officials included Roberto D'Aubuisson, the intellectual author who planned Archbishop Romero's assassination, and Domingo Monterrosa Barrios, the military commander who carried out the El Mozote massacre (Gill 2004; Hodge and Cooper 2004; Nelson-Pallmeyer 2001). Besides these two officials, SOA-trained Latin American soldiers from the *entire* hemisphere were implicated in military coups, massacres, and human rights violations throughout the entire Cold War period (1945–90) and beyond (1990–present) (Gill 2004).

Given the "school's" less-than-stellar reputation, it engendered tremendous controversy, with activists associated with School of the Americas Watch (SOAW) demanding its closure every November (timed to coincide with the 1989 UCA massacre). Starting with just nine people who went on a thirty-five-day water-only fast outside Fort Benning's gates starting in September 1990, the movement rapidly expanded over the next decade, including nearly 20,000 people in the early 2000s (Gill 2004).[7] The actual protest begins with a single name (for example, Óscar Romero) and a collective response, "*Presente!*" Reading so many names takes hours. During that time, some activists commit civil disobedience, climbing over or under the barbed-wire fence into Fort Benning. Within the movement, this high-risk activity is known as "crossing the line"; before the terrorist attacks in the United States on September 11, 2001, thousands freely walked over the painted yellow line, as the penalties were far less severe back then (many who trespassed were issued a simple citation and released shortly thereafter). However, after 9/11, Fort Benning became even more militarized; additional barriers were erected that made crossing the line nearly impossible, but some succeeded and typically received a six-month jail sentence and $5,000 fine (Koopman 2008a, 2008b; Riegle 2013).[8]

In 2005, I traveled to Fort Benning with eight students from a class I was teaching on globalization, sweatshops, and transnational labor organizing. During the course, we read Mark Danner's *Massacre at El Mozote* (1993), and many were stunned and horrified, particularly when they discovered how the sole survivor, Rufina Amaya, hid among the bushes while her children were butchered in December 1981 (75–76). When they heard that the massacre could be traced back to the SOA, the students mobilized, planting crosses all over campus, passing out flyers and fact sheets about the SOA, and reenacting the actual events, with one student dramatically reading Amaya's gripping testimony. Still hungry for justice, a smaller subset went to Georgia to participate in the annual demonstration to shut down the SOA. During the funeral procession, when the names were being recited, we saw an elderly, blind white man approach the barbed-wire fence. Two people were holding his arms as he walked. He seemed resolute, like nobody could turn him around.[9] I watched him carefully and then helped lift the fence, and he crawled under.[10] I thought for a moment, "here's your chance, cross over," but I looked at my students' faces and wondered what they might do. Would they follow me? I thought about my immediate family, including my wife and five-month-old daughter, our house, and my job as a Chicana/o studies professor at UC Santa Barbara, and slowly backed away. I felt angry and ashamed for not crossing the *actual* line, but recognized that we had crossed many *other* lines—overcoming our fears and momentarily setting aside personal challenges and circumstances. We didn't change the world that day (the SOA is still open), but *we* changed.[11]

The anti-SOA movement transformed and sustained me for many years. Like many other global-justice-movement protests in the 1990s and 2000s, the annual protest in Fort Benning included numerous workshops and films on Latin American politics, music, nonviolent direct action, faith, and spirituality.[12] Those spaces were just as invigorating and life-changing as the actual demonstration itself. I especially found an alternative Mass, with inclusive liturgy and inspiring music, presided over by a Roman Catholic woman priest deeply moving because I favored women's ordination and "open-table worship" where *all* are truly welcome (Bourgeois 2013; Raab 2000; Spellers 2006).[13] During the Mass, I realized that the anti-SOA movement, like the Central American solidarity and sanctuary movements, had been strongly influenced by a progressive, even radical, version of Christianity that has deep roots among African

Americans and Latinas/os throughout the Americas (Aquino 1993; Berryman 1987; R. Brown 1984; Coleman 2008; Cone 2011; Gutiérrez 1988; Isasi-Diaz 1996; West 1982).[14] I found this Christianity, often called "liberation theology," refreshing and affirming. I always knew that Jesus was a troublemaker who not only spoke about "feeding the hungry and clothing the naked," he actually did those things, expanding his base of followers and upsetting the Roman Empire, which ultimately oversaw his torture and execution (Crossan 2008, 2009). Having fasted for forty days, Jesus also rejected fortune, fame, and power. He embraced a more simple, austere, but still joyful lifestyle and worked to create a world "turned upside down," a world where the "last will be first and the first will be last" (Matthew 20:16).[15] Despite great risk, Jesus pressed on (sometimes reluctantly), sacrificing himself with the hope that his life and death might inspire others to go and "do likewise," as he suggested in the parable of the Good Samaritan.[16]

In following Jesus and many other high-risk activists (Óscar Romero, Martin Luther King, Rigoberta Menchú, among others), some might ask themselves, "How far should *I* go? Should I go far as these people did? Should I cross the line and get arrested? Should I stop eating? Should I put my life on the line, despite having children and a 'good' life?"[17] In our political culture, citizens can make their voices heard by writing to their elected officials or daily newspaper. Beyond these traditional tactics, people can post their concerns on many different social media websites, such as Facebook and Twitter. These low-risk actions have produced positive but limited results, raising a haunting question that Quaker peace activist Norman Morrison asked his wife, Anne, shortly before he immolated himself to protest the Vietnam War in November 1965, "What can we do that we haven't done" (Morrison Welsh 2008: 4).[18]

That's the question many California college students from all racial backgrounds on public and private university campuses found themselves asking in the late 1980s and early 1990s. Faced with a prolonged and painful economic recession, hostile anti-immigrant legislation, racial scapegoating, budget cuts, rising fees and tuition, sweatshop labor, and the rapid expansion of the military- and prison-industrial complexes, among other things, they resisted, organizing teach-ins, sit-ins, rallies, protests, demonstrations, and makeshift "shanty-towns" (Ervin 2011; Featherstone 2002; E. Martínez 1998; Mora 2007; Phillips 1990; Rhoads 1998; Soule 1997). Despite these efforts, the neoliberalization of the public and private university and the concomitant evisceration of the middle class continued (Newfield 2008).[19] Given this situation, some University of

California, Los Angeles (UCLA), UC Santa Barbara (UCSB), and Stanford University Chicana/o and Latina/o students took even bolder and more dramatic measures, going on hunger strikes in 1993 and 1994. Hunger strikes also took place at the University of Colorado, Boulder; UC Irvine; and UC Berkeley in the 1990s.[20]

With the exception of the UCLA hunger strike, these high-risk, nonviolent actions have escaped scholarly attention.[21] This study seeks to fill this gap by rigorously examining the hunger strikes that took place at UCLA, UCSB, and Stanford in the 1990s. Two key questions guide this work—what prompted these students to go on hunger strike, risking their physical and academic well-being, and were they effective?[22] As will be demonstrated later, I contend that they, and their allies and supporters, sacrificed their lives hoping that their actions might create a more dignified university, state, nation, and world.[23] Dignity is a contested, elusive, and slippery concept. Following John Holloway (1998: 184–85), I claim that those who press for dignity typically have revolutionary aspirations, although they often make practical demands as they did in these three hunger strikes, calling for, among other things, the establishment or expansion of Chicana/o studies departments.

Indeed, the students that went on hunger strikes at UCLA, UCSB, and Stanford all made this particular demand in various forms, but their concerns extended *beyond* such issues. Chicana/o studies was critical, but so were obtaining better wages and working conditions for farm workers; creating safe spaces where students and low-income immigrant families could organize and mobilize to stop budget cuts, deportations, and unscrupulous landlords; lowering student fees; and establishing a more diverse student body and faculty. Inspired by diverse figures such as Antonia Castañeda, Rudolfo Acuña, Cecilia Burciaga, Chela Sandoval, and Subcomandante Marcos, as well as their own grandparents, parents, siblings, friends, and partners, these students had had enough.[24] They had been humiliated and rendered invisible, and they demanded not what Canadian philosopher Charles Taylor (1994) called "recognition," but *justice*—a "world where many worlds fit," as Marcos and the Zapatistas famously put it.[25]

These university-based movements and hunger strikes were imperfect and contained many internal contradictions, as will be seen; nevertheless, they partially succeeded. They helped make their respective campuses more dignified (for example, creating and strengthening Chicana/o studies departments and expanding student and faculty diversity), but maintaining and expanding that dignity has been challenging as budget cuts, apathy, fear, and internal conflicts have limited further progress. As Holloway (1998: 168) has argued, dignity can never be fully achieved in a (capitalist) society that is based on the denial of dignity.[26] Dignity, therefore, is impermanent; it must be constantly struggled for through sacrificial, "spectacular" actions like these three hunger strikes that embody "the scream," which can often mobilize or arouse people (Holloway 2010: 1–10). As Indian revolutionary activist Bhagat Singh said, "It takes a loud voice to make the deaf hear" (Noorani 2001: 30).

In subsequent chapters, I narrate and fully analyze the UCLA, UCSB, and Stanford hunger strikes, but before doing so, I start with a historical and theoretical overview of the tactic, focusing on its geographical, gendered, spiritual, and temporal origins and framing it conceptually as a form of "spectacular speech." Having done that, I examine in the following chapter the social and political context that sparked these three hunger strikes. A complex mix of global, national, state, campus, and personal processes are crucial for understanding why these actions took place. While chapter 2 focuses on the macro, sociopolitical environment, chapters 3 through 5 emphasize the more micro, or local factors that shaped and influenced these protests. The final chapter briefly explores the University of Colorado, Boulder; UC Irvine; and UC Berkeley hunger strikes and offers some reflections on the struggle for dignity in an increasingly undignified world—a world where fewer and fewer people fit.

HUNGER STRIKES:
A LONG BUT BRIEF HIS/HERSTORY

Genealogical narratives are often inherently problematic because they invariably reflect the storyteller's subject-position. When examining the history of hunger strikes, the names that typically appear are men. Mohandas Gandhi, César Chávez, Bobby Sands, and Nelson Mandela are perhaps the most iconic and well-known hunger strikers. Even Jesus and Moses were famous men who fasted. White women and women of color are rarely mentioned despite the fact that Irish, English, and American women suffragists like Hanna Sheehy-Skeffington, Emmeline Pankhurst, Alice Paul, and Dorothy Day, among others, went on hunger strikes to obtain "votes for women" in the early 1900s.[27] In her seminal text, *Chicana Power: Contested Histories of Feminism in the Chicano Movement*, Maylei Blackwell (2011: 28–30) contends that most (male) social movement scholars have consciously or unconsciously reinforced specific biases (namely sexism) in how they have periodized these movements. Until recently, for example, most Chicano Movement texts (books, articles, films, etc.) claimed that Chicana feminism(s) emerged *after* 1975, when the movement supposedly declined or disappeared.[28] Such framing makes it seem as if challenging sexism was not integral to the Chicano Movement, when in fact it was (A. García 1997). Calling themselves Hijas de Cuauhtémoc after a similarly named Mexican revolutionary feminist organization that was established in the early 1900s, Chicana college students at California State University, Long Beach confronted racism *and* sexism in the late 1960s (Blackwell 2011: 100–109). Many other Chicana organizations were also established during that era, continuing their efforts into the 1970s and beyond (Blackwell 2011). Moreover, the Chicano Movement was also focused on class and labor issues, but union organizing campaigns did not start with the United Farm Workers (UFW) in 1965; they harken back to the 1930s (if not earlier), as historians such as Ernesto Galarza (1964), Vicki Ruiz (1998), Zaragosa Vargas (2005), Devra Weber (1994), Tomás Almaguer (1984), and Carey McWilliams (1939) have shown.

Following Jacquelyn Dowd Hall (2005), Blackwell and these latter scholars have shown that the Chicana/o Movement was "long" rather than "short." Temporally defined movement narratives can be quite useful, but they often obfuscate more than enlighten. Taking a "long" social movement perspective enables one to see that movements often have multiple goals (such as challenging racial, gender, and class inequality) and multiple actors (namely, women, as well as queer people, another oft-overlooked group in most movement narratives).[29] Movements are also geographically based, sparking unique dynamics and concerns across space, further complicating facile assertions about their scope and meaning. Despite these complexities and nuances, most social movement researchers have reinforced what Blackwell (2011: 28–30) calls the "great man narrative," creating the mistaken impression that time "began" and "ended," for example, with Chávez, King, and Gandhi. Gandhi was not the first hunger striker, as some might assume given his revered stature. Such accounts erase women's agency and underline Blackwell's (2011: 1–13) important assertion, "the telling is political."

To better understand the gendered and historical "origins" of the hunger strike, it is critical to reflect on how attitudes toward hunger shifted in early-twentieth-century England (Vernon 2007). Whereas before the twentieth century, people that died from starvation, hunger, and malnutrition were blamed for their own fate, that social Darwinist position became increasingly untenable after the devastating famines that left millions dead in Ireland and India (both British colonies) in the middle and late nineteenth centuries (Ó Gráda 2009; Vernon 2007). Along with hunger and famine overseas, many British soldiers came home after serving in the Boer War in South Africa in the early 1900s without sufficient resources for food. To raise public awareness about their plight, they organized hunger marches, much like U.S. World War I veterans did in Washington, DC, during the Great Depression in the 1930s (Vernon 2007). Shortly thereafter, British women also relied on nonviolent direct action, organizing hunger strikes to obtain voting rights as part of the militant suffragist movement (Grant 2006, 2011; Mayhall 2003).

"Hunger communicates," as Russell (2005: 73) has argued. Famine, hunger marches, and hunger strikes conveyed a clear message—the British government was brutish and unforgiving. Whereas previously, mass society might have believed that hunger and famine were natural outcomes, such logic imploded as hunger permeated the British Empire (internally and externally) in the early 1900s. Rather than condemn the hungry, more and more people turned their focus and ire toward an imperialist, antidemocratic, and cold-hearted state that generated widespread hunger, misery, and suffering inside and outside its national borders.

While social and economic deprivation explains why *hunger* emerged as a form of "political critique" in early-twentieth-century England, why did British women embrace hunger strikes as their proverbial "weapon of the weak" (Scott 1985)? Focusing on Russian hunger strikers in the late nineteenth century, Vernon (2007: 60) briefly mentions how they influenced British suffragists and how the tactic diffused, spreading transnationally in the early 1900s. Expanding on this argument, Kevin Grant (2006, 2011) has shown that male and female political prisoners in Russia went on hunger strikes and immolated themselves, even taking poison to protest Tsarist authoritarian rule in the 1870s and 1880s. Some Russian activists escaped capture and detention, migrating to England where they denounced the treatment of political prisoners and publicized the use of hunger strikes. These activists later formed coalitions and alliances with British suffragists, labor union leaders, elected officials, and other radical political activists to protest an official state visit between Russian Tsar Nicholas II and his uncle, British King Edward VI, in August 1909 (Grant 2011).

Several weeks before this meeting between the two heads of state, Marion Wallace Dunlop, a member of the British suffragist organization the Women's Social and Political Union (WSPU), wrote part of the 1689 Bill of Rights ("It is the right of the subject to petition the King and all commitments and prosecutions for such petitioning are illegal") on the walls of Parliament, prompting her arrest in June 1909 (Grant 2011; Tickner 1988).[30] Several days later, she went on a short but successful hunger strike to demand that she be classified as a "political prisoner," as Russian activists (male and female) had previously done (Grant 2011: 114).

Shortly after Wallace Dunlop's hunger strike, more British suffragists followed suit, prompting the British government to start force-feeding them (see figure 1). Such practices generated even greater moral outrage as suffragists likened the tactic to torture and rape. Having initially relied on nonviolent parades and pageants that emphasized their "ornamental bodies" (wearing dresses and adopting "feminine" norms), suffragist hunger strikers publicized their plight in newspapers, magazines, and pamphlets, displaying their "docile bodies" (B. Green 1997). The "spectacle" of starving, disenfranchised, mostly middle-class women being fed under great duress generated great sympathy, even though the British government undertook such measures to stop them from dying (B. Green 1997; Tickner 1988).[31] Strategically trapped, officials passed the Prisoners Temporary Discharge for Ill Health—or "Cat-and-Mouse"—Act in 1913, which temporarily freed frail hunger-striking prisoners, allowing them to physically recover before they were taken back to finish their sentences (see figure 2).

Such "cat-like" measures did not stop the "mice" from resisting, however. WSPU activists persisted (doing things like breaking windows and destroying property), inspiring Hanna Sheehy-Skeffington and Margaret Cousins, along with other women *and* men, to establish the Irish Women's Suffrage League (IWFL) in the early 1900s (C. Murphy 1989; Owens 1984).[32] Living up to its slogan, "suffrage first above all else," the IWFL generally favored nationalist "home-rule" bills on the condition that they included provisions for enfranchising "property-owning, middle-class" women (Matthews 2010: 66). Placing greater emphasis on independence over women's suffrage, Sinn Féin, a masculine-oriented nationalist Irish Republican organization, did not support IWLF activists like Sheehy-Skeffington who went on hunger strikes between 1912 and 1914, calling them a "womanish thing" (Banerjee 2012; Vernon 2007: 62). Not all male Irish nationalists supported this position. James Connolly, a radical socialist with strong internationalist and pro-suffragist views, for example, reportedly told his daughter, "what was good enough for the suffragettes to use . . . is good enough for us" and went on a weeklong hunger strike after he was arrested for

FIGURE 1. *Torturing Women in Prison: Vote Against the Government.*
National Women's Social and Political Union, David Allen and Sons, Ltd.,
1913/British Library, London, UK/Bridgeman Images.

FIGURE 2. *The Cat and Mouse Act*. National Women's Social and
Political Union, David Allen 1914, © Museum of London.

supporting a general strike in Dublin in 1913 (W. Murphy 2014: 30; Nevin 2006). Three years later, Connolly and his comrade, former Irish Republican Brotherhood president Thomas Ashe, were arrested after the failed Easter Rising, which called for Irish independence from British colonial rule (Grant 2011; McGarry 2010; W. Murphy 2014).[33] Shortly after being released, Ashe was rearrested on charges of sedition and went on hunger strike. He died just five days after prison officials tried to force-feed him (W. Murphy 2014). Besides Ashe and Connolly, thousands of Irish Republicans (male and female) went on hunger strikes between 1916 and 1923, the most notable perhaps being Terence MacSwiney, Irish Republican Army (IRA) commander and Lord Mayor of Cork, who died after a seventy-four-day hunger strike in October 1920 (Biggs 2004b; Costello 1995; Hannigan 2010). Before he died, MacSwiney famously stated, "It is not those that can inflict the most, but those that who can suffer the most who will conquer" (Hannigan 2010: 10–11).

MacSwiney's actions and those of his (male) comrades were reported widely in the Indian press (Banerjee 2012; Grant 2006; Nair 2009). In the early 1920s, several Punjabi Sikhs, protesting British rule and the brutal 1919 Amritsar massacre, went on a hunger strike, which prompted one British medical official to openly wonder if they should be force-fed or left to die as was done with MacSwiney (Grant 2006: 245).[34] While the latter option was ultimately rejected but not the former in that particular situation, Jatindra Nath Das, who was deeply involved with Bhagat Singh's revolutionary socialist movement (which was based in Punjab and northwestern India), later died after a lengthy and widely publicized sixty-three-day hunger strike on September 13, 1929. Despite multiple attempts, Das refused force-feeding, as did Singh, but officials finally overcame his objections (Rana 2005: 71–72). Known as the "Indian Terence MacSwiney," Das's family received letters of support and sympathy from the late mayor of Cork's family, and the Indian government passed legislation after his death that improved prison conditions along the lines of the hunger strikers' demands (Grant 2006: 257; Nair 2009: 665).

This "long" historical narrative suggests that the hunger strike underwent a transnational tactical diffusion process, migrating from Russia to Britain to Ireland to India in the late nineteenth and early twentieth centuries (Grant 2006, 2011; Sharp 1973; Soule 1997; Vernon 2007). Based on this trajectory, Gandhi's reliance on what Sharp (1973: 367–68) calls "satyagrahic" fasting warrants some reinterpretation. While most accounts emphasize his mother's numerous fasts and his spiritually eclectic (although deeply rooted within Hinduism) views and practices, some have noted that Gandhi traveled from South Africa to London

in July 1909 for several months, attending WSPU meetings and greeting suffragist hunger strikers who had just been released from prison (Alter 2000;
Pratt and Vernon 2005; Gandhi 1993; Grant 2006: 258). Gandhi appreciated
the WSPU's tenacity and courage, but he disagreed with property destruction
and armed struggle (therefore he opposed MacSwiney, Singh, and Das's hunger
strikes since they were members of revolutionary organizations that sometimes
relied on violence) (Grant 2006: 260; Nair 2009: 670–78). Focusing on the no-
tions of conversion and "soul-force," Gandhi claimed that his fasts, unlike the
WSPU's, were noncoercive; that is, they were designed to transform the hearts
of multiple audiences or targets (followers, bystanders, and elite opponents).[35]
Regarding the followers, he hoped that his actions might reenergize those who
had questioned or even rejected the strategic and moral value of nonviolence.
With the respect to the latter two groups, Gandhi tried to persuade them with
self-sacrifice and suffering to passively or actively support nonviolent ("satyagrahic") social movements by passing compassionate policies based on love, equality,
and justice for all (Erikson 1993; Fischer 1954; Gandhi 1993, 2001). Despite these
claims, he recognized that his first public fast (involving striking textile workers) could be construed as coercive (Gandhi 1993: 432). Because his many subsequent public fasts were based on "soul-*force*," one could reasonably claim that
they too were coercive (and hence violent), but Gandhi stated that they were
"acts of love" designed to mitigate widespread violence (Juergensmeyer 2005:
46–49, 54–55, 151–55).

The fact that Gandhi learned directly about the strategic power of fasting
from militant British suffragists (whom he sometimes disagreed with) and that
hunger strikes have a transnational, modern, and *feminist* origin stemming from
Britain's imperialist and antidemocratic policies is compelling and seldom recognized. Despite this gendered legacy, the hunger strike became masculinized
over time for reasons that I explore below. Tracing the hunger strike's roots back
to male and female Russian revolutionaries in the late nineteenth century is
a critical intervention, but this raises the question—who influenced *them*? In
other words, if Marion Wallace Dunlop inspired Hanna Sheehy-Skeffington
who inspired James Connolly who inspired Terence MacSwiney who inspired
Jatindra Das and Bhagat Singh, who inspired and influenced these "original"
Russian hunger strikers? Calling the genesis of these hunger strikes in the 1870s
and 1880s "obscure," Grant (2011: 123) suggests that fasting associated with the
Russian Orthodox Church may have been instrumental, while Sharp (1973: 360)
claims that starving Russian peasants often laid down in the fields until they

received food. Whatever the case, something mysterious remains about the genealogy of the hunger strike. Grant's (2006, 2011) work provides tremendous insights, but his analysis and approach are still quite Anglo- and Eurocentric (aside from his analysis of hunger strikes in India in the 1920s) and secular.

FASTING, SACRIFICE, GENDER, AND CHRISTIANITY

Traveling backward temporally, one can see how hunger striking, fasting, and religion are inextricably linked. While not all hunger strikers have been devoutly, moderately, or even tepidly religious, nearly every major faith tradition practices fasting (Rogers 2004; T. Ryan 2005).[36] Within Christianity, Jesus fasted, as did John the Baptist and his followers, as did Moses, who went without food and water on Mount Sinai before God gave him the Ten Commandments.[37] I realize that focusing on Jesus may reinforce patriarchal, Eurocentric narratives of hunger strikes that valorize "great (white) men" like MacSwiney, Ashe, Connolly, Sands, and others, but seen from a radical perspective, Jesus was a colonized male subject of color who sometimes reproduced and challenged sexism (Blum and Harvey 2012; Crossan 2008, 2009; Jencks 2009).[38] He inspired and continues to inspire oppressed peoples all over the world. His life and death, therefore, merit greater scrutiny.

In Matthew's Gospel, the author claims that after Jesus was born and fled with his family to avoid death squads who wished to execute him (2:13–18), he fasted for forty days in the "wilderness" (4:1–11).[39] While often framed as an individualistic allegory and triumph over "evil," I contend that Jesus's fast might be read politically as a rejection of empire and an affirmation of what the late Latina liberation theologian Ada María Isasi-Diaz (1996) called the "kin-dom of God," an egalitarian, nonsexist world where the "last shall be first and the first shall be last." Having barely escaped death and living amid widespread misery and injustice in first-century Roman-occupied Palestine, Jesus could have played it safely, "making life" and surviving as most people did under those arduous circumstances (Crossan 2009; Flacks 1976, 1988). When offered fortune, fame, and power, some might understandably be tempted and accept those entreaties, knowing that they could lead to a "better life." Jesus rejected the "devil's" overtures, however, forgoing not only food but comfort and privilege.[40]

Shortly thereafter (following Matthew's Gospel), he started "making history," as Dick Flacks (1976, 1988) might put it, calling his first disciples who immediately "left their nets and followed him" (Matthew 4:18–22). With these and other supporters, Jesus began working alongside the "least of these," empire's victims (the physically and mentally ill, poor people, women, prostitutes, tax collectors, racialized others, homeless people, and others), healing and curing them (Matthew 4:23–25). While often ridiculed and rejected as quaint, unrealistic miracles, Jesus's actions were countercultural in occupied Palestine. As biblical scholar Walter Brueggemann (2001: 45) has argued, "Empires live by numbness. . . . Jesus penetrates this numbness by his compassion and with his compassion he takes the first step toward making visible the odd abnormality that had become business as usual." By healing the wounded, Jesus not only "saved" them, he implicitly critiqued the "domination system" that produced so many wounded people in the first place and inspired many to imagine that another world, a world with far less misery and suffering, was possible (Borg and Crossan 2006: 7–9; Brueggemann 2001: 105). Jesus's words and deeds attracted huge crowds, making the "powers and principalities" extremely uneasy (Ephesians 6:12).[41] Fearing revolutionary change, Jesus was arrested, tortured, and executed (Borg and Crossan 2006; Howard-Brook 2010). Despite his brutal death, his female disciples (particularly Mary Magdalene) spread the "good news" that he had risen from the dead, which some of his male followers questioned (Matthew 28:1–10; Mark 16:10–11; John 20:27).[42] Women and men within the "Jesus movement" continued seeking nonviolent transformation after he was killed, even though some suffered the same fate (Stegemann and Stegemann 1999).[43]

While this narrative is generally well known, few recognize that Jesus apparently fasted just once (abstaining from food for forty days). When John the Baptist's followers asked him about his disciples' fasting practices, he replied that they would fast more often after he died (Matthew 9:14–17). Speaking metaphorically about "new wine being put into fresh wineskins," Jesus implied his followers would fast in a completely unique manner. Rather than abstain from food, they would abstain from their old lives, just as Jesus did, to "bring good news to the poor" and create a more just world, despite great personal risk.

Jesus's vision closely resembles Isaiah's. When asked about fasting, the Old Testament prophet boldly declared, "Is not this the fast that I choose: to loose the bonds of injustice, to undo the thongs of the yoke, to let the oppressed go free, and to break every yoke? Is it not to share your bread with the hungry, and bring the homeless poor into your house; when you see the naked, to cover them?" (Isaiah 58:6–7). Fasting, therefore, was not initially about forgoing food, it was about justice. Jesus and his followers hungered for a world without violence, poverty, and injustice. Despite this unequivocal call and the repeated emphasis on serving the "least of these," Christian leaders embraced a depoliticized form of fasting under Roman emperor Constantine starting in the early fourth century. Transitioning from a state-opposed to state-sanctioned religion, Church officials defused its explosive nature and radical orientation (Maurin 2010; West 2004). Rather than "going and selling" all that they had and working for the "kin-dom of God," devoted followers refrained from eating red meat during Lent, holy days, and Fridays (Fagan 2006).[44]

Having once been associated with challenging injustice and breaking *every* yoke (racism, sexism, capitalism, etc.), fasting became institutionalized and routinized. Christians were encouraged to focus on individual salvation (from one's "sins"), not collective liberation. Given this general orientation, one can see why Marx famously said that religion was the "opiate of the masses"—because Christianity encouraged its followers to stop eating certain foods rather than "feeding the hungry, clothing the naked, caring for the sick, welcoming the stranger, visiting the imprisoned, giving drink to the thirsty, and burying the dead."[45]

This new defanged and deradicalized version of fasting trivialized sacrifice within Christianity, prompting some, starting in the early 1960s, to swap a McDonald's Big Mac for a Filet-O-Fish sandwich (Clark 2007). From the Cross to the Golden Arches, it has been a long, strange trip, one that some—most notably women—never accepted. Despite the fact that some women were Jesus's closest friends and the priesthood was initially open to all, Christianity became increasingly patriarchal over time. Because their voices were so often muted, many women, starting in the Middle Ages, went on prolonged fasts and died (Bell 1987; Bynum 1987; Vandereycken and Van Deth 1994). While seemingly irrational, many women were canonized as saints shortly after their deaths. These "hunger strikes" were therefore a subtle form of resistance against sexism within the Catholic Church. Fasting was virtually the only way that women could fight back and be heard within this male-dominated bastion.

Given that possibility, male church leaders banned canonization based on self-starvation. Women thus turned to "tireless charity" to challenge injustice and make their voices heard, but many continued fasting (Vandereycken and Van Deth 1994: 31).[46] From "fasting saints" to "fasting girls," women have gone without food for centuries. Such practices have almost always been scorned, mocked, and ridiculed. In the late nineteenth century, medical "experts" claimed that female self-starvation stemmed from hysteria, melancholia, and other psychological disorders (Brumberg 2000). Food abstinence became known as "anorexia nervosa," a dangerous, potentially life-threatening medical condition. Having once gone without food to protest sexism (in the Catholic Church and wider society), women activists who starved themselves were now classified as "insane" or "suicidal" in the early 1900s (Brumberg 2000).

Such framing influenced British suffragist hunger strikers who knew that government officials force-fed mentally ill prisoners and criminals in the late nineteenth and early twentieth centuries (Grant 2006, 2011). Seeing themselves as neither, suffragists claimed that they were political prisoners that should not be force-fed without their consent. Despite this assertion, the practice continued, although it was slightly modified (under the Cat-and-Mouse Act). Publicizing these actions as "spectacular confessions" in newspapers, pamphlets, and books, suffragists believed that force-feeding would enrage the public, particularly since they represented themselves as patriotic mothers (Green 1997; Vernon 2007). However, focusing on the suffragists' penchant for property destruction, the British government and press out-maneuvered them, framing them as extremists and thereby limiting their appeal among potential "third-party" supporters (Grant 2011: 134; Lipsky 1968).

Because starving women's bodies had been ridiculed for so long, suffragists faced a skeptical public even though they were being brutally force-fed. This legacy has persisted, as Irom Sharmila, an Indian woman who has been on hunger strike for *fifteen years*, has discovered. After Indian paramilitary forces shot and killed ten suspected "militants" at a bus stop in Malom, Manipur (Northeast India), Sharmila went on an indefinite hunger strike on November 2, 2000 (Mehrotra 2009). Before the Malom massacre, Sharmila had been investigating the effect of the Armed Forces Special Powers Act (AFSPA), which was implemented in Manipur in September 1980 after guerrilla organizations seeking independence from India emerged (Mehrotra 2009). The AFSPA provides Indian military and paramilitary forces with a "state of exception"; that is, they can operate freely, committing human rights abuses, because they are targeting "terrorists" and protecting "national security" (Agamben 1998; Buxi 2011: 67). Sharmila wants the AFSPA repealed because it has spawned extrajudicial killings and violence. She, like English suffragists a century ago, has been imprisoned and force-fed for her actions. When her health recovers, she is released but is rearrested when she resumes fasting because of claims that she is suicidal (Peer 2014).

Totally ignoring this rich historical context and a nonviolent Manipuri women's movement that has existed for much more than one hundred years, the

Los Angeles Times published a story titled "In India, Love Tests World's Longest Hunger Strike" (Magnier 2011; Mehrotra 2009).[47] Noting that a prominent elderly male anticorruption activist named Anna Hazare received far more press attention for his twelve-day fast in August 2011 than Sharmila, the *Times* acknowledged that her much longer strike had been "largely ignored" in the mainstream press (Magnier 2011; Roy 2011). Rather than focus on the issues that sparked Sharmila's historic fast, the *Times* concentrated on her fiancée and his alleged attempts to undermine the movement she has been deeply involved with for many years.

Had a male activist been on hunger strike for fifteen years, he probably would have achieved iconic, legendary status, but Sharmila remains a little-known, obscure figure. While the personal lives of political activists warrant some attention, it is striking to observe that during Gandhi and Chávez's fasts very few people mentioned their wives, partners, or children. Their actions were seen as brave, courageous, and heroic, despite the fact that they could have died, leaving their loved ones without a husband and father. Such concerns have long tormented female activists who have been sometimes called "bad mothers" for abandoning their children while participating in high-risk actions such as hunger strikes and demonstrations (Morales 2009). In contrast, IRA member Bobby Sands, who left behind a young son, wife, and extended family after he died after a sixty-six-day hunger strike in May 1981, is a venerated figure around the world (O'Hearn 2006). As that hunger strike dragged on, more male IRA members died, prompting some mothers to sign medical release forms to stop their sons from suffering a similar fate (George 1996; Morrison 2006). These actions generated far greater media attention than did the female IRA prisoners who also went on a hunger strike with their male comrades in 1981 (Loughran 1986; Roulston 1989).

These and countless more examples vividly illustrate Sharman Russell's (2005: 78) pithy observation, "hunger communicates," but what does an emaciated *female* body communicate versus a male one?[48] When celebrated pop singer Karen Carpenter died from anorexia nervosa in the early 1980s, many felt shame, sympathy, and even revulsion (Schmidt 2011). It was hard to look at her extremely thin body before she passed away. Was this because she was a woman and her body therefore invited scorn, rather than compassion? Contrast her body with those of Sands, Chávez, Gandhi, or even Jesus. What do these male bodies communicate—strength, valor, bravery, or courage perhaps? The gendered distinction between male and female bodies is significant because the latter are often seen as hysterical, irrational, insane, and anorexic, thus they do not typically generate much third-party support, but powerful targets still fear them based on patriarchal norms. For example, the British government force-fed female suffragist hunger strikers, keeping them alive, but it let MacSwiney (a terrorist, in its eyes) die and released Gandhi (a "half-naked fakir") before he could do so.[49]

These outcomes indicate that while "hunger communicates," the message is often scrambled and confused. That is, depending on who is starving (and possibly dying) and how the target(s) responds, concessions may or may not be forthcoming. The hunger strike is a constantly evolving cat-and-mouse game of "political jiu-jitsu" that shifts over time (Scanlan, Stoll, and Lumm 2008; Sharp 1973). Bodies with softer voices may become more audible through force-feeding, whereas louder bodies may be drowned out by elite "framing processes" (Benford and Snow 2000). Final outcomes depend on *all* the bodies (strikers, allies, family, bystanders, targets, etc.) involved and may dramatically change even after the strike has officially ended.

As will be shown below, the hunger striker hopes that "the whole world is listening" and can hear their scream for dignity.[50] Because women's hungry, starving, and emaciated bodies have been so often mocked and demonized over time (even when force-fed), some have opted for tireless charity over fasting and hunger striking. The tactic therefore has become heavily masculinized despite the fact that women largely pioneered it. Against all this *his*-story, many women of color (namely Chicanas and Latinas) still went on hunger strikes on college campuses in the 1990s, as will be shown later in this book. Recognizing that the "telling is political," I document and analyze the role that women played as fasters, allies, negotiators, and even "targets" in the UCLA, UCSB, and Stanford hunger strikes in the hopes that I do not perpetuate the "great man" narrative as has been done for decades in Chicana and Chicano studies as well as many other fields (Blackwell 2011: 1–13, 28–30).

HUNGER STRIKES AND SOCIAL MOVEMENTS: A THEORETICAL APPROACH

The social movement literature on hunger strikes and the Chicana/o Movement is thin. While many books have been published on both, very few have relied or drawn on key social movement theories and concepts.[51] Despite strong criticisms and new developments, the political process model, which emerged in the early 1980s, remains the leading social movement perspective (Gamson and Meyer 1996; Goodwin and Jasper 1999; McAdam, McCarthy, and Zald 1996; V. Taylor 2010). Political process theorists contend that social movements may emerge when opportunities arise (McAdam 1982; Tarrow 1994; Tilly 1978). Opportunities provide space for organizing and challenging powerful social groups. When they narrow or contract, social movements decline or disappear. Logically speaking, hunger strikes apparently cannot occur without opportunities—without a "favorable political climate."

Two relatively recent, widely reported mass hunger strikes contradict these claims. In 2013, California prisoners and Guantánamo Bay "detainees" went on hunger strikes, protesting extended solitary confinement and prolonged unjust imprisonment respectively (Mizner 2013; Harris, McVeigh, and Townsend 2013).[52] Despite being considered the "worst of the worst" (convicted murderers, violent felons, and "terrorists") and having little or no freedom, they resisted and stopped eating, generating substantial public attention and even some sympathy.[53] These actions, along with many others under similar circumstances, demonstrate that social movements can occur with or without opportunities (Gamson and Meyer 1996; Scanlan, Stoll, and Lumm 2008). Indeed, hunger strikes often emerge when opportunities are virtually nonexistent. The old adage "desperate times call for desperate measures" metaphorically embodies the hunger striker's situation.

One might assume that political factors are superfluous when exploring hunger strikes, but that is not the position I am taking here. Political *inopportunity* often sparks hunger strikes because established channels for redressing grievances have been blocked (Scanlan, Stoll, and Lumm 2008). Once under way, hunger strikes can exploit preexisting intra-elite divisions or generate new fissures between administration officials, as happened at UCLA in 1993 (Almeida and Stearns 1998; Jenkins 1985; McAdam 1982; Tarrow 1994). Hence, opportunities do matter, but they often come from below, not above. Hunger strikes generally produce unique opportunities and create space for extracting concessions from seemingly intractable, omnipotent social groups. They are also usually effective (Scanlan, Stoll, and Lumm 2008: 299).

Having partially unraveled the political process model's "winding and snarling vines" and having created space, what comes next?[54] Without effective "mobilizing structures," social movements may not take off (McAdam, McCarthy, and Zald 1996: 8). Mobilizing structures are movement organizations that attract human and financial resources; without both, social movements cannot emerge (McCarthy and Zald 1977). Movements simply and plainly need people;

as the chapters on the three hunger strikes will illustrate, non-hunger-striking students performed essential tasks—making flyers; creating alliances and constructing coalitions; gathering and building tents; supplying water; writing memos and negotiating with administration officials; providing security and emotional support; and being present for rallies and demonstrations (T. Gutiérrez 2011; Valencia Sherratt 2011). The hunger strikes also needed money for paper, pens, banners, blankets, press releases, faxes, phone calls, and so on.

Strong mobilizing structures and sufficient opportunities are seen as necessary (but not sufficient) preconditions for social movement emergence, but the former may not always be present (McAdam, McCarthy, and Zald 1996: 8). In the UCLA and UCSB hunger strikes, for example, the two main mobilizing structures experienced severe internal conflict and atrophy, but they persevered and were relatively successful. Without many opportunities and robust mobilizing structures, how can social movements develop, let alone be effective?

Within social movement discourse, opportunities and mobilizing structures are seen as macro-level or structural processes. When both are present, the "objective" conditions for movement takeoff are ripe. Movements cannot emerge, however, without a third, micro-oriented or "subjective" factor known as "framing processes" (McAdam, McCarthy, and Zald 1996; Benford and Snow 2000). Snow contends framing processes are "conscious strategic efforts by groups of people to fashion shared understandings of the world and of themselves that legitimate and motivate collective action" (McAdam, McCarthy, and Zald 1996: 6). For example, a multiracial group of activists in the 1940s claimed that the prosecution of Mexican American men and women on a variety of criminal charges was "fascist" (Armbruster-Sandoval 2011; Barajas 2006; Escobar 1999; Polletta 2006; C. Ramírez 2009).[55] Such framing practices effectively mobilized supporters and generated financial resources, but they predictably sparked counterframing efforts as local political leaders argued that the coalition's members were "communists" who were defending "blood-thirsty criminals" or possibly affiliated with fascists in Mexico (Barajas 2006; Leonard 2006). This example illustrates that social movements can devolve into "frame contests" as opposing sides seek to "control the narrative" or "define the situation" on terms that generally favor them (Benford and Snow 2000: 626–27; Gitlin 1980).

In the three hunger strikes examined in this book, activists relied on specific framing processes, targeting multiple actors. Hoping to capitalize on widespread indignation stemming from higher tuition rates and budget cuts in the UC system in the early 1990s, UCLA students discovered that high-ranking university officials were eating expensive publicly subsidized meals at an exclusive members-only club while resources for ethnic and women's studies programs were stagnating or being reduced. Calling the elite bureaucrats "fat cats," one *Daily Bruin* (1993b) writer captured the campus-based class struggle with the following headline: "They Feast; We Fast." UCSB students also focused on fee hikes, framing their strike in "universal" terms since that issue cut across race, affecting *all* students, not just raza. That strategy prompted some white students and other students of color to support the strike, but others remained indifferent, bewildered, or even hostile (G. Green 2011a; Yelles 1994). Unless frames are properly "aligned," they will not resonate or stimulate action (Snow et al. 1986).

The foregoing analysis indicates that opportunities, mobilizing structures, and framing processes are critical for understanding social movement formation. Taken separately and collectively, these theoretical concepts provide unique insights, but they still cannot fully explain the field's central question—what makes people move? Frames do arouse people—the poster depicting the suffragist activist being force-fed while imprisoned effectively singled out the government, but that wasn't sufficient for facilitating action. The graphic image morally outraged people, breaking people's hearts and prompting them to take action to stop women from being tortured. The poster was a powerful emotional trigger that strengthened the suffragist movement (McAdam 1982). It broke their hearts and affected them emotionally, provoking them to act, to stop women from being tortured and to empower them with "votes."

Starving, hungry bodies thus often move people. Despite their weakness and frailty, they can generate substantive social change. As Sharman Russell (2005: 73–74) has cogently and elegantly written,

Hunger is a form of communication. When we fast for health, we are having a conversation with the body. When we fast as a Jew or Catholic, Muslim or Hindu, we are having a conversation with God. These are *private* discussions and are often silent. Hunger strikes are different. Almost always, they are loud and public like a messy family argument that the whole neighborhood can hear. The man or woman fasting for change wants the world to know and judge. To know and act. The conversation is with the world. Hunger is a demand, a cry, and if that cry is ignored, hunger will only call out more urgently, seeking its audience until they begin to call and cry and demand, and there are *many* voices now, and hunger has become *theater*—a tragedy, perhaps, or a farce. In a hunger strike, the end is not yet written. The play unfolds. Hunger strikers believe that the voice of hunger has a power disproportionate to its source. *Hunger can strengthen the weak, inspire the timid, bully the powerful.* The voice of hunger can free the oppressed and right injustice. It can alter history. In the story of David and Goliath, hunger is David's stone. Thousands of lives will change because of one man's [*sic*] hunger. And this is true. This has happened. (emphasis added)

Relying on similar but slightly different language, sociologist Michael Biggs (2004a) has claimed that hunger strikes and self-immolations are forms of "communicative suffering" and self-sacrifice. Suffering has long been valorized within certain activist and spiritual/religious circles because of its redemptive qualities and transformative potential, which some feminists have challenged, stating that it perpetuates gender-based oppression by encouraging women to suffer even more than they already have (Starhawk 2002: 219–20). While valid, what explains the power of suffering? In one of his most memorable quotes, Gandhi stated, "I have come to this fundamental conclusion, that if you want something really important to be done, you must not only satisfy the reason, you must move the heart too. The appeal to reason is more to the head, but the penetration of the heart comes from suffering" (Easwaran 2011: 196–97). Borrowing from Old Testament prophet Ezekiel (11:19), one could say that Gandhi hoped that his fasts might transform people's "hearts of stone" into "hearts of flesh." Through self-sacrifice, he hoped his actions would "strengthen the weak, inspire the timid, and bully the powerful." In other words, he, like all hunger strikers, wanted to "change the world" (Russell 2005: 91).

What the hunger strike frames, therefore, is the body. A starving, hungry body (depending on race, gender, sexuality, citizenship, and many other factors) communicates bravery, courage, commitment, and a willingness to die for one's beliefs. Starving bodies have been used consciously and deliberately in hunger strikes in a spectacular and performative fashion. Much like "hunger artists" in the late nineteenth and early twentieth centuries, hunger strikers want to grab the public's attention, but they want people to do more than simply watch a "circus show" or macabre spectacle of self-starvation. They want them to be concerned, to express sympathy and compassion, and above all, to act, because if they do not, the hunger striker, who genuinely wants to live, will die (P. Anderson 2004, 2010).

In relying on their bodies as nonviolent "weapons of the weak" (Scott 1985), hunger strikers hope to pierce numb hearts and an indifferent world, to provoke emotional responses among their allies, supporters, and third-party bystanders (as well as their opponents). Like those that have immolated themselves (such as Thich Quang Duc, Alice Herz, Norman Morrison, and Mohamed Bouazizi), hunger strikers are like physicians performing open-heart surgery; with their self-sacrifice and suffering they hope to "revive the patient," morally shocking them with their emaciated bodies in the hopes that they will wake up and take action.[56]

There has been an emotional and affective turn within the social movement literature over the past twenty years (Goodwin and Jasper 1999; Jasper 1997; Nepstad 2004; V. Taylor 2010); many scholars have shown that moral outrage and moral shocks often stimulate or trigger individual and collective action (Nepstad 2004). To illustrate how this process works specifically, I will provide two concrete examples from chapters 3 and 5. When Stanford University fired Cecilia Burciaga, the campus's highest-ranking Latina administration official and a long-time civil rights and women's rights advocate—in March 1994, when students were away on Spring Break—many were outraged. Burciaga was a positive role model, mentor, friend, and de facto mother-like figure to many Stanford Chicana/o and Latina/o students. Her dismissal, combined with some students yelling "beaners, go home" during a screening of the UFW's documentary film *No Grapes*, generated widespread anger. Similar feelings emerged after UCLA chancellor Charles Young decided, after many years of struggle and deliberation, to not establish a Chicana/o studies department just four days after César Chávez died. These actions generated strong emotions, leading some students to put their bodies on the line by forgoing food. These high-risk, sacrificial actions consequently affected many nonstriking students emotionally, sparking their involvement as allies and supporters. As one can see, emotions are crucial for understanding these hunger strikes, as well as the others examined in this book.

SPECTACULAR SPEECH AND DIGNITY: SCREAMING AND STARVING FOR JUSTICE

To sum up the argument so far, the hunger strike has complex temporal, spatial, spiritual, and gendered origins. It often occurs when opportunities are few and people feel great moral outrage. Once under way, hunger strikes typically move followers and third-party supporters emotionally, generating a larger and stronger social movement that can more effectively pressure targeted actors and institutions. Finally, most hunger strikes are generally effective, as one comprehensive study, analyzing nearly fifteen hundred such actions over almost one hundred years (1906–2004), discovered (Scanlan, Stoll, and Lumm 2008: 290, 299).

The fact that so many hunger strikes have generated positive outcomes merits greater attention. Many scholars and writers have noted that hunger strikes and other forms of self-starvation often produce multiple messages and meanings that are not altogether clear; that is, starving, emaciated bodies are generally indeterminate (P. Anderson 2010; Ellmann 1993; Kafka 1995). Hunger does "communicate," as Russell (2005: 78) has argued; therefore, hunger strikes are an "act of speech," but not everyone hears what is being articulated in a consistent and universal manner (Fierke 2013, 37). In *The Hunger Artists*, Maud Ellmann (1993: 17) contends that "self-starvation is above all a performance . . . it is staged to trick the conscience of its viewers [third-party supporters], forcing them to recognize that they are implicated in the spectacle that they behold." In her article on hunger strikes among Red Army Faction prisoners and members in West Germany in the 1970s and 80s, Leith Passmore (2009, 33–34) powerfully expands this argument:

> Whether the food practices of medieval spirituality; the demonic self-starvation of the Reformation; the eighteenth century naturalization of hunger with the rise of empiricism; the spectacle of "hunger artists" and "living skeletons" of the late nineteenth and early twentieth century; the emergence of medicalized anorexia nervosa in the late nineteenth century; or the particularly twentieth century phenomenon of the political hunger strike, self-starvation has been successfully approached as a symbolic language, a performative act within a specific cultural context.

Because of their self-sacrifice, hunger strikers are speaking without using words, without talking, but what is it that they want us to hear (Fierke 2013: 37)? Because the sounds that their hungry bodies make are so spectacular, dramatic, and loud, they can leave one with their ears ringing, questioning hunger strikers' sanity and emotional well-being. Relying on Judith Butler's *Excitable Speech* (1997), Jane Nicholas (2008) addressed this issue: "Written on the body, the voluntary act of self-starvation is often analytically troubling, given its ritualistic and often silent forms. Such a form of corporeal speech gives rise to the risk of psychiatric appropriation and erasure of the subject." Nicholas goes on to quote Judith Butler (1997: 136, emphasis added): "If the subject speaks impossibly, speaks in ways that cannot be regarded as speech or as the speech of a subject, then that speech is *discounted and the viability of the subject is called into question*. The consequence of such an irruption of the unspeakable may range from a sense that one is 'falling apart' to the intervention of the state to secure criminal or psychiatric incarceration."

Given their spectacular, performative nature, hunger strikes and other forms of self-starvation often generate crowds of curious onlookers, as Kafka (1995) mordantly observed in his classic short story, "The Hunger Artist."[57] While morbid fascination with the grotesque perhaps explains their gaze, most people do not know what the hunger strikers want, nor do the strikers sometimes. That is, despite the fact that hunger strikers usually release a series of demands, press releases, and manifestos, they may be pushing or reaching for something that they cannot fully articulate. What they want is something ephemeral, almost mystical, which is hard to put into actual words. In fact, some hunger strikers see words as suspect because they relied on them in the past, during rallies, meetings, and marches, but since they were unsuccessful, they stopped speaking. Yet still they "speak"—or more accurately, still they *scream*.

What is the "scream?" In John Holloway's (2010: 1) evocative words,

In the beginning is the scream. We scream. When we write or when we read, it is easy to forget that the beginning is not the word, but the scream. Faced with the mutilation of human lives by capitalism, a scream of sadness, a scream of horror, a scream of anger, a scream or refusal: NO.

The starting point of theoretical reflection is opposition, negativity, and struggle. It is from that rage that thought is born, not from the pose of reason, not from the reasoned-sitting-back-and-reflecting-on-the-mysteries-of-existence that is the conventional image of the thinker.

We start from negation, from dissonance. Our dissonance comes from our experience, but that dissonance varies. Millions of children live on the streets of the world. In some cities, street children are systematically murdered as the only way of enforcing respect for private property. In 1998, the assets of the 200 richest people were more than the total income of 41% of the world's people (two and half billion). In 1960, the countries with the wealthiest fifth of the world's people had per capita incomes 30 times that of the poorest fifth, by 1990, that ratio had doubled 60 to 1 and by 1995 it stood at 74 to 1. The stock market rises every time that unemployment does. Students are imprisoned for struggling for free education while those that are actively responsible for the misery of millions are heaped with honors and given titles of distinction, General, President, and so on. The list goes on and on. It is impossible to read a newspaper without feeling rage, without feeling pain. You can think of your examples. Our anger changes each day, as outrage piles upon outrage.

The easiest thing for those with power to do, as Butler's quote suggests, is to discount or disregard the hunger striker's scream or "spectacular speech" and to question their sanity (such arguments echo Gandhi's famous dictum, "first they ignore you, then they mock you, then they fight you, and then you win").[58] This process can be clearly seen with the 2011 Occupy Movement when activists were maligned and criticized for their supposedly unintelligible message (Xu 2013). While perhaps not crystal clear, their occupation of public spaces and chants ("We are the ninety-nine percent") were "screams," or defiant *gritos*—but what were they screaming *for*? Moreover, what were the hunger strikers in this study screaming for? While such generalizations are inherently problematic because of the widespread differences between the students that were involved in these high-risk actions, I contend that they were screaming for dignity.

Dignity is a contested term for women, people of color, working-class people, disabled people, queer people, and other oppressed peoples. César Chávez often spoke about dignity, focusing on how farm owners typically abused, exploited, and mistreated farm workers, treating them like "rented slaves" and "beasts of burden." To address this situation, Chávez stated that dignity could only be obtained through sacrifice (Dalton 2003: 79). He understood that systemic injustice generated numerous indignities and that dignity for all could not be achieved without radical social transformation (77).

That revolutionary spirit and vision for creating a new world informed the Zapatista National Liberation Army, who also called for dignity in their first communiqué issued on January 1, 1994 (Holloway 1998: 159). Recognizing the term's ambiguity and complexity, Holloway (1998: 169–70, emphasis in original) expresses dignity in the following poetic manner:

> Dignity is the lived experience that the world is *not* so, that this is *not* the way things are. It is the lived rejection of positivism, of those forms of thought that start from the assumption, "that's the way things are." It is the cry of existence of that which has been silenced by "the world that is." Dignity is the cry of "here we are!," the "here we are!" of the indigenous peoples forgotten by neoliberal modernization; the "here we are!" of the growing numbers of poor who somehow do not show up in the statistics of economic growth and the financial reports, the

"'here we are!" of the gay whose sexuality was for so long not recognized, the "here we are!" of the elderly shut away to die in the retirement homes of the richer countries, the "here we are!" of the women trapped in the role of housewife, the "here we are!" of the millions of illegal migrants who are not where, officially, they should be, the "here we are" of all those pleasures of human life excluded by the growing subjection of humanity to the market. Dignity is the cry of those who are not heard, the voice of those without voice. Dignity is the truth of truth denied.

Seen from this perspective, the struggle for dignity isn't about "recognition," as Charles Taylor suggested during the academic culture wars in the early 1990s (when these hunger strikes discussed in the following chapters occurred); it is about transforming an unjust capitalist, racist, sexist, heterosexist, and imperialist system that has made the "wretched of the earth" unrecognizable historically and presently (Maldonado-Torres 2008; Newfield 2008). These hunger strikers wanted more than mere "recognition," more than expanding and creating Chicana/o studies departments, as they themselves stated in press releases, newspaper articles, interviews, and so on. They wanted that which did not exist— a more dignified university, state, nation, and world. To achieve those goals, they called for tangible reforms, but they also wanted something *more*—a new department, university, and world where all people were treated with respect and dignity.

Through self-sacrifice, they and their allies and supporters partially succeeded. They transformed some "hearts of stone" into "hearts of flesh," prompting university officials to meet most of their demands, which extended into local, low-income immigrant communities, California's "factories in the fields" where farm workers were exposed to toxic chemicals, and beyond (even into Chiapas where the Zapatistas were located).[59] Those fleshy hearts hardened over time, however. Gains eroded with budget cuts, and new challenges emerged. These three campuses, the state, the nation, and the world became increasingly undignified as fees skyrocketed, immigrants were targeted, prisons were built, and bombs were dropped all over the world, killing hundreds of thousands of people from the mid-1990s until today. These hunger strikes therefore gradually "slowed down the machine of destruction," but it is incredibly resilient and insatiable.[60] Its hunger for even greater power and wealth has not gone unnoticed, as students, faculty, staff, and the wider public have shown that they too are hungry—hungry for dignity and justice. The struggle for both is a perpetual one that will be explored in the book's final chapter.

METHOD

This book examines three hunger strikes that took place at UCLA, UCSB, and Stanford University in the 1990s. I started with my home campus, UCSB, where I have worked for seventeen years as a faculty member in the Chicana and Chicano Studies Department. Having been hired just four years after the hunger strike ended, I knew that the students who were involved with this hunger strike called for more Chicana/o studies faculty as one of their six core demands. Without their sacrifices, I would have never been hired, a fact that weighed heavily on me. Many Chicana/o student activists who were involved with El Congreso (the key group that organized the strike) stated that someone should write "something" about it before too much time had elapsed and memories faded. More than a decade (1998–2008) passed before I started formally collecting "data" on this hunger strike. I initially talked with two key hunger strikers, Naomi García and Edwin López, who not only spoke with me for several hours over multiple occasions but generously loaned their personal archival materials (memos, photos, notes, etc.) on the hunger strike.

   With these oral history interviews and primary sources, I began piecing together the narrative of this hunger strike. While mapping out the bigger picture, I quickly discovered that this action was a collective, not solitary, affair. That is, upon speaking with Alma Flores—a hunger striker who also shared with me her extensive, meticulous, and invaluable personal collection of administrative, departmental, and organizational memos—I realized, as El Congreso member Lisa Valenica Sherratt (2011) stated, "The strikers were our heart, but the strike involved the entire body." Thus I interviewed critical El Congreso leaders, such as Chairperson Abel Gutiérrez, and all three hunger strike negotiators. I also spoke with members from the administration's negotiating team, including Social Science Dean Donald Zimmerman, who played a critical role in shaping the Chicana/o Studies Department both before and after the strike ended. I finally talked with several departmental colleagues (current and former) who shared with me their recollections on the strike. Overall, I conducted and transcribed twenty-two oral history interviews on the UCSB hunger strike, totaling more than forty hours.

   Beyond students' personal archives, I relied heavily on El Congreso's multiple filing cabinets, which are located in El Centro Arnulfo Casillas (also known as Building 406). El Centro is the place where everything began at UCSB—the

Chicano Studies Department, the Center for Chicano Studies, the Chicano Educational Opportunity Program, El Congreso, and the Colección Tloque Nahuaque (Chicano Studies Library)—in the early 1970s. Congresista activists have maintained a substantive, although sometimes unwieldy, collection of newspaper articles, pamphlets, and other materials inside El Centro's back offices. I combed through these files, along with the California Ethnic and Multicultural Archives collection on the 1994 hunger strike. I combined all these materials with the extensive oral history interviews to assemble a case study rich with "thick description" and analytical insights (Geertz 1973). As chapter 4 demonstrates, the UCSB hunger strike was effective, but major issues remain unresolved, particularly within the Chicana/o Studies Department.

After concluding research on the UCSB hunger strike, I turned toward the UCLA hunger strike, which took place one year earlier, in May 1993. Unlike UCSB, I had very limited ties with UCLA student activists, faculty members, and administrative officials. I fortunately established good rapport with Chicano Studies Research Center (CSRC) librarian Lizette Guerra, who provided me with extensive access (read: plentiful low-cost copies) to CSRC archival materials on the 1993 hunger strike. While reviewing articles from the *Daily Bruin*, *Los Angeles Times*, and *La Opinión*, two names were repeatedly mentioned—Milo Alvarez and Marcos Aguilar. Both were committed, long-time MEChA (Movimiento Estudiantil Chicano de Aztlán) members, but only Alvarez agreed to be interviewed. He spoke for several hours, tracing the strike's long historical roots back to the mid-1980s, as well as discussing its strengths and weaknesses. Alvarez also emphasized the involvement of Chicanas and Latinas and offered critical information for contacting hunger strikers and other key players.

Following Alvarez's helpful suggestions and insights, I conducted oral history interviews with Cindy Montañez and Joaquín Ochoa, two hunger strikers. I also spoke with former UCLA neurobiology professor and hunger striker Jorge Mancillas from Switzerland where he worked with Public Services International, an international federation of public-sector unions. I also talked with student activists such as Michelle Téllez, Blanca Gordo, Scott Kurashige, Horacio Roque Ramírez, and Santiago Bernal, among others. Interviews with UCLA faculty members, administration officials (including the former chancellor, Charles Young), community activists (such as John Fernández), and an elected official (Tom Hayden) broadened and deepened my understanding of this hunger strike. While I wish that I could have had conversations with Marcos Aguilar, Mindy Ferguson, and UCLA History Professor Juan Gómez-Quiñones (all of whom played crucial roles during the strike), I still conducted twenty-seven oral history interviews on the UCLA hunger strike, totaling more than fifty hours.

Through interviews and archival materials, I developed a substantive, nuanced narrative of the two-week action. While other scholars have examined this strike, this study is the first comprehensive account that includes oral history interviews from multiple perspectives.[61] What also makes it unique is the fact that it draws on theoretical insights from the social movement and hunger strike literatures. As chapter 3 illustrates, the UCLA hunger strike was successful, but some still hope that the Chicana and Chicano Studies Department will focus more on generating and facilitating radical social change, both on and off campus.

Like UCLA, I had very few contacts with Stanford students, faculty, and administration officials. I had never actually been on the "Farm," the lush, private Palo Alto campus that railroad tycoon and former California governor Leland Stanford and his wife Jane Stanford founded in 1885. Relying on a tip from UCSB hunger striker Naomi García, I initially contacted Eva Silva, her close childhood friend from Salinas, California. Silva was a Stanford hunger striker, as was Elvira Prieto, whom I spoke with at El Centro Chicano, a key campus cultural space established in the late 1970s. I later spoke with two other hunger strikers, Tamara Alvarado and Julia González Luna, in San Jose, California, but could not contact the final hunger striker, Felipe Barragan (the only male student who fasted during the three-day action) in a timely manner.

Beyond these oral history interviews, I talked with former Stanford University president Gerhard Casper, former dean of students Michael Jackson, former vice-provost for student affairs Cecilia Burciaga, Casa Zapata Fellows Chris González-Clarke and Gina Hernández-Clarke, and professors James Leckie, Alberto Camarillo, Luis Fraga, Ramón Saldívar, and Miguel Mendez. I also spoke with Alma Medina, a longtime key student activist who provided invaluable information about the hunger strike and actions that preceded it. Despite multiple requests, former provost Condoleezza Rice never replied when asked to be interviewed for this study. While her testimony and those of other critical players (such as Jorge Solis, who was a dedicated MEChA member and acted as a hunger strike negotiator) would have enriched the case study, I still conducted eighteen oral history interviews on the Stanford hunger strike, spanning more than forty hours.

I also relied on a series of newspaper articles from the *Stanford Daily* that Eva Silva kindly loaned to me. El Centro Chicano also was an invaluable resource, as it had pieces from the *Stanford Review*, *San Jose Mercury News*, *San Francisco Chronicle*, and *El Aguila* (MEChA's newsletter) on the 1994 hunger strike. I also leaned heavily on secondary sources, such as Steve Phillips's (1990) historical overview of the Stanford Black Student Union, Donovan Ervin's (2011) master's thesis on the campus antiapartheid movement in the 1970s and 80s, and Chris González-Clark's short paper (2006) on the establishment of Stanford's Comparative Studies in Race and Ethnicity Program (CSRE), which actually emerged from the hunger strike. Former Stanford president Richard Lyman's (2009) memoir was also quite helpful for understanding the 1960s student movement.

Using these various sources, I constructed a rigorous narrative of the 1994 Stanford hunger strike. With one shallow exception (Condoleezza Rice's 2010 autobiography), this action has never been written about. I contend that this omission partially stems from the fact that nearly all the Stanford hunger strikers were Chicanas. Women hunger strikers, as shown above, have been typically marginalized, mocked, and ignored. Despite this history and the strike's relative brevity (it lasted just three days, whereas the UCSB and UCLA strikes lasted nine and fourteen days, respectively), it generated positive outcomes—the CSRE was established—but many issues were left unaddressed. Grapes were still on campus and the East Palo Alto Latina/o community still lacked a space to fight back to obtain better living and working conditions. Recognizing the hunger strike agreement's limitations, Tamara Alvarado and Julia González Luna literally screamed when the action ended because they knew how high the stakes were. They knew how destructive the 1980s and 90s had been for communities of color, women, workers, and people in the developing world. When they stopped eating, they "spoke about destruction" and temporarily slowed the "machine" down, but they knew that dignity for all remained elusive, so they screamed and sobbed because they sacrificed their lives not for a comparative ethnic studies department (they wanted a full-fledged, independent Chicana/o studies department) but for justice—"a world where many worlds fit."

While unique factors and events on these three campuses helped spark the hunger strikes that eventually took place in the 1990s, students confronted a seemingly consistent, intractable, and omnipotent system all across the state and nation, so they starved themselves and spoke spectacularly. To better understand why they put their lives on the line and to grasp the grave situation that they faced some twenty years ago is the subject of the next chapter.

2

"SPEAK ABOUT DESTRUCTION"

Coloniality, Humiliation, and Self-Sacrifice

This is a world destruction, your life ain't nothing.
The human race is becoming a disgrace.
The rich get richer.
The poor are getting poorer.
Fascist, chauvinistic government fools . . .
Nationalities are fighting each other.
Why is this? Because the system tells you . . .
Speak about destruction.

TIME ZONE, "WORLD DESTRUCTION"

INTRODUCTION

THE STUDENTS, COMMUNITY MEMBERS, PARENTS, AND PROFESSORS that went on hunger strikes on California college campuses in the 1990s faced an extremely hostile political climate. Long beset with racial tensions and violent conflicts, the Golden State partially resembled Mississippi in the 1960s, as mostly white voters "rioted" electorally, passing divisive ballot measures such as Propositions 184, 187, 209, 227, and 21 between 1994 and 2000 (Ly. Chávez 1998; Mi. Davis 2002; Lipsitz 1998; Martinez HoSang 2010). These initiatives largely targeted immigrants, people of color, and youth, limiting educational opportunities for social mobility and expanding the prison-industrial complex. The state's transformation into a virtual "golden gulag" began ten years earlier as spending on incarceration grew steadily while funding for higher public education declined in the 1990s (Anand 2012; Gilmore 2007). Twelve prisons (two specifically for women) were opened during the decade, but just one public university campus (California State University, San Marcos) was built (A. Davis 2005, 2010; Gilmore 2007).[1]

Seeing these state-level trends and the national shift to mass incarceration, young activists of color began calling for "schools not jails," "critical resistance," and prison abolition (Alexander 2010; A. Davis 2010; Kwon 2013; E. Martínez 2000; Tilton 2010).[2] UC Riverside students built, for example, a makeshift prison located near the campus's bell tower, highlighting the state's misguided budget priorities (Gómez 2012). Despite this and many other similar actions in the 1990s, the "warfare" state (which includes the military- *and* prison-industrial complexes) survived (even after the Soviet Union collapsed in 1991); as funding for social programs was dramatically cut, scarce resources were found for prison beds and "humanitarian interventions" (Chomsky 1999; Mauer 2006; Meeropol 1998).

Exactly one year before he was assassinated, Martin Luther King, in perhaps his most radical and controversial speech, titled "A Time to Break Silence," declared, "A nation that continues year after year to spend more money on military defense than on programs of social uplift is approaching spiritual death."[3] King recognized that the United States could not win the "war on poverty" while simultaneously fighting the Vietnam War. He also understood that despite the Civil Rights Movement's achievements, poor people from all racial backgrounds were suffering economically in the middle and late 1960s (Harding 2008; King 1967; Smiley 2010, 2014). The Poor People's Campaign, he reasoned, would unleash a "radical revolution in values" that might save the nation from its "tragic death wish" (Honey 2007; Mantler 2013; McKnight 1998).[4] Before he could attend a militant, multiracial, and dramatic nonviolent demonstration in the nation's capital, however, he was killed while supporting striking black sanitation workers in Memphis, Tennessee, on April 4, 1968 (Estes 2006; Honey 2007).

King's death underscored deep racial and class divisions that existed in the United States in the late 1960s. Polls showed that the iconic civil rights leader's approval ratings were quite low just months before he was assassinated (Smiley 2010). The white "counterrevolution" that emerged after the 1954 *Brown v. Board of Education* decision and the 1955 Montgomery bus boycott took off and became increasingly consolidated after King was killed (Alexander 2010). His dream of an economically and racially just America gradually evaporated post-1968. Over the next twenty-five years, as the nation experienced three significant recessions and the nascent welfare state morphed into the full-fledged warfare state, nightmarish conditions developed.[5] Homelessness surged. Racial, class, and gender inequality widened. Unemployment and poverty rose. Over time, the "mean season" became bipartisan as the Democratic Party essentially embraced the Republicans' draconian social and economic policies, opening space for Bill Clinton's election and eventual eight-year presidency (1993–2000) (Block et al. 1987; Bluestone and Harrison 1988; Meeropol 1998; Mishel, Bernstein, and Schmitt 1999; Sklar 1995; Wolff 1996).

Tracing these three hunger strikes on California college campuses in the 1990s backward to King's death may seem rather circuitous, so let me state my argument as clearly as I can. The nation turned even harder to the "right" in 1968 as both political parties gradually adopted policies that exacerbated inequality on all levels (racial, class, and gender) (Omi and Winant 1994). Given this hegemonic consensus, very little space existed for organizing and generating substantive social change. In chapter 1, I argued that hunger strikes are more likely to occur when opportunities are few and moral outrage is extensive. Moral outrage and anger were widespread in the 1980s and 1990s because social programs were being eviscerated; more prisons were being built than schools; corporations were shedding jobs, moving overseas, and hiring more temporary workers with little or no benefits; unions were under attack and largely ignored workers of color (especially immigrants); college tuition kept rising; racially charged ballot propositions easily passed; mostly white Los Angeles Police Department (LAPD) officers beat Rodney King and were found not guilty; five men of color were falsely convicted of raping a white female jogger in New York City's Central Park in 1989; and the United States supported repressive regimes in Central America and apartheid in South Africa.[6] Tensions ran especially high in California, particularly in Los Angeles, a "city on the edge," as one local labor union proclaimed in a documentary film that examined the racial and class divisions that helped ignite the 1992 "riots" (HERE 1992).[7]

Having been collectively humiliated for twenty-five years, culminating for Latinas/os with the Save Our State (SOS) ballot measure that later became known as Proposition 187 in 1994, these students and their allies had had enough. Despite the decidedly unfavorable political climate, they creatively "made a way out of no way," going on hunger strikes to restore their dignity (Coleman 2008; Mieder 2010).[8] In *Political Self-Sacrifice: Agency, Body, and Emotion in International Relations*, K. M. Fierke (2013: 52–53) contends when an "external [colonial] power places constraints on the sovereignty of a community, which represents a lowering of their status and thus a humiliation . . . this represents a form of silencing." To be heard, subjects that have been humiliated and colonized often rely on what I call "spectacular speech," hoping that their sacrificial actions will transform "hearts of stone" into "hearts of flesh" (Ezekiel 11:19). Because these students were being repeatedly pushed around and ignored, they took control of the one thing that remained relatively free—their bodies. By refusing to eat, they became *decolonial* hunger artists who raged against the "machine." Their acts of speech, or "screams," were sometimes mocked, scorned, and disregarded, but they effectively reclaimed their dignity and helped make their campuses more dignified. Their gains could not be sustained over time, however, as new indignities and injustices emerged on all three campuses after the hunger strikes concluded.

The fact that they, their families, and their communities had been attacked and silenced for so long (going back five hundred years before King's assassination) was humiliating and infuriating. Given these desperate times, these students adopted desperate measures. However, it wasn't just state, national, and global events that sparked these intense feelings and emotions; it was the daily conditions they faced on their local campuses, combined with their own personal challenges and self-development, that prompted them to risk their lives.

Before exploring those latter issues, I first examine the "mean" climate that emerged more fully after King's death and the humiliating circumstances that these students faced on a global, national, and state level. These conditions primed the pump, generating anger and moral outrage. Additional, humiliating campus-level events exacerbated those feelings, fueling the hunger strikes that occurred. In other words, both macro- and micro-oriented processes are crucial for understanding these high-risk actions. The former are substantively analyzed below, while the latter are more fully described in chapters 3 through 5.

LIVING IN THE EIGHTIES:
MISTER REAGAN AND MOURNING IN AMERICA

Unlike the turbulent 1960s, the 1980s are often stereotypically remembered for materialism, greed, and apathy, even though the decade was rife with opposition and dissent.[9] Activists mobilized against nuclear weapons and nuclear power plants, U.S. intervention in Central America, apartheid in South Africa, AIDS, and many other issues (Martin 2011; Sirota 2011; C. Smith 1996; Soule 1997). More often than not, these social movements targeted one specific person—Republican president Ronald Reagan—blaming him for the country's woes, particularly the deep economic recession that began in the early 1980s.

For many, Reagan was a long-time foe, going back to his time as California governor (1967–1975) when he collaborated with FBI director J. Edgar Hoover to spy on liberal (read: "potentially communist") UC president Clark Kerr and pressured the UC regents to fire him in January 1967 (Mt. Davis 2007: 94–97; Kerr 2003: 283–330; Rosenfeld 2012: 368–78).[10] Having campaigned on the promise to "clean up the mess at Berkeley," he also called on the regents to impose tuition for the first time in the UC's nearly one-hundred year history (which Kerr vigorously opposed on the grounds that the UC system, under the 1960 California Master Plan for Higher Education that he helped craft, should remain "free" and open to all top-tier academically qualified students regardless of their economic circumstances) because of his desire to cut spending on all state agencies by 10 percent (Kerr 2003: 319; Rosenfeld 2012: 369). Higher fees, incidentally, put pressure on some "beatniks, radicals, and filthy speech advocates"—his words for student activists—to work rather than organize marches (Cohen 2014).[11] With relentless fervor, Reagan continued his anticommunist purge, pushing the regents (after UCLA Chancellor Charles Young refused to do so) to fire philosophy professor and U.S. Communist Party member Angela Davis in October 1969 and condemning UCSB Chancellor Vernon I. Cheadle for "capitulating" and agreeing to establish black studies and Chicano studies departments after black students nonviolently occupied North Hall in October 1968 (Dundjerski 2011: 180–81; Gardner 2005: 42; Lynch 2013; Y. Márquez 2007: 534). He later declared a "state of extreme emergency" after a local Bank of America branch was burned down in Isla Vista (where many UCSB students lived) during a militant antiwar protest in late February 1970 (Biskind et al. 1970; Gardner 2005; Gault-Williams 2004; Rt. Kelley 1981; Lodise 2008; Whalen and Flacks 1989). Reagan, a former union president, also famously mocked the UFW and hence the larger Chicano Movement by eating "scab" grapes on television during the union's bitter five-year grape boycott in the late 1960s (Mt. García 2012: 129).

A ubiquitous lightning rod and shape-shifter (e.g., despite being Screen Actors Guild president in the late 1940s and early 1950s as a Democrat, he fired ten thousand striking air traffic controllers in 1981 shortly after winning the presidency as a Republican), Reagan favored what then presidential candidate George H. W. Bush famously called "voodoo economics."[12] Relying heavily on Milton Friedman's conservative economic policies that he and his Chicago School colleagues unsuccessfully championed in the 1950s and 60s, the former New Dealer slashed social programs, cut taxes on the wealthy, and sharply increased military spending (Block et al. 1987; Harvey 2005; N. Klein 2007).[13] Reagan also scaled back environmental, health, and safety regulations, nominated antiunion appointees to the National Labor Relations Board, and facilitated deindustrialization and globalization through bilateral and multilateral free-trade agreements and "structural adjustment policies" that his administration favored (Bello 1994; Bluestone and Harrison 1988; Bonacich et al. 1994; George 1991; Gross 1995).[14] Stubbornly rejecting substantial evidence that showed his policies had essentially generated greater inequality and misery, Reagan proclaimed during his victorious 1984 reelection campaign that it was "morning again in America" (Troy 2007). The nation's "long, dark night of the soul" (Watergate, Vietnam, and the Sixties) was supposedly over.[15] *Happy Days* wasn't just a hit television sitcom, it was a new, popular, national "reality show."[16] This triumphal narrative obscured the nearly incontrovertible fact that "trickle-down economics" generated tremendous *mourning* and suffering in the 1980s (Bluestone and Harrison 1982, 1988).

Those trends continued under President Bush, who initially mocked and later ironically embraced his predecessor's economic and foreign policies. Despite calling for a "kinder and gentler nation" and a "thousand points of light," he established no new social programs and bombed Panama and Iraq, kicking the "Vietnam syndrome" and "wimp factor" in two relatively short years (1989–91) (Trent 1992).[17] Although he enjoyed high approval ratings after the short but bloody Persian Gulf War, Bush was swept out of office mainly because he never seriously addressed the recession that emerged in the early 1990s, which Bill Clinton skillfully exploited with his unofficial campaign slogan, "it's the economy, stupid."[18]

Coming into office as a "New Democrat," President Clinton initially backed health care reform, but later he "ended welfare as we know it" and declared the "era of big government is over" (Chappell 2010; Meeropol 1998). He also vigorously supported corporate-friendly NAFTA and signed legislation repealing the Depression-era Glass-Steagall Act (Kay 2011; McArthur 2000; Prins 2009; Stiglitz 2004).[19] That decision helped fuel rampant financial and real estate speculation, sparking the Great Recession (2006–8) during President George W. Bush's second term (Prins 2009: 141–44). While poverty, unemployment, and homelessness declined under Clinton's presidency (1993–2000), middle- and working-class income stagnated and CEO (chief executive officer) pay skyrocketed (Collins and Yeskel 2005; Mishel, Bernstein, and Schmitt 1999; Sklar 1995).[20]

Bush Sr.'s and Clinton's policies indicate that "Reaganomics" could exist without Reagan. While the hip-hop/funk/punk music group Time Zone turned "Mr. Reagan" into a convenient punching bag, every president since Nixon has embraced neoliberalism, which David Harvey (2005: 46) simply defines as a strategy to restore "class power." To illustrate this argument, consider that in 1975, the top 1 percent owned 20 percent of all the nation's wealth and CEOs earned forty times more than the average worker. In 2001, the top 1 percent owned 33 percent of all the nation's wealth and CEOs earned four hundred times more than the average worker (Collins and Yeskel 2005: 43–45, 51–53; Sklar 1995; Wolff 1996).[21] Class power, which the New Deal and Great Society had supposedly weakened, had indeed been restored.

FIGHT THE POWER: RACIAL NEOLIBERALISM AND THE NEW JIM CROW

Neoliberalism wasn't and still isn't merely an economic or class project; it is a racial one designed to perpetuate white supremacy, albeit in a more nuanced manner (Goldberg 2011).[22] As the late scholar-activist Manning Marable (1984) argued thirty years ago, the United States experienced a "Second Reconstruction" from 1965 (after the Civil Rights and Voting Rights Acts were passed and signed into law) to 1981 (when Reagan took office). During that period, people of color (specifically African Americans) made limited gains, just as they did under the first Reconstruction (1865–1877) (Du Bois 1935). Interracial working-class solidarity terrified white economic elites, however, prompting Reconstruction's demise and the emergence of Jim Crow (racial apartheid) in the South. Michelle Alexander (2010) has suggested that a similar process occurred in the post–Civil Rights Movement era with King's short-lived Poor People's Campaign (PPC).[23] King hoped that the PPC might facilitate the "radical revolution in values" he called for one year before he was assassinated, but internal divisions and government repression limited its effectiveness (Honey 2007; McKnight 1998).[24]

Seeking to forestall subsequent radical movements, what became known as the New Right in the early 1980s began focusing more forcefully on "crime" and "law-and-order" (Alexander 2010; Omi and Winant 1994). Such coded language, while "color-blind," had clear racial overtones as people of color were often seen as dangerous criminals for committing civil disobedience and breaking unjust, discriminatory laws during the social movements of the 1950s and 1960s

(Alexander 2010: 40–41). That trope persisted with the War on Drugs, which began modestly under Nixon in the early 1970s but rapidly accelerated during Reagan's first presidential term a decade later.[25] Focusing on the so-called crack epidemic, Reagan and his cabinet officials racialized and spatialized this war, generating the mistaken impression that illegal drugs and crime were an inner-city (black) problem (Alexander 2010: 40–58).[26] Such framing sparked the mass incarceration of people of color, mainly young African American and Latino men. With more than 2 million people behind bars, the United States has the highest rate of incarceration in the world. Beyond the walls, another 5 million people categorized as permanent felons face countless legal forms of discrimination (housing, employment, voting, etc.) that limit their freedom and life chances (Alexander 2010: 60, 94, 140–165). These new barriers constitute what legal scholar Michelle Alexander (2010) has called the "New Jim Crow."

The New Jim Crow is just one manifestation of racial neoliberalism. Besides targeting "criminals" (mostly black and brown men of color), Reagan condemned the so-called welfare queen who supposedly had "80 names, 30 addresses, 12 social security cards, and had a tax-free income of over $150,000" (Alexander 2010: 48–49). This "post-racial" discourse (which singled out working-class women of color based on "neutral" language), combined with similar attacks on "busing" (integrated public schools), "quotas" (affirmative action), and "illegal aliens" (unauthorized migrants), often paid dividends for Republicans *and* Democrats in the 1980s and 1990s as politicians from both parties deliberately crafted their campaign messages to attract middle- and working-class white voters (Edsall and Edsall 1991; Omi and Winant 1994). Given their declining economic fortunes, such appeals generally found fertile ground. Having embraced the bipartisan (but mostly New Right) premise that people of color, immigrants, women, and "big government" were responsible for their woes, the Second Reconstruction ended as white supremacy and (capitalist) class power were gradually reestablished.

CALIFORNIA ÜBER ALLES: PETE WILSON, HIGHER EDUCATION, PRISONS, AND PROPOSITION 187

Racial and economic neoliberalism did not operate solely on the federal level; both processes "trickled down" to states like California, particularly under Republican governor Pete Wilson.[27] Having succeeded Republican governor George Deukmejian (1982–90), a fiscally conservative, tough law-and-order, anti-labor official, Wilson's first term in office coincided with the economic recession in the early 1990s.[28] While the nation slowly "recovered" (according to macroeconomic indicators that often overlook the tangible struggles that most working people face on a daily basis) over time, California's economy remained feeble. The end of the Cold War partially crippled the aerospace and defense industries, reducing tax revenues (Walker 1995). Fewer resources (combined with continued low taxes on the wealthy) generated significant budget deficits ($14.3 billion), prompting Wilson to pass several creative tax measures and slash funding for social programs, primary (K–12) education, and the CSU and UC systems in 1991–92 (Lustig and Walker 1995). Notably, prison spending increased despite the tough economic climate (Anand 2012).[29] Sharply criticizing these decisions, the Bay Area–based, multiracial, radical hip-hop band Disposable Heroes of Hiphoprisy released an updated version of the Dead Kennedys' classic punk anthem, "California Über Alles," stating,

> I'm your Governor Pete Wilson, ya know. The baddest governor to ever grab the mic and go BOOM! Gimme a budget and watch me hack it! Gimme a beat and I'll show you how to jack it! I give the rich a giant tax loophole and I leave the poor living in a poophole. At a time when AIDS is in a crisis, I cut health care and I raise prices. Sales tax, snack tax, excise tax. Information attack with a newspaper tax. Hit the pocket books of working families, increase tuition at the universities. . . . I'm so proud to know the Great Communicator, wanna be known as the Great Incarcerator. I'll keep cutting public education, even though we rank 45th in the nation. I've got a plan for all the minorities, send 'em to the California Youth Authority. From San Francisco Urban Elementary [school] to Pelican Bay State Penitentiary. There they can work for the master race and always wear a happy face. . . . Now it's 1992, knock, knock at your front door. . . . People starvin' and livin' in the streets, because they tried to mess with me President Pete.[30]

Faced with $900 million in cuts from Sacramento between 1990 and 1995, the UC regents laid off five thousand employees, froze and cut salaries, offered early retirement packages, and raised tuition (Pelfrey 2012: 60). Student fees increased more than 125 percent over the same five-year period, rising from $2,000 to slightly more than $4,400 (Schrag 2004). Higher costs presaged the privatization of the UC system, which has rapidly accelerated over the past twenty years.[31] When Wilson graduated from UC Berkeley's Boalt Law School in the early 1960s, fees were nominal. The 1960 California Master Plan for Higher

Education was based on the premise that the UC system would automatically admit the top 12.5 percent of graduating high school seniors in the state. Under this model, working- and middle-class students, who could not afford Stanford or Harvard, could attend UC Berkeley or UCLA tuition-free and still obtain an equally rigorous and prestigious degree as they would from these and similar private, elite colleges. Higher fees upended this plan, however, affecting students from all racial backgrounds, but they hit students of color harder since most were first-generation college students who came from working-class or lower-middle-class homes (Newfield 2008: 1–2). UC Student Association president and UCSB graduate student Marisela Márquez (who played a key role during that campus's 1994 hunger strike) spoke about these issues before a 1992 regents board meeting: "A public University of California is the greatest of gifts that each generation of Californians passes on to the next, but every time student fees go up, every time you allow more of the burden to be shifted from the state to the individuals, the university loses some of that essential quality, its public nature" (L. Gordon 1992a).[32]

Higher fees generated great moral outrage, sparking large student protests on nearly every UC campus in the early 1990s. What many found even more offensive was the generous and largely secretive $2.4 million retirement package that the regents offered then–UC president David P. Gardner in March 1992 (Merl 1992).[33] Equally irksome were closely held documents that revealed many top-paid UC officials received significant pay increases despite fiscal austerity and student-fee increases (L. Gordon 1992b; Frammolino 1993). Democratic state senator Tom Hayden critiqued these decisions, stating, "I see budgets being slashed and doors being closed on students . . . and the more privileged sectors helping themselves to more and more of the reward. They model themselves after Harvard, Stanford, IBM and General Motors. And the irony is they are not even buying competence with these inflated salaries. We have seen a whole series of embarrassing stumbles" (Frammolino 1993). Such disclosures fueled student concern that while elite UC officials were enjoying higher salaries, bonuses, and other perks, the academic programs and departments (the EOB, Chicana/o studies departments, ethnic studies libraries, etc.) that they relied on and were passionate about were being financially starved. As will be seen in chapters 3 and 4, financial starvation sparked self-starvation, as nearly two dozen Chicana/o and Latina/o UCLA and UCSB students went on hunger strikes in 1993 and 1994, demanding, among other things, no more fee increases and the establishment and/or expansion of Chicana/o studies departments.

The state's prolonged economic crisis, combined with draconian budget cuts, sank Wilson's approval ratings, limiting his chances for reelection in 1994.[34] Having previously favored less restrictive immigration policies as a U.S. senator in the middle and late 1980s, the former San Diego mayor (1971–83) "flip-flopped," claiming that unauthorized migrants and their U.S.-born children (citizens under the Fourteenth Amendment) helped prompt the state's deep economic crisis (J. Klein 1993).[35] Relying on what Leo Chávez (2013: 23–47) has brilliantly called the "Latino threat narrative," Wilson asserted that total spending (for health care, education, corrections, etc.) on "illegal immigrants" cost California $3 billion annually, which he demanded that the Clinton administration provide given immigration matters fall under the federal government's jurisdiction (Nevins 2002: 72). Wilson also embraced *mainstream* anti-immigrant discourse, declaring that illegal immigration constituted a "silent invasion" and covert *reconquista* and voicing support for a ban on birthright citizenship to "children born in the United States to illegal immigrant parents" (Le. Chávez 2013; Inda 2006: 91–92; J. Klein 1993).[36] Given these views, his support for a far-right ballot initiative, initially known as "Save Our State" in 1993 and later becoming Proposition 187, wasn't too surprising (Martinez HoSang 2010; Santa Ana 2002).[37] The measure would have eliminated virtually all educational, social, and health care services for undocumented immigrants (including in-state tuition for undocumented community college, CSU, and UC students) and would have required teachers, social workers, nurses, and doctors (among others) to report any *suspected* noncitizen to the Immigration and Naturalization Service (Ono and Sloop 2002: 83–86).[38] The politics of racial scapegoating paid dividends, as white middle- and working-class voters overwhelmingly backed Proposition 187, securing Wilson's landslide reelection victory (Martinez HoSang 2010: 160–200).

Although later ruled unconstitutional, Proposition 187 reflected nationwide anti-immigrant sentiment, as Democratic president Bill Clinton enacted Operation Gatekeeper in 1994 (Nevins 2002). Gatekeeper militarized the U.S.-Mexico border, pushing unauthorized migrants from the San Diego-Tijuana checkpoint to the sweltering Arizona desert, where thousands have died over the past twenty years (Nevins 2002; Urrea 2004).[39] Despite this state-sanctioned violence, "they kept coming," fleeing poverty and high unemployment, spurred by U.S. support for neoliberal economic reforms and structural adjustment policies within Mexico that were first instituted in the early 1980s (Barry 1995; LaBotz 1992). Backed into a corner, their livelihoods compromised by cheap corn exports from huge U.S.-based agribusiness companies, indigenous farmers rose up and formed the Zapatista National Liberation Army, which came out into the open on January 1, 1994, the same day NAFTA went into effect (Bacon 2004, 2008; Barry 1995). While the UCLA hunger strike occurred six months before the Zapatistas publicly emerged, their call for dignity echoed and re-echoed across many social movements, including the UFW, the Mexican Revolution, and almost any place where the "wretched of the earth" have demanded their freedom and liberation (Callahan 2004; Khasnabish 2006; Fanon 2004; Holloway 1998).

THE YEAR OF THE BOOMERANG: HIGHER LEARNING, POLITICAL CORRECTNESS, AND THE CULTURE WARS

Proposition 187, Operation Gatekeeper, NAFTA, and the Zapatistas produced a unique *coyuntura* (historical moment) in 1994.[40] Latino stand-up comedian Carlos Mencia crudely but accurately captured the underlying message behind the popular ballot measure, stating, "I can take racism from one or two people, but when a *whole state* tells you get the fuck out . . . fuck."[41] Proposition 187 collectively humiliated the entire Latina/o community. *They* keep coming, destroying *our* state; save *our* state from *them*. That same logic, ironically, governed the so-called culture wars in the 1980s, as some leading conservative and liberal scholars (William Bennett, Dinesh D'Souza, Allan Bloom, Arthur Schlesinger Jr., among others) claimed that calls for establishing multicultural education and diversifying the (white, male, heterosexual, Eurocentric) canon would *disunite* the United States, causing irreparable damage (J. Wilson 1995). Often framed as the struggle over political correctness, the culture wars deeply affected public and private universities, including the nine-campus UC system and Stanford. As chapter 5 will demonstrate more fully, the debate on multiculturalism generated nationwide headlines when Rev. Jesse Jackson and more than five hundred Stanford students marched on Martin Luther King Day in January 1987, demanding the elimination of the year-long required freshman class Western Culture (Lindenberger 1990; Pratt 1990; Troy 2007; J. Wilson 1995). That movement partially overlapped with a campus-based antiapartheid movement to press the Stanford administration to divest from South Africa, as the UC system did in 1986 (Ervin 2011; Masaover 2014; Soule 1997). Bowing to student pressure, Stanford partially divested and replaced Western Culture with Cultures, Ideas, and Values (CIV) (Ervin 2011; Pratt 1992).[42]

Controversy surrounding political correctness spilled over into the popular culture, specifically Hollywood, in the early 1990s. While *PCU* (Bochner 1994) satirically mocked campus- and society-wide struggles for racial and gender equality, *Higher Learning* (Singleton 1995) exposed deep fissures on a mythical campus named "Columbus University." Racial tensions turn deadly when a white male supremacist student tragically opens fire and kills two students during a campus peace festival. Such outcomes, although exaggerated for dramatic effect, accurately depicted the intense conflict or "low-intensity" war that existed on many college campuses in the early 1990s.

Analyzing the political correctness controversy from a class-based perspective, UCSB English professor Chris Newfield (2008: 6) contends that the "culture wars were economic wars." Starting with a California Senate Fact-Finding Committee on Un-American Activities (headed by longtime president pro tempore Hugh Burns) report released in 1951 stating that the UC system had "willingly or unwittingly . . . aided and abetted the international communist conspiracy in this country," J. Edgar Hoover demanded that UC President Robert Sproul take action (Newfield 2008: 51–52).[43] He appointed UC Berkeley's first chancellor, Clark Kerr, as the agency's "contact man" (an insider or "snitch") in the early 1950s, but he never named names, making him "subversive" and "un-American" in Hoover's, and later Ronald Reagan's, eyes (Kerr 2001: 49–53; Rosenfeld 2012). The Free Speech Movement and subsequent antiwar movement exacerbated Hoover and Reagan's concerns about the UC, prompting government repression and partial co-optation through what Randall Collins (1979) called the "credential society." However, too much credentialing threatened white supremacy and ruling-class power. The coming multiracial, middle-class majority, imbued with "noncapitalist" values and "imagining post-capitalist alternatives," was a "pervasive and at times shocking threat to the business and political leadership that had thrived during the cold war" (Newfield 2008: 13, 47).

Given the post-1960s political climate, the ruling elite could not overtly erect institutional barriers to limit admission, so liberal and conservative intellectuals and media pundits like Bennett, D'Souza, Bloom, Scheslinger, and many others mounted a subterranean battle on the university, attacking politically correct "tenured radicals" (student activists from the 1960s turned powerful college professors) who subversively challenged the canon (Kimball 1990; Sykes 1992). The culture wars, therefore, revived the long-standing trope that the UC was harboring dangerous "un-Americans" who sought to possibly overthrow the government. Such framing helped delegitimize public support, and mostly importantly funding, for higher education, sparking budget cuts and higher tuition. Fee hikes eroded the power of the "mass" middle-class, as Newfield (2008: 19–30) calls it, reinforcing white supremacy and elite rule.

Seen from this lens, the culture wars represent what Carlos Mencia said about Proposition 187, as public and private universities effectively told students from marginalized communities, "Get . . . out now. We don't really want you here. Should you be admitted, do not count on learning new forms of knowledge that may disrupt capitalism, racism, sexism, and imperialism." That was the elite's unstated fear—that the *mass* (multiracial) middle-class might decolonize their minds, bodies, and spirits and later the very structures and institutions that governed America, transforming it into the land where "every man [person] is free," as Langston Hughes (2004) stated in his classic 1935 Depression-era poem, "Let America be America Again."

WE DIDN'T CROSS THE BORDERS, THE BORDERS CROSSED US: COLONIALITY, FREEDOM, AND SELF-SACRIFICE

Therefore the stakes were quite high in the 1980s and 1990s. Many students of color (particularly black and brown) recognized, twenty-five to thirty years after the Civil Rights and Chicana/o Movements, they were still not completely free. They realized that while they were no longer colonized, coloniality and inequality still existed (Mignolo 2000; Quijano 2000). Even after colonialism was abolished in the "core" and "periphery," coloniality persisted post-1960s (Quijano 2000). Racism is a project of colonialism, imperialism, and modernity, spanning more than five centuries and persisting beyond the 1960s when legislation supposedly eliminated disparate treatment (Galeano 1997; Maldonado-Torres 2008; Omi and Winant 1994; Rodney 1981). Coloniality was ubiquitous in America during this so-called post-racial era—four mostly white LAPD officers being found not guilty after beating an African American motorist in March 1991; poorly funded, resegregated public schools; mass incarceration; Proposition 187; the widening gap between the rich poor; attacks on "welfare queens" and affirmative action; and a highly biased Eurocentric "canon." Speaking about the latter, the multiracial, radical, hip-hop/metal, Los Angeles–based band Rage Against the Machine acidly observed in their 1994 song "Year of the Boomerang,"

> Seems like I spent the 80s in a Haiti state of mind. Cast me into classes for elec-
> tro shock. Straight incarcerated, the *curriculum's a cell block*. I'm swimming in half-
> truths and it makes me wanna spit. Instructor come separate the healthy from
> the sick. You weigh me on the scale, smellin' burnt skin. It's dark now in Dachau
> and I'm screamin' from within. 'Cause I'm cell locked in the doctrines of the right.
> Enslaved by dogma, talk about my birthrights. Yet at every turn I'm running into
> hell's gates. So I grip the *cannon like Fanon* and pass the shells to my classmates.
> (emphasis added)

Coloniality also existed, not surprisingly, on the "left," as several major la-
bor unions in Los Angeles largely ignored Latina/o immigrants who had fled
U.S.-fueled economic and political violence in Mexico and Central America
(J. González 2000; Hamilton and Chinchilla 2001; Milkman 2006). Led by
older white men in the early 1980s, HERE (Hotel Employees and Restaurant
Employees Union) Local 11 often closed its offices early, printed its materials
in English only, and did not provide Spanish translation during its meetings
(Acuña 1996: 182). After winning a contested internal election, a rank-and-
file group led by former Chicana student activist María Elena Durazo took
over HERE Local 11.[44] Transforming it from a staid, service-oriented "business union" into a militant "social movement" union that "organized the unor-
ganized," Local 11 successfully targeted (albeit briefly) Hyatt and New Otani
in the late 1980s and early 1990s (Geron 1997).[45] Aside from HERE Local 11,
SEIU (Service Employees International Union) Local 399's Justice for Janitors
(J4J) campaign shook the notoriously antiunion city, particularly after more
than one hundred LAPD officers viciously beat nonviolent demonstrators in
Century City on May 15, 1990 (Cranford 1998, 2001; Laslett 2012; Milkman
2006).[46] That incident, which left sixteen people injured and caused two women
to miscarry, morally outraged many, generating sympathy for low-wage,
mostly Latina/o, primarily Spanish-speaking immigrant janitors (Acuña 1996:
186). Over the next several years, Local 399 organized nearly every single office building in Los Angeles, but internal conflicts soon emerged as a multiracial (black and brown) coalition of union activists challenged Local 399's white
male leaders, organizing a hunger strike outside the union's local offices (Acuña
1996: 187–88; Nazario 1995). These divisions prompted SEIU's top leaders to

place Local 399 under trusteeship, but it eventually recovered and continued, securing solid contracts for janitors through the 1990s and into the early 2000s (Milkman 2006: 159–62).[47]

These labor struggles are crucial for understanding the broader context behind the 1993 UCLA hunger strike. As the following chapter will demonstrate more clearly, before that strike occurred, student activists "scaled up," creating the United Community Labor Alliance (UCLA), which included HERE Local 11, SEIU Local 399, and many other labor, community, and civil rights organizations (Houston and Pulido 2002). Some state and local politicians, professors, and labor leaders (Gloria Molina, Rudy Acuña, César Chávez, among others) joined UCLA too.[48] During the actual hunger strike, Local 399 members offered their support, joining protests and press conferences, just as some hunger strikers and student organizers had done during previous SEIU labor actions. While seemingly incongruous, what temporarily united the student and labor movements was their shared rejection of racial neoliberalism (Mora 2007). Racial neoliberalism perpetuated coloniality, generating moral outrage and anger.

Coloniality is profoundly humiliating. It constitutes, as Maldonado-Torres (2008: 217–18, emphasis added) has argued, "life in hell," where Fanon's *damned* experience unrelenting war-like precariousness, given the "*permanent* state of exception" that emerged in 1492. Hellish conditions have often engendered anticolonial or decolonial "cries" (Fanon 2004), "screams" (Holloway 2010), and "wails" (Bob Marley) for dignity and respect. Despite the "damned's" impassioned pleas for life and liberty, they are often condemned as "whiners" who do not have "legitimate critiques and grievances" about inequality and injustice.[49] Given racism and colonialism's apparent demise, it became extremely challenging for the "subaltern" to speak in the late 1980s, as Spivak (1988) famously noted. When they did speak, their claims about institutionalized discrimination often fell on deaf ears, as many believed that American society had become post-racial or color-blind after the 1960s (Alexander 2010; Bonilla-Silva 2003; Brown et al. 2003). To be heard, Chicana/o and Latina/o university students (which constitute the subaltern or "damned" in this book) in the 1990s practiced self-sacrifice, starving themselves to reclaim their dignity and create a more dignified world (Fierke 2013).

Like their comrades in the labor unions mentioned above, these students spoke (in Time Zone's words) about the "destruction" of coloniality and racial neoliberalism—both on and off campus. They screamed, cried, and wailed about Chicana/o studies (its absence or feebleness), higher fees, toxic pesticides and unsafe working conditions in the fields, Proposition 187 and immigrant-bashing, globalization, "free trade," deindustrialization, the ever-increasing gap between the rich and poor, the prison-industrial complex and mass incarceration, and imperialism. Turning toward hip-hop bands like Aztlán Underground, many embraced indigenismo and decolonial politics, chanting "we didn't cross the border, the border crossed us!"[50] They spoke and screamed without speaking, without actually using their mouths. Because their words were so often ignored, ridiculed, and twisted, they spoke with their bodies, hoping to be heard—hoping not only to be recognized as Chicanas/os but to transform colonial relations of power that leave *all* colonized peoples unrecognizable and invisible (Maldonado-Torres 2008: 150–59). These students (specifically the UCLA hunger strikers) have typically been characterized as provincial when their concerns were broader, although they sometimes did adopt narrow or questionable positions and practices (E. Martínez 1998; Mora 2007; Rhoads 1998; Soldatenko 2005). Given the unstable *coyuntura* that existed in the early 1990s, these strikes were messy—they were inclusive and exclusive, democratic and antidemocratic, nonsexist and sexist, and coherent and incoherent. The Fanonian boomerang that they threw sometimes came back and hit them. Despite these contradictions and the fact that they were not fully prepared, these students felt like they had no other choice. "Life in hell" had become simply unbearable. They had been repeatedly humiliated on a global, national, state, and local level. Full of emotional energy, passion, anger, and love, they stood poised to put their bodies on the line.[51] All they needed was one more match, one more destructive, morally outrageous event (which eventually happened on their respective campuses) to prompt them to act, to scream, to speak spectacularly by going without food. How that process unfolded at UCLA is the subject of the next chapter.

3

UCLA

"Hungry for Justice"

I want a strike where we can all go out.
A strike of shoulders, legs, hair,
a strike born in every body.
I want a strike of workers, of drivers, of technicians, of
doctors, of doves, of flowers, of children, of women.
I want a big strike that includes even love.
A strike where everything is shut down:
the clocks, the factories, the nursery, the schools, the bus, the hospitals, the
harbors.
A strike of eyes, hands, and kisses.
A strike where breathing is banned.
A strike where silence will be born in order to hear
the departing footsteps of the tyrant.
                    GIOCONDA BELLI, "STRIKE" (1978)

INTRODUCTION

ON APRIL 28, 1993, UCLA chancellor Charles Young made a fateful and ill-timed decision.[1] After carefully consulting with faculty leaders from the campus division of the Academic Senate and discussing the matter with high-ranking university officials, such as Dean of Social Sciences Scott Waugh and Vice-chancellor for Academic Development Raymond Paredes, he chose *not* to create a Chicana/o studies department.[2] Coming just five days after César Chávez's death and one day before his funeral, Young's statement morally outraged, shocked, and humiliated many students, faculty, staff, and community members who had been seeking to establish such an academic unit for years, if not decades (M. Alvarez 2011a; Fierke 2013; Jasper 1997; Mora 2007; Mora-Ninci 1999; J. Ramírez 1993; G. Ramos 1993).

Chávez died on April 23, 1993, in San Luis, Arizona. Several days before, he testified against Bruce Church Incorporated in nearby Yuma (his birthplace). Church sued the United Farm Workers (UFW), claiming the union's lettuce boycott that it launched in the mid-1980s was based on libelous assertions that cost the company millions of dollars (Ferriss and Sandoval 1997: 253–54; Pawel 2014: 468–72). Church's lawsuit could have bankrupted the long-admired but increasingly feeble union (Bardacke 2011; Ferriss and Sandoval 1997; Mt. García 2012; Pawel 2009, 2014). In the middle and late 1960s, the UFW relied on strikes and a transnational boycott of grapes to obtain contracts for farm workers that improved their wages and working conditions (Bardacke 2011; Dunne 2007; Ganz 2009; Mt. García 2012; Pawel 2009, 2014). During that bitter five-year campaign (1965–70), some union activists and workers questioned the strategic efficacy of such nonviolent tactics, prompting Chávez to undertake the first of his many fasts in February 1968 (Bender 2008; Dalton 2003; M. García 2007; Matthiessen 2000; Pawel 2009, 2014; Orosco 2008; Shaw 2008).

Having read Gandhi and been strongly influenced by two Mexican Catholic women (his mother and grandmother), Chávez understood the symbolic and moral power of fasting and personal sacrifice (Dalton 2003; M. García 2007). Hoping to transform his supporters' "hearts of stone" into "hearts of flesh," Chávez fasted for twenty-five days, consuming nothing more than a daily communion wafer, water, and some bouillon (Ferriss and Sandoval 1997: 144). In a widely publicized and soon-to-become iconic moment (see figure 3), Chávez broke his fast on March 10, 1968, with Democratic senator and presidential candidate Robert F. Kennedy; his wife, Helen Chávez; and his mother, Juana Chávez at his side (Bender 2008).

Over the next twenty-five years (1968–93), Chávez would fast many more times, with perhaps the most notable lasting thirty-six days in 1988. Deeply concerned about reports of farm workers living in makeshift caves in Salinas, California, and the growers' heavy reliance on dangerous (cancer-causing) pesticides, Chávez hoped what he called the "Fast for Life" might rejuvenate the flagging union as well as his own spirits (Ferriss and Sandoval 1997; Pawel 2009, 2014; R. Pérez and Parlee 2014). Despite his lengthy sacrifice, the "wrath of grapes" continued, poisoning farm workers and their children as well as consumers and the general public (Ferriss and Sandoval 1997: 238). While he received careful medical attention during this fast, his body and physical well-being were deeply affected, and so, when he fasted several years later during the Church trial in April 1993, he noted that he felt "drained and exhausted" rather than refreshed (254). Just hours after breaking his short fast, he died in his sleep.

FIGURE 3. Robert F. Kennedy breaking fast with César Chávez,
Helen Chávez, and Juana Chávez at far left and far right,
respectively, March 10, 1968, *Los Angeles Times*.

The untimely death of the celebrated, charismatic, and sometimes autocratic labor and civil rights leader led tens of thousands of people to flock to Delano, California, symbolic birthplace of the UFW in the mid-1960s, to attend Chávez's funeral, which was scheduled to take place on April 29, 1993 (Bardacke 1993, 2011; Mt. García 2012; Pawel 2009, 2014). Some who made the trek had been involved in the movement to establish a Chicana/o studies department at UCLA (Gordo 2012a; Mabalon 1993a; Mora 2007; J. Ramírez 1993).[3] Upon hearing the news that Chancellor Young had not done so, they became deeply upset because they knew that Chávez had embraced their *causa*, sending the top UCLA official a letter several years earlier supporting departmentalization.[4] Young's decision, therefore, effectively poured salt on raw wounds, inflaming students who were already charged up by Chávez's sudden and unexpected passing (R. Collins 2004).

As chapter 1 indicated, social movement scholars have increasingly observed that moral shocks often generate intense emotional responses, or "triggers," facilitating critical self-transformation and activism (Jasper 1997; Nepstad 2004).

Indeed, just two weeks after receiving two such shocks (Chávez's death and Young's decision), a new, multiracial coalition of both male and female students, calling themselves Conscious Students of Color (CSC), organized a march and conducted a sit-in at the UCLA Faculty Center, occupying it for several hours on May 11, 1993 (Gordo 2012a; L. Gordon and Dundjerski 1993a; Mabalon 1993b; Mora 2007). While not solely focused on the establishment of a Chicana/o studies department, the CSC undertook this militant action because of a purported third moral shock—reasonable suspicions that the budgets for the UCLA Chicano Studies Research Center Library and ethnic and gender studies programs were about to be substantially cut (Gordo 2012a; Téllez 2011).

Based on safety concerns for the retired faculty members who were inside the building eating lunch, Executive Vice-chancellor Andrea Rich (2011), acting in place of Young, who was in Japan on a fundraising trip for the new School of Management, called the LAPD to stop the occupation because the center was privately owned and thus not under the jurisdiction of the campus police department (Mora 2007: 135). Clad in riot gear and carrying tear gas canisters, LAPD officers arrested ninety-nine students who were all finger-printed, strip-searched, booked, and jailed on trespassing and vandalism charges (the latter stemming from a broken window, ripped painting, and the words "Chicano Studies Now" and "Fuck Chuck," which were written on the center's walls during the demonstration) (Mabalon 1993b; Mora 2007).[5] Female students spent the evening at the Sybil Brand Institute for Women in East Los Angeles, while male students were housed at the downtown jail (Mora 2007: 134).

This fourth moral shock proved decisive, as some UCLA students, including Mark (Marcos) Aguilar, began exploring more radical actions, such as a hunger strike (Fuentes Salinas 1993).[6] The scant secondary literature that exists on the UCLA hunger strike often mentions Aguilar and Mindy ("Minnie") Ferguson, overlooking the fact that other individuals such as Milo Alvarez, Bonnie Chávez, Blanca Gordo, Alicia Molina, Jackie Mendoza, Michelle Téllez, Leo Estrada, Steven Loza, Cynthia Telles, Jorge Mancillas, Scott Kurashige, Richard Chabrán, John Fernández, Arturo ("Pastel") Mireles, and many more were also involved as students, staff, faculty, and community members (Acuña 1996, 2011a; Rhoads 1998).[7] This was no heroic one- or two-person show that exclusively relied on "Chingón politics," as some writers, activists, and scholars have maintained (E. Martínez 1998; Soldatenko 2005: 269). Some strikers and organizers embraced exclusionary, patriarchal positions, but this movement included diverse people with many different viewpoints and aspirations, making such sweeping assertions problematic.

The students who organized this hunger strike had been repeatedly humiliated on and off campus. Racial neoliberalism was highly destructive, sharply rolling back the gains that people of color, women, and queer people had made twenty-five years earlier. Budget austerity "trickled down," undermining the academic programs, student services, and decolonial "safe spaces" (e.g., ethnic studies libraries) that challenged the status quo and provided them with dignity. During the LA uprising one year earlier, thousands "spoke about destruction," burning down stores and taking basic necessities. While violent, these actions can also be interpreted as "spectacular speech."[8] National, state, and local leaders heard their revolutionary screams and cries for justice, even though they stifled them through repression and co-optation.

The 1992 LA uprising demonstrated that the city was on the edge (HERE 1992). Despite its Westside location, UCLA was not immune from these tensions. Revolution was in the air in the early 1990s as Latinas/os rose up, taking over unions and challenging corporations and "public" universities through militant civil disobedience (Elbaum 2002; Mora 2007). The UCLA hunger strikers were involved, however haphazardly, with this citywide social movement, which was violent *and* nonviolent, reformist *and* revolutionary.

Given this charged and chaotic atmosphere, these students sought out tactics, practices, and discourses that might weaken or dismantle coloniality (see chapter 2). Even though he never adopted radical, anticapitalist views and often alienated and pushed out his former allies from the union he co-founded, César Chávez's presence lingered like a "ghost" over the UCLA hunger strike (A. Gordon 2008; Pawel 2009, 2014). Borrowing, or "sampling" (much like hip-hop artists did in the 1980s and 1990s), from his nonviolent tool kit, they embraced his most risky and dangerous tactic—the fast, or "hunger strike," as they called it (Blackwell 2011; M. García 2007).[9] They also found his emphasis on dignity appealing because they struggled not only for departmentalization but also for a more dignified campus, city, state, nation, and world. Besides Chávez, indigeneity and the "decolonial imaginary" strongly influenced many students who saw their movement as one that had been going on for more than five hundred years (E. Pérez 1999). The quincentennial of the "discovery" of the Americas helped spark an "indigenous turn" in the early 1990s, affecting not only students but also the musical groups (such as Rage Against the Machine and Aztlán Underground) that inspired them (Francoso 2012; R. Hernández 2012).

The 1993 UCLA hunger strike occurred within this fluid, unstable context. While certain tendencies were prevalent, the strike cannot be simply dismissed as nationalist or reduced to identity politics since it involved multiple actors who had broad "freedom dreams" that extended beyond departmentalization (R. Kelley 2002; Rhoads 1998). In the following sections, I flesh out this argument, narrating the actual strike with primary sources and interviews, but before doing so, I explore UCLA's history and the crucial events that preceded it.

WHITEWASHING THE IVORY TOWER: HIGHER EDUCATION AND THE RIGHT TO THE UNIVERSITY

Despite the city's name, Los Angeles has historically treated its Mexican, Mexican American, Chicana/o, Latina/o, and indigenous residents in a decidedly un-angelic manner. Before the Spanish arrived in the mid-sixteenth century, there were approximately 300,000 indigenous people living in California (Simmons 1998: 48).[10] When the first mission was constructed in San Diego, more than two hundred years later, there were about 30,000 indigenous people living in Southern California. By 1910, there were less than 1,300 (McWilliams 1946: 28–29). Without uttering the word that Raphael Lemkin first coined during World War II, civil rights attorney, writer, and activist Carey McWilliams (1946: 29, emphasis added) sharply criticized this *genocidal* process, stating, "With the best theological intentions in the world, the Franciscan padres eliminated Indians with the effectiveness of *Nazis operating concentration camps.* . . . So far as the Indian was concerned, contact with the Missions meant death."[11] In "Los Angeles," there were about five thousand Tongvas (also known as Kizh and later as Gabrielinos) living in Yang-Na (the city's pre-colonial name) before the Spanish conquistadores "discovered" California in the 1540s (W. Estrada 2008: 16). They had lived there for centuries until the Spanish settlers virtually eliminated them through coerced labor, starvation, disease, and sexualized violence (Castañeda 1993; Cook 1976).

The Kizh/Tongva spoke Takic, a Northern Uto-Aztecan language that was often called "Shoshonean" for many years (Golla 2011: 169, 179–80). The Aztecs, who apparently migrated from the contemporary Southwestern United States ("Aztlán") into the Valley of Mexico (known as Anáhuac, which later included Tenochtitlán, located in modern-day Mexico City) in the eleventh century, spoke Nahuatl, a Southern Uto-Aztecan language (170).[12] This linguistic affinity made the Tongvas and Aztecs "distant relatives" who were also politically related through colonization and genocide.[13] The indigenous population in Central Mexico (which includes Tenochtitlán) fell from 25 million people in 1519 (when Hernán Cortés and his conquistadors arrived) to 1.3 million in 1595 (Stannard 1992: 85). Despite these cultural and historical ties, after Mexico became independent in 1821, the new government provided former Spanish elites (not the Tongvas or other California Indians as was guaranteed under legislation governing mission secularization) with huge land grants called ranchos (Castañeda 1993; Chávez-García 2006; McWilliams 1946). While they should have been owners, the Tongva/Kizh became workers, performing strenuous, back-breaking labor just as they had done ever since settler colonialism emerged in Southern California (Hixson 2013).[14]

Shortly after the U.S.-Mexico War ended, a new multiracial working class developed in the greater Los Angeles area. Chinese workers competed with mostly Mexican and white workers, sparking the 1871 Chinatown massacre and the 1882 Chinese Exclusion Act (Saxton 1971; Zesch 2012). Japanese workers replaced the Chinese, but under the Gentleman's Agreement enacted in the 1900s, Japanese immigration into the United States was not allowed (Kurashige 2008; Takaki 1989). With very few Asian and indigenous workers, capital could have turned toward black labor, but their numbers were still relatively small (Flamming 2005; Sides 2003). Fleeing a decade-long revolution that the United States helped facilitate by supporting long-time Mexican dictator Porfirio Díaz (1876–1911), Mexicans filled this void, becoming the region's proletariat, working in factories and in the fields (Gilly 1983; González and Hernández 2003). While they were granted full citizenship rights under the Treaty of Guadalupe Hidalgo, Mexicans faced tremendous discrimination, transforming them into second-class citizens (Griswold del Castillo 1990).

From the early 1900s onward, the city's white leaders practiced ethnic cleansing, "whitewashing the adobe" (Deverell 2004). In the 1920s, Mexican children attended segregated, poorly funded public schools where they were forcibly assimilated and banned from speaking Spanish (G. González 1990; Sánchez 1993). Several years later, Mexicans were blamed for the Great Depression and more than a million were deported nationally (Balderrama and Rodríguez 2006; Guerin-Gonzáles 1994). During the "good war" (World War II), Mexican American youth were targeted for murder, incarcerated, and stripped of their clothes and hence their dignity (L. Alvarez 2008; Mazón 1984; Pagán 2003; C. Ramírez 2009). While the nation was fighting the Red Menace during the Cold War, Mexican Americans were uprooted from their homes (even though many served during World War II and the Korean War), opening space for the construction of freeways and Dodger Stadium (Avila 2004; R. López 2009; Normark 1999; Parson 2005; Yosso and García 2007). Chicana/o youth fared no better in the 1960s, as many were pushed out from public schools and tracked into vocational, non-college-prep courses (García and Castro 2011). They were also taught that they were culturally deficient and were poor because of their customs and traditions (Yosso 2006). They never learned about colonialism, white supremacy, and how the city's Mexican and Mexican American community—and other communities of color, workers, women, and queer people—had struggled for decades for dignity, respect, and freedom (Gottlieb et al. 2005; Pulido, Barraclough, and Cheng 2012).

In the early 1900s, *Los Angeles Times* publisher general Harrison Otis envisioned Los Angeles as the nation's "white spot," just as the University of Southern California's (USC) second president, Joseph Widney, did when he proclaimed (in his 1907 book *Race Life of the Aryan Peoples*) that the city was "destined to become the world capital of Aryan supremacy" (Avila 2004: 22; Bernstein 2011: 22–23).[15] Located in what was then known as West Los Angeles (now called South Central Los Angeles), USC initially enrolled very few students of color. Residential and educational segregation kept the Methodist-oriented campus lily-white, male, and mostly upper-middle class (Epting 2013; Flamming 2005: 92–93).[16] Aside from USC, several private four-year postsecondary institutions (Loyola, Occidental, Whittier, Redlands, Pomona, La Verne, Throop Polytechnic, and Immaculate Heart) existed in Southern California in the early 1900s (Hamilton and Jackson 1969: 2). A two-year teacher-training institution called the Los Angeles State Normal School also operated in downtown Los Angeles (where the Los Angeles Public Library currently resides).[17] Given its ever-expanding enrollment, the Normal School moved *west* to a larger, more modern campus on Vermont Avenue in 1914.[18] Several years later, because of the region's rapid population growth (more people lived in Southern California than the Bay Area in 1915), Los Angeles State Normal School president Ernest Carroll Moore and *Los Angeles Express* editor and UC regent Edward Dickson successfully lobbied the California state legislature and Republican governor William Stephens to establish a "Southern Branch" (Berkeley represented the "Northern Branch," but it was never called that) of the University of California on the Normal School's grounds on Vermont Avenue. The University of California, Southern Branch thus came into existence in 1919 (Dickson 1955; Dundjerski 2011; Moore 1952; Scott and Soja 1996).

The Southern Branch grew quickly, sparking intense debate about possible new locations for the campus. UC president William Campbell established a "citizens committee" that included seventeen members of the city's power elite. Having explored five key sites, they eventually selected the "Letts" property (near Beverly Hills), which Edwin and Harold Janss owned (Dundjerski 2011: 36–37; Hamilton and Jackson 1969: 40–41). Broadway department store owner Arthur Letts bought the 3,300 acre property, called the Wolfskill Ranch, in 1919 for $2 million. When Letts died, his son-in-law, Harold, and his brother, gained control of his estate, placing it under control of the Janss Investment Corporation (Wanamaker 2010: 7). Former state senator John W. Wolfskill had "originally" purchased it for $10 an acre in 1884, but before he owned it, a Spanish soldier named Don Máximo Alanis obtained it from Mexican governor Manuel Micheltorena through a land grant in 1843 (Hamilton and Jackson 1969: 40; Wanamaker 2010: 7–9). He called the property Rancho San José de Buenos Ayres (see figure 4). Alanis, however, wasn't the *original* owner; the Tongvas or "Shoshones" were. The 1993 UCLA hunger strikers knew that the campus was located on "occupied territory," stating in a flyer passed out two years before the actual event, "Let's remind Chuck (Chancellor Charles Young) whose land he is on" (Boyarsky 1993).[19]

After securing funding, construction began and UCLA (its name was formally changed by the regents in 1927) was opened in September 1929 (Dundjerski 2011: 45–46, 52–53). Despite being public and relatively "free," the campus was initially racially homogenous (reflecting the then nearly all-white Westside that included the aptly named Westwood and nearby Santa Monica).[20] While prominent African Americans such as Ralph Bunche, Jackie Robinson, and Tom Bradley attended and graduated from UCLA over time, it remained "whitewashed" for decades (Ramón and Hunt 2010). During that time (1930–60), the campus experienced several controversies, including the suspension of four students affiliated with the National Student League (which included many communists, socialists, and radicals) who "requested permission to hold a forum" on the 1934 gubernatorial race between Upton Sinclair (a socialist running as a Democrat that was opposed by the party establishment) and Republican Frank Merriam (Cohen 1993: 121–29; Dundjerski 2011: 76–77; Kerr 2001: 124–25). UCLA provost Ernest Carroll Moore's decision to suspend the four (he dismissed Celeste Strack, who was a member of the Young Communist League), along with the student body president, for merely seeking an open

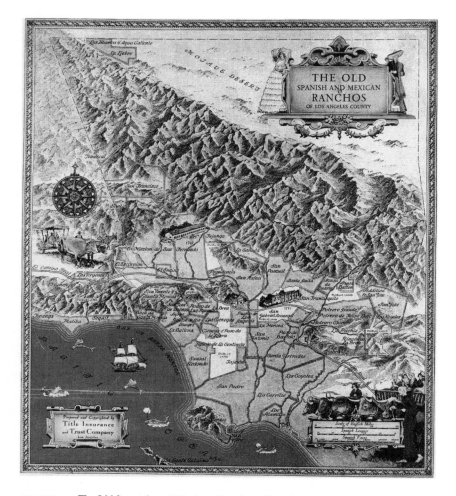

FIGURE 4. *The Old Spanish and Mexican Ranchos of Los Angeles County.* Title Insurance and Trust Company, USC Special Collections Library, California Historical Society Collection, 1860–1960 (CHS-13060).

dialogue over the upcoming election, sparked significant pushback as more than three thousand students protested, the "largest political demonstration ever seen at UCLA" (Cohen 1993: 121).[21]

Nearly ten years later, during the Red Scare, the regents instituted a loyalty oath (banning all UC employees from belonging to organizations that "advocate or teach the overthrow of the United States government" as well as membership in the Communist Party) that four UCLA faculty members did not sign, prompting their dismissal (Dundjerski 2011: 120–23). The California Supreme Court later declared that the oath was unconstitutional, but the regents and UC president Robert Sproul continued their war on the "Red Menace" by appointing Raymond Allen as UCLA's first chancellor in 1952 (Dundjerski 2011: 126; Rosenfeld 2012). Before taking that post, Allen served as president of the University of Washington, where he recommended that two "self-admitted communist" professors be fired (Dundjerski 2011: 120). Once in office, he became the "contact man" between UCLA and the California state senate Fact-Finding Committee on Un-American Activities, a role that UC Berkeley Chancellor Clark Kerr rejected, generating concerns in J. Edgar Hoover's eyes that the future UC president might be "red" (Dundjerski 2011: 127; Kerr 2001: 49–76; Rosenfeld 2012: 7–8).[22] Had Allen's reputation not been tarnished by an athletic scandal involving the UCLA football team, he, rather than Kerr, might have become UC president, replacing Sproul, who resigned (after serving for nearly thirty years) in 1958 (Dundjerski 2011: 130).[23]

Under Chancellor Franklin Murphy (1960–68), UCLA's student population and physical presence expanded (Dundjerski 2011: 134). Thanks to his close ties with the city's power elite and several UC regents that lived in Southern California, the university's reputation, power, and visibility increased, emerging from Berkeley's long shadow (Mt. Davis 2007). Despite those strides, the campus, like the city itself, was not immune from social unrest. In August 1965, Watts exploded, revealing deep, historical racial and class inequalities that had existed for decades in the African American community in South Central Los Angeles (Horne 1997). Having been mistreated for so long (even though they helped "officially" establish the city when it was "founded" on September 4, 1781), African Americans were claiming, as they had for many years previously through music, culture, activism, and politics, that they had a "right to the city" (Abdullah and Freer 2010; W. Estrada 2008; Harvey 2008, 2012; Johnson 2013; R. J. Smith 2006).[24] That sentiment surfaced three years later in East and South Los Angeles, when ten thousand mostly Chicana/o students walked or "blew out" from their high schools in March 1968 (Berta-Ávila, Tijerina Revilla, and Figueroa 2011; Blackwell 2011; Delgado Bernal 1998; García and Castro 2011). Those students received some assistance and support from UCLA Chicana/o students that were affiliated with the campus chapter of the United Mexican American Students (UMAS), who several months later demanded that UCLA establish a Chicano studies department (Macías 2011). Demanding their "right

to the city," these high school students called for more Chicana/o teachers, counselors, and administrators; relevant, non-Eurocentric course materials; and
something seemingly small, but quite important, for bodily integrity and personal dignity—more bathrooms (García and Castro 2011; Harvey 2012). Because nearly one-half of all Chicana/o students dropped out, or were "pushed-
out" because of institutional racism within the Los Angeles public school
system in the 1960s, UCLA had very few Chicana/o students, even though they
were the second largest ethnic group in the region during that era. The university
thus, on the eve of great upheaval, was much like the city, a "white spot."

Given the Watts riots, the high-school blow-outs, and other social movements and protests, UC president Charles Hitch (who took over after the regents fired Clark Kerr in 1967) instituted the Urban Crisis Program to increase
the number of students and faculty of color (Collisson 2008: 128; Dundjerski
2011: 178–79). After Murphy resigned (because of deep UC budget cuts and tuition increases that Governor Ronald Reagan pushed through as well as Murphy's disappointment in not being named Kerr's replacement), his close ally,
thirty-six-year-old Charles Young (1968–97) took over as chancellor and established the Faculty Development Program, which recruited Communist Party
member Angela Davis to teach at the university in fall 1969 (Mt. Davis 2007:
106; Dundjerski 2011: 178–79). After being challenged by student activists to
increase African American and Chicana/o student enrollment, Young created
the High Potential Program (HPP), and during the summer of 1968, students
like Daniel Johnson, a key Black Student Union leader, went out and helped
recruit fifty black students and fifty Chicana/o students (Collisson 2008: 1;
Dundjerski 2011: 182–86). Black Panther Party members Elaine Brown, Al-
prentice ("Bunchy") Carter, and John Huggins were three of those recruits who
attended UCLA as HPP students (Collission 2008: 1). They, along with other
black students, called on Young to create the Center for Afro-American Studies (CAAS), which he agreed to in 1968. A bitter dispute over who would lead
the new unit soon ensued, however, sparking a shoot-out at Campbell Hall
(where the HPP was located) on January 17, 1969, that left Carter and Huggins
dead (S. Brown 2003: 164–67; Collission 2008: 150–51). Their deaths were attrib-
uted to UCLA alumni Maulana Karenga's United Slaves (US) organization,
although many still believe that the FBI *and* US were both involved, which has
still not been verified (S. Brown 2003: 96–97; Collisson 2008: 139).[25] The killing
of Carter and Huggins, combined with Angela Davis's eventual firing (which
Young and Hitch vigorously opposed), occurred within the context of the FBI's
counterintelligence program (COINTELPRO) that systematically decimated

the Black Panthers and other radical political organizations in the 1960s and 1970s (Alegría 2011; Churchill and Vander Wall 1990).

Much like their black counterparts, Chicana/o students demanded that they had a "right to the university" too, as UMAS activists called on Chancellor Young to create a "think tank" similar to the CAAS (Macías 2011). Once again, he agreed, and the Chicano Studies Research Center (CSRC) was established in fall 1969 (Tasch 2010: 16). In a revealing comment, however, Young was quoted—almost immediately after the Asian American and American Indian Studies Centers (AASC and AISC, respectively) were created under the Ford Foundation–funded Institute for American Cultures (IAC), which also provided partial backing for the CAAS and CSRC—as not favoring the formation of full-fledged ethnic studies departments, stating, "[I] agree with the faculty, this is not *the right way to go*" (Tasch 2010: 16, emphasis added).[26]

Despite his opposition (he repeatedly blamed the faculty over the next few decades, claiming that they were the main stumbling block regarding this issue), Chicana/o students continued pushing for departmentalization, as they had been doing since 1968 (Macías 2011). On May 5, 1970, Chicana/o students affiliated with MEChA (Movimiento Estudiantil Chicano de Aztlán, which replaced UMAS in 1969) called for a Chicano studies department.[27] Taking place on Cinco de Mayo (when the underdog Mexican Army defeated the powerful French military in the Battle of Puebla on May 5, 1862), the students occupied the main campus administration building, framing their action in anti/decolonial terms (Hayes-Bautista 2012; Macías 2011; Mora 2007). That same day, just hours after four white Kent State University students were shot and killed by National Guardsmen while protesting President Nixon's escalation of the Vietnam War into Cambodia, thousands of students held a protest outside the UCLA Reserve Officers' Training Corps (ROTC) office.[28] That protest turned violent when LAPD officers beat several students and faculty members. The police also forcibly removed Chicana/o student activists, ending their action (Macías 2011; Mora 2007). Shortly after both demonstrations, a campus-wide emergency was declared and Governor Reagan (who called for a "blood-bath" and "no more appeasement" shortly *before* Kent State) ordered all California universities and colleges to be closed down for four days (Mora 2007; Perlstein 2014: 90; UCLA 1970).

Aside from repression, Chancellor Young and his administration relied on more subtle measures, creating a feeble, understaffed Chicano Studies Inter-Departmental Program (IDP) under the CSRC's auspices in 1973 (Macías 2011).

Not a full-fledged department, any student could major in the program, taking classes from faculty that worked in traditional fields and disciplines (history, sociology, English, political science, etc.) and specialized in Chicana/o studies issues and themes (Macías 2011). The CSRC directors initially managed the IDP, but since its focus was primarily on research, most could not strengthen it without more financial and human resources from Murphy Hall (the main administration building), particularly the dean of social sciences, who oversaw the fledgling program (Mitchell-Kernan 2011; Waugh 2011).

Through activism and pressure, UCLA Chicana/o students gained their "right to the university" in the 1960s and 1970s, making it slightly less white-washed. That right was circumscribed, however, as the IDP illustrated their continued colonized, second-class status even in an emerging "post-racial" America. It took twenty more years before the IDP was transformed into something unique—the Center for Interdisciplinary Instruction (CII). That nomenclature, seen as a victory by many, indicated that it was still too early for an unequivocal right to the university, despite the fact that UCLA resided on land that had been taken away from their indigenous ancestors nearly five hundred years before. These stubborn facts (explored more fully below) galvanized many Chicana/o students in the late 1980s and early 1990s as their struggle for dignity turned them into decolonial hunger artists, starving for justice.

FRAMING THE IDP: BENIGN NEGLECT VS. CULTURAL DEFICIENCY, 1973–1990

The 1993 hunger strike can be traced back to the IDP's structural weaknesses. Having already publicly declared his opposition, Chancellor Young supported the IDP as a concessionary measure that might quell discontent and block future calls for full-scale departmentalization. Without office space, staff, full-time faculty, flyers, brochures, and financial resources that might raise the program's profile, the Chicano studies IDP floundered over the next seventeen years. Fiscal austerity generated more, not less, conflict over that period. Falling under the CSRC's auspices, there was confusion and tension around the center's mission—was it primarily a research unit focused on publishing materials that might address and transform the challenging realities (coloniality) that Chicanas/os faced in Los Angeles and the Southwest, or was it responsible for teaching and offering classes on Chicano studies? The center's long-time director, pioneering historian Juan Gómez-Quiñones (1974–84), felt that it could do both, but without sufficient funding, it could not properly focus on the latter.[29] In a June 11, 1979, memo sent to College of Letters and Science dean Eugene Weber, he called for a large introductory course on Chicano studies, a theoretically based undergraduate seminar class, and a senior seminar, but his proposal was considered dead on arrival given that future resources were not forthcoming. Weber therefore never even forwarded Gómez-Quiñones's proposal up the bureaucratic chain of command for further consideration (*La Gente* 1990; Suk 1990).

That decision would come back and haunt Chancellor Young and his cabinet more than ten years later when the Academic Senate Committee on Undergraduate Courses and Curriculum (CUCC) stated in a February 1990 report that while the IDP had a "remarkable group of young Latino faculty," the program itself was a "random collection of courses, with no coherence or depth" (De Andreis 1990b).[30] On the basis of its findings, the CUCC recommended that admissions into the major be suspended until "certain improvements were made," including the addition of the very same courses that Dr. Gómez-Quiñones had called for back in 1979 (De Andreis 1990b). Had top UCLA officials provided funding for those classes ten years earlier, the 1993 hunger strike might have been avoided, but rather than augment the puny $1,500 budget that the IDP received in 1989–1990, the university spent $40,000 for a new lawn outside Royce Hall and $170,000 on the Office of Fraternity and Sorority Relations (Bernal 2011; De Andreis 1990a; Hagstrom 1990a; *La Gente* 1990; E. Martínez 1998). That latter expenditure offended many Chicana/o students after it was discovered that some fraternities regularly held Mexican "theme parties" that degraded Mexican women through offensive, violent, and misogynist lyrics found in "Lupe's Song" (Acuña 1996; de Alba 1998; D. González 2001; Suk 1992).[31]

Seen from this perspective, the IDP had been financially starved, limiting its potential and sparking possible elimination. Relying on "racism" as their key frame or trope, Chicana/o activists, staff, and even high-ranking officials repeatedly targeted the UCLA administration, especially Chancellor Young, for the program's shortcomings. Former IAC and CAAS Director and Graduate Division Dean Claudia Mitchell-Kernan (2011), for example, stated that UCLA "benignly neglected the program, never providing it with adequate funding, but you know what? Neglect is never benign. It wasn't benign in the 1960s when the federal government systematically disinvested in urban areas where many African Americans lived after the Moynihan Report came out, and it wasn't benign in the 1990s either. Neglect is cruel and it had obvious consequences here and there."[32]

Small budgets for organized research units (ORUs)—the CAAS, CSRC, AASC, and AISC—therefore sometimes generated interracial and even intraracial conflicts, as one former Chicana/o staff member asserted:

> I see it this way—if you have a family of two people and you have seventy-five thousand dollars to maintain it, it can be done, but when you have twenty people in that same family and the same seventy-five thousand dollars to raise, you can't do it. So they were starving the program (IDP). This caused a lot of in-fighting. There were different [faculty] camps or cliques. Yes they existed, but the conflicts that existed blossomed since there was no institutional leadership. If UCLA's top leaders had just listened to those people who were calling for a department, it would have been a much different place. They were so arrogant.

The UCLA administration countered those claims, framing Chicana/o faculty and students as the villain. Current executive vice-chancellor Scott Waugh (2011) (who attended Angela Davis's lectures as an undergraduate student in 1969 and later served as dean of social sciences during the 1993 hunger strike) stated that conflicts between political science professor Raymond Rocco and history professor Juan Gómez-Quiñones weakened the IDP.[33] Waugh (2011) also noted that the campus's Chicana/o faculty showed little interest in the program, focusing more on their "home" disciplines, where they served on committees and taught their courses. Finally, the university's official periodical, *UCLA Today*, along with liberal mainstream newspapers and publications such as the *Los Angeles Times*, *New York Times*, and *Chronicle of Higher Education*, all pointed out that the program had few majors (Mitchell 1991). Just two students graduated from the IDP from 1983 to 1988, *UCLA Today* pointedly observed, demonstrating its apparent unpopularity (De Andreis 1990a, 1990b). Such data, combined with faculty conflicts and perceived apathy, generated a compelling story or "majoritarian narrative": "We gave them what they wanted, but they just haven't taken good care of it. It's not our fault, it's theirs."[34]

Such logic blamed the victim, echoing liberal and conservative arguments made after segregation was dismantled in the 1960s and 1970s. Focusing on alleged cultural deficiencies in communities of color, some scholars and writers (particularly Daniel Patrick Moynihan, starting in the mid-1960s) claimed that inappropriate values and behaviors, rather than racism, benign neglect, and deindustrialization, explained persistent poverty in the 1980s and 1990s.[35] While quite popular, especially among white middle- and working-class voters, such discursive reasoning ignored the fact that when segregation ended, people of color were not completely free, as a new system of racial inequality (called "color-blind racism" or the "New Jim Crow") emerged shortly thereafter (Alexander 2010). People of color's lives were still marked by coloniality in the post-1960s era, which many UCLA Chicana/o students, staff, and faculty understood, but whose cries often fell on deaf ears (Maldonado-Torres 2008). UCLA's top administrators were responsible for the IDP's woes (just as the country's mostly white elites were culpable for the injustices that existed in ghettoes and barrios), but they deftly shifted the blame to the colonized.

These frame battles persisted, with MEChA Officer Alicia Molina stating, "How can students be attracted to the major when the university has set it up to be a phantom? Even if you are interested in it, you get discouraged" (Anima 1990b). Coloniality works most effectively as an "absent referent," like a ghost concealing unequal power relationships that perpetuate historical and contemporary injustices (A. Gordon 2008; A. Smith 2005). Operating from the margins, the colonized initially seek to unmask the fact that they are "living in hell" through deliberation and reason, but since their voices are so often dismissed or drowned out, they typically turn to spectacular speech by organizing rallies, protests, and when all other options have been exhausted, hunger strikes (Maldonado-Torres 2008).

CHICANO STUDIES NOW! TRUE GENEROSITY VS. FALSE GENEROSITY, APRIL–JULY 1990

Despite being discouraged, Molina and one hundred mostly UCLA Chicana/o students, staff, and faculty organized a demonstration outside Campbell Hall (site of the 1969 Carter-Huggins shooting) before marching over and occupying Chancellor Young's office in Murphy Hall to protest the CUCC's decision to suspend admissions into the Chicano Studies IDP (Anima 1990b; S. Hernández 1990). Joining this MEChA-organized action were students from the Afrikan Student Union, the Asian Pacific Coalition, MEChAistas from nearby CSU Northridge, and some graduate students (S. Hernández 1990).[36] While camped outside his doorway and chanting "What do we want? Chicano

Studies! When do we want it? Now," MEChA requested a meeting with the
chancellor, but he declined, even though he was inside his office and could
have spoken with the students (Anima 1990b). Two days later, the MEChA
Chicano Studies Committee met with Chancellor Young, Executive Vice-
Chancellor Murray Schwartz, College of Letters and Science Provost Raymond
Orbach, Vice-chancellor for Academic Advancement Raymond Paredes, and
Spanish professor Guillermo Hernández to demand that "CUCC's decision to
suspend admissions into the major be reversed; that immediate and permanent
funding be provided to strengthen the major; and that a Chicana/o Studies
Department be created" (Suk 1990).[37] Taking those concerns into consideration, Chancellor Young established a special Provost's Advisory Committee
on Chicano Studies (with Orbach as chair), which included faculty, students,
and staff (Anima 1990c).

Concerned about the backlash against affirmative action and the lack of student and faculty diversity in public higher education, the National Association
for Chicano Studies called for a nationwide day of action on May 7, 1990. More
than three hundred students walked out of their classes that day (two weeks after the April 25 protest), claiming UCLA was "institutionally racist in its policies of retention, financial aid, faculty recruitment, and admissions" (Hagstrom
1990b). Many were concerned that the Academic Advancement Program
(AAP), which replaced the HPP in the 1970s and was located inside Campbell
Hall, might close down given its budget shortfall. Without the AAP, the campus would become even less diverse than it already was. Because of the AAP
and IDP's troubles, many students of color were morally outraged and emotionally charged. Chancellor Young poured more fuel on the fire on May 10 when
he restated his opposition to departmentalization, saying Chicano studies is
"not a traditional discipline" (Anima 1990c).

Despite taking this position, Young set aside, in collaboration with the Office of Instructional Development (OID), $10,000 to hire a graduate research
assistant to restructure the IDP's curriculum over a three-year period. He also
provided six faculty members with released time from teaching to develop that
proposal (Anima 1990d). Assistant professor of history and Chicano studies
IDP chair George Sánchez, associate professor of sociology Vilma Ortiz, and
sociology graduate student José Calderon had applied for OID monies before
the February 1990 CUCC report was released and the April 25 action took place
(Ortiz 2011).[38] MEChA education coordinator Mark Aguilar condemned
these moves, calling them "completely unsatisfactory" (Anima 1990d). In a

position paper, MEChA called the temporary, one-time funds from OID and the Provost's Advisory Committee "insignificant." Several days later, on May 15, MEChA met with Paredes, the highest-ranking Latina/o official within Young's cabinet who shared the chancellor's views on departmentalization. Calling him a "sell-out," MEChA claimed the session was a "waste of time" (Anima 1990c).

Before the spring 1990 quarter ended, nearly one hundred students, wearing red-and-black "Chicano Studies Now" T-shirts, held a candlelight vigil outside Chancellor Young's home on May 31 (Anima 1990f). This action indicated that despite Young's co-optive measures, the cat-and-mouse game or tactical interaction process that social movement scholars have written about continued, with students not relenting from their primary demand (McAdam 1983). One week later, on June 6, two hundred students protested AAP's relocation from the second and third floors to the first floor and basement inside Campbell Hall. Having once occupied the entire building, many students of color interpreted this move, combined with no additional financial aid despite recent fee increases, as further proof that they were no longer welcome and that UCLA was practicing low-intensity "warfare" on them (Dinh 1990).[39] The day before that action, ironically, faculty members on the Provost's Advisory Committee released a statement backing departmentalization, but Orbach remained opposed even though he agreed that the IPD needed office space and funding for a part-time administrator and part-time academic counselor (Anima 1990g).

Over the summer, tactical interaction continued as Chancellor Young held a closed-door meeting with several Latina/o faculty on July 2. MEChA sharply criticized this decision, stating that it violated shared-governance procedures, with MEChA Women's Unit Coordinator Mindy Ferguson adding, "Many of the faculty that [Young] is meeting with are *Latino*, so they don't understand our Chicano history. *We* have a different history. *They* don't understand *our* struggle" (Hagstrom 1990c, emphasis added). Ferguson's remarks underscored growing concerns that MEChA was too nationalist and exclusionary, claims that were repeatedly mentioned before, during, and after the hunger strike (E. Martínez 1998; Soldatenko 2005). Only six of the invited fourteen Latina/o professors actually attended this meeting. Professors Gómez-Quiñones, Sánchez, and Ortiz (who is Puerto Rican) boycotted the meeting after they discovered that students had not been invited and were not allowed to participate (Hagstrom 1990d). Echoing Ferguson's comments, Aguilar stated, "There are several faculty who probably would not want to see Chicano Studies become powerful because it is the study of *Mexican people and their descendants in the United States*" (Hagstrom 1990d, emphasis added). While seemingly innocuous, this statement ignored UCLA's Central American students who were increasing in the early 1990s and had a shared colonial history (Bernal 2011). MEChA's discourse alienated some Central American- *and* Mexican-descent students, as will be seen below.

Shortly after this meeting, Young announced (reiterating Orbach's previously announced proposal) that the IDP would receive funding for "one staff member, one researcher, office space, and supplies" (L. Ramos 1990). When combined with the OID grant, the university provided the IDP with $150,000 to $200,000, temporarily expanding its tiny budget. Having made additional concessions that would strengthen the program's foundation and visibility, Young declared that students could once again major in Chicano studies and praised the student activists for their efforts (L. Ramos 1990). Seeing these measures, in Paulo Freire's (2000: 44–46) words, as "false generosity," Aguilar flatly rejected Young's moves, stating, "This meeting is a deviation from the process that we began ourselves" (L. Ramos 1990). Freire (2000: 55) understood that the oppressor can never free the oppressed; "true generosity" is liberating and decolonial, frightening the colonizer. When pressed, ruling elites can "buy peace," like Young tried with these initiatives, but "peace cannot be bought; peace is experienced in solidary and loving acts which cannot be incarnated in oppression" (146). The chancellor hoped that the "rejects of life" would extend their "trembling hands" and be content, but he was sorely mistaken, as he would soon discover (45).

TAKING IT TO THE NEXT LEVEL: SCALING DOWN AND UP, AUGUST 1990–JANUARY 1991

Despite the university's "benevolence," MEChAistas like Marcos Aguilar, Milo Alvarez, and Minnie Ferguson kept their eyes on the prize—departmentalization. Over summer and fall 1990, these three, along with Bonnie Chávez and several other MEChAistas, began drafting an extensive proposal to create a Chicana/o studies department at UCLA (Alvarez 2011b).

Alvarez was born in East Los Angeles in September 1970, just "one month after the Chicano [Anti-War] Moratorium," he proudly noted. He grew up in a Mexican working-class family that lived in Alhambra and Rosemead during his formative adolescent years. While his parents were not overtly involved in politics, he observed that his mother had a feminist sensibility, calling on him to do "traditional gender-specific" work (such as washing dishes and vacuuming the house). Calling his father a Reagan Democrat, he too was taken as a high school student with Reagan's speeches, and he embraced conservative, hard-work ethics and ideals. His political views began shifting, however, after he enrolled in the AAP's Freshman Summer Program (FSP) in 1988. The FSP included workshops on racial diversity, and participants watched powerful films on Central America, South Africa, and the Israeli-Palestinian conflict (Alvarez 2011b).

Salvadoran UCLA student Santiago Bernal saw those films too. The one on Central America hit home, as his family fled El Salvador in 1980 after his brother, who was involved in radical social movements, was killed (Bernal 2011). Upon arriving, his family rarely discussed the country's brutal civil war, but they remained leftists. After watching these films and going through FSP, Bernal started changing, becoming more politicized, as did Alvarez, who went from quasi-conservative to dedicated MEChAista. Aguilar underwent a similar self-transformation, coming into UCLA as a "surfer from Redondo Beach and leaving as an Aztec warrior" (Alvarez 2011b; Bernal 2011). He also attended FSP and later joined MEChA, changing his first name from Mark to Marcos and then to Huitzilihuitl (Nahuatl name meaning "hummingbird feather," also the name of Tenochititlán's second ruler in the early fourteenth century). Such name changes were common in the late 1980s and early 1990s, cutting across race, as some UCLA African American students and staff adopted African or Muslim-inspired names (Bernal 2011). During this period, many black and brown students wore African and Aztlán medallions, listened to politicized hip-hop bands like Public Enemy and Aztlán Underground, and started spelling "Chicano" with an *x* and "African" with a *k*. While seemingly minor, such changes reflected an emerging decolonial consciousness and praxis, echoing Malcolm X's decision to drop his "slave last name" (Little) in 1950.[40] Aguilar, Alvarez, and Bernal, incidentally, all worked as part-time AAP counselors in the late 1980s.

Given its strategic importance, many students of color were concerned that the AAP's budget was being cut back and that its director, Adolfo Bermeo, was changing its ethos by making plans to "professionalize" its counseling staff. Seeing these decisions (combined with the move to the Campbell Hall basement) as radically downsizing and depoliticizing the program, MEChA, the Afrikan Student Union, Asian Pacific Coalition, and the American Indian Student

Union all broke their ties with AAP, creating their own outreach, recruiting, and retention programs (Alvarez 2011a; Bernal 2011; Maldonado 2010; Roque Ramírez 2012). MEChA also called for expanding the campus-wide Chicana/o retention program, named Mariposa, and placing it under the new Chicana/o Studies Department in its proposal, which was released on December 1, 1990. That document also included nearly one hundred courses, on topics including gender, sexuality, mass media, labor, education, law, politics, the arts, and field studies. Most tellingly (belying claims that the 1993 hunger strike was overly "male-centered, patriarchal, homophobic, and nationalist") the working draft of the proposal stated,[41]

> Because the history and perspective of Chicanas has traditionally been *excluded* from Chicano Studies courses (wherever they have existed), our proposal recognizes the need and demands the implementation of courses designed to recognize the role of women in the historical process of the Chicana and Chicano movements both in Mexico and the U.S. This proposal is unique in that women have not only been included in the development of the curriculum and vision, but have substantially impacted the actual content of the courses. Chicanas have been *starved* of a program which is inclusive of our histories, as well as of a program which acknowledges and gives merit to the fundamentally inherent role of Chicanas/Mexicanas. (emphasis added)

This discourse does not mean that this proposal and the movement that produced it were free from sexism and heterosexism—nor nationalism for that matter. Indeed, the text, which specifically called for a Chica*na* and Chicano studies department (demonstrating its feminist ethos and the strength of the MEChA Women's Unit, as it was then called), focused exclusively on Mexicans, Chicanas, Chicanos, and "people of Mexican descent" (MEChA and UCLA 1990). Central Americans and other Latinas/os were never mentioned, a glaring omission that would later haunt the organization as many Chicana/o, Guatemalan, and Salvadoran students found the organization's politics too narrow, opting instead for multiracial groups that focused on common interests without forgoing unique concerns (Bernal 2011; Téllez 2011).

Aside from the Mariposa retention program and the broad-based but ethnically specific curriculum, the proposal called for the "immediate hiring of a senior-level professor to chair the department," "recruiting fifteen core faculty," and "establishing a junta directiva . . . that would *operate independently of university guidelines with full authority over all aspects of the department*" (MEChA and United Community Labor Alliance 1990, emphasis added). This last demand addressed the false generosity and co-optation that Aguilar foresaw just months before, potentially establishing a decolonial institution within the larger colonial institution. Those two logics could not operate simultaneously, however. Relying on neutral, bureaucratic language, the university claimed that the *junta directiva* (board of directors) would have violated its policies and procedures for managing academic departments and stated that all proposals for departmentalization must come from faculty, not students or community members (Waugh 2011). Calls for community control over Chicana/o and black studies programs and departments have often generated considerable friction (Rojas 2007). The most "successful" ones have often distanced themselves from community-based concerns, which many MEChAistas recognized and hoped to remedy through the junta directiva and the establishment of a community action center that might transform Los Angeles from a "city on the edge" to a "rebel city" based on social justice for all oppressed people (Alvarez 2011b; Harvey 2012).

Despite its certain rejection, MEChA released its proposal on the very same day Alvarez attended a crucial MEChA Central Meeting held at CSU Northridge. In the mid-1980s, the League of Revolutionary Struggle (LRS, also known as the Liga), a Maoist group that emerged from the Chicana/o August 29th Movement, the Asian American I Wor Kuen, and the African American Revolutionary Communist League in the late 1970s, reportedly "infiltrated" and took over the California statewide MEChA (Licón 2009: 88–100). MEChA groups that opposed the Liga formed "MEChA Summit" chapters. UCLA was a MEChA Summit chapter, and in 1985 and 1986 it, along with other MEChA Summit chapters, denounced the Liga and disrupted a National Chicano Student Conference held at UC Berkeley on grounds that it was a secretive, undemocratic organization that limited freedom of speech (92). After this conference, anti-Liga MEChA chapters left the California statewide MEChA, leaving the Liga to consolidate its power over the next three years (1986–89). In 1989, the Liga MEChA faction passed a new California MEChA constitution and published a new manifesto, called El Plan de MEChA, which reaffirmed Chicano nationalism but also emphasized class struggle and multiracial coalitions, especially with African Americans and Asian Americans (93). El Plan de MEChA also criticized their opponents for being too ultranationalist.

MEChA Summit chapters rejected this new plan and embraced the organization's founding document, El Plan de Santa Barbara, which some in the middle and late 1980s saw as nationalist, sexist, and anachronistic (Licón 2009; Pardo 1984). Calling themselves the "real" or "true" MEChA, MEChA Summit chapters rallied to "take back" MEChA from the Liga, initially focusing on Southern California–based campuses. The CSU Northridge LA County MEChA Central meeting on December 1, 1990, thus was a high-stakes battle. MEChA Summit chapters became a voting majority at the meeting, pushing aside Liga chapters like the one that existed at CSU Los Angeles (Licón 2009: 96). Over the next two years, MEChA Summit chapters took over the California statewide MEChA as the Liga collapsed after China brutally repressed pro-democracy activists in June 1989 and the Soviet Union and other socialist countries fell apart in the early 1990s (98–101). With Marxism, Maoism, and other radical ideologies discredited, some Chicana/o students gravitated toward nationalism and indigenismo, which became even more popular as the quincentennial of the conquest of the Americas approached (Alvarez 2011b).

With this intense schism within MEChA in the late 1980s, one can perhaps understand why UCLA MEChAistas worked so diligently to establish a Chicana and Chicano Studies Department. They viewed El Plan de Santa Barbara, which called for such units to be placed under the control of a junta directiva as their sacred, iconic text. It was very symbolic, therefore, that on the very same day that UCLA MEChA released its plan for departmentalization based on El Plan de Santa Barbara, Alvarez, one of its key leaders (who wrote several sections of the actual proposal), helped empower other Chicana/o student activists within the LA County MEChA that held similar beliefs.[42]

Having successfully "scaled down" (ousting their internal opponents democratically), UCLA MEChAistas "scaled up," spatially expanding their movement into the wider off-campus community; specifically, the city's historic Mexican heart—East Los Angeles and the Placita (Plaza) in downtown (Herod 2001; Houston and Pulido 2002). Partially on the basis of preexisting ties between Vivién Bonzo (owner of La Golondrina Mexican Café and head of the Olvera Street Merchants Association), Marcos Aguilar, and Minnie Ferguson (who had all been working together, along with others, for several years to stop Los Angeles from redeveloping or "whitewashing" the historic downtown area), the United Community Labor Alliance (UCLA) was formed in December 1990 (Acuña 1996: 23–30; J. Fernández 2011).[43] The coalition included more than fifty labor, civil rights, immigrant rights, and community-based organizations such as One Stop Immigration, the Coalition for Humane Immigrant Rights, Mothers of East Los Angeles, SEIU Local 399 ("Justice for Janitors"), HERE Local 11, and the United Teachers of Los Angeles (UTLA). Prominent

supporters included California state senator Art Torres, California state as-
semblyperson Tom Hayden, Bert Corona, César Chávez, and professors Rodolfo Acuña and Juan Gómez-Quiñones (the latter two were also involved
with the battle over Olvera Street).[44] Long-time UTLA activist and East Los
Angeles (Roosevelt) high school teacher Dr. John Fernández, the very first student to graduate from UCLA with a bachelor's degree in Chicano studies in
1977, co-chaired UCLA with Bonzo. Fernández (2011) also worked closely with
Gómez-Quiñones, who was deeply involved with the coalition.

Like many labor unions in the 1980s and 1990s, UCLA MEChAistas recognized that they could not win without external allies. Having not been heard,
they took their struggle to the next level, bringing what Public Enemy called
the "noise."[45] In Alvarez's words, "It seems for the university to listen to us, we
have to bring East L.A. to UCLA" (Hagstrom 1991). UCLA and MEChA am-
plified their voices by releasing the proposal for departmentalization together,
making their spectacular speech more credible and therefore more audible.
UCLA's name, moreover, cagily demonstrated that "another UCLA," one where
Chicanas/os finally fit (more than seventy years after the university was first
established in 1919), was possible.[46] On another level, the organizations that
were involved with UCLA were part of a citywide, mostly Latina/o-led social
movement that emerged in the 1980s and 1990s, spilling over into workplaces,
union halls, classrooms, and universities (Meyer and Whittier 1994; Milkman
2006; Mora 2007). For the first time since the U.S.-Mexico War ended in 1848,
Los Angeles was no longer the nation's "white spot," as people of color became
the demographic majority in the 1990s (Dear 2000: 15). While UCLA became
slightly less visible over time, it included many organizations that were later
involved in the large march against Proposition 187 in downtown Los Angeles in October 1994. Former One Stop Immigration executive director José
Gutiérrez (2011) stated that the movement for Chicana/o studies and the subsequent hunger strike actually provided the momentum and inspiration for
that historic action.

THE WAITING GAME AND THE RISE AND FALL OF
MEChA: FEBRUARY 1991–APRIL 1993

After jointly releasing the proposal for departmentalization with UCLA,
MEChA continued scaling up, holding a news conference with several UCLA
representatives on Olvera Street on February 1, 1991. Aguilar understood the

site's spatial and strategic value, stating, "This is symbolic because this is where the Mexican community in Los Angeles began. This is a less hostile environment than the UCLA campus. This is a better place to extend our campaign into the community" (Mitchell 1991). Just hours before this news conference was held, twenty-five mostly Chicana/o staff and faculty sent a letter to Chancellor Young, President David Gardener, and Vice-President for Academic Affairs Eugene Cota-Robles Sr. (the highest-ranking Latino official in the UC system) supporting departmentalization.[47] These coordinated actions illustrated that the campaign for Chicana/o studies was becoming increasingly sophisticated, further amplifying MEChA's voice. Despite the louder volume, Vice-chancellor Paredes claimed that most Chicano students were simply not interested in taking Chicano studies classes; the IDP's weaknesses, therefore, were not the university's responsibility (Mitchell 1991). MEChA literally turned the music back up several weeks later with a rally outside Murphy Hall that included the Chicano hip-hop group Lighter Shade of Brown and Danza Mexica Cuauhtémoc. Flyers for this event stated, "Let's remind Chuck whose land he's on," underscoring the campaign's decolonial imagination, which included but also went beyond Chicana/o studies and UCLA (E. Pérez 1999). For some, the real prize wasn't just an academic department; it was a new university, city, state, nation, and world—"a world where many worlds fit," as the Zapatistas stated several months after the UCLA hunger strike ended (Marcos 1996).

Shortly after the press conference and rally, the Provost's Advisory Committee on Chicano Studies released its findings in April 1991. Seven of the fourteen committee members voted for departmentalization, four to maintain the IDP but to review it again in three years, and three to keep it as is with no future review (Wee 1991). MEChA and UCLA saw those results positively, holding a victory celebration at Bonzo's La Golondrina Mexican Café on Olvera Street. Paredes saw the outcome differently, however, stating, the "vote is clearly split" (Moran 1991). Provost Committee co-chair and IDP chair Vilma Ortiz countered that view, saying, "I see it as eleven to three against continuing the way things are" (Wee 1991).

Despite this lopsided, favorable result, Young remained steadfastly opposed, but he stated he would consider proposals from faculty. Seizing this opportunity, eleven Chicana/o and Latina/o professors released their plan for departmentalization on January 28, 1992, which included (much like MEChA and UCLA's 1990 document) provisions for fifteen faculty members, recruiting and retention programs for undergraduate majors, and a community advisory board to oversee and manage the new unit.[48] Within hours, Provost Orbach and Academic

Senate chair Seymour Feshsbach released memos opposing the plan, as did Chancellor Young, although he stated, "I'm prepared to be persuaded to change my mind" (G. Ramos 1992). University officials framed their opposition on a familiar old trope, claiming that Chicana/o faculty did not favor departmentalization. Such logic mirrored earlier arguments that the IDP's weaknesses stemmed from internal squabbles between Chicana/o and Latina/o faculty. Paredes reinforced that view, stating, "I don't know any [Latina/o] faculty members who have agreed to participate full-time in a department" (*Daily Bruin* 1992). Ortiz once again rebutted the highest-ranking Latino campus official, saying, "It is very unfair to demand that faculty make a commitment to a department knowing how against this idea the administration is" (*Daily Bruin* 1992).

Just days before the Los Angeles "riots," Young still had not read the full faculty proposal, although several departments (English, Spanish, Portuguese, sociology, history, geography, education, economics, and political science) did. Besides history, all voted against it, citing concerns about "ghettoizing" Chicana/o faculty, staff, and students in a separate unit and having a community advisory board govern it.[49] Former History Department chairperson Scott Waugh (2011)—who later became dean of social sciences in July 1992 and then executive vice-chancellor in 2008—claimed that the university was more concerned about the latter rather than the former. In his chair's memo, however, he articulated another critical issue:

> I believe that UCLA should acknowledge the importance of ethnic studies, especially in the wake of the *social turbulence we have recently experienced* [the April 1992 riots]. It is clear, for better or worse, some faculty understand "acknowledgement" as meaning specifically "departmentalization." . . . The danger, however, is that each ethnic studies program along with women's studies programs will clamor for departmentalization once a Chicana/o Studies department is formed. It is a problem similar to the ones faced in the language departments. *Can UCLA afford a proliferation of departments at this time?* The answer depends, in part, on the relative costs of IDPs and departments, but I worry that a *multiplication of departments* would lead not only to *higher costs*, but ironically, to the isolation of those faculty, rather than their integration into the community as a whole. (emphasis added)[50]

This passage reveals that UCLA was facing a significant fiscal crisis in the early 1990s. Budget cuts from Governor Pete Wilson and the California legislature sparked plans for eliminating or consolidating several long-standing, prestigious programs (UCLA graduate programs in public health, architecture and urban planning, social welfare, library and information science, and nursing); the graduate student teaching-assistant union was consistently rebuffed; faculty were offered early retirement packages; and fees increased dramatically (Mora 2007; Newfield 2008). UCLA administrators could have stated that the state's economic woes forced them to make "tough choices" (no Chicana/o studies department), but they knew that because of UC president David Gardner's controversial "golden parachute" and reports that top campus officials were dining on fine publicly subsidized meals at exclusive clubs, such claims would have fallen on deaf ears (*Daily Bruin* 1993b). The university, therefore, relied on a more liberal, paternalist argument, saying that departmentalization might generate greater isolation or "ghettoization." Chicana/o staff, faculty, and students countered that claim, stating that UCLA could create a Chicana/o studies department *and* hire more Chicana/o faculty in traditional academic departments. It wasn't either-or; it could be both, which the university opposed, having ghettoized the Chicana/o and Latina/o community in the first place decades before (Chabrán 1993).

As the 1992–1993 academic year began, MEChA continued calling for departmentalization and held a rally in October 1992 to protest sexually explicit and extremely degrading songbooks from the Theta Xi fraternity (Acuña 1996: 295–97; de Alba 1998; D. González 2001). Commenting on the lyrics, Blanca Gordo, a MEChA member and double-major in sociology and Chicano studies, said, "There's no money to fund Chicano Studies, but there's money to fund fraternities who instill these [sexist and racist] thoughts through these songs" (Suk 1992). MEChA Women's Unit Coordinator Laura Manzano echoed Gordo's views, saying, "It's not just a Mexican issue or a women's issues; it's both" (Suk 1992). This action challenges the assertion that the 1993 hunger strike was unequivocally patriarchal; the campaign for Chicana/o studies took several years and involved many students who held diverse views.

One month after this protest, Dean Waugh forwarded a lengthy list of challenging questions to nearly all the faculty who submitted their proposal for departmentalization back in January 1992.[51] The questions were financial, pragmatic, and pedantic, indicating that prospects for approval were slim. Two anonymous professors—named El Kukuy (The Bogeyman) and La Llorona (The Weeping Woman) from the Departmento de los Muertos (Department of Death) responded in a sarcastic but measured tone, noting that racial tensions that sparked the 1992 "riots" could have partially been defused through departmentalization.[52] Several weeks later, MEChA and UCLA demanded a community meeting "with Chuck at Placita Olvera."[53] Young never replied, but Waugh issued his final decision, stating that the university should have a "Chicano Studies *program* second to none." He also called for a "renewed commitment to the IDP from the administration, departments, *and* Chicana and Chicano faculty" (emphasis added).[54]

Nonstop activism and the waiting game that the university masterfully played took a personal and academic toll on Milo Alvarez and Alicia Molina. Alvarez (2011b) recalled, "Alicia gave these speeches about her parents who worked so hard. Her father worked like eighty hours a week. I remember that. We kept on going because we had been disrespected and knew we were valuable as human beings." Nevertheless, he temporarily stepped back because of his family's financial struggles and his strong desire to stay closely involved with his family. That decision generated some controversy since MEChA's militant, all-or-nothing ethos demanded unwavering commitment. Such dedication, while laudable, was not sustainable, and its exclusive focus on "Mexicans" alienated Salvadoran gay students Santiago Bernal and Horacio Roque Ramírez, who later worked with other Central American and South American students to create the Latin American Student Association (LASA) in the late 1980s. While seen as a purely apolitical, "social" organization, LASA organized films and lectures on the civil wars in Central America (Alvarez 2011b; Bernal 2011; Roque Ramírez 2012). Bernal (2011) also felt that MEChA did not welcome him because of his sexuality. Tensions also erupted between Alvarez and Aguilar, with the latter almost being forced from MEChA in a very close vote. Aguilar later left on his own, remaining very active in the campaign for Chicana/o studies.[55]

Given this volatile context, a new mobilizing structure known as the Conscious Students of Color (CSC) emerged in April 1993. Because it included African American, Asian American, Chicana/o, Native American, and Middle Eastern students, men and women, queer and straight, Soldatenko (2005: 270) claimed that the CSC represented an "epistemic break in Chicano Studies and U.S. education in general." While overly effusive, that argument underscores perhaps the fundamental difference between CSC and MEChA: the former was multiracial while the latter was "monoracial" or nationalist. While nationalism can be progressive and revolutionary, the Chicano Movement twenty-five years earlier was often masculine and excluded Chicanas and queer Chicanas/os (Blackwell 2011). In the long struggle for a UCLA Chicana and Chicano studies department in the early 1990s, MEChA addressed sexism and hetero-sexism, but Aguilar, its most vocal and visible spokesperson, alienated some with his seemingly incomprehensible attack on University of Colorado ethnic studies chairperson Evelyn Hu-Dehart, a respected scholar whose first two books focused on Yaqui Indians under Spanish, Mexican, and American rule. Paredes had invited her to speak at a one-day conference titled Rethinking Chicano Studies in November 1990, which the UC Chicano/Latino Faculty Association organized. After Aguilar stated it was "very disrespectful of you to invite an Asian American woman to a conference on Chicano Studies," the audience "booed and hissed" (Anima 1990h).[56] UCSB Chicano studies and women's studies professor Antonia Castañeda (a crucial figure in the 1994 hunger strike on that campus) critiqued Aguilar's comments, saying that they "pained her" (Anima 1990h).

While certainly questionable, Aguilar *and* Chicano studies librarian Richard Chabrán criticized the Rethinking Chicano Studies conference because it included only faculty (Anima 1990g). Students, staff, and community members were "excluded," although they could speak from the audience. Given this arrangement, the conference looked like more false generosity, but Aguilar's comments only fueled more speculation that MEChA was becoming ultranationalist and sectarian. His embrace of indigenismo also inspired some, but repelled others. Because Aguilar embodied MEChA (even though he was nearly kicked out of it and eventually left), it became a fragmented caricature; multiple perspectives existed within the organization, but they became less audible and visible over time. CSC, in contrast, represented something "new," a nonhierarchal collective focusing on Chicano studies *and* other ethnic and women's studies programs. Based on CSC's flexibility and MEChA's weaknesses and perceived rigidity, the former gained traction as many students flocked to its first action (a candlelight vigil held for "people that had been killed by all forms of violence in this society") on April 14, 1993 (Mora 2007: 139).

THE FACULTY CENTER OCCUPATION AND AFTERMATH, MAY 11–24, 1993

Over the next two weeks, CSC and MEChA activists received two powerful moral shocks—César Chávez died on April 23, 1993, and five days later Chancellor Young declared that he still opposed departmentalization, reaffirming the same position he took twenty-five years before. Despite this decision, Young backed plans for strengthening the Chicano Studies IDP through joint appointments, which would have expanded the program's course offerings. Acting CSRC Director David López (1992–93) criticized the proposal as more false generosity, calling it nothing more than a "consolation prize" (Mabalon 1993a).

Young's decision angered many MEChAistas, fueling calls for a May 12 rally. However, after speaking with Chabrán about proposed cuts to the CSRC Library, where many CSC activists met and created a safe space, CSC decided to hold a separate rally and march to the Faculty Center on May 11. These two actions reflected the tensions that existed between MEChA and CSC, but having publicly announced its action (which it could have abandoned given MEChA's already planned event), CSC moved forward, issuing several demands—no cuts to the CSRC Library; full funding for ethnic and gender studies programs (which were also facing budget cuts); a full-fledged Chicana/o studies department; and the removal of López as acting CSRC director (Alvarez 2011b; Mabalon 1993b; Mora 2007).[57]

Michelle Téllez was a CSC member who attended the May 11 rally. Before she arrived on campus in fall 1991, Téllez lived in San Diego and was senior class president and prom queen at her high school. During her first quarter on campus, she attended one MEChA meeting and marched to Chancellor Young's home, but she never went back, stating, "I didn't feel like that was my environment. I was just trying to find myself and be Chicana." Téllez (2011) found multiracial groups focused on unjust incarceration and recruiting students of color more appealing, joining CSC as a second-year student because of her friendship with Mario Valenzuela and Christine Soto, two leading CSC activists. When asked why she marched on May 11, she replied,

This was the time, more or less, when the film *Higher Learning* came out.[58] It was shot at UCLA and it was an accurate representation of the racial tensions that existed on campus. There were race-themed Greek parties on campus; Pete Wilson was in office; there was this state-wide hysteria around immigration, and so with the library we were worried about a domino effect. Had the library shut down, others [gender and ethnic studies programs] might be next. We thought, "If we don't act now, what will become of us?" We thought this [cut] represented the beginning of the end.

FIGURE 5. Michelle Téllez, center with baseball hat backward,
UCLA Faculty Center, May 11, 1993, *Los Angeles Times.*

Téllez remembered a poignant conversation with her father, with whom she had a very close relationship, right after she had been released from jail. Hoping that no one had noticed her involvement, she stated,

> I got my cousin to cover my shift for me at the campus financial aid office so I could go to the protest. I really wanted to be there. Well, as it turned out, I was on the cover of the *LA Times,* wearing a T-shirt that said, "brown and proud," with my hat on and brown Converse shoes [see figure 5]. My family in LA saw the picture and they called my sister in San Diego and she said, "She's in jail." My dad then got on the phone and got really quiet. He was disappointed and asked me to not tell my mother. I finally told her on her birthday and she got upset and lectured me. She said that she worked three jobs at once sometimes and I told her, "That's why I did it," because they were working so hard. I wanted to make their lives better. My dad eventually came on board, but not my mother. My dad then died from a heart attack in June 1993.

Téllez's testimony illustrates many key issues, one being how students sometimes hide their activism from their families. Despite trying to hide it from her family, Téllez still took action because she knew how high the stakes were despite potential risks and consequences. Coming days after Young's decision on Chicana/o studies, Chávez's death and funeral, the 1992 Los Angeles "riots," fraternity theme parties, anti-immigrant hysteria, and a long and bitter three-year fight for Chicana/o studies, the proposed budget reduction to the Chicano Studies Library (an almost "sacred space" for an energetic, politicized, multiracial group of students that often gathered there) was simply *too much*—they had been pushed too far and been humiliated one too many times.

So they marched—from Campbell Hall (home of the embattled AAP) to the Faculty Center, where some retired professors were having lunch with Executive Vice-chancellor Andrea Rich. While the Center's General Manager Ali Tabrizi (2011) felt the action was quite irrational, students deliberately selected the site because Young had stated he could not create a Chicana/o Studies Department without faculty approval. The Faculty Center was an exclusive club for faculty and administrators; most students felt that critical decisions were being made in such settings, behind closed doors, without their input. They literally broke down those doors, breaking one window, ripping a painting, and writing "Chicano Studies Now" and "Fuck Chuck" on the Center's walls.[59] These tactics generated great media attention, but most student activists nonviolently occupied the center, only breaking trespassing statutes. With Chancellor Young away on a fundraising trip in Japan for the graduate school of management, Rich called the LAPD to break up the demonstration. Clad in riot gear, police officers arrested ninety-nine students, all of whom had the charges dropped against them, except for seven who faced significant vandalism charges stemming from property damage (Mora 2007).

Rich's decision poured even more fuel on the fire, as more than one thousand students attended a rally outside Royce Hall (in the center of campus) the day after the Faculty Center occupation. This protest generated considerable local and national media attention, with Spanish-speaking news stations Univision and Telemundo covering it extensively (Mabalon 1993b). Marching alongside the students were one hundred striking Justice for Janitors (J4J) members who joined the action despite the fact that they were involved in their own labor dispute. J4J organizer Rocío Saenz explained the union's participation in the May 12 action: "We have had a lot of support from MEChA and UCLA. Many times we are fighting the same racist issues. We are returning their support. Whenever we see something that is unjust, we have a responsibility to fight it, not only in the workplace, but for students too" (Loo 1993). During this action, Chicano Studies Program Academic Counselor Ruben Lizardo voiced the frustration that many others felt, stating, "They treat us like wetbacks on our own campus. Young is the Daryl Gates of the UC system. This is the apartheid of Aztlán" (Mabalon 1993c).

Time sped up over the next two weeks. In this highly dynamic and fluid context, two more organizations emerged—Students for Revolutionary Action (SRA) and the Network for Public Education and Social Justice (Mora 2007). The Network had been created in 1991 to stop the neoliberalization of higher education and mostly involved graduate students of color, while SRA was established in April 1993 and included radical or socialist undergraduate students of color that favored participatory democracy. Because MEChA and CSC continued squabbling after the protests on May 11 and 12, a horizontal (nonhierarchal) general assembly, which included all students, faculty, staff, and community members, was established (Mora 2007: 143). Soon thereafter, California state senators Art Torres and Tom Hayden, California assembly-women Hilda Solis and Marguerite Archie-Hudson, and actor Edward James Olmos (among others) met with Rich and Young at the Faculty Center. During that session, Torres threatened to delay $838,000 that had been set aside for expanding the campus law library (Gordon and Dundjerski 1993b). Young coolly replied he didn't care for that "kind of action." Shortly after the meeting ended, Olmos told the students "UC Irvine students are fasting for the creation of an Asian American Studies Department" and that they should adopt the "same form of protest" (Farley 1993). Olmos also said, "Bring pictures with you of Martin Luther King, César Chávez, Gandhi, and Jesus Christ." The actor made these remarks after students marched from Kinsey Hall to the Faculty Center, where Joaquín Ochoa addressed the crowd: "The students that were arrested on May 11 looked tired on the outside, but they were spiritually whole. The marches went on for days, weeks, months in the 1960s. The boycott of the buses too. We must never forget that" (Snyder 1993a). Just days later, Ochoa went on hunger strike.

Senator Torres addressed the UC regents one week later, on May 20, asking the board to establish a Chicano studies department, stating "it is more than UCLA now; it has taken on a symbolic nature" (Kong 1993). The next day, on May 21, more than two thousand people attended the largest protest over the entire three-year campaign for departmentalization. Held outside Royce Hall, the protest included state legislators, UFW co-founder Dolores Huerta, MEChAistas from UCLA and nearby universities, CSC, J4J, HERE Local 11, and many other organizations and individuals (Dundjerski 2011: 232–33; Mabalon 1993e).

One such group, calling itself Asian Americans for Relevant Education—later known as the Concerned Asian Pacific Students Association (CAPSA)—along with the AASC, passed out flyers titled "Why Asian Students Should Join the Chicana/o Studies Struggle" at the rally.[60] Former UCLA graduate student Scott Kurashige (2011), who was involved with CAPSA, attended the event and recalled tutoring Joaquín Ochoa, whom he called "one of the leaders of CSC," at AAP. Ochoa's involvement with CSC and his admiration for key CSC activists (see below) once again challenges claims that the eventual hunger strike was nationalist and one-dimensional (Soldatenko 2005). Such assertions ignore the fact that the strike involved complex individuals who articulated and embodied multiple perspectives.

THE HUNGER STRIKE: STAGING SPECTACULAR SPEECH, MAY 25–JUNE 6, 1993

One day after the huge rally, Neurobiology Professor Jorge Mancillas announced (in *La Opinión*, not the English-language *Los Angeles Times*) that some students and faculty had decided to go on an "indefinite hunger strike until a Chicano Studies Department was opened" (Comesaña Amado 1993a). How this decision came about is not entirely clear. While Aguilar apparently mentioned the possibility of a hunger strike after he was arrested during the Faculty Center takeover, it may have emerged after an indigenous sweat lodge ceremony that some students attended before the May 21 demonstration (Gordo 2012b). Still others claim that Torres and Olmos's comments about the UC Irvine hunger strike for Asian American Studies might have planted crucial seeds. Stating the obvious, most students knew that the recently deceased César Chávez relied on fasting as a nonviolent "weapon of the weak" (Bender 2008; Ferriss and Sandoval 1997; M. García 2007; Griswold del Castillo and García 1995; Pawel 2009; Pérez and Parlee 2014).[61] Whatever the case, one humiliating event after another pushed many over the edge, prompting calls for more radical measures. Having generated substantial momentum and emotional energy and with the spring quarter quickly winding down, the time for action was upon them, before students, staff, and faculty left campus for the summer.

The strike began on May 25, 1993. The strikers included five UCLA students: Aguilar, Balvina Collazo, María Lara, Cindy Montañez, and Joaquín Ochoa.

One high school student, Norma Montañez (Cindy's sister); one professor, Jorge Mancillas; and one community member, Manuel Montañez (Cindy and Norma's father) joined them (the latter stopped after four days, but two others, Pastel Mireles and Arturo Diaz López, stopped eating soon after it began) (Comesaña Amado 1993b). They had three key demands—no budget cuts for ethnic and women's studies programs, a full-fledged Chicana and Chicano studies department, and dropping all charges against those arrested during the May 11 Faculty Center protest (Mora 2007).

Aside from her sister, Cindy Montañez was the youngest hunger striker. She grew up in the San Fernando Valley with her parents, who migrated to the United States in 1970. Noting how her parents, especially her father, emphasized education and political engagement, Montañez (2011) also recognized that her brother, Miguel, also deeply influenced her. "I remember, as a high school student," she said, "going with him, Mom, and Dad to protests on lots of different campuses; that was exciting to me. I wanted to go to UCLA where I could continue being me, which meant being involved with community activism."

During her very first week on campus, in fall 1992, Montañez attended a candlelight vigil that MEChA organized, protesting Mexican theme parties, which she called "frightening and disgusting." Despite her brother's extensive involvement with UCLA MEChA and her friends who were MEChAistas, Montañez (2011) remained unaffiliated. While concerned about the struggle for Chicana/o studies, she found CSC's multiracial approach appealing and noted that while internal politics within MEChA existed, it was not the reason why she remained on its periphery. When the strike began, Montañez was a nineteen-year-old freshman student, full of passion and energy, seeking a diverse student body and curriculum (see figure 6).[62]

Joaquín Ochoa's background intersects and diverges from Montañez's. Having grown up in a Mexican-immigrant working-class household in Watsonville, California, Ochoa (2011) stated, "This wasn't new territory for me. I grew up in a Chicano Movement family; my dad was active in 1960s, my mother too with the UFW. Lots of kids came from similar backgrounds; meaning they came from Chicano Movement families." Ochoa knew that others had been fighting for Chicano studies many years before he stepped foot on campus. He felt strongly about the department: "We were right in our cause. Who could deny that it was wrong?" Stating he was "never really part of MEChA," Ochoa (2011) found CSC's methods attractive, noting, "It was a multicultural group,

FIGURE 6. First-year UCLA student Cindy Montañez outside tents,
UCLA Daily Bruin, 1993.

with African Americans and Middle Eastern students. I was close to Ghassan Hassan and Shiva Thornton, who were both arrested after the Faculty Center protest. Ghassan's views really influenced mine; he was so much more advanced than me. I come from Watsonville, which is about 80 percent Mexican. We never thought about a more inclusive people's movement there, but they did. They saw this as a struggle that could benefit all students of color, not just Chicano students."

When asked why he joined the hunger strike, he stated,

There had been racist paraphernalia on campus, with "Lupe's Song" and the frat houses. All that pissed me off. Then events unfolded with the department. I asked a few people like Marcos and Minnie for their advice, and Balvina [Collazo], too. I knew her from Watsonsville; we both had worked in the fields and had gone to the same high school together. So we knew each other, but we weren't very close. We knew each other from danza too, but I wasn't too involved with that either. I was always my own guy; what mattered to me most was whether or not it was important for people. That's what my father taught me—if it's important for others, then do it. Ghassan and Shiva understood that too. I was so focused on Mexicans first, but they had a bigger worldview and understood why coalitions were so important. (Ochoa 2011)

Without explicitly criticizing MEChA, Montañez and Ochoa's comments indicate that some Chicana/o students found its politics problematic. Having gone all out for three years, some MEChAistas pulled back, focusing on their grades, while others graduated or dropped out. Despite their previous friendship, Aguilar and Alvarez got into a physical altercation before the hunger strike. After being nearly kicked out and then having left the organization, Aguilar continued working with Calmécac, MEChA's indigenous-based recruiting and retention program that emerged in the early 1990s from internal conflicts within AAP. He also developed ties with Danza Mexica Cuauhtémoc's (DMC) spiritual leader, Pastel Mireles. DMC is a "political Aztec dance organization with branches in Southern California, Arizona, and Minnesota" (Valadez 2012: 73–74). First established in the early 1980s after one of Cuauhtémoc's descendants (Salvador Rodríguez) gave Mireles and two other *capitanes de danza* (dance leaders/teachers) soil from the last Aztec ruler's apparent resting place, DMC was involved in crucial marches and rallies for labor, civil rights, and immigrant rights in Los Angeles in the early 1990s (Alvarez 2011a; Valadez 2012: 73). While some found its ostensibly decolonial politics and spirituality empowering, others found it too much like the old Chicano Movement—patriarchal, sexist, masculinist, and overly romantic (glossing over the Aztecs' problematic practices, which included oppressing other indigenous groups within Mexico before the Spanish Conquest).[63]

Social movements depend on relatively cohesive mobilizing structures; organizational bodies recruit physical bodies through framing processes that can include body art, tattoos, costumes, and even people's names (McAdam, McCarthy, and Zald 1996). During the hunger strike, the key historical mobilizing structure, MEChA, was fragmented, and two new, alternative organizations, CSC and SRA, had just been created, reducing prospects for a successful outcome. Given this situation, DMC's role became more pronounced, as Mireles gave Balvina Collazo, Cindy Montañez, and Norma Montañez Nahuatl names during the two-week protest. Aguilar and Mireles often wore Danza Azteca or indigenous clothing, and DMC provided security and danced throughout the event. While Cindy Montañez (2011) found these practices "attractive, because that's who we are as a people," Ochoa and Jorge Mancillas disagreed.

Born in Durango, Mexico, Mancillas lived in Ensenada, Baja California, until he moved to the United States when he was seventeen. He received his bachelor's degree in psychology from UC Berkeley and PhD in neuroscience (which was a new interdisciplinary field, much like Chicana/o studies) from UC San Diego (Levine 1993). UCLA hired him, and he began working as an assistant professor in the Neurobiology Department in 1989. Before arriving on campus, Mancillas had been very active politically, providing his scientific expertise to the UFW, Mothers of East Los Angeles, and the Labor/Community Strategy Center, who all fought "environmental racism" (dangerous pesticides, a toxic waste incinerator, and oil refineries) in LA County and beyond in the 1980s and 1990s. Spanish-language media like Telemundo and *La Opinión* regularly interviewed him on a wide range of public health issues that affected the region's Latina/o community (Mancillas 2011b). Most notably, he also served on Provost Orbach's Advisory Committee on Chicano Studies and voted for departmentalization in April 1991.

Given his extensive involvement with social movements, Mancillas understood the crucial role that the mass media played. After discussing how a prolonged fast might physically affect their bodies, Mancillas (2011a) joined the strike, but not before telling the students, "they needed the best MEChA organizers and the hunger strikers had to be irreproachable; good students with good GPAs and from families that supported them." Following the "politics of respectability," Mancillas knew that one "bad apple" or negative image might torpedo the strike with the public, so he often dressed conservatively, wearing a red, white, and blue sweatshirt during one press conference. Before another televised audience, he unconsciously folded his arms, covering up an eagle feather that someone else handed him. Seeing that gesture as intentional, the person that gave it to him said, "You're ashamed of your roots," sparking a tense exchange. "I have no Aztec roots," Mancillas (2011b) said, "I know my background and indigenous roots are not Aztec, they are Tarahumara from Durango. The Tarahumara hated the Aztecs who tried to conquer them, but they failed. Please respect my convictions."

Mancillas's stance illustrates he wasn't the strike's mastermind, as many had alleged. Such assertions ignore the fact that the strike was "their idea," as he stated, and that the students had ideas and practices that he privately disagreed with (Mancillas 2011b). While he respected their choices, he knew that he would attract more media attention given his academic position (untenured faculty member) and role as a father of two children. Displaying his children's pictures outside the tents that had been pitched outside Murphy Hall, Mancillas dramatically stated on the strike's first day, "This is not a symbolic act, this is not a political statement. Either we get a department of Chicano Studies or you will see us die before your eyes" (*Los Angeles Times* 1993). Despite that declaration, the strike generated little media attention over the next several days, until *Los Angeles Times* reporter Bettijane Levine wrote a human-interest story titled "Ultimate Sacrifice" on Mancillas that was published on June 1. Levine quoted Mancillas's daughter, Monica, as saying, "I support my father; he's an absolutely brilliant man. He spoke to me at great length about what is happening and I am proud of the stand that he and the students are taking. I am not prepared for his death and I will never be. But if the time comes when he has to choose between life and death, I will not ask him to change his decision" (Levine 1993). The same day that this article appeared in the *Times*, local Latina/o news reporters Bob Jimenez and Diane Diaz (from English-speaking channels 13 and 4, respectively) interviewed Mancillas and aired stories on the hunger strike during evening news programs.

The media's focus on Mancillas reflects the hunger strike's gendered history (see chapter 1). Rather than being criticized (as many mothers have been) for potentially leaving his children without a father, Levine's article praised him for making the "ultimate sacrifice." While extremely problematic from a gender-based viewpoint, the *Los Angeles Times* story increased the strike's visibility, as did reports that Cindy Montañez "blacked out and had muscle cramps and dry heaves" on the strike's fourth day. Despite her weakened condition, the first-year business economics major refused emergency medical treatment, including intravenous nourishment. "They recommended that I go to the [hospital]," she said, "but because I am determined to stay here until the end, until we get the department, it's better for me to stay" (Snyder 1993b). Margarita Montañez supported her daughter's decision, but she stated, "I feel depressed, but at the same time happy because they're not fighting amongst themselves. They're fighting for a better future, for [coming] generations" (Snyder 1993b). Montañez's decision inspired community members and students ("third-party supporters" in social movement discourse) who began appearing outside the tents and showed UCLA officials that the strike was not a mere publicity stunt (Mancillas 2011b).

Providing even more media attention was Cindy Montañez's younger sister, Norma, who was a sixteen-year-old junior at San Fernando High School when the hunger strike began. In an interview with *Los Angeles Times* reporter Josh Meyer (1993), she explained why she took such a risk: "I know that I'm a minor, but this is my decision. I really strongly believe that I am doing the right thing. I am willing to die for it. In high school, junior high school, and elementary school they don't teach anything about us and our people. We have been ignorant of our culture for a long time and I think that it is time that they teach us who we are, where we come from and what our history is." Titling his article "Young Believer," Meyer wrote, "Because of her age and her articulate and unhesitant word of conviction, Montañez has become a media darling, a spokeswoman for the protest underway." Montañez's age therefore helped make the invisible (for example, coloniality and repeated humiliation) visible. While women of color have been especially ignored in the literature on hunger strikes, Montañez was *not*, indicating that a young, starving female body of color's scream/cry can be heard (Fanon 2004; Holloway 2010).

Despite the increased "volume," Chancellor Young essentially plugged his ears, stating,

> That's the way that I have always been with my daughter. As long as I did what she wanted, I was a great daddy; anytime that I didn't, I was an ogre to be castigated. Sometimes you get what you want in the process, sometimes you don't. . . . I don't think that anyone is going to starve to death. There are very few cases of people fasting and starving to death. (*Daily Bruin* 1993a)

Dean Waugh echoed those comments, observing "We gave them [the strikers] electricity, sent medical workers to check on their condition, and had extra police protection so no one gets hurt. It's all very picturesque, but it's tantamount to someone walking in with a gun to his own head and saying, 'give me what I want or I will shoot'" (Levine 1993). Showing great indifference, even after she called the LAPD during the May 11 Faculty Center occupation (inflaming many students), Executive Vice-chancellor Rich said, before the strike actually began, "All things considered, I would rather be at the beach" (Farley 1993).

Rich, who ironically wrote a book on interracial communication and another on the "rhetoric of revolution" with Arthur Lee Smith (who later changed his name to Molefi K. Asante, a seminal Afrocentric scholar) in the early 1970s, knew the hunger strikers were gaining the "moral high ground" through the press.[64] The *Los Angeles Times* eventually delivered the coup de grâce, from her perspective, printing a full-page photograph that showed Rosa María Mancillas comforting her increasingly frail son (see figure 7 below). Calling it "sheer genius," Rich and Mancillas both saw it mimicking Michelangelo's famous

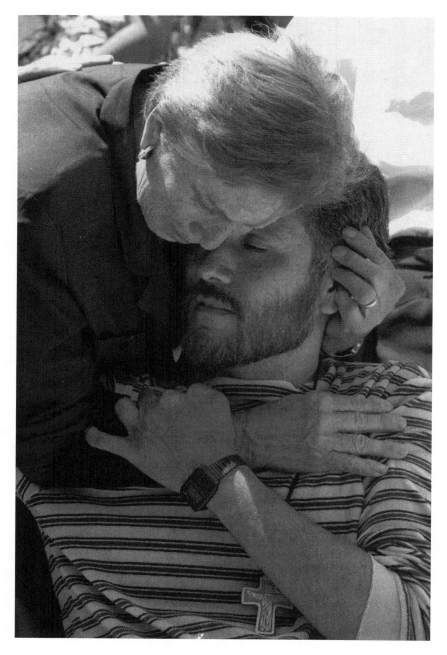

FIGURE 7. Rosa and Jorge Mancillas, UCLA, June 1, 1993. Axel Koester.

Pietà (which depicted Mary cradling Jesus after he had been crucified). Speaking dramatically, she stated,

> It is Christ and his mother; the way his beard was cut, it rips you apart. It was perfect. I thought "Who is going to argue with this?" This man is starving. He is going to die in his little peasant mother's arms, so whatever our arguments were, this became right. Everything became *highly emotional*, completely transcending whatever the issues were. (Rich 2011, emphasis added)

Mancillas (2011b) viewed the picture from a different perspective. Having just passed the crucial seven-day mark, when their bodies could have been seriously compromised and suffered long-term damage, the strikers and their supporters called for a press conference on June 1st. Before it began, Mancillas, who had blood in his urine and could not walk without assistance, was pushed over in a wheelchair to use the restroom. When he returned, he was placed next to his mother. "Just then," he said, "she reached over to hold me and I leaned my head on her shoulder and she did the same. I held onto her hand with my eyes closed. It became the iconic photo of the strike. It wasn't planned at all. It became a real human story. Someone's life was at stake; a mother was in pain and suffering and she was supporting her son. It was a powerful image, it prompted people to take action" (Mancillas 2011b).

Mancillas' narrative underscores a crucial point: hunger strikes are highly performative (see chapter 1). While not deliberately scripted, they are often "staged" (as Waugh sarcastically noted). Much like early-twentieth-century "hunger artists," the UCLA hunger strikers generated curiosity and elicited increasing public sympathy as they put their bodies on display (Russell 2005). The *Los Angeles Times* photo was, as Rich (2011) metaphorically stated, a "game changer"; it turned up the sound several decibels higher, just as pictures depicting force-feeding nearly a century earlier had done for the suffragist movement (B. Green 1997).

While the hunger strikers were transforming "hearts of stone" into "hearts of flesh" through self-sacrifice, they would not have been as effective as they were without MEChA. Even though not one striking student was an active MEChAista, women within the organization performed crucial tasks. "Blanca Gordo, Cindy Sotelo, and Gabby Valle were everywhere, making the strike happen," Soldatenko (2005: 260) stated. Claudia Ganados also did exemplary work with the media, writing press releases and doing interviews with English- and

Spanish-language media (Mancillas 2011c). Acting as MEChA external coordinator, Jackie Mendoza (2011) helped bring MEChA chapters and Chicana/o and Latina/o students from nearby universities to campus to support the strike. She also worked with other students, networking with HERE Local 11, J4J, Art Torres, Tom Hayden, Edward James Olmos, and the Nation of Islam, all of whom extended their solidarity and support (Alvarez 2011b; Mabalon 1993e).

Through these activities and relationships, the hunger strike turned into front-page news. Having momentarily gained the upper hand, strike organizers went for the knockout blow, calling for a fourteen-mile march from Olvera Street to UCLA on June 5, 1993 (Gordon and Nazario 1993). Spatially symbolic, the protest enabled "UC to meet LA" as one *LA Weekly* writer aptly put it (Lee 1993). Despite a steady, cold rain, more than one thousand people marched, holding Mexican flags, Virgen de Guadalupe banners, and picket signs saying "Chicano Studies Now!" The protest generated even more favorable press attention, further isolating Young, Rich, Paredes, Waugh, and other top UCLA officials.

Backed into a public-relations nightmare and concerned about Torres's threats regarding the campus law library, Young's cabinet officers began searching for a resolution—even before the June 5 march. On the strike's fifth day, for example, even though he later mocked the hunger strike, Waugh and College of Letters and Science vice-provost Carol Hartzog visited the tents. During this meeting, both apparently got teary-eyed (Hartzog 1993; Mancillas 2011c). Having asked the strikers how they might end the protest, Hartzog contacted psychology professor Cynthia Telles, and they collaborated with Academic Senate chair David Kaplan to develop a unique proposal that would eventually become known as the César Chávez Center for Interdisciplinary Instruction (CII) in Chicana and Chicano Studies (Mancillas 2011c).

While those conversations were taking place, the hunger strikers developed ties with urban planning professor Leobardo ("Leo") Estrada who previously served on the Provost's Advisory Committee on Chicano Studies and voted for departmentalization in April 1991. Not trusting anyone else, Estrada became the strikers' faculty representative during negotiations with the campus administration. Although professors Steven Loza, Cynthia Telles, Gina Valdez, and Juan Gómez-Quiñones were also involved with these talks, along with Waugh, Hartzog, Kaplan, Young, Paredes, Claudia Mitchell-Kernan, and Vicechancellor for Student Affairs Winston Doby, Estrada played a critical role.

Recalling one of the early meetings between the strikers' representatives (which included student organizers, community members, and faculty), Estrada (2011) said, "We were all sitting in a circle and you could see how angry Young was. The student reps told us why they believed what they did and it was incredibly powerful. I was deeply impressed, but Young basically said, 'not over my dead body' and that was it."

Both sides (minus Young) met the next day (June 4). That session included Vivén Bonzo, One Stop Immigration executive director José Gutiérrez, and all the strikers, who now included Mireles and Diaz López (a community activist and DMC member). Torres, Hayden, and SEIU Local 660 general manger Gil Cedillo also attended this meeting (Sotomayor 1993). Frustrated with the slow negotiating process (which threatened their health), the students "vented" and the meeting was quickly adjourned (L. Estrada 2011). Shortly thereafter, Estrada accidentally bumped into Hartzog outside the Faculty Center. Hartzog told him, "We might have something for you. It's called a CII. We don't use it very often, but we can make things happen with it" (L. Estrada 2011). Estrada had been on campus since 1977 and had never heard of a CII before. "I don't believe that it really existed before that moment," he chuckled.

Once Waugh finished drafting the proposal, Estrada presented it to the strikers and organizers. Because they had been so focused on departmentalization, it generated extensive debate and discussion. The students eventually asked Waugh and Hartzog to come out to the tents and provide greater clarification. During that meeting, Waugh reportedly stated, "If you want a department, we can't do that for a while, if you want this other option (the CII), we can start working on that tomorrow and we can have something in place as early as next quarter (Fall 1993)" (L. Estrada 2011). The CII proposal split the strikers, who felt relieved that administration officials assured them that gender and ethnic studies programs would not be cut back, but they worried that several students were still facing charges from the Faculty Center occupation. After resolving that latter issue, student organizers, hunger strikers, Bonzo, Gutiérrez, and several other representatives met and voted on the proposal (Estrada waited outside the room, as the students requested). After some debate, a motion was made and passed to accept the CII.

Having voted for the proposal just before midnight on June 6, the students pushed for ending the strike the following morning, hoping for greater media coverage. Chancellor Young angrily rejected that plan because he could not "control the situation," as Mancillas (2011c) stated. The students hoped that both sides could sit down as a "community of equals" and sign the agreement together, but the strike embarrassed Young, who faced fierce opposition. His office was flooded with postcards and letters opposing departmentalization. Relying on racist discourse, one simply stated, "We taxpayers are fed up with this crap! Let them go the University of Mexico [*sic*] and study their culture. We need money to be spent on American Studies—plus we're already making cuts in courses that we need more than Chicano Studies. We're furious. Don't give in!"[65] Commenting on Rich's elimination and consolidation of several crucial programs, which Young approved several days *before* he reluctantly signed the CII proposal, several anonymous students made and distributed a flyer, stating, "First things first. Finance pre-existing programs. Save Nursing! Save Library Science! Demand academic and administrative integrity, not political correctness."[66] Young also received a letter from the Los Angeles Association of White People, backing his position on departmentalization.[67]

The latter correspondence must have startled the "liberal" chancellor, who courageously backed Angela Davis's appointment in 1969 and would later work diligently to maintain affirmative action after Regent Ward Connerly and Governor Pete Wilson began calling for its elimination in 1994 (Dundjerski 2011: 234–37). Despite these positions, Young remained staunchly against departmentalization, explaining that Waugh, Hartzog, and other officials created the CII as a face-saving gesture. Knowing he would never back a full-fledged department, they conjured up the CII at the last second, which the strikers and organizers interpreted as a de facto victory. Indeed, when informed that the Center's name would include three C's (the other two were for César Chávez), the students started playfully shouting, "Sí, sí, sí" (Mancillas 2011c).

Young's opposition meant there would be no joint news conference on June 7. Instead, two separate news conferences were held, one with the nine hunger strikers, Doby, Hartzog, Mitchell-Kernan, Paredes, Waugh, Torres, and Hayden, and the other with no one but Young. All parties eventually signed the pact separately. It provided the new César Chávez CII in Chicana and Chicano Studies with $800,000 to hire four full-time faculty members (one senior, three junior) in 1993–1994 and two more (open rank) in 1994–1995 (Ceniceros 1993). Full funding for ethnic and gender studies programs and libraries was also secured, and the university asked city district attorney James Hahn to drop charges against all but seven of the students who were arrested during the Faculty Center takeover. During the "student" news conference, Mancillas stated, "We did this to keep alive the flame that César Chávez ignited. We continue his work for dignity and justice. This is just the first step" (L. Gordon 1993b). Shortly thereafter, they had a huge celebration on campus, eating tortillas dipped in salsa. The strike was over.

For Mancillas, however, such pronouncements were premature. Given his weakened physical condition, he could not walk without assistance nor defend himself or his elderly parents. He recalled feeling "terrified" after the strike based on fears that white fraternity members might attack him or his parents—they had made threats during the strike that they would forcibly remove them from Schoenberg Plaza, where their tents were located. While they made it home without incident, One Stop Immigration provided him with assistance for two weeks until his body recovered (Mancillas 2011c).

THE STRUGGLE CONTINUES: FROM CENTER TO DEPARTMENT, 1993–2014

Despite having chanted "sí, sí, sí" after the strike, some hunger strikers, faculty, staff, and community members said "no, no, no" as the new center experienced significant growing pains during its first five years. These various constituencies assumed that the new unit would focus on activist scholarship, social transformation, and Chicana feminism (among other things), as previous proposals had outlined.[68] They also believed that a junta directiva would help govern it. These views indicate that this movement had far-reaching goals. Partially rooted in a radical citywide social movement against racialized and sexualized neoliberalism, the struggle for Chicana/o studies paradoxically wasn't about Chicana/o studies per se. It was about creating a new university, city, and world— a decolonial, "upside-down" world where the "last will be first and the first will be last" (Matthew 20:16). Such "freedom dreams" were often camouflaged; the movement's exclusive focus on "Mexicans" and "Chicanas/os," along with its emphasis on iconic *male* leaders (Che Guevara, Emiliano Zapata, César Chávez, among others) was problematic, but nationalism is not always regressive (R. Kelley 2002; Mariscal 2005; E. Martínez 1998; Soldatenko 2005). "Nationalist-internationalism" can be revolutionary, as the Zapatista *National* Liberation Army demonstrated several months after the UCLA hunger strike ended when they came out into the open in Chiapas in January 1994 (R. Martínez 1993; Ronfeldt et al. 1999; Zugman Dellacioppa 2009).

Sensing just how high the stakes were, the university conceded, but only partially. New faculty (namely, Chicana feminist scholars Alicia Gaspar de Alba, Aída Hurtado, and Judith Baca, along with Camille Guerin-Gonzáles, Otto Santa Ana, Abel Valenzuela, and later Eric Avila) and staff were hired and courses were expanded, but the CII's first few directors had opposed departmentalization before the hunger strike (Valenzuela 2011). Waugh and Paredes, for example, ran the center (separately) for short periods between 1993 and 1998, enraging many, given their previous views. Paredes became even more vilified after he fired the Center's academic counselor, Jovita Cardenas, who monitored students' academic progress and provided crucial emotional support (Mejia 1998). Decisions like this, combined with the fact that the junta directiva model was immediately rejected because of "university regulations," indicated that coloniality had not been eliminated. Like the IDP, the CII circumscribed the "right to the university" that Chicana/o students had been proclaiming for more than twenty-five years.

This new humiliation spawned a new movement (involving some veterans from the 1993 hunger strike and even earlier struggles), the Coalition for Chicana/o Studies (CCCS), in 1998 (Fernández 2011). During a press conference held outside Murphy Hall on August 12, 1998, "thirty-five students held signs that read 'Save Chicano Studies,' 'Defend Our Education,' and 'Paredes Equals Broken Promises.'" Former hunger striker and CCCS member Cindy Montañez critiqued Paredes's appointment as center director, saying, "He is not a scholar in the field of Chicano studies. He is a vice-chancellor. The administration has basically appointed people with Spanish surnames who have a loyalty to the administration." UCLA co-chair John Fernández, who was deeply involved with CCCS, echoed that view, declaring, "Putting Raymond Paredes as chair was a mistake. He is basically there to make sure the Chávez Center doesn't grow into a department. He's a custodian." Disputing those claims, Waugh asserted, "Raymond Paredes has always been a strong supporter of Chicano Studies," adding, "I think that we've got a wonderful program. We've worked hard for five years to develop it into outstanding Chicano Studies *program*. It has got the full support of myself and the chancellor's office" (emphasis added).

Waugh's choice of words revealed the university still opposed departmentalization even under a new chancellor, Albert Carnesale (1997–2006). Despite that fact, the dean of social sciences hired former UC Santa Barbara Education professor Reynaldo Macías as CII director in 1998–1999.[69] A seasoned "insider" with "outsider" credentials (he served as UC director for linguistic minority research from 1992 to 1997 and called for a Chicano studies department as a UCLA undergraduate MEChAista and UMAS member back in the late 1960s), Macías had what organizational sociologist Neil Fligstein (1997, 2001) calls "social skill." He understood that while the university's intricate, frustrating bureaucratic structure often thwarted social change, it still contained apertures that could be exploited, generating positive results. Recognizing the CCCS's and the university's concerns, Macías (2011) sought consensus, meeting with all relevant stakeholders and developing a ten-point action plan that included maintaining regular CII office hours, expanding course offerings, hiring more faculty and staff, and "growing" the CII. Macías also established research-based community-action courses and Nahuatl-language classes, addressing issues that concerned the CCCS. Over time, Macías helped create a stable, engaging center that became a full-fledged department, with support from Carnesale and Waugh, in 2005 (Macías and O'Byrne 2006).

With fifteen faculty, more than one hundred majors, and a strong PhD program, the César E. Chávez Department of Chicana/o Studies looks quite successful today.[70] The department has brought about greater dignity for Chicanas/os and Latinas/os, but coloniality remains present both on and off campus as higher fees and the deep economic recession have pummeled *all* students, but especially Chicana/o and Latina/o students from working-class households. The fact that the 1993 hunger strike and the long campaign that preceded it did not generate radical social change is certainly lamentable, given disturbingly high levels of inequality and injustice, and one could blame some students for being too narrow-minded (nationalist), but the movement was relatively effective. Coloniality was tempered; dignity was restored, but only temporarily. Singling out or criticizing the colonized as they struggle for their liberation and freedom is crucial, yet what about the colonizer or tyrant (Belli 1978)? Aren't they responsible for spinning a virtually inescapable and seemingly indestructible "web of power" (Holloway 2010)? Why haven't the powers that be (within Murphy Hall) been as rigorously critiqued as the students, professors, staff, and community activists that were involved with this movement?

The students could have established their own autonomous universities, mitigating age-old worries about co-optation, but sustaining them would have been challenging, as some have discovered (Valdata 2006).[71] Creating a decolonial department based on dignity inside a colonial, imperial, neoliberal, and militarist institution like the UC system isn't easy (Chattarjee and Maira 2014;

D. Rodríguez 2012). It is a complex tightrope that many have carefully walked and some have fallen from because of multiple factors, including incredible pressure to publish, produce, and become upwardly mobile. The UCLA hunger strikers and student organizers knew all this. They understood that the colonizer might tame their "wild tongues" with concessions, but their insatiable "hunger for justice," as Balvina Collazo eloquently put it on the strike's thirteenth day, kept them moving, even after the strike ended (Anzaldúa 1987; Mabalon 1993f). Their movement got others moving, inspiring UC Santa Barbara students to organize their own hunger strike for dignity, as the next chapter will demonstrate.

4

UC SANTA BARBARA

"We Offer Our Lives as a Moral Protest"

Students must take the initiative; they should not be mere imitators. They must learn to think for themselves. Real education should consist of drawing the goodness and best out of our students. What better books can there be than the book of humanity? Once social change begins it cannot be reversed. You cannot uneducate a person who has learned to read—you cannot humiliate the person who feels pride. You cannot oppress the people who are not afraid anymore. We have seen the future and the future is ours.

CÉSAR CHÁVEZ

INTRODUCTION

ON APRIL 27, 1994—a little more than one year after César Chávez's untimely death—nine Chicana/o and Latina/o students at UC Santa Barbara (UCSB) took the initiative. Putting their bodies, as Berkeley Free Speech Movement leader Mario Savio memorably stated some thirty years earlier, "upon the wheels and levers of the machine,"[1] these students risked it all, as their UCLA counterparts did some ten months before, consuming nothing more than water over the next nine days. During that time, some students' bodies became noticeably weaker and required wheelchairs for assistance (see figure 8), while others attended classes, prepared for medical and graduate school, prayed, danced, kissed, marched, gave speeches, played board games, and kept journals, all in an effort to maintain their spirits and, when possible, their grades. Outside the highly visible—but extremely cold and drafty—tents located outside Cheadle Hall, the main UCSB administration building, three students met with four campus officials to negotiate an agreement that might be amenable to both sides. Aside from the hunger strikers and negotiators, many other students performed key

FIGURE 8. Naomi García and Edwin López outside Cheadle Hall, facing Campbell Hall. Used with permission from Lisa Valencia Sherratt, UC Santa Barbara Library Special Collections Department, California Ethnic and Multicultural Archives (CEMA).

tasks—writing press releases; making flyers, banners, and posters; taking pictures; creating coalitions and alliances with campus- and community-based organizations; maintaining the security and safety of the fasters; doing health checkups (monitoring key vital signs including blood pressure, pulse rate, and body weight); and gathering water, blankets, and other necessary supplies (Flores 2011a; A. Gutiérrez 2011; Valencia Sherratt 2011).

This was no heroic one-*man* show. Most people assume that hunger strikes are solitary, isolated events, involving one great, iconic man (like Mohandas Gandhi, Bobby Sands, César Chávez), when nearly all such actions are rooted in mass (including women, queer people, and other marginalized groups) social movements that have been struggling for social change for years (Blackwell 2011). This particular hunger strike mirrored that reality. Unlike their UCLA counterparts, UCSB students had a Chican*o* Studies Department.[2] It had been established in 1970, but nearly twenty-five years later, it was still incredibly tiny and deeply divided. While many Chicana/o and Latina/o students took great pride that the UCSB Chicano Studies Department was the first and only one that existed in the UC system at that time, they felt humiliated that it was so small and remained seemingly oblivious and separate from the broader disturbing realities that Chicanas/os and Latinas/os faced in the early and mid-1990s.

When pressed, most people might assume that the controversial, widely publicized, and unsuccessful hiring of CSU Northridge (CSUN) Chicana/o studies professor Rodolfo ("Rudy") Acuña in June 1991 might have facilitated this action (Acuña 1998). While many students found this decision morally outrageous and became heavily involved in his subsequent and ultimately successful lawsuit (*Acuña v. Regents of the University of California*), such explanations are facile and reductionist. The students did not go on strike "for" Acuña; they went on strike because student fees had sharply increased while top UC officials, including then–UC president David Gardener, saw their salaries and retirement benefits dramatically rise in the early 1990s;[3] because Immigration and Naturalization Services (INS) agents were conducting raids that targeted low-income, mostly Chicana/o and Latina/o families in nearby Isla Vista; because support services for retaining Chicana/o and Latina/o students were being cut; because eligible, local Chicana/o and Latina/o students from San Luis Obispo, Ventura, and Santa Barbara counties were not being recruited heavily enough into UCSB; because plans for expanding the campus library would have demolished a historic "counter-space" called El Centro, home to El Congreso (the campus's leading Chicano student organization), the Center for Chicano Studies, and the Chicano Educational Opportunity Program (EOP); because the Department of Chicano Studies was falling apart and losing faculty; and because farm workers, especially those picking grapes, were being poisoned and sickened by dangerous pesticides and toxic chemicals. These were just some of the reasons why these nine students took this dramatic and dangerous action that could have had negative long-term health consequences.

While no one called for an indefinite hunger strike that could have proved fatal, the hunger strikers and student organizers were serious, passionate, and committed. Most knew that a multiracial group of students, along with two professors, had gone on a hunger strike five years before, pressing the administration to institute a campuswide general-education ethnicity requirement for all undergraduate students in February 1989 (N. García 2011; G. Gutiérrez 2011).[4] Many were also aware that another multiracial coalition of students, including El Congreso's first chairperson, Arnulfo Casillas, had taken over the university's computer center located in North Hall in May 1975 (Acuña 2011: 110–11; Y. Márquez 2007). Eight years before that protest, black students organized the first computer center takeover, occupying North Hall in October 1968 (Gardner 2005: 38–45). Several months later, more militant protests, involving Chicana/o, black, and white students took place, which led to the creation of a short-lived alternative "free university" and the establishment of the Chicano studies and black studies departments (Y. Márquez 2007; Moreno 2009).[5]

Given El Congreso's focus on "internal education," most hunger strikers understood that there was a "long" movement for social justice on campus that existed for decades and included not only Chicanas/os but also students from all racial backgrounds (Hall 2005). One student who definitely recognized the connection between the past and present was history major and 1992–1993 El Congreso co-chairperson Naomi García. A gifted, rigorous feminist scholar whom Professors Yolanda Broyles-González, Antonia Castañeda, and Zaragosa Vargas had mentored, García (2011) placed the 1994 hunger strike in a broader context: "This was not an isolated event. It was the continuation of a long history of activism on this campus. People like Arnulfo Casillas, Gabriel Gutiérrez, Mateo Latosa, all previous leaders within El Congreso, made sure we knew our history. They made sure we had institutional memory." The UCSB hunger strike, therefore, was not about Rudy Acuña (although his case lingered over the campus and department for many years before, during, and after the strike, galvanizing many students, including many fasters and several of its key organizers). Unlike the UCLA hunger strike, there was no one overarching dramatic event that "triggered" this action. Students had multiple grievances that had been accumulating for three decades, producing the following demands: no more fee increases, more Chicana/o studies faculty and a PhD program, stronger recruiting and retention programs for local Chicana/o students, the establishment of a community center for families in Isla Vista, maintaining and renaming El Centro after Arnulfo Casillas, and the banning of grapes from campus.

These goals indicate that the students had broader objectives that extended beyond the Chicano Studies Department and UCSB. While they were mocked for starving themselves over purportedly inconsequential matters, they hungered for dignity, not only for themselves, but for all people. Seen from this perspective, they had one utopian demand or decolonial "freedom dream"— a new department, university, state, nation, and world (R. Kelley 2002). They had simply been humiliated one too many times. By going without food, they gained back their dignity, but only temporarily. Over time, new indignities arose because of fiscal austerity and internal conflicts. Those humiliations ignited subsequent struggles for dignity, including several rallies and fasts.

To better understand this hunger strike, I start with a brief historical overview of the UCSB Department of Chicana and Chicano Studies, focusing on the "frame battles" or competing narratives that were used to explain its weaknesses, much like the previous chapter examined with regard to the UCLA Chicano Studies Inter-Departmental Program (IDP). While the strike wasn't entirely about the department, it was one of the students' most important demands, and some of its faculty were deeply involved with the strike, taking opposing viewpoints that had long-lasting consequences. Having established this contextual backdrop, I explore the hostile climate that existed on campus in the early 1990s that helped ignite the strike, and then analyze the strike itself. I conclude by focusing on the post-strike fallout, including the contentious removal of the department chair, the establishment of the world's first PhD program in Chicana and Chicano studies, lingering coloniality, and the struggle for social justice.

FROM CHICANO POWER TO CHICANO STUDIES: A BRIEF HISTORY OF UC SANTA BARBARA, THE CHICANO STUDIES DEPARTMENT, AND THE CHICANO STUDENT MOVEMENT, 1891–1990

UCSB originated from the Anna S.C. Blake Manual Training School for Girls—a teacher training school that was established in 1891.[6] Santa Barbara native Ednah Rich became the school's principal in 1896 and took over as president after Blake died in 1899. Rich ran the school over the next seventeen years (Redmon 2010; L. Wilson 1913). In 1909, the Blake School became the Santa Barbara State Normal School of Manual Arts and Home Economics and offered a two-year program that included classes on teaching training, home economics, industrial arts, and foreign languages. The campus moved four years later from downtown Santa Barbara to the hilly, affluent Riviera neighborhood located near the Santa Barbara Mission. In 1919, its new president, Clarence Phelps, expanded its curriculum for elementary school teachers, and the school changed its name to the Santa Barbara State Normal School. In 1921, it became a four-year institution and was rechristened as Santa Barbara State Teachers College (Starr 1990: 284). Upon offering liberal arts degrees, the school underwent yet another name change, becoming Santa Barbara State College in 1935 (Rt. Kelley 1981: 1–3).

Shortly thereafter, two city power brokers, newspaper publisher and editor Thomas Storke and conservationist Pearl Chase (who graduated from the Blake School in 1908), lobbied California governor Earl Warren, the state legislature, and the UC regents to incorporate Santa Barbara State College into the UC system (Rt. Kelley 1981: 4–6). On July 1, 1944, the University of California, Santa Barbara College came into being, and when World War II ended a year later, its enrollment swelled. While the old teachers college owned property on the mesa and drew up plans for relocating there in the early 1930s, that changed after the Marines sold their former four-hundred-acre base on Isla Vista to the UC regents for $10 in 1948 (Lodise 2008: 10). Before the Spanish Conquest, a large, established Chumash community lived in what they called Anisq'oyo for many years. Colonization and missionization decimated the Chumash, who survived and often resisted but were eventually separated from their ancestral lands (Sandos 1985, 1991). Under Mexican rule, Isla Vista was part of the huge 15,000-acre Rancho Dos Pueblos land grant made to Nicholas Den in 1842. The Den family hung onto the land until the 1920s when land speculators and oil companies bought it, hoping to turn it into a lucrative beach resort community. Those efforts failed, however, leaving Isla Vista "pretty much uninhabited" before World War II (Lodise 2008: 10).

After a Japanese submarine shelled a nearby oil field in February 1942, the Marines took over Isla Vista, building a sewage processing facility over a bulldozed Chumash sacred cemetery. Such machinations, combined with Santa Barbara's historic mistreatment of its Mexican, Mexican American, and Chicana/o residents, underscore the city and university's settler-colonialist and white-supremacist foundations (Camarillo 1979; McWilliams 1946).[7] Six years after buying the land from the Marines, UCSB opened its doors in Isla Vista in 1954 with a planned enrollment of 3,500 students. Under Samuel Gould, the campus's first chancellor (1959–62), that threshold was surpassed, reaching nearly 4,000 in fall 1961 (Rt. Kelley 1981: 16).[8] Despite his positive record and a construction boom on campus, Gould often clashed with the Academic Senate, and he stepped down after serving just three years.

Vernon I. Cheadle, a renowned botanist from UC Davis, replaced him, serving as UCSB's longest-serving chancellor (1962–77) until Henry Yang (1994–current). Upon assembling a strong administrative cabinet, the campus grew exponentially because of Cheadle's leadership. Beyond more than a dozen new permanent structures on campus and the explosive growth of the campus library, student enrollment nearly tripled from 4,780 in 1962–1963 to 13,254 in 1969–1970. In just one year, 1965–1966, two hundred faculty members were hired, facilitating departmental expansion, including the establishment of many new master's and doctoral programs (Rt. Kelley 1981: 22–23). While impressive, the campus was an "almost wholly white enclave," with blacks and Chicanas/os making up just 1.1 percent of the student body in 1968 (Rt. Kelley 1981: 36; Moreno 2009: 158). In early 1968, a small group of Mexican American students, led by freshman Cástulo de la Rocha, a student activist from Roosevelt High School in East Los Angeles, came together and created a local, campus-based chapter of the United Mexican American Students (UMAS), which had been founded in May 1967 at Loyola Marymount University in Southern California (Casillas 1986; Y. Márquez 2007: 171; Moreno 2009: 160). Despite being quite small, UMAS organized outreach-related conferences, such as La Raza and Higher Education and Educación por Todos, that brought Chicana/o high school students to UCSB with the hope that they might become inspired and gain knowledge to pursue higher education (Y. Márquez 2007: 311; Moreno 2009: 166–67). These efforts, combined with the EOP's recruiting activities, generated slightly greater diversity, but the campus was still lily-white in the late 1960s.

Shortly after UMAS was created, twelve Black Student Union (BSU) members took over the university's computer center (where sensitive documents were stored) in North Hall on October 14, 1968 (Gardner 2005: 38–41; Rt. Kelley 1981: 40; Moreno 2009: 178).[9] The students unofficially renamed the building Malcolm X Hall and issued several demands, including hiring more black faculty and staff, establishing a black studies department and center for black studies, and creating an investigative committee to study racism on campus. While some administration officials and faculty favored harsh measures (expelling the student activists), Cheadle and Dean of Students Lyle Reynolds took a softer, conciliatory approach, creating the Committee on Ethnic Studies, with history professors Otey Scruggs and Jesús Chavarría acting as co-chairs, shortly after the occupation (Gardner 2005: 40; Y. Márquez 2007: 122; Moreno 2009: 183–84).[10] Despite this concession (which Governor Reagan opposed), the BSU, UMAS, and the mostly white-led Students for a Democratic Society (SDS) came together and formed the United Front, partially because promises for increasing black and Chicana/o student enrollment had not yet materialized (Rt. Kelley 1981: 40). The multiracial student coalition met with Cheadle, Assistant Chancellor David Gardner (who later became UC president in 1982), and Vice-chancellor for Student Affairs Stephen Goodspeed, but slow progress prompted it to break off negotiations. The United Front subsequently took over the University Center, creating a short-lived "New Free University" in February 1969 (Rt. Kelley 1981: 40–41). It also demanded (notwithstanding serious internal divisions within the United Front) that the administration immediately establish black studies and Chicano studies departments (Moreno 2009: 191). Favoring "persuasion over coercion," Cheadle once again compromised, supporting two faculty hires in each department (Gardner 2005: 44; Y. Márquez 2007: 136).

Several months later, Chicana/o educators, teachers, and students met at UCSB, in the privately owned and operated Francisco Torres Residence Hall, in mid-April 1969 to write a highly influential document known as "El Plan de Santa Barbara," which called for the establishment of Chicano studies centers and departments on college campuses and universities (Y. Márquez 2007; Moreno 2009).[11] Chavarría and UMAS had issued their own similar plan *before* the El Plan conference took place (Y. Márquez 2007: 189–91; Moreno 2009: 201).[12] After being fully evaluated and reviewed by the Academic Senate and other relevant agencies, Cheadle successfully submitted a revised version of that latter proposal to UC president Charles Hitch and the UC regents on July 30, 1969 (Moreno 2009: 223). In early 1970, the Center for Chicano Studies (CCS) officially opened with Chavarría as its director and College of Letters and Sciences academic counselor Fernando de Necochea as its associate director.[13] In fall 1970, the Chicano Studies Department offered its first classes with several part-time faculty.[14] While Chavarría and a junta directiva oversaw the CCS, the Chicano Studies Department was "governed by a chairperson that the Chancellor appointed" (Moreno 2009: 219).[15]

Despite these positive steps, the university cut back funding for Chicana/o student admissions and proposed reducing Chicano Studies Department faculty and teaching assistant positions, sparking renewed protests in May 1973 (Y. Márquez 2007: 267). MEChA (Movimiento Estudiantil Chicano de Aztlán—the Chicano student organization that replaced UMAS shortly after the El Plan de Santa Barbara conference ended) spearheaded those actions. Two years later, Chicana/o faculty, students, staff, and community organizations filed a class-action lawsuit, hiring then–civil rights attorney Leon Panetta, against UCSB and the UC regents for failing to treat Chicanas/os in an equitable and just manner.[16]

As these events unfolded, a split emerged within the Chicana/o student community between MEChA and La Raza Libre, an offshoot of MEChA established in 1971 that quickly formed close ties with a new community-based organization called La Casa de la Raza, which was located on Santa Barbara's eastside, a long-standing Mexican working-class barrio (Camarillo 1979;

Ornelas 2000). Although there is an ideological division between the two groups, with MEChA being labeled as "nationalist" and La Raza Libre as "third worldist or internationalist," Arnulfo Casillas, El Congreso's founding chairperson and Vietnam War veteran, framed the conflict around El Centro (Building 406), a World War II–era barracks that housed EOP, CCS, the Chicano Studies Department, and the Colección Tloque Nahuaque (Chicano Studies Library) in the early 1970s. Distinctively Chicano, Casillas opposed a proposal that La Raza Libre supported that would have transformed El Centro into a multiracial space. Having previously collaborated with the BSU and white radical student organizations, Casillas supported multiracial coalitions, but he maintained that the Chicano campus community must organize and sustain itself independently before making such alliances.[17] Casillas recognized that the bitter, almost violent conflict between MEChA and La Raza Libre weakened both organizations. Seizing the opportunity, he worked alongside other Chicana/o student activists and helped establish El Congreso in October 1974 as a new unified Chicana/o student organization, supplanting MEChA and La Raza Libre (Y. Márquez 2007: 234).[18]

In May 1975, El Congreso, along with the BSU, Asian American Student Alliance, Women's Center, Gay Student Union, Young Socialists of America, Native American Student Alliance, Isla Vista Community Council, and Arab Student Union, formed an eclectic, multiracial coalition called Students for Collective Action (SCA) (Y. Márquez 2007: 287). SCA took over the North Hall computer center on May 4, 1975, demanding the hiring of a new CCS director and new Chicano Studies Department chairperson; the establishment of an Asian American studies department; the continued operation of the Center for Black Studies; and the resignation of Cheadle, Goodspeed, Affirmative Action Coordinator Raymond Huerta, and other campus officials (298). While this action produced few tangible results, Cheadle established a committee to hire a new CCS director and appointed a new Chicano Studies Department chairperson (301–2).[19]

Before Eugene García took over in January 1977, the department had multiple chairpersons. Dean of Letters and Sciences Bruce Rickborn served as acting Chicano Studies Department chairperson (1975–76) after Carlos Ornelas's term ended in June 1974. Preceding Ornelas were Carlos Zamora, Amado Padilla, and four faculty members from the Chicano Studies Department that functioned as an executive committee (Y. Márquez 2007: 82).[20] García served as chair until 1979, when Professor Isidro Ortiz took over as acting chair for six months. Dean of Letters and Science David Sprecher replaced Ortiz and served as chair for two years before stepping aside in 1981, when yet another acting chair, anthropology professor Manuel Carlos (who came from outside the Chicano Studies Department), was appointed (Y. Márquez 2007).[21]

All told, the department had nine chairs during its first eleven years in existence. Such high turnover, combined with its small size and conflicts with the CCS and El Congreso, limited its effectiveness. Nevertheless, the department began slowly expanding in the mid-1970s after Marío T. García was hired in fall 1974. García had a 50 percent appointment in the Chicano Studies Department and a 50 percent appointment in the History Department. Joint appointments were standard operating procedure for all faculty hires in Chicano Studies until the early 1990s.[22] While such arrangements were seen as professionally beneficial for young, emerging scholars, and some relished being active in two departments/disciplines, others saw joint hires more critically as being reflective of Chicano second-class citizenship within the colonial university. By comparison, when the UCSB Religious Studies Department was established in the mid-1960s, it included three full-time faculty members.[23] In other words, that academic unit's faculty members, along with subsequent hires, were given more power and freedom than Chicano Studies, which perhaps underscored administration officials' lingering concerns that the latter department would become too politicized with full-time faculty. Joint hires thus helped prevent Chicano Studies from engaging more fully with community-based organizations and radical social transformation. Having been pressured by students shouting "Chicano Power" and demanding "Chicano Studies" in the late 1960s, the UCSB administration acted to blunt its impact and influence (Rojas 2007).

Chicano studies and spanish and Portuguese professor Francisco Lomelí (2011) understood the delicate dynamics around these issues. Having majored in Chicano studies and Spanish at CSU San Diego (CSUSD) and been involved in social movements in the late 1960s, he recalled the department's early days:

I was hired in 1978 with a joint appointment in Spanish along with Guadalupe San Miguel Jr. (education) and Inés Talamantez (religious studies).[24] This was when we were trying to *build and formalize* Chicano Studies. Gene García was pushing for the idea of a major because before we were not really yet a department; it was looser, more like a program. After we three were hired, we had six professors and we had a more solid foundation. We knew the old days of being a battling unit, not having much respect on campus, might be behind us. We wanted to establish our academic bona fides, *but still have ties to the community.* This was ambitious and quite difficult. (emphasis added)

In the early 1980s, under Dean David Sprecher's chairship, the Chicano Studies Department unexpectedly moved from El Centro to Phelps Hall.[25] While seemingly innocuous, Lomelí (2011) recognized this spatial transformation had broader implications, stating, "We were treated like a regular department from that moment on. We later gained even greater legitimacy when we moved to South Hall in 1998." Academic units often move without much fanfare, but this one coincided with broader structural change within the department. Formerly unified within El Centro, the Chicana/o campus community splintered, with Chicano Studies faculty focusing more fully on their scholarly productions and personal careers. While ties between its different units (the CCS, the department, the library, the EOP, El Congreso, and community groups) were often strained, El Centro was the glue that bound them as they worked for the social transformation El Plan de Santa Barbara and the Chicano Movement had envisioned. That model, while utopian and sometimes exclusionary, presented the colonial university with a decolonial challenge—a challenge it defused with deftness (Soldatenko 2009).

Seeking limited change, the university provided the Chicano Studies Department with more physical space, but with the expectation that it become more "professional and academic" and less "community-oriented," as former chairperson Isidro Ortiz put it (Y. Márquez 2007: 340–42). A Faustian bargain was struck between the campus administration and the Chicano Studies Department in the 1980s; the former provided more resources for faculty hires and the latter focused more on academic pursuits and stabilizing internal departmental affairs. While this did not mean that all faculty muted their progressive political views and activism, the department and discipline changed during this time.

After Manuel Carlos's chairship ended, Mario T. García replaced him. A well-established scholar, García helped oversee the hiring of six new faculty members—Yolanda Broyles-González, Denise Segura, Antonia Castañeda, Rosalinda Fregoso, Ramón Favela, and Zaragosa Vargas—during his five years as department chair.[26] All had joint appointments in other departments, with the exception of Vargas, who had a 75 percent position in the Department of History. These hires effectively institutionalized and stabilized the department after the turbulent 1970s. External and internal review panels

welcomed and praised these developments. Calling for 6.0 new *full-time* equiv-
alent (FTE) faculty positions, García sent Vice-chancellor for Academic Affairs Robert Michaelsen a hopeful memo on December 23, 1987:

> This department during the last five years has turned a crucial corner. We are now
> a solid academic unit. To continue this development, it is imperative that we ob-
> tain commitments for future FTEs. Together with much patience and commit-
> ment, we have produced a quality Department of Chicano Studies here at UCSB
> that is, in our opinion, unrivaled in the country. We now have the opportunity
> to create . . . perhaps the most outstanding ethnic studies program in the United
> States.[27]

García also noted that with these new faculty members the department could
develop the first Chicano studies doctoral program in the entire country.[28]

SOMETIMES THERE IS NO OTHER SIDE: RUDY ACUÑA AND THE CHICANO STUDIES DEPARTMENT, 1990–1994

Yolanda Broyles-González succeeded García as department chair in fall 1990,
becoming the first Chicana to lead the department. She was also the only Chicana department chair in the entire UC system at that time. While not as well
known as leading Chicana feminist theorists and writers such as Gloria Anzaldúa and Cherrie Moraga, Broyles-González (1994) gained increased recognition for her seminal book on El Teatro Campesino (the iconic Chicano theater
group that supported the farm workers movement), which sharply critiqued its
founder, Luis Valdez, for ignoring Chicanas as well as reinforcing harmful bi-
nary representations about them. A long-time supporter of the United Farm
Workers (UFW), Broyles-González helped bring César Chávez to campus,
where he taught for the only time a quarter-long class on farm-labor organizing and the new grape boycott that emerged in the middle and late 1980s. Many
El Congreso students who were involved with the 1994 hunger strike took this
course from the iconic civil and labor rights activist (E. López 2011a).[29]

On the basis of his scholarly credentials and extensive ties to social justice organizations like the UFW, Broyles-González supported CSUN Chicano Stud-

ies professor Rodolfo ("Rudy") Acuña, who applied for a position in the UCSB Chicano Studies Department in fall 1990.[30] Best known for his foundational text, *Occupied America* (1972), Acuña helped establish the celebrated CSUN Chicano Studies Department in the late 1960s. He also had close ties with Casa de la Raza (located on Santa Barbara's eastside Chicana/o community) and El Congreso founder Arnulfo Casillas. Despite his strong progressive political views, Acuña generally did not focus on gender or sexuality in the first two editions of *Occupied America* or his other publications, making his choice somewhat curious given the department's emerging feminist "turn" in the early 1990s (Orozco 1997: 266).[31]

Nevertheless, Broyles-González, Castañeda, and Favela voted for Acuña, while Fregoso, Segura, and Lomelí abstained.[32] While these results (3–0–3) were positive, others saw them much differently. Interpreting the abstentions as "no" votes, campus officials claimed that the department was split and established a secret, ostensibly objective, ad hoc committee (which included faculty from outside the Chicano Studies Department) to review Acuña's materials.[33]

Calling him a "cult professor" and focusing on his age, committee members questioned his "thin" publication record and noted he had not supervised any doctoral dissertations. The latter charge was particularly nonsensical given that CSUN granted no doctoral degrees. That jaundiced assessment (which also noted he would run the UCSB Chicano Studies Department in a "dictatorial" manner), combined with College of Letters and Science provost David Sprecher's equally skeptical and biased appraisal, spelled doom for Acuña.[34]

What happened next is fairly well known (Acuña 1998). In September 1992, Acuña sued the UC regents, claiming that the university had discriminated against him because of his age, racial background, and political beliefs (Enriquez 1992). His lawsuit generated national attention and placed the UCSB Chicano Studies Department under great scrutiny. Many wondered how the flagship Chicano studies department in the UC system could deny the field's arguably most prominent scholar a senior-level position.[35] While some claimed the department already had several historians, it bears mentioning that Acuña would have shaken up the department, university, and community. Acuña represented a radical vision of Chicano studies that many El Congreso students found appealing (four of the nine hunger strikers and two of the three student negotiators were heavily involved with his subsequent successful lawsuit and campaign).[36] After the racialized neoliberalism and the profound hostility they encountered on and off campus, many Chicana/o students felt that they needed someone like Rudy Acuña to challenge the status quo.

However, radicalism was not very effective in the 1970s, as the UCSB Chicano Studies Department reeled under frequent leadership changes and clashes with El Congreso and the CCS. Having become relatively more stable in the 1980s, the department took a significant risk under Broyles-González's leadership, not only seeking out Acuña but also focusing more on gender and sexuality too. Such dynamics affected the entire field in the late 1980s and early 1990s, as some Chicana/o students and academics pushed the National Association for Chicano Studies to change its name to the National Association of Chicana and Chicano Studies, which took place in 1995 (Blackwell 2011: 33). Alongside gender and sexuality, indigeneity also resurfaced in the early 1990s, which for some was a mostly masculinist project, but various Chicana feminists reinterpreted indigeneity in a more inclusive and liberatory manner (S. Ramírez 2002).

Given these debates around gender, sexuality, and indigeneity, and the hostile climate that existed on many college campuses in California, the United States, and the Americas (broadly speaking), Chicano studies was a contested project in the early 1990s when Broyles-González chaired the UCSB Chicano Studies Department. Those who embraced a more traditional, liberal, civil rights-oriented version of Chicano studies were on the defensive (I. García 1996), while those who favored a more radical vision of the field, focusing on gender, sexuality, indigeneity, and transnational solidarity, were energized. Those perspectives were not neatly dichotomous, but these cleavages were profound and helped tear apart the Chicano Studies Department just as much as Acuña's nonsuccessful hiring.

These deep tensions led Fregoso and San Miguel Jr. to resign from the Chicano Studies Department in 1991 and 1992, respectively. In her letter, Fregoso noted, "There was a split in the department between those of us who supported a new direction for Chicano Studies and those content with things as they were."[37] She later pointedly stated that Broyles-González was not the reason for her departure. San Miguel Jr.'s comments differed slightly: "Especially significant in my decision not to return to UCSB is the university's politically inequitable treatment of Rudy Acuña as well as its failure to act in the best interests of the Chicano Studies Department. These actions, as well as its lack of official concern for my well-being, point not only to a continuing pattern of institutional non-acceptance of Chicano Studies scholars and scholarship, but also one of indifference."[38]

Vargas and Segura soon followed their two colleagues, but rather than leave UCSB entirely as Fregoso and San Miguel Jr. did, they separated from Chicano Studies. Castañeda then expressed major concerns when UCSB did not offer her husband, Arturo Madrid, a highly-respected modern languages and literature professor and founding president of the Tomás Rivera Center (a key Latina/o public-policy think tank), a "spousal hire." With her options limited, she contemplated leaving the university and was on leave when the strike began in April 1994. Thus, as Lomelí (2011) describes it, in a few short years the department "imploded," undermining the gains that were made in the 1980s.

Under Mario T. García's chairship, the department reached an all-time high of 4.25 FTE (nine faculty overall: eight part-time and one with a quarter-time appointment), but it had fallen to 3.5 FTE when the hunger strike began in April 1994.[39] Masking those numbers were the two-year leaves that Castañeda and Lomelí were on, however.[40] Therefore, in 1993–1994 it had just four present, physical bodies, or 2.5 FTE. Broyles-González, García, and Favela all had half-time appointments, while newcomer Chela Sandoval was the unit's first full-time faculty member (she was hired two years after Acuña was turned down). With the hallways often empty and office doors typically shut, Broyles-González quipped that the department resembled a ghost town in a memo she sent to Dean of Social Sciences Donald Zimmerman calling for additional faculty resources. Noting the newly created, but still unfilled, Luis Leal Endowed Chair position and the department's highly regarded faculty, Broyles-González candidly wrote Zimmerman and UCSB provost Llad Phillips,

> The aforesaid circumstances speak to the inordinate *potential* of our Chicano Studies Department. That is, we are positioned such that we could easily move into the top five Chicano Studies programs nationally. For the time being, however, we perceive a declining trend: the lack of institutional support has prevented the UCSB Chicano Studies Department from capitalizing on its existing strengths. Only through additional FTE allocations will our department emerge from its present state of marginalization. We are a tiny department, the smallest on the UCSB campus. Although UCSB has taken the important—and in the UC system—singular step to create a Chicano Studies *Department* it should logically move to make our departmental presence more than a *token presence*.[41]

The department's emaciated status sparked an intense frame battle, much like the one that engulfed the UCLA Chicano Studies IDP. From Broyles-González's perspective, institutional racism eroded the department's strength. However, some campus officials and department faculty blamed her, claiming she had poor managerial skills. Similar sentiments were expressed about previous chairs.[42] Segura (2011) claimed that both factors—institutional racism and ineffective leadership—weakened the department. Finally, longtime education professor J. Manuel ("Manny") Casas verbalized a widely held assertion about the unit's woes: "It has been this way for a long time. There has been nothing but personality conflicts. When are they going to act like adults, take responsibility and stop acting like children?" (Cornfield 1994b). While reasonable, such assertions effectively blamed the "victim" rather than the system that generated nearly endless internal bickering. Casas's comments echoed the administration's, chastising his colleagues while remaining silent on the broader structural issues that exacerbated these departmental conflicts.

For its part, El Congreso generally supported Broyles-González, with 1993–1994 El Congreso Chairperson Abel Gutiérrez (2011) and Alma Flores (2011b) agreeing with her that the Chicano Studies Department was a mere "symbolic token." Twenty-five years after it was first established, it had fewer active FTE in 1994 than 1970. This situation mirrored what was taking place in the wider society; people of color were still colonized in the early 1990s, a generation after the turbulent 1960s. Coloniality, both on and off campus, was profoundly humiliating. The department's condition, combined with Acuña's unsuccessful hiring, sparked great moral outrage. That anger kept building with each new demeaning event (see below) until it reached an emotional tipping point that eventually resulted in the hunger strike. Seeking substantive change, El Congreso called for a "critical mass of faculty" and a department that was more engaged.

Engaged departments and universities seek to address the national reality; that is, they push for broad-based social change (Hassett and Lacey 1991; Macías and O'Byrne 2006).[43] While one could reasonably argue that all faculty in the UCSB Chicano Studies Department partially or wholly embraced this ethos, the department was not organized *collectively* around that vision. Because they believed they were under siege, with racialized neoliberalism affecting their everyday lives, El Congreso hoped that the Chicano Studies Department would not only include more "brown faces"—it longed for a department that addressed all forms of injustice, inside and outside the United States. Its vision of Chicano Studies, therefore, mostly overlapped with Broyles-González and Acuña, but El Congreso activists acted autonomously; they did not always make their decisions with guidance and assistance from these two professors, as some mistakenly assumed.

Once the strike began, most people didn't realize who the hunger strikers were. Because this action occurred quickly (as will be explained below), there wasn't sufficient time to disseminate biographical information about the fasters and their motivations for taking such great risks. Flores (2011a) spoke about her gradual self-transformation and the climate that existed during her first few years on campus:

> I was born in Guadalajara, Mexico, and grew up in South Gate [California]. I had a hard first year. I couldn't relate to other El Congreso members at first. I grew up Mexican, not Mexican American. No one called themselves "Chicano." That wasn't really a great word. When I went to Campbell Hall [a huge lecture hall that seats eight hundred people], it was a complete culture shock. Almost everyone was white. Over time, I learned we were not as bad as everyone said we were. Francisco Lomelí actually taught that class. The more that I learned, the angrier I became. . . . During my second year, Rudy's case hit me hard. I really believed in the cause. He helped create Chicano Studies. We felt that they would hire him because they wanted what was best for us and he was the best. But we were wrong.

While stating she "adored Rudy," Flores (2011b) also declared, "I would never go on a hunger strike over him. What was going on back then was much greater than Rudy." What she wanted was relatively modest: "a place where you get a well-rounded education, with faculty that knew our names; it was that simple." Gutiérrez (2011) claimed he wanted a more "politically and ideologically diverse Chicano Studies Department that focused on the community," with second-year El Congreso member Lisa Valencia Sherratt (2011) stating she merely wanted more classes; the department's offerings were frequently meager. The request for more courses and more humble faculty collaborating with community-based organizations may not have seemed too radical, but a stronger Chicano Studies Department would have provided students with knowledge to counter anti-Mexican and anti-immigrant discourse and practices, which were pervasive in the early 1990s (L. Chávez 2013). A more robust and engaged Chicano Studies Department would have also offered students sanctuary, a safe space where they could decolonize their minds, bodies, and spirits.[44] Having done that, they might work for broader decolonial change after graduating from UCSB.[45] The demand for a stronger Chicano Studies Department, therefore, was not about Chicano studies per se; it was about radical social transformation—changing themselves, the university, and the world.

"OUR GRIEVANCES ARE MANY": RACIAL AND GENDERED NEOLIBERALISM ON AND OFF CAMPUS

Aside from the Chicano Studies Department, the students who were deeply involved with the hunger strike claimed "our grievances are many" in its declaration issued on April 27, 1994. The university's unwillingness to retain Antonia Castañeda with a "spousal hire" for her husband, Arturo Madrid, was one of those grievances that many found especially flagrant. While claiming that it didn't have sufficient resources to provide Madrid with a faculty position, the students cogently noted, "UCSB has already pumped over one million dollars into defending itself in Acuña vs. University of California, [but] it fails to hire and retain faculty such as Prof. Antonia Castañeda, leaving the numbers of Chicana women faculty at 4 and the number of white male faculty members at 600."[46] Many Chicana/o students greatly admired Castañeda, a leading Chicana feminist historian and supportive mentor to many Chicano Studies and Women's Studies Department majors. Failure to retain her further weakened the former and hurt the latter (leaving it with *no* Chicana faculty).

Academic Senate chairperson Laurence Iannaccone poured more fuel on the fire when he stated that Barbara Uehling was hired as UCSB Chancellor in June 1987 primarily because of her gender (Cornfield 1994a). Having come into office after her predecessor, Robert Huttenback, resigned after embezzling university funds to refurbish his private residence, Uehling was arrested on drunk driving charges before she was officially inaugurated as UCSB chancellor (L. Gordon 1988). Generally seen as distant and aloof, students of color and progressive white students found her largely disengaged regarding racial issues when they went on a hunger strike in 1989 (G. Gutiérrez 2011). Four years later she stated she would resign on June 30, 1994. During the 1993–1994 academic year, therefore, she was a "lame duck," which generated a power vacuum within the administration that El Congreso skillfully exploited. Before Uehling was officially replaced, former UCSB Chicano Studies Department chair Eugene García's name came up as a potential successor. Iannaccone again objected, claiming that García was being considered mostly on the basis of his racial background rather than his academic credentials. His comments about Uehling and García sparked the following line in the hunger strike declaration: "The recently published and never retracted racist and sexist remarks made by the UCSB Chair of the Academic Senate are part of the hostile climate that we face on a daily basis."[47]

The racial battle fatigue and microaggressions that many Chicana/o and Latina/o students felt on campus in the early 1990s were exacerbated by UCSB's 1990 long-range development plan (LRDP) that called for El Centro's demolition (W. Smith 2004).[48] A "temporary building" first erected when the U.S. Marines essentially occupied Isla Vista during World War II, El Centro represented sacred ground (despite the fact that it physically "resembled an INS detention center")[49] for many Congresistas who held their weekly Thursday evening meetings there. Many Chicana/o and Latina/o students spent countless hours inside El Centro (or Building 406, as it is known on campus) studying, watching films, organizing, and meeting with Chicano EOP counselors who helped retain thousands of students by providing them invaluable assistance and mentoring.[50] During this period, the CCS, Colección Tloque Nahuaque, EOP, and El Congreso (along with its many subcommittees) also called El Centro home.

The LRPD included expanding the main campus library, which is located next to El Centro. Governor Pete Wilson's draconian budget cuts to higher public education in the early 1990s ironically scuttled that project, but only temporarily. Chicana/o and Latina/o students understood that should California's economy recover, construction and deconstruction would commence. Uncertainty regarding El Centro's future and the possibility that dwindling resources would force the Chicano EOP to be folded into one integrated program, as Arnulfo Casillas feared in the mid-1970s, took a toll. "Each year we are threatened with its removal," the hunger strike declaration noted, "as well as the collapse of Chicano EOP into a diluted central unit."[51] Fewer EOP staff meant Chicana/o and Latina/o students might not be retained or recruited. Given its motto ("Keeping the doors open for those yet to come"), El Congreso rallied hard behind El Centro.[52] Its preservation was crucial for sustaining and expanding student diversity and even creating a better world, as many student organizations seeking social change met there.

Beyond El Congreso, CEPAN (Cultura Educación para Avanzar Nuestros Niños [Cultural Education for the Advancement of Our Children]) held its meetings at El Centro. Because of turnover and graduation and fatigue stemming from the Acuña case, activism within El Congreso waned in 1993–1994, opening space for CEPAN to emerge (A. Gutiérrez 2011; E. López 2011a). CEPAN focused on tutoring Isla Vista school children and developed close ties with the community's Latina/o families (Leiva 2011; E. López 2011a). Through those relationships, its members (including future hunger strikers Naomi García, Edwin López, Claudia Leiva, Salvador Barajas, and Tino Gutiérrez) discovered that INS officials were knocking on people's doors and deporting those who were undocumented. They also heard from numerous families that while their apartments were generally substandard and their rental payments were sky-high, they remained silent given their citizenship status (Leiva 2011). Concerns such as these were reflected in the hunger strike declaration: "It is also apparent that the university has reneged on one of its most primary responsibilities: to be a resource to the larger Isla Vista and Santa Barbara communities."[53]

The university not only ignored low-income, mostly immigrant families in nearby Isla Vista, it overlooked Latinas/os working in the state's agricultural fields. Deeply concerned about farm worker rights and sometimes having come from farm worker families and communities, some El Congreso members took César Chávez's class on farm labor organizing in spring 1992. Those lectures inspired and mobilized many Chicana/o and Latina/o students who became involved in the UFW's "new" grape boycott. Launched in the mid-1980s, this campaign never generated as much attention and change as the original one in the middle and late 1960s, but it successfully raised consciousness, especially among young Chicanas/os and Latinas/os who recognized that not much had changed despite all the sacrifices that Chávez and so many more made a generation before (Pérez and Parlee 2014). Given their backgrounds, this issue was critical, but when Chicana/o and Latina/o students approached university officials, they were often dismissed. "This university ignores the decade-long grape boycott that is presently being waged by the United Farm Workers of America," the hunger strike declaration stated. "It continues to serve table grapes and has ignored our requests to support the grape boycott which protests the pesticide poisoning of farm workers and consumers."[54]

While all these events were transpiring on and off campus, UC fees skyrocketed, negatively affecting all families, but especially working-class Latina/o ones who often had modest incomes. Higher fees and the backlash against affirmative action (as Iannaccone's remarks on Eugene García and Barbara Ueh-

ling made clear) generated suspicions that the UC system was effectively telling students of color, especially Chicanas/os and Latinas/os—*get out!* That was
the same message behind the Save our State ballot (SOS) initiative that later
became Proposition 187—*leave now!* In the post–Civil Rights Movement era,
the UC system could not practice overt racial discrimination, so it did so dis-
creetly, limiting the Chicano Studies Department's growth (by not retaining
Antonia Castañeda and pushing other faculty away) and cutting back funding
for Chicana/o, Latina/o student recruiting and retention programs. Fewer faculty and counselors, El Centro's planned demolition, higher fees, and the university's disregard for Latina/o families and farm workers all added up—raza's
presence on campus was being erased.

Given this dire situation, El Congreso announced,

> The systemic presence of discrimination must be addressed and ended through
> *action*. Much blood has been lost in the past, and will continue until we are liber-
> ated from our shackles. In the spirit of César Chávez, co-founder of the United
> Farm Workers of America, El Congreso declares a hunger strike until our de-
> mands are met by the University of California, Santa Barbara. We offer our lives
> as a moral protest and act of non-cooperation with a university that has relegated
> us to a status of *invisibility* and *second-class citizenship*. We urge faculty, staff, and
> community members to actively support our demands. (emphasis added)[55]

"WHEN ARE WE GOING TO TAKE DIRECT ACTION?": PRE-STRIKE ORGANIZING, MARCH–APRIL 1994

The hunger strike was ignited around the Eternal Flame, the campus monument (located just a few steps from El Centro) dedicated to Martin Luther
King, Robert Kennedy, and John Kennedy. While discussing plans for a forthcoming protest against Proposition 187, Naomi García (2011), a graduating senior and former El Congreso chairperson (1992–93) who was born and raised
in Salinas, California, where her parents picked lettuce for many years, asked
the students who had gathered around the fire, "When are we going to take
direct action?" Despite the upcoming demonstration, García felt something
more dramatic was needed. She recalled,

> It was all coming to a huge tipping point—immigration, student fees, the Chi-
> cano Studies Department, the PhD program, community center, and the grape

boycott. We started an institutional trail; writing letters to the provost, chancellor, and so on. After we worked on these issues for two years, we thought they would eventually listen, but they never did. I wondered "what is it going to take?" I felt that we need more direct action. Having meetings, talking and talking, meeting with the chancellor, writing letters—all that hadn't worked. Nothing had changed. On the contrary, things were getting worse. So we needed to take direct action to bring about real change.

Edwin López (2011a), a Central American student from Glendale, California, whose parents migrated from Guatemala to the United States in the late 1960s and whose sister, Silvia Argueta, was one of Rudy Acuña's attorneys, vividly recalled García's words:

Naomi spoke up and said, "when are we going to do direct action?" But the meeting just continued, so she said it again, "when are doing to do some sort of direct action?" Let me give you some background here. There were a lot of things going on back then. People like Rudy were not being hired; people were not being retained;[56] the department had only three and a half FTE. So Naomi made her call for direct action and some people agreed with her, but not me. Because I was one of the main organizers of the upcoming protest against Proposition 187, I got really upset. I felt like her comments were taking us off on a tangent. Sometime later, someone said "what about a hunger strike?" Many people liked that idea because it was a nonviolent, peaceful way to address our concerns. *I just kept quiet because I didn't support it.* (emphasis added)

After this initial discussion, five students—Naomi García, Edwin López, André Vásquez (a freshman, first-year student from Fillmore, a working-class Mexican community located in Ventura County), Salvador Barajas (a transfer student from Oxnard, another predominantly working-class Mexican community that included many farm workers and was the place where César Chávez worked with the Community Service Organization in the late 1950s), and Claudia Leiva (a Guatemalan student who grew up in Los Angeles, specifically the Central American community located in the Pico-Union area)—held a meeting at García's Isla Vista apartment and decided to go on hunger strike.[57] During that much smaller and more intimate session, these five students poured out their hearts, with García and Leiva talking about their grandmothers who had recently died. While their deaths influenced García and Leiva's actions, López (2011a) felt like he had reached a personal crossroads: "I saw this as a personal test. It was like, 'When the time comes, am I willing to stand up for what I really believe in or not? It took a while for me to say 'yes.'"

Having crossed the line, the five began discussing their demands. While initially "long and comprehensive" (López 2011a), they were whittled down over time without much input from El Congreso or the broader Chicana/o and Latina/o student community. With the exception of Vásquez, all of the original strikers were members of CEPAN, a new organization whose members (particularly López and Tino Gutiérrez, who later joined the strike) found Marxism, class-based analysis, and radical social movements like the Zapatistas attractive. With memories of previous divisions within El Congreso and the California statewide MEChA still fresh in many people's minds, some worried that a new split might be eminent. El Congreso chairperson from 1993 to 1994 Abel Gutiérrez (2011) did not share those concerns, but he acknowledged that the organization experienced a "lull" that year compared to previous years when it held huge rallies around Rudy Acuña's lawsuit. Given these complicated dynamics, the five (who were all Congresistas, incidentally) kept the hunger strike a virtual secret until April 18, 1994, when they issued press releases under the banner "Indigenous Resistance for Social Justice," stating it would begin at midnight on April 19, the day of the already planned demonstration against Proposition 187 (*Daily Nexus* 1994). López (2011a) felt the Proposition 187 action (which included Rudy Acuña, Silvia Argueta, Naomi García, Jorge Mancillas, and Rogelio Trujillo as speakers) would generate favorable media coverage for the forthcoming hunger strike.[58]

While the press releases alerted the media, they also roused the broader Chicana/o and Latina/o community, which came out for an emergency 7 p.m. meeting on April 18 at El Centro, just five hours before the strike was scheduled to begin. Lisa Valencia Sherratt (2011), a second-year, biracial (Chicana and white) student from Anaheim Hills, California, attended it, clearly remembering the heartfelt "emotional energy" that existed inside the discussion circle:

Everyone was there. I was still pretty new to the group and was fairly quiet. A small group of strikers told the full Congreso body that they had gotten together and were down for the strike. Things were really bad they said and would not get better unless we acted. All of them had decided to go on a hunger strike, but not as Congreso per se. They pretty much presented their idea and said "here it is, we are going to do it anyway, if you like it or not." You could cut the air with a knife at this meeting—it was really intense. There was no joking, it was all serious. People were willing to die. This was not some idle threat. During the discussion, everyone had their turn, all voices were heard. It was a solemn, serious, reverent, strong, and sacred space; it was like people were going into battle, with strikers on the front lines. It was scary, seeing your friends willing to do that. There was a combination of respect and admiration. Some people were upset since they were not involved in the initial hunger strike discussions. It was a long, long night.

Valencia Sherratt's narrative highlights the internal divisions that existed within El Congreso. López (2011a) said nothing about the hunger strike because, should it fail, El Congreso might suffer irreparable damage. Gutiérrez (2011) found such reasoning less than credible given that all five hunger strikers were Congresistas; hence the organization would have been held responsible regardless. On a deeper level, Gutiérrez found López somewhat naïve and overly eager (even though he had been politically active for several years), not recognizing why El Congreso had become more quiescent in 1993–1994. Given López's personality, Gutiérrez reacted skeptically when he heard about the fast, which he generally questioned as too "ego-driven," matching his interpretation of the 1993 UCLA hunger strike. Beyond these concerns, Flores (2011a) felt that the strike was premature, stating that other options had not been exhausted. Graduate Student Association (GSA) vice-president Marisela Márquez (2011) shared Flores's views, suggesting a delay until fall 1994, when UCSB's new chancellor (Henry Yang) would take office.[59]

These arguments nearly torpedoed the strike until García, who had more influence than López because of her role as previous El Congreso chairperson, suggested that the five students would wait a week if Congreso agreed to help organize and endorse the action. The El Congreso general body (including those present at the hastily arranged meeting on April 18) agreed, hastening several significant changes with the planning process, including first revising the demands. Following suggestions from Mike Muñoz, a former El Congreso chairperson (1991–92) who had been a member of a Trotskyist organization called Socialist Action while he was a student at Garfield High School in East Los Angeles, nationalist-oriented discourse was excised (E. López 2011a). The call for a community center for *Latina/o* families in Isla Vista, for example, became a community center for *low-income* families. A new demand (to stop fee increases), designed to attract students from all racial backgrounds, was also added (E. López 2011a). Such class-based and racially neutral discourse might have emanated from some students' Marxist leanings. Regardless, social movement scholars have long stressed the strategic value of broad-based frames because of their ability to mobilize and move people (Benford and Snow 2000).

The second noteworthy change was the new organizational form that El Congreso adopted for the hunger strike. Gutiérrez (2011) explained this issue:

> We had elected officers. We were very democratic. We held elections and had meetings and did things according to Robert's Rules of Order. We followed the language of the university. We did away with all that. We created an executive council that handled all the strike logistics. I was chair of that council during the strike, not El Congreso. Our motto for the strike was "One action, one voice, one people—we are one."

The executive council included some fifteen subcommittees in charge of community outreach, campus outreach, documentation, external outreach, funds, security, spokespeople and the information table, legal observers, auxiliary committee, media, medical services, public relations, research, staff outreach, and supplies (Valencia Sherratt 2011).[60] These microorganizations illustrate this action was no "ego-driven, one-man" show; it was a collective effort. Without the labor and sacrifice of all the unnamed people that were involved with these subcommittees, the hunger strike would have never taken place and been as successful as it was.

The third crucial change that emerged from the April 18 meeting focused on moral leverage. Sensing the need for greater public support and positive media coverage, the students launched a last-ditch effort to resolve their differences with university officials (E. López 2011a). While they knew such efforts would prove futile, they wrote letters, made appointments, and pleaded their case, but the administration did not budge. Having gone the "extra mile," the students captured the "high ground," saying that they had exhausted all existing mechanisms for redressing their grievances before embarking on such a radical and dangerous action.

The fourth key shift was the selection of three student negotiators. El Congreso recognized the hunger strikers could not effectively bargain and meet with university officials because prolonged fasting would compromise their physical and mental well-being. Gutiérrez (2011) felt that the UCLA hunger strike could have been more effective had student negotiators been involved from the outset. Given this interpretation, the strike executive council carefully chose three people with distinct skill sets.[61] The first negotiator was Benjamin ("Benny") Torres. Torres was a previous chair of El Congreso (1989–90) who had been deeply involved in Chicana/o student and community politics for many years and was extremely active in the campaign around Rudy Acuña. Torres was charismatic, gregarious, and greatly admired for his bluntness and militancy. The second negotiator was Mike Muñoz, another past El Congreso chair and MEChAista at East Los Angeles College before transferring to UCSB. Muñoz adroitly helped revise the hunger strike demands and was someone the fasters deeply trusted (E. López 2011a). The third and final negotiator was Marisela Márquez, a UCSB political science graduate student who previously served as UC Student Association president in 1991–1992. Having been on campus for the 1989 hunger strike, Márquez had long been involved in campus politics and knew the arcane inner workings of the Academic Senate, which many students found opaque (M. Young 2011).

The fifth and final change that occurred was expanding the number of hunger strikers. Aside from the original five students (Naomi García, Edwin López, Claudia Leiva, André Vásquez, and Salvador Barajas), four more (Tino Gutiérrez, Alma Flores, Heather González, and Gilberto Límon) joined their ranks. Gutiérrez was a transfer student from Ventura College who worked extensively with the campus Multicultural Center after arriving at UCSB in fall 1992.[62] He was external co-chair of El Congreso in 1993–1994 and became very involved with CEPAN that same year. After discussing the issue with his then partner, Lisa Marie Navarro, he decided to go on strike because "it all seemed very logical for me to ask to take part in it; all the people that I knew, Edwin, Naomi, were involved in it and it was closer to my politics, which were more radical and action-oriented" (T. Gutiérrez 2011). Flores (2011a) was perhaps an unlikely choice, as she said, given that she was a cheerleader in high school, but she had been politically active as a junior high school student. After visiting Chicano EOP staff counselors during her rocky first year on campus, she gained self-confidence and started taking more Chicano studies classes. Those courses partially transformed her, as she became deeply involved with the Rudy Acuña case and was elected 1993–1994 El Congreso internal co-chair. She felt strongly that one of the organization's key leaders should join the strike, so Flores (2011a) made the decision, stating, "The people not fasting were smarter than me; they were going to do the hard work. I was like, 'I can do go without eating.' I knew my family (outside the tents) was going to take care of me day and night and that's why I agreed to do it."

Unfortunately, I had no contact information for Heather González and Gilberto Límon and thus did not interview them for this study.[63] Naomi García (2011) stated that her close friendship with González helped sustain her during the strike and Vásquez (2011) said that Límon provided fellow hunger strikers with vital health-related information that he learned while preparing for medical school.[64]

"THAT REALLY HURT US": THE STRIKE BEGINS, APRIL 27, 1994–APRIL 29, 1994

After making all these critical adjustments and organizing almost nonstop since the April 18 emergency meeting, the hunger strike began on Wednesday, April 27, 1994, at 3 p.m. That same day, at a press conference held at 11:45 a.m. in front of Cheadle Hall, El Congreso released its hunger strike declaration, along with the following six demands:

- Stop fee hikes for the fiscal 1994–1995 year; save EOP from budget cuts.
- Establish a community center for low-income families.
- Hire 15 FTE and establish a PhD program in Chicano studies.
- Recruit and retain more local, eligible Chicano and Latino students.
- Preserve El Centro and rename it after Arnulfo Casillas.
- Support the UFW grape boycott.[65]

Right after the press conference ended, the hunger strikers joined a rally against fee hikes that included Democratic California state senator Tom Hayden and UCSB Associated Students president Geoff Green. Early the next morning, Edwin López tried to wake his fellow fasters at 6:30 a.m., enthusiastically declaring "comrades, we must wake up at sunrise and meet the sun!" López and two other students then went outside to pray and express gratitude to the Creator, as many students did earlier in an indigenous sweat-lodge ceremony that was held shortly before the strike began.[66] Later, around 9:30 a.m., García and López, along with several other students, met with Academic Senate Affirmative Action chairperson Walter Yuen and Academic Senate vicechair Douglas Morgan, where they discussed the students' demands. While impressed with the former, calling him "sincere and supportive," García found the latter problematic, claiming he was cold and insensitive.[67]

Several hours later, Gutiérrez read the hunger strike declaration during an Academic Senate meeting, deliberately emphasizing the phrase, "*The recently published and never re-tracted racist and sexist remarks made by the UCSB Chair of the Academic Senate are part of the hostile climate we face on a daily basis.*" While Senate Chair Laurence Iannaccone had earlier claimed that he had been misquoted, Gutiérrez's comments exacerbated the tension that existed in the room. Taking front-row seats traditionally reserved for faculty, several hunger strikers, student organizers (including "Big" John Delgado, who was rather tall and served on the security subcommittee), and Benny Torres became upset when Iannaccone asked them to move to back of the room. After reluctantly complying, Torres stood up and "implored the Senate and university administration to produce a team of negotiators to deal with the situation quickly."[68] Iannaccone rather surprisingly agreed with Torres, stating he would begin making plans for handling specific proposals the Senate might receive on the basis of a future joint settlement.

Feeling positive after that unexpected development, the hunger strikers, organizers, and Torres walked back to the tents only to find that Mario T. García, Francisco Lomelí, and Inés Talamantez, along with Affirmative Action Coordinator Raymond Huerta, published a letter in the *Santa Barbara News-Press* explaining why they opposed the strike.[69] While focused on the hunger strikers' health and well-being, many fasters and El Congreso members viewed the letter with disdain. Reflecting later that day, Naomi García stated, "That really hurt us. The university wants us to be divided, so the letter helped them. If you don't support us, fine, but don't hurt us. They should have pressured the administration to settle if they were so concerned about our health."[70] Having initially targeted the campus affirmative action officer in the mid-1970s, El Congreso generally distrusted those (minus Talamantez) who signed the letter (N. García 2011; E. López 2011a). Such animosity stemmed partially from political, ideological, and generational differences, as El Congreso vigorously challenged inequality in the early 1990s just as Chicana/o activists did in the late 1960s. Twenty-five years after El Plan de Santa Barbara was published, Congresistas such as García felt it was time to act, and so she and her comrades did, even though many (including most within Cheadle Hall) disagreed with them. The day after this letter was published, Huerta wrote another piece that was published in the *Santa Barbara News-Press*, stating, "We support the students' demands," but he was noticeably silent on their means. Such sleight-of-hand gestures further upset El Congreso (N. García 2011).

Given these tensions, most El Congreso members were not too surprised when they learned who signed the initial letter, but when they discovered that Talamantez's name was on it as well, some were taken aback. A well-respected indigenous elder who focuses on American Indian religious traditions and practices, Talamantez went into the hunger strikers' tents outside Cheadle Hall on the strike's second day (when the first letter was published in the city's daily newspaper) to bless the fasters with sage and copal. Seeing her actions as contradictory, Edwin López (2011a) was incensed. He asked her to leave, but other El Congreso members intervened, stating her intentions were good (S. Barajas 2011).

These interactions indicate that relations between Chicana/o faculty and Chicana/o students were complex. Sociology professor Denise Segura understood just how fragile the terrain was in the Chicano Studies Department in the early 1990s. When asked why she didn't sign the letter along with her other colleagues, she stated, "I knew it would be misunderstood and not be seen as a caring gesture, but as a real betrayal." Viewed suspiciously after her abstaining vote on Rudy Acuña, Segura (2011) acted cautiously, working behind-the-scenes with fellow sociologist and social science dean Don Zimmerman and other faculty and students to broker an agreement. Segura later played a crucial role fulfilling the demand of establishing an Isla Vista community center, but some never forgave her for her previous actions (E. López 2011a).

"WHERE ARE WE, AS WOMEN, SAFE?": GENDER, INDIGENEITY, AND THE UCSB HUNGER STRIKE

While the *Santa Barbara News-Press* letter stung, another critical event happened later that same day. Around midnight, nonstriking El Congreso members went into the strikers' tents and turned on the lights, waking everyone up. Deeply disturbed, the nonstriking students stated that someone associated with the Harmony Keepers, a Los Angeles–based group that focuses on indigenous ("Mexica") spiritual and cultural traditions, reportedly touched Alma Flores inappropriately during a sweat lodge ceremony before the protest began.[71] The Harmony Keepers had ties with Danza Mexica Cuauhtémoc (DMC) and Aztlán Mexica Nation and initially provided the UCSB hunger strikers with security.[72] They were liked by some Congresistas but made others uncomfortable with their masculine-oriented indigeneity and posturing (Torres 2011).

After these allegations, the students had an intense conversation about gender and sexual harassment. Some demanded that the Harmony Keepers leave, while others stated that they felt that the organization had made some positive contributions before and during the hunger strike (N. García 2011). García was especially torn, as she recognized that several Chicanos within El Congreso were not viewed as skeptically as the Harmony Keepers, even though they had also previously mistreated women. This inconsistency bothered her, with her stating in her audiotaped journal, "Where are we, as women, safe?"[73]

Finally, after much internal debate, El Congreso decided that it would tell the Harmony Keepers that they no longer needed their assistance with security. Conveying that message would be no easy task given that the Harmony Keepers were quite enthusiastic and deeply committed to the action. Nevertheless, Salvador Barajas and Benny Torres approached several Harmony Keepers members, including former UCLA hunger striker Marcos Aguilar. Barajas (2011) recalled what happened next:

I was aware and agreed with the concerns other Congresistas voiced about the Harmony Keepers. The safety issues raised by Alma Flores and other women troubled me. When we met with the Harmony Keepers, I knew that asking them to leave was the right thing to do. Out of respect to Marcos, I wanted to be part of the group who met with them that evening, but it was hard since he had such a strong influence on my development as a student activist. I told them we appreciated their presence, but we had to do this on our own.[74]

Torres (2011) remembered the incident slightly differently:

Initially there was a sense of trust with the group after the sweat [lodge], but the guys in the group were these big dudes, ex-Marines, they were body-builder types and went around looking for snipers. They made us feel uncomfortable. Then the whole thing that happened at the sweat was just weird. This was the first big test for us as a group; we became much more united after they left. They drove to Los Angeles and got their tents and said we are ready to do security and we said Sonia Rosas [a first-year student] is our security person, so we don't need you. Please respect our decision. As we were talking to them, they turned their backs on us. That was a huge sign of disrespect. Marcos finally said, "I don't agree with your decision. We're disappointed, but we will leave you alone." So they left.

This episode illustrated that while indigeneity resurfaced in the early 1990s within Chicano/o student organizations and Chicana/o Studies, it was a complex project. For some, it resembled old-school Chicano nationalism, which romanticized and valorized masculinist nationalism, but Chicana feminists deconstructed and reconstructed indigeneity, making it much more inclusive and empowering (S. Ramírez 2002). El Congreso students knew that *indigeneity* was a fluid, oppositional term; indeed the *Daily Nexus* (1994) reported that the hunger strikers initially called themselves "Indigenous Students for Social Justice" before the protest began. While seemingly harmless, some El Congreso members were concerned that DMC and the Harmony Keepers might "colonize" the hunger strike and possibly El Congreso, much like some Marxist groups tried to do with MEChA and El Congreso in the 1970s and 1980s (Licón 2009; Muñoz 2011). As more seasoned activists, Gutiérrez (2011) and Muñoz (2011) expressed reservations about newcomers—"born-again indios," the former sarcastically called them—but they also understood indigenous spiritual practices could also be fulfilling and transformational.

Like most social justice organizations, El Congreso was complex and diverse. While fairly progressive on issues of gender and sexuality, some members were not as tolerant or open-minded as others. Moreover, a gendered division of labor often existed, with Chicanos often taking on public leadership roles. Nevertheless, Chicanas acted, in Dolores Delgado Bernal's (1998) words, as "grass-roots leaders." They made flyers and banners, provided security, took pictures, organized rallies and demonstrations, delivered speeches, and established links with social justice groups on and off campus. Yet their contributions were still obscured, as figure 9 indicates, which shows Rudy Acuña speaking with a reporter while Chicana students are busy making posters for the hunger strike. Without this picture, one might mistakenly assume that a few "great men" organized the hunger strike or that it was primarily about them (Blackwell 2011). While some Chicanos were heavily involved, Chicanas were even more pivotal, a fact that has not been widely acknowledged (Flores 2011a; N. García 2011). Alma Flores, Naomi García, Heather González, Claudia Leiva, Marisela Márquez, Claudia Monterrosa, Sonia Rosas (Santos), Aída Salazar, Lisa Valencia Sherratt, and countless other Chicanas made great sacrifices, ensuring the strike's eventual success.[75]

Thus, while the sweat-lodge incident was the catalyst, when the lights were turned on around midnight, they illuminated several ghosts (A. Gordon 2008).

FIGURE 9. Rudy Acuña speaking with reporter outside El Centro (on left).
Women students making posters (on right). Used with permission from
Lisa Valencia Sherratt. UC Santa Barbara Library Special Collections
Department, California Ethnic and Multicultural Archives (CEMA).

The tents were haunted—with the Chicano Movement and its exclusion of women and queer people, with the perception among many Congresitas that DMC had undermined the UCLA hunger strike with its heavy emphasis on masculine-oriented indigeneity, with the complicated role of religion and spirituality in the Chicana/o and Latina/o community, and with lingering memories and concerns about "infiltrators" within the Chicana/o student movement. Such complicated dynamics could have torpedoed the hunger strike, but the students remained relatively unified and kept pressing for substantive social change (Flores 2011a; N. García 2011; E. López 2011a).

TACTICAL INTERACTION: THE CAT-AND-MOUSE GAME RESUMES, APRIL 30–MAY 5, 1994

With the Harmony Keepers gone and the hunger strike in its third day, strike organizers held a rally on April 30, 1994, that included many speakers such as

Rudy Acuña, black studies professors Claudine Michel and Otis Madison, Antonia Castañeda, and several of the strikers' parents. In a powerful speech, Michel asked the crowd, focusing on the Chicano Studies Department's weaknesses and the students' deeper decolonial politics, "Where is Rosalinda Fregoso? Gone! Where is Guadalupe San Miguel? Gone! Where is Antonia Castañeda? About to leave! Where is Rudy Acuña? Not hired! What these students want is simple: *they want an education in a land that was once theirs*" (emphasis added).[76]

Before that moment, top university officials refrained from making any public statements on the strike. Having effectively called their bluff, UCSB assumed the students might call it off, but on the contrary, the strike executive council scaled up, much like the UCLA hunger strikers did when Chancellor Young proved implacable (Houston and Pulido 2002). Holding nightly rallies, posting flyers all over campus, and establishing ties with campus, community, and student organizations from all over the country, key Chicana/o student organizers took the strike to the next level, generating greater awareness and putting more pressure on UCSB. The Associated Students Commission on the Status of Women, for instance, issued a statement supporting the strike, asserting, "Currently there are nine people risking their lives, to be given a voice, so that the people on the top floors of Cheadle Hall will not only listen to what they are asking for but also to take appropriate action. This is not some radical, sensational, irrational act. For years students have been going through all the 'proper' channels . . . after all this time nothing has changed for the better, only for the worse."[77] Beyond UCSB, the Alliance, a multiracial group of undergraduate students from the University of Colorado, Boulder, who had just conducted and concluded an effective six-day hunger strike that called for the creation of an ethnic studies department, called on university officials to negotiate and settle the strike.[78]

Meanwhile, back on campus, as the nine hunger striking students remained inside their tents, several student organizations—including the Lesbian, Gay, Bisexual, and Transgender Alliance; Concerned Students; Hillel; CalPIRG (California Public Interest Research Group); and the Asian American Student Alliance—pitched "solidarity tents" outside Cheadle Hall (N. García 2011). This nascent multiracial coalition indicates that El Congreso wasn't as nationalist as some had alleged (E. López 2011b). Progressive white students and students of color generally supported the strike, but many who were not politically engaged were indifferent, if not outright hostile, as evinced by letters that the campus *Daily Nexus* published. William Yelles (1994), for example, mockingly wrote,

> Today we want to inform you of the enormous injustices we face every day here at UCSB. We call for the end to discriminatory policies historically committed by this elitist institution against us, the left-handed Jewish films studies majors of UCSB. Brothers and sisters, we can no longer remain silent. There are virtually no left-handed desks in classrooms on campus. . . . As the great Ferris Bueller said, "Life moves around pretty fast, if you don't stop to look around once in a while, you could miss it." It's extraordinary to possess convictions you're willing to die for, but I'd rather sit on the beach and watch the sun set.

Brett Orlanski (1994) took a less sarcastic tone, arguing,

> Some things are worth fighting for, but an increase in an already existing department is not. Would it be reasonable for me to strike to get back our football team—something many students would rather have than a larger Chicano Studies Department? Clearly this would seem ridiculous. Some things are just not worth it and a larger Chicano Studies Department is one of them.

Lest one dismiss these letter-writers as the work of misguided students, others such as AS Commission president Geoff Green (2011b), who was born and raised in Fremont, California, and had been deeply involved in a multiracial campus coalition called Concerned Students (which strongly opposed Governor Wilson's budget cuts and their impact on all students), also expressed strong reservations about the strategic logic behind the hunger strike:

> There was a cultural history and lineage behind that tactic, but it seemed like a foreign strategy to me. I wasn't fully aware of the UFW's history. I had discussions with Edwin [López] and Tino [Gutiérrez] about the strike, but I did not comment publicly on it. I supported the demands, but was not sure about the tactic. I think there was a tiny group of students who were active around the strike, but even among Latino students at UCSB, I am not sure how well communicated the strike was across campus. If I had those questions about it and I follow politics fairly well, then I know what the average student was probably saying, "What the hell are you doing?" Well-meaning people didn't get it; they

were like, "how does this connect—no fee hikes and no grapes—what?" It just didn't make sense.

While ideologically far apart, Green, Orlanski, and Yelles all made remarkably similar claims—the hunger strike was unwarranted (although Green was much more sympathetic and raised sound concerns about messaging and organizational strength). Seeing lower fees, no more grapes on campus, and a stronger department (or more desks for left-handed students) as their ultimate aim, all three misinterpreted what many students were actually struggling for—dignity—or in other words, a new department, university, state, nation, and world. One campus-based hunger strike involving less than 1 percent of the student body could never achieve those goals, but that was their "freedom dream," which was not always clearly articulated given the multiple crises that these students were facing in the early 1990s. Without sufficient time, they "screamed" and spoke quickly and spectacularly, with such volume that it split some people's eardrums or left them confused and feeling like they were the victims (Holloway 2010; R. Kelley 2002). Rather than having their "hearts of stone" turn into "hearts of flesh," many simply ignored the strike, just as the university and media initially did.

Despite these obstacles, one group provided the hunger strikers with generally unyielding support (see figure 10). The students' parents rallied behind their sons and daughters even though many were not initially aware that they had stopped eating, which generated great worry and concern. Because of their parents' own delicate health, some students considered not going on hunger strike and some deliberately kept that information from them. Salvador Barajas (2011) recalled his own internal decision-making process regarding these issues:

I was concerned about my mother's [Josefina Barajas-Maldonado] health. She had diabetes and for one day I thought, "Should I really do this or not?" I was worried that when she found out, she might become even sicker. I talked with my older brother and realized that it had to be done. There were very few other options to bring about change. I told my brothers about it first and then they explained it to my mother. I told them to tell her "I am being careful as possible. This isn't really a big deal." My job ultimately was pretty easy; stay inside the tents and talk with media, professors, and so on. Those who were outside the tents sacrificed more than we did.

FIGURE 10. Parents supporting hunger strikers. Juanita Gutiérrez holding sign,
"my son is a hunger striker." Used with permission from Lisa Valencia Sherratt,
UC Santa Barbara Library Special Collections Department, California
Ethnic and Multicultural Archives (CEMA).

Barajas-Maldonado later met with Executive Vice-chancellor Donald
Crawford, Dean of Social Sciences Donald Zimmerman, Vice-chancellor for
Student Affairs Michael Young, and Academic Senate Vice-chair Douglas
Morgan inside El Centro on May 1, 1994. Dean of Students Gladys de Necochea was also involved from the administration side, particularly after Young
had knee surgery while the hunger strike was still going on.[79] The students' parents called for this meeting, marking the first time both sides sat down with each
other since the strike actually began. After exchanging pleasantries, Barajas-
Maldonado told the four university officials, "I am here to check on my son, to
see if he is OK or not. You better pray that nothing happens to him, because if
it does, I will go on strike to make sure his sacrifice wasn't wasted" (S. Barajas
2011). Shortly after the intense ninety-minute session ended, the hunger strikers' parents released a letter, which stated,

> At this moment nine lives are in danger. We do not want to see our children
> and colleagues dead from hunger; therefore, we demand your intervention as

administrators now that the lives of these nine students are in your hands. We cannot stand watching our children suffer for demands that could have been resolved a long time ago; nevertheless, they are determined to do what is necessary to achieve their goals and we support them with all our hearts. We extend our voices through this letter. We have sacrificed to send our children to the university and we are very proud of their achievements. Taking all this into account, we feel that it is not necessary for our children to have to go on a hunger strike to gain something that is fair. The requested demands are just and necessary and are possible for the institution to grant.[80]

While they presented themselves as a "united front" during the meeting, tensions emerged shortly thereafter. Torres (2011) recalled what took place after the session ended: "Some strikers felt that it would be over fast, but I knew it wouldn't be. There was money involved—right? I remember after the officials left, Claudia's [Leiva] dad came up to me and said, 'If something happens to my daughter, I will kill you.' He was supportive before, but when he realized it wasn't going to be easy he came after me because I did all the talking."

Leiva's father wasn't the only parent who found the strike disturbing. Alma Flores (2011a) remembered a conversation that she had with her father:

I called him during the strike and he said, "Quieres morir [Do you want to die]?" This is so weird [starts crying]. I have not discussed this in a long time. My parents were saying, "We're sacrificing and you are going to throw that all away?" I'm a parent now and I understand what they were saying. My dad may not have understood because he didn't see all things that I went through at UCSB. But during one negotiating session, I remember my dad saying, "You need to settle today because if you don't, we [as parents] will be on strike too." That was just so powerful.

Having met the students' parents and seeing the unity that existed publicly between them and the hunger strikers, negotiations between the four-person administration team and the three student negotiators finally got under way on May 2, 1994. The following day both sides met for nearly four hours (Muñoz 2011; Torres 2011). Before adjourning, the four UCSB officials presented the strike executive council with their proposal, addressing all six demands. This abrupt turnaround warrants some explanation. Serious health risks can emerge after not eating for one week (Russell 2005). On the morning of May 3, a UCSB medical staff member examined the students and noted several were experiencing physical difficulties.[81]

André Vásquez (2011) developed severe abdominal pain, for example. He recalled how the strike and his father's absence during the May 1 meeting affected his body:

> I lost ten, fifteen pounds in ten days, a pound a day. I was not a thick person to start with. Gilberto Límon educated us about how the fast would impact our bodies and told us to drink a certain amount of fluids. . . . One day I said, "This has gone on too long, you have to make this end." My judgment wasn't too sharp. My dad was working and couldn't come [to UCSB], so that upset me and I stopped drinking water for one day. My body freaked out and got red and hot. People got scared. I just wasn't thinking too clearly. I was just a little *mocoso* [snot-nosed kid]. I was just nineteen years old.

Even though López and Vásquez's struggles were most evident, UCSB medical staff and the hunger strikers' supporters strongly encouraged all nine to use wheelchairs while going to class and using the restroom. Most understood and accepted that advice, but following it was challenging because of the students' unique personalities. Flores (2011a) became slightly irritated, for instance, when she was told to stop dancing because "people might get the wrong idea that I wasn't suffering, when I really was." This comment underscores the fact that fasting bodies are more effective, in terms of generating public sympathy, when they are docile, weak, and emaciated (P. Anderson 2010; B. Green 1997; Russell 2005).

Flores complied, but she did not become idle. She prayed regularly, as did García and Leiva. For both, the deaths of their grandmothers strongly influenced their decision to go on hunger strike. García (2011) explained the circumstances behind her grandmother's death:

> She was struck by a hit-and-run driver and was killed. We had been telling the city, "We need stop signs. Kids cross through here. The library and elementary school are nearby." Then my grandma got hit in January 1994. Soon after she died, the city finally put in the stop signs and lights. With all these other things going on, I was like, "That's it," I had been pushed too far. Someone had to do something, even if it meant putting our bodies on the line. We felt it was a personal attack on us.

Leiva's (2011) grandmother died one year before the strike began, in Guatemala. Unlike García, she didn't have close ties with her, but her passing wounded her deeply:

> I never grew up with her. I didn't get that bond with her. I yearned for it and missed it as I grew up. She was spiritually the reason why I made that choice—I wanted to offer some sort of sacrifice for the sacrifices that she made for my mom and the other children she had too. That was the offering that I did and it was for her. I asked her for guidance throughout the entire process. I still had not processed her death when the strike began.

Commenting more on the role of prayer and maintaining her spirits as the hunger strike went into the second week, García (2011) recalled,

> We woke up, did danza, prayed, and meditated. We focused on our bodies while the negotiators did what they were doing. We had to preserve our strength and spirit no matter what. I felt in my heart of hearts that whatever happened would be better than what happened before. . . . I just knew, based on other people who had committed the ultimate sacrifice, the hunger strike would change something, one way or the other.

In no less powerful a manner, Gutiérrez (2011) found a creative way to keep his spirits up with his partner, Lisa Marie Navarro (a fellow Congresista). In a playful, but telling manner, he expressed what kept him going on a personal level:

> We played games. I talked with my mom, tried to read and keep up with my classes. Lisa and I had tried before to get married in Mexico, and we thought we were because we paid eighty dollars, but we never got the certificate. So right after the hunger strike ended, we went to Las Vegas. I was still delirious when we got married. We didn't discuss all this during the strike [their future plans for eloping], but we were making out a lot, kissing a lot, that's a form of nonviolence—right? *Love kept it going.* (emphasis added)

The hunger strikers' deteriorating bodies (held together with spiritual practices and the love they received from their friends, parents, and fellow students), combined with increased media attention and significant pressure on and off campus, had a cumulative effect. After virtually ignoring the hunger strike during its first three days, university officials became much more engaged, presenting an extensive proposal to the students to consider. Reaching that moment was complicated and laborious given Chancellor Uehling's lame-duck status. Vice-chancellor for Student Affairs Young (2011) stated that far from purposefully dragging its feet, the university had trouble assembling its team because of this leadership vacuum. Once established, Young quarreled with Academic Senate Vice-chair Morgan, who had better rapport with Dean of Students de Necochea (2011). She consequently helped convince Morgan that the students' demands were legitimate. Professor Segura (2011) played a similar role with Dean of Social Sciences Zimmerman, providing him with unique insights about the Chicano Studies Department and its faculty. These behind-the-scenes conversations indicate that Chicanas were not only involved as hunger strikers, student organizers, and negotiators, but they also played crucial roles as faculty and administrative insiders.

With the ball now back in their court, the students debated the university's proposals and found them deficient. The document included no specific, unequivocal language on bolstering the Chicano Studies Department with additional faculty members, creating a PhD program in Chicano studies, establishing a community center in Isla Vista, banning grapes from campus, lowering or freezing fees, and maintaining El Centro. The only initial tangible guarantee was a promise for hiring more Chicano EOP counselors. All other demands were addressed, but only in vague, conditional terms, prompting serious concerns from many hunger strikers and strike organizers. The three negotiators (who sometimes privately disagreed with each other, just like the four university administrators did) understood those fears but felt that the final agreement would be much more favorable and contain concrete results (Muñoz 2011; Torres 2011). With that assessment and concerns about the strikers' health, they pressed them to accept it, which effectively meant calling off the strike without having ironclad promises on all that they wanted. That uncertainty prompted some intense soul-searching, as some students favored continuing while others supported ending it. The strikers eventually chose to end the protest (Leiva 2011; E. López 2011b, Vásquez 2011).

Having made this decision, the nine-day hunger strike ended on May 5, 1994. In a highly symbolic and emotional ceremony, the striking students wore black-and-white Arnulfo Casillas T-shirts and sat down at a table covered with Professor Antonia Castañeda's face (see figure 11). Standing behind them

FIGURE 11. Hunger strikers breaking fast. Students (left to right) Tino Gutiérrez, André Vásquez, Edwin López, Alma Flores, Claudia Leiva, and Naomi García. Naomi García personal collection.

were Abel Gutiérrez, Benny Torres, Marisela Márquez, Donald Crawford, and Douglas Morgan. After some initial remarks, both sides signed the agreement. With hundreds of spectators, the strikers' parents, and press looking on, the students and administrators sipped apple juice and nibbled on bread that Barajas (2011) said tasted like paper. García (2011) recalled that moment: "We all started crying, family members, faculty, and community members; Michael Young (who was on crutches after his knee surgery) and Gladys de Necochea did too." López (2011b) remembered how he felt emotionally, stating, "When we signed the agreement, that was a big collective high. The fact that we got the university to bend to our demands was actually more exciting than eating."

Couching the signing in historic, anti-imperialist, and probably overly idealistic terms, Torres claimed, "It's difficult to overlook the significance of this battle and not to compare it to the Battle of Puebla," referencing the celebrated battle when the much weaker Mexican Army defeated the powerful French military on May 5, 1862.[82] Adopting a more cautious and subdued approach, Barajas (2011) stated that the ending of the strike was "anticlimactic, given that as we were finishing the strike, another one was starting [at Stanford]; other students were also struggling in the state and elsewhere too."[83]

Having gone nearly nine days without food, what did the hunger strikers and El Congreso achieve? On student fees, UCSB stated that while it "regretted the fact that the Regents have raised [them] steeply in recent years," it claimed it could do very little other than increase financial aid, grants, and scholarships.[84] Regarding recruitment and retention, UCSB set aside funds for filling four vacant full-time counseling positions in EOP and established a three-year plan for admitting more eligible Chicana/o and Latina/o students from the Tri-Counties region (Ventura, Santa Barbara, and San Luis Obispo).[85] The university also pledged to expand the department's FTE from 3.5 to 7.0 and create a PhD program by 1997–1998 and conduct an external search for a new chair when Broyles-González's term ended.[86] UCSB also promised to collaborate with relevant local agencies, such as the Isla Vista Redevelopment Agency, to make the Isla Vista Community Center a concrete reality.[87] Campus officials agreed, moreover, to consult El Congreso before removing El Centro, stating that the Academic Senate's History and Traditions Committee would "fully and expeditiously consider" a proposal to rename Building 406 after its founding chairperson, Arnulfo Casillas. Finally, the university claimed that it would offer grapes only when customers specifically requested them.[88] Summing up these results, the *Santa Barbara Independent* (1994) tartly noted that the students "Got little more than already existed."[89]

THE OTHER SHOE DROPS: OCCUPIED AMERICA, OCCUPIED UCSB, 1994–1996

While much more critical than Torres's sanguine assessment, events soon made the *Independent*'s words look tame, as a new crisis emerged.[90] Two weeks after the strike ended, Dean Zimmerman asked the Chicano Studies Department to consider accepting five professors as "term transfers" on a temporary three-year basis to bolster it in the short-run before reaching the longer-term goal of 7.0 permanent FTE by 1997.[91] Those five faculty members had already embraced this proposal in a memo called the "Coalition Plan" issued to "the hunger strikers and their representatives" on May 5, 1994.[92] These same five professors, along with Reynaldo Macías (education), Richard Durán (education),

Chela Sandoval (Chicano studies), Carlos Ornelas (Chicano studies), Yolanda Broyles-González, and Mario García, sent a letter to Chancellor Uehling and Executive Vice-chancellor Crawford on May 2, 1994, calling for a "concrete [prompt] resolution acceptable to all parties."[93]

This memo was remarkable given some of these faculty members took contrasting positions before the hunger strike began. Unfortunately, this consensus did not last long. Seeing Zimmerman's proposal as a neocolonial imposition that abrogated departmental autonomy and potentially threatened the new vision of Chicano Studies that had been pursued over the past few years, Broyles-González, along with Antonia Castañeda, Ramón Favela, and Chela Sandoval in a two-thirds majority vote, favored approving the five term transfers as "affiliate appointments" (0.0 FTE) rather than on a 0.2 FTE basis, which would have accorded them full voting rights.[94] The department majority also expressed a preferred willingness to focus on filling the newly created Luis Leal Endowed Chair position and then offering current half-time faculty the option of becoming full-time faculty members as the hunger strike stipulated. The four professors also favored focusing on the forthcoming and arduous external program-review process and supported retaining Castañeda through a spousal hire.[95] The recent hire of Rafael Pérez-Torres (who started teaching in the department full time in 1994–1995), moreover, mitigated (from the majority's perspective) the pressing need for courses that the five professors might have taught between 1994 and 1997.[96] Given their significant differences with Broyles-González, the department's other two faculty members opposed all these proposals and filed a minority report documenting their support for the Coalition Plan.[97] Zimmerman (2011) found the department and later El Congreso's rejection of the faculty term transfers puzzling since he thought they would have strengthened it. As the former Social Sciences dean quipped, "It was like snatching defeat from the jaws of victory."

Moving quickly, Zimmerman took action, writing to Broyles-González on June 7, 1994:

> I regret to inform you that I have lost confidence in your ability to exercise the constructive leadership necessary to implement the recent provisions of the recent agreement between UCSB and the student hunger strikers. . . . I have therefore forwarded my recommendation to Executive Vice Chancellor Crawford that you not continue as Chair past expiration of your current term on June 30, 1994.[98]

Because of his assumption that the administration and three student negotiators had agreed on the term transfer plan before the strike ended, Zimmerman felt confident that the Chicano Studies Department and El Congreso would embrace it with little opposition. How he could have thought so is puzzling given the hunger strike agreement clearly stated, "Depending on the response of the faculty, and *after consultation with the Department of Chicano Studies,* term transfer of appropriate faculty from other departments into the Chicano Studies Department will be funded" (emphasis added).[99] Reading "consultation" as mere notification, Zimmerman apparently thought that the department would rubber-stamp his proposal. When it did not, he removed Broyles-González as chair on the grounds that she opposed the hunger strike agreement when, in fact, she was probably its most vocal faculty supporter. That decision created a toxic environment, with El Congreso chairs Abel Gutiérrez and Alma Flores writing lengthy memos opposing the Coalition Plan and Broyles-González's nonreappointment as department chair.[100] Professors Castañeda, Favela, and Sandoval also resisted Zimmerman's decision regarding Broyles-González.[101] Castañeda especially defended her accomplishments as department chairperson, noting how she transformed it into a "democratic academic unit in which ALL faculty and students—regardless of gender and rank—are equally valued."[102] She added,

> The structures and the principles and practices that sustain them have defined one individual—Professor Broyles-González—a woman of color and the only Chicana full professor in the history of UCSB as well as the only female chair of a Chicano Studies Department in any research institution, as the "problem" in Chicano Studies. In doing so, they deliberately ignore the historical and contemporary problems rooted in the institutional history and corollary relationships within and without the Department long before Dr. Broyles-González became chair. In doing so, they replicate the highly conflictive history of Chicano Studies at UCSB. The student's hunger strike is rooted in these historical and contemporary problems—not in Professor Broyles-González's chairship. *By defining one individual in this case, Dr. Broyles-González as the "problem" and proposing her non-reappointment as the "solution,"* the institution abdicates responsibility for addressing institutional structures, principles, and practices of sexism, racism, and other inequities that have historically resulted in administrative intervention and the usurpation of the authority and autonomy of the Department of Chicano

Studies. It does not address the fundamental issues and relationships. Instead, it sustains and reproduces the same structures, the same patterns, the same issues, and the same relationships of power and inequality.[103]

Castañeda's memo revealed what had been largely unspeakable. Broyles-González was a feminist activist-scholar who favored social justice inside and outside the department. Fearing change, some faculty members and campus officials opposed her. Speaking about Zimmerman's decision, Broyles-González called her nonreappointment "backlash for the hunger strike" and "defamation" that impugned her "excellent leadership abilities" (M. Burns 1994; Tutt 1994).[104] New El Congreso chair and former hunger striker Alma Flores also saw Zimmerman's decision as a retaliatory gesture: "I think that it is a direct response to the hunger strike. . . . They want someone passive, someone they can manipulate" (Tutt 1994). Castañeda framed the matter in similar terms, stating, "Dr. Broyles-González is not the problem and removing her is not the solution."[105] Threatening to resign should the term transfers be approved, she said, "We have been begging and pleading with them for the past four years to commit more resources to the department. But we want to be consulted" (M. Burns 1994).

The final act in this messy and tragic affair took place when Crawford released a status report on August 24, 1994, describing what progress had been made regarding the implementation of the hunger strike agreements.[106] In this five-page, single-spaced memo, UCSB's second highest-ranking official made at least two fateful decisions. First, on the basis of his understanding of the "El Centro" concept (first outlined in 1969 in El Plan de Santa Barbara), Crawford created an Implementation Coordination Committee, which was designed to include representatives (that he himself approved) from the Department of Chicano Studies, the CCS, Colección Tloque Nahaque, Chicano EOP, and El Congreso.[107] Second, acting on Zimmerman's previous recommendation, Crawford removed Broyles-González as department chair and called on Letters and Sciences provost Gretchen Bataille to "consult with the department to appoint an acting chair for 1994–95."[108] Having received strong objections from Sandoval, Castañeda, Favela, and Broyles-González, Bataille could not select the department's other two faculty members as chair without inciting even greater internal conflict and division.[109] She could have alternatively recommended that Sandoval and Pérez-Torres, who were both assistant professors, serve as acting co-chairs, as five faculty members suggested.[110] Bataille rejected this proposal, however, instead appointing Zimmerman as acting chair, marking the *third* time the Chicano Studies Department had been placed in "administrative custody" in its relatively short twenty-five-year existence.[111]

Both moves morally outraged the five-person departmental majority and El Congreso. Crawford's actions regarding El Centro transgressed the inviolable principle of self-determination. El Congreso chair Abel Gutiérrez further noted in his June 9, 1994, letter to Crawford, "Dr. Broyles-González has firmly defended the Department of Chicano Studies against administrative intervention. It has become an autonomous, democratically-run department instead of one controlled by the administration. As the only Chicana chair within the University of California system, this attack on Dr. Broyles-González is undoubtedly a sexist, racist, and elitist act designed to punish those who question the administration's views."[112]

Gutiérrez's comment underscores a crucial point. Many students, community members, and some faculty felt that the Chicano Studies Department had become neocolonized and had lost its radical edge over time. In the early 1990s, it was becoming decolonial, from Gutiérrez's perspective, focusing more explicitly on gender, sexuality, and social justice issues. Before such shifts could be consolidated, however, campus officials struck back. Crawford supported Zimmerman, a white male sociology professor, to lead the department. Soon thereafter, posters with the dean's face appeared on campus, stating, "Funny, you don't look Chicano!" with others declaring, "Occupied America, Occupied UCSB, Zimmerman Out!"[113]

The brazen takeover of the Chicano Studies Department sparked resistance, with El Congreso organizing a rally called Take Back Your History, Take Back Chicano Studies that more than one hundred people attended on November 16, 1994. Zimmerman (2011) recalled how El Congreso framed him as the proverbial enemy, stating, "I was not thrilled. I was being painted as a blue-eyed devil and so that affected me, but you had to get beyond that. I could not help but be who I was born." The day after the rally, the *Santa Barbara News-Press* (1994) indirectly chastised Broyles-González and other faculty, stating, "Those who choose to can easily manipulate the sensibilities of impressionable students and that appears what is at work in the most recent protest."

Framed from this perspective, Chicana/o and Latina/o students had no agency; inspiring, charismatic professors were wholly responsible for everything. While Broyles-González and Acuña were influential, the hunger strikers acted independently, even opposing El Congreso's leaders before reconciling with them before the protest began. El Congreso thus embraced and questioned *all* faculty members, even its closest allies as well as those that it especially mistrusted. It critically interrogated everyone and recognized that the Chicano Studies Department had been troubled for many years, as most people understood. It realized, however, unlike some administration officials and faculty members, that the problem could not be simply resolved by removing Broyles-González, which it vigorously opposed. The key issue, from its perspective, was coloniality—a department, university, state, nation, and world that limited their self-determination and ability to be free. That was the problem, along with endemic structural violence that was harming farm workers, immigrants, tenants, students, people of color, women, and other marginalized communities.

A twenty-one-year-old UC Davis student named Óscar Gómez Jr. understood these issues and sympathized with El Congreso. Because of his charismatic personality and deep involvement with MEChA and social justice issues, some called him a "young César Chávez." Nicknamed "El Bandido," Gómez Jr. hosted a popular UC Davis campus radio program titled "La Onda Chicana" (The Chicana/o Wave), and he had followed the UCSB hunger strike and subsequent events. He actually attended the Take Back Chicano Studies rally; the protest took place just one week after Proposition 187 passed, which had further upset many Chicana/o and Latina/o students. After the event, Gómez Jr. met some friends in Isla Vista. The next morning, his body was found "floating in shallow water below a bluff near UCSB's Engineering Department" (Wallace 1994). While the *Santa Barbara News-Press* reported his blood-alcohol level was .21 (more than twice the legal limit at that time), it failed to mention, as another newspaper article did, that he was "involved with a demonstration where Latino students were protesting the hiring of a Caucasian [*sic*] professor to head that school's Chicano Studies Department."[114] The *News-Press* article implied that Gómez Jr. was simply an unfortunate, but irresponsible, drunk student who fell from the cliffs in Isla Vista and died (Wallace 1994). That narrative didn't sit well with El Congreso and his family members, who suggested that Gómez Jr. had been possibly killed or assassinated given his outspoken political beliefs. Sensing foul play, Óscar Gómez Sr. demanded a substantive investigation into his son's death, but the Santa Barbara County Sheriff's Department refused to do so, claiming he died from "blunt force trauma to the head" (Valles 1995; Wallace 1995). Presumably that fatal injury came from falling off the cliffs while intoxicated, but questions regarding Gómez Jr.'s death still linger, even twenty years later (Valencia Sherratt 2011).

Gómez Jr.'s death—or murder, as some called it—deeply affected El Congreso's members, who organized a memorial service on his twenty-second birthday (January 9, 1995). Beyond grief, some became frightened and edgy, taking extra precautions regarding their personal safety. "I remember carrying a little knife while I was riding my bike between UCSB and Isla Vista," Flores (2011a) recalled. While nothing was ever definitively proven, some Congresistas pulled back, spending less time on the struggle to "take back" the Chicano Studies Department as well as the other hunger strike agreements (Valencia Sherratt 2011).[115]

With overt pressure diminishing over time, Zimmerman stepped aside, appointing assistant professor Rafael Pérez-Torres as departmental vice-chair in winter 1995.[116] Pérez-Torres continued serving in that capacity for one more year (1995–96) while the department carried out two unsuccessful searches, one for chair, the other for the Luis Leal Endowed Chair. UC Berkeley ethnic studies professor Norma Alarcon was offered the former position, but she turned it down.[117] El Congreso opposed her nomination, backing Pomona College Chicano Studies Department chairperson Deena González instead (Valles 1996).[118] Given the already delayed external program review and the upcoming deadline for submitting the PhD proposal, Zimmerman consulted with departmental faculty and temporarily put aside the ongoing external search for a new chairperson. While this decision technically violated the hunger strike agreement, Zimmerman appointed Francisco Lomelí as new department chair for 1996–1997 based on his extensive experience on campus.[119]

Given Lomelí's vote on the proposed hiring of Rudy Acuña and the *News-Press* editorial he co-signed opposing the hunger strike, El Congreso expressed deep concern when it found out he had been appointed as chair (Vásquez 2011). His selection was a painful reminder that two years after the strike ended, UCSB had not followed through on any of the hunger strike agreements, except for Chicano EOP and possibly El Centro (Valles 1996). Former hunger striker and 1995–1996 El Congreso internal co-chair André Vásquez spoke about the challenges associated with putting the agreements into practice: "It's hard as students because there's so much stuff to do—we dropped everything we were doing for the strike at that time. It's just one thing after another and we knew that going in; you can only do so much, you have to pick your battles. I really don't want to see something drastic happen again" (Valles 1996). Former hunger striker and 1995–1996 El Congreso external co-chair Tino Gutiérrez echoed this latter comment, implying direct action might once again be necessary: "Unless we push it, they're really not going to do anything. It really pisses us off because they want us to be good Mexicans and keep our mouths shut. El Congreso is not about keeping our mouths shut" (Valles 1996).

Challenging El Congreso's grim assessment, Executive Vice-chancellor Crawford issued a second, largely upbeat, progress report on the hunger strike agreements on July 24, 1996.[120] Noting that while the Luis Leal Endowed Chair position was still unfilled and the 7.0 FTE level probably would not be reached by the July 1, 1997 deadline, he declared with Lomelí as the newly installed chair, "the department is now positioned to undergo a program review and to develop, in conjunction with the review, a Ph.D. proposal." Crawford also emphasized that Chicano EOP staff positions were not cut back and funding for recruiting Chicana/o and Latina/o students from the Tri-Counties region was expanded. Finally, Crawford argued that "UCSB has honored its commitments to work with governmental agencies to seek funding for the Isla Vista Community Center. Despite these efforts, funding has not been secured." El Centro, the grape boycott, and student fees were not addressed in this memo.[121]

MOVING FORWARD, SLOWLY: TWO STEPS FORWARD, ONE STEP BACK, 1996–2016

Depending on one's viewpoint, either very little or moderate change occurred in the two years after the hunger strike ended in 1994. Over the next twenty years, a different, though still mixed, picture emerged. During Lomelí's chairship, the department hired three new full-time assistant professors (Edwina Barvosa, Jonathan Inda, and me) in 1997–1998. Those hires, combined with María Herrera-Sobek, who had been named Luis Leal Endowed Chair in 1996–1997, brought the department's FTE to 8.0 for 1998–1999, surpassing the 7.0 mark established in the hunger strike agreement. In addition, the department in the late 1990s, under the guidance of Professors Inda and Herrera-Sobek, drafted a new, expanded PhD proposal (Broyles-González wrote an earlier version, with assistance from Naomi García and other faculty, in March 1994) and submitted it to the appropriate reviewing agencies. After an uncommonly large number of revisions and edits, the program was finally approved in 2003. The first graduate students in the department started to take classes in fall 2004. The first three

PhDs in Chicana and Chicano studies in the entire world were awarded in June 2012. Since then, ten more students have received their doctoral degrees in Chicana and Chicano studies.[122]

Regarding Chicana/o student enrollment, after the controversial elimination of affirmative action in the UC system in July 1995, many thought that the numbers of students of color might plummet. UCSB Executive Director of Admissions William Villa and his staff worked tirelessly, however, relying on the "comprehensive review" process, to maintain high Chicano/Latino enrollment.[123] UCSB became a Hispanic Serving Institution (HSI) (making it eligible for increased federal funding), with Chicana/o and Latina/o undergraduate enrollment reaching 27 percent, in 2014–2015 (L. Gordon 2015). This is a remarkable feat when one considers that less than 1 percent of all students were Chicana/o in the late 1960s and only 10 percent were Chicana/o or Latina/o when the strike occurred in 1994.[124] With additional funding for recruiting and retaining eligible, local Chicana/o and Latina/o high school students, UCSB has become more diverse partially because of the hunger strikers' sacrifices.

The Isla Vista community center was established, but not without considerable struggle. Initially designed as a space where low-income families might organize and challenge immigration raids and unscrupulous landlords in Isla Vista, the community center became a more service-oriented "teen center," which the Channel Islands YMCA currently operates. First opened in 1998, the Isla Vista Teen Center offers sixth to twelfth grade youth recreational, cultural, and leadership services. It also offers teens (especially those considered "at-risk") with a safe, alternative space where they can hang out after school and do their homework, watch movies, and be with their friends until their parents come from work. The center also offers dance, music, theater, and parenting courses (Reyes 2013). Originally located in a dilapidated trailer for years, the Isla Vista Teen Center was recently replaced by the St. George Family Youth Center, a much more modern and spacious building constructed by local real estate developer and philanthropist Edward St. George with his own funds (L. García 2015).

While the Teen Center may not have been what the hunger strikers and some El Congreso members had initially envisioned, some were later involved with a critical study under CCS Director Denise Segura's leadership. Titled *Latinos in Isla Vista: A Report on the Quality of Life Among Latino Immigrants*, Marisela Márquez (hunger strike negotiator), Claudia Leiva (a hunger striker who pushed hard for the community center demand), John Delgado (a Congresista who provided security during the hunger strike), and Angel Valdivia (who was briefly involved with the Harmony Keepers), among others, conducted interviews and collected survey data on Latino families in Isla Vista (Segura 1999). Isla Vista was long seen as a party town for young college students, but *Latinos in Isla Vista* documented, for the first time, the challenging living and working conditions that Latina/o families faced, providing policy makers and activists with substantive information to press for better services and more effective programs. Márquez later taught a two-quarter undergraduate community-research-methods seminar in the Chicano Studies Department, which focused on a wide variety of issues facing the Chicana/o and Latina/o community in Isla Vista. Students from this course eventually produced a pamphlet on housing conditions and renters' rights.[125]

Neoliberal austerity, ironically, helped save El Centro (which was eventually named after Arnulfo Casillas) from demolition. Originally slated for removal under UCSB's 1990 LRDP, it survived, precariously, over the next twenty years. In November 2010, the UC regents approved UCSB's new 2025 LRDP, increasing student enrollment and earmarking necessary resources for the long-delayed 1990 LRDP's completion (Kettmann 2010). This decision unnerved many Congresistas, who assumed that UCSB would immediately drop the wrecking ball on El Centro. When construction began three years after the LRDP was ratified, however, it remained intact, although the building's interior and exterior looked quite shabby. Despite this fact, El Centro remained a vibrant, safe space where all students could study, meet with EOP counselors, and organize outreach events, rallies, and protests. Indeed, a multiracial coalition met there after George Zimmerman (the security officer who shot and killed Trayvon Martin in February 2012) was declared not guilty in July 2013. After one of those meetings, the words "deportation = justice; deport illegals now" were written on El Centro's sliding glass doors. Because IDEAS (Improving Dreams, Equality, Access, and Success), a campus-based organization that supports undocumented students, held its regular meetings in El Centro, Chancellor Henry Yang and Vice-chancellor for Student Affairs Michael Young strongly condemned the offensive and degrading graffiti, calling it an "act of vandalism" (Wenzke 2013). Yang also supported funding for repainting the building; it has also been recently upgraded with new carpeting and furniture. A new organization, La Mesa Directiva, which includes representatives from all entities that have office space inside El Centro, has also emerged over the past few years. La Mesa Directiva is based loosely on the original El Centro concept, first outlined in El Plan de Santa Barbara. It relies on consensus-based decision-making procedures and seeks to keep Building 406 a "convivial space" where students can organize and challenge injustice.[126]

The record on the last two issues (grapes and fees) is decidedly more problematic. While the UFW ended its sixteen-year grape boycott in 2000, making this a moot point from the university's perspective, pesticide poisoning remains widespread among farm workers. Most are nonunionized, receive very little pay, and work long hours under arduous conditions (Holmes 2013). The fact that farm workers are no better off than they were in 1994 mirrors the situation for students who have seen their fees increase 300 percent since 2000, when rates started skyrocketing (reaching more than $12,000 per year in 2012–2013). These exorbitant hikes have essentially priced out students from all racial backgrounds, but especially students of color, who are often first-generation college students who come from working- and lower-middle-class families. Despite assurances from the administration that low-income students will graduate with the "least amount of indebtedness possible," more and more UCSB students are taking out massive loans, reflecting national trends on student debt (Mitchell and Jackson-Randall 2012). Repeated fee hikes sparked massive student protests on several UC campuses, with protests, rallies, a "die-in," and a one-day fast taking place at UCSB in fall 2009 (Bachman 2009). In November 2015, more than one thousand UCSB students participated in the nationwide Million Student March, which demanded student debt cancellation, tuition-free education, and a $15 minimum wage for all campus workers (Fried 2015).

While these protests have increased public awareness, not much tangible change has taken place. Indeed, massive budget cuts enacted over the past decade have been devastating. With classes being eliminated; staff, clerical, and custodial workers being laid off or given additional job duties without any pay increase; and a virtual freeze on faculty hires, the UC system has reached a critical juncture (J. Medina 2012). The crisis has severely strained the UCSB Chicana and Chicano Studies Department. After reaching an all-time high of 13.5 FTE in the mid-2000s, the department currently has 10.0 FTE (9 full-time and 2 part-time). Some faculty left for personal reasons, but internal conflicts within the department also influenced some departures. A staggered voting system, which was established after the hunger strike, that favored senior faculty members and disenfranchised associate and assistant professors, was especially troublesome, generating significant tension. Personnel reviews—based on disparate standards—were especially bitter, making promotions in rank challenging.[127] Finally, after numerous painstaking efforts, the department's by-laws were revised in fall 2013, making it possible for all faculty, regardless of rank, to vote on all cases.

Despite this recent development, the Chicana and Chicano Studies Department still faces significant challenges. Since Lomelí's five-year term as chair ended in 2001, María Herrera-Sobek, Claudine Michel, Chela Sandoval, Juan Vicente-Palerm, Aída Hurtado, and Denise Segura have all served in that capacity. While all six did well under challenging circumstances, constant leadership changes have taken a toll on the department.[128] In May 2015, Executive Dean of the College of Letters and Sciences and SAGE Sara McCune Miller and Dean of Social Sciences Melvin Oliver placed the Chicana/o Studies Department under administrative receivership, appointing UC Irvine education professor Gilberto Conchas as acting chair for 2015–2016 and freezing graduate student admissions for 2016–2017. These two decisions were made on the assumption that the department's weaknesses stem mostly from internal conflicts rather than draconian budget cuts from Sacramento and Oakland. Self-inflicted wounds have definitely sapped the department's growth, but so too has benign neglect, as campus officials have not focused on leadership development from within. Without sufficient resources and bodies, department faculty have taken on multiple responsibilities and are severely overburdened, although they still have published award-winning books and articles and provided exemplary teaching and service. Generally speaking, it is a demanding, draining, and precarious space that has left many people (faculty, staff, students, and so on) wounded. Twenty-plus years after the hunger strike and forty-five years after first being established, the Chicana and Chicano Studies Department is still troubled and viewed with suspicion, even derision.[129] It emerged from and was strengthened by struggle. To revive it from its most recent crisis, more struggle may be needed.

CONCLUSION: LA LUCHA SIGUE (THE STRUGGLE CONTINUES)

The 1994 UCSB hunger strike was relatively successful. Chicana/o and Latina/o student enrollment expanded, more Chicana and Chicano Studies Department faculty were hired and a PhD program was established, a community center was opened, and El Centro was maintained and renamed after Arnulfo Casillas.

Tuition soared, however, and the department experienced renewed turmoil. And while UCSB became a Hispanic Serving Institution, many Chicana/o and Latina/o students still reportedly feel like outsiders because of the campus's largely dominant, white, affluent culture. Chicana/o and Latina/o families, moreover, are still being displaced by spiraling rents and unjust evictions in Isla Vista (S. Burns 2011; Villegas 2015).

Despite these varied results, the hunger strike had an overall positive effect on campus (M. Márquez 2011). Without it, UCSB would look much different than it does today. Seen dismissively as a narrow struggle for more departmental faculty members or an incoherent plea, this hunger strike was a "scream" for a new world, a world where life is sustained and nurtured rather than extinguished by endless budget cuts, tokenism, sexism, and racism (Holloway 2010). While not wholly successful, it partially decolonized the campus and made it possible for many students to live a more dignified life. Colonial practices proved resilient, but this does not diminish what these students achieved under very challenging circumstances. They spoke spectacularly about "destruction" and inspired Stanford University students to go on their own hunger strike, as will be seen in the next chapter.

5

STANFORD

"Things Aren't Right Here"

Chávez was our hero. We had grown up in Salinas. Everyone believed in him and the cause. We thought it was common sense what he was fighting for—the short-handed versus long-handed hoe, having bathroom breaks, and water. He risked his life for these issues. We realized that the only way we would be taken seriously was by doing this [a hunger strike]. Students had been struggling for years for a Chicano Studies Department; they had done many petitions, but no one listened to them. We thought that what we were calling for made common sense too.

EVA SILVA, STANFORD HUNGER STRIKER (2012A)

INTRODUCTION

ONE DAY BEFORE THE UCSB HUNGER STRIKE ENDED, another one began at Stanford University. While they had multiple grievances, the unexpected firing of Cecilia Burciaga on March 22, 1994, shocked and humiliated many Chicana/o and Latina/o students. The highest-ranking Latina administration official on campus, Burciaga had been at Stanford for twenty years, serving as associate dean for student affairs and development officer for student resources when she was dismissed (see figure 12). She and her husband, José Antonio ("Tony") Burciaga, a celebrated Chicano writer, poet, and artist, were also resident fellows (RFs) at Casa Zapata, a Chicana/o themed dorm. Casa Zapata housed Tony Burciaga's well-known mural, "Last Supper of Chicano Heroes," which included iconic and unheralded figures such as Stanford Chicana/o students, gardeners, and housekeepers.[1]

Beyond her job titles and official responsibilities, Cecilia Burciaga provided many students with invaluable assistance, counseling, and mentoring. Countless Chicanas saw her as a "mother-like figure" that lifted their spirits through

FIGURE 12. Cecilia Burciaga outside the quad during the hunger strike. Used with permission of *San Jose Mercury News*.

her wisdom, support, and encouragement (Alvarado 2012; González Luna 2013a). Given the campus's stark racial and class divisions in the early 1990s, Burciaga became a beloved confidant and Casa Zapata a safe space where Chicanas/os and Latinas/os could simply exist without being constantly attacked.

Much like UCLA Chancellor Charles Young's decision to not establish a Chicana/o studies department the day before César Chávez's funeral, Burciaga's firing was the emotional trigger that helped spark the Stanford hunger strike (Jasper 1997; Nepstad 2004). Having been bombarded with racial microaggressions (explained more fully below) for years, these students had sought redress through bureaucratic channels without any success (Silva 2012a; Yosso 2006). Repeated denials took a toll, generating anger and desperation.

These feelings were exacerbated several weeks after Burciaga was fired when some students sarcastically laughed during a screening of the United Farm Workers (UFW) documentary film, *No Grapes* (Ellman, Parlee, and Bourin 1992). Focusing on the relationship between toxic pesticides and cancer clusters in California's San Joaquín Valley, the ten-minute video depicted physically handicapped farm worker children, some of whom were born without limbs. Hoping that those heartbreaking scenes might generate greater sympathy, the Chicana/o and Latina/o students who organized the film screening were outraged when their classmates shouted, "Beaners, go home!"

Coming from farm worker, immigrant, and low-income families in Salinas, Reedley, Escondido, and Burbank, four Chicana students—Tamara Alvarado, Julia González Luna, Elvira Prieto, and Eva Silva—found that racist discourse morally repugnant (see figure 13). After budget cuts targeting El Centro Chicano (a historic counter-space much like UCSB's El Centro Arnulfo Casillas) and Burciaga's firing, they saw little difference between these comments and decisions that top university officials, such as Provost Condoleezza Rice and President Gerhard Casper, were making. They had been effectively told "Beaners, go home" many times since first setting foot on Leland and Jane Stanford's old "farm," but rather than do that, they resisted and fought back—demanding a Chicano Studies Department, a ban on grapes, a community center in nearby East Palo Alto, and Burciaga's rehiring.

Starting on May 4, 1994, Alvarado, González Luna, Prieto, and Silva all stopped eating. For three days, they, along with many other students, occupied

FIGURE 13. Chicana hunger strikers (left to right) Elvira Prieto, Eva Silva, Tamara Alvarado, and Julia González Luna, May 5, 1994. Stanford Daily Inc.

the main campus quad, located steps away from the university's historic, ornate Memorial Church and the provost and president's offices. Given its aesthetic splendor and Stanford's lucrative brand, the quad is a popular destination for tourists, weddings, and other crucial campus events. Hunger strikes have traditionally (especially in Ireland) occurred on the doorstep of power (Beresford 1987; Russell 2005). Spatial proximity "turns up the volume," making the hunger striker's spectacular speech even louder, generating greater media coverage and public attention (Johnson 2013).

Having just recovered from an embarrassing financial scandal involving charges that Stanford defrauded the federal government out of millions of dollars, the university could ill afford any more negative publicity (Casper 2014; Celis 1994; Kennedy 1997; Merl 1991).[2] Thus, while Rice and Casper initially took a hard-line stance toward the hunger strikers (claiming fiscal austerity limited increased budget expenditures for new departments and programs), they eventually relented, partially because of the favorable press that the strikes received. Most hunger strikes involving women, especially women of color, are ignored or ridiculed, even though they largely pioneered the tactic in the early twentieth century (see chapter 1). Alvarado, González Luna, Prieto, and Silva suffered similar fates, but they persisted and obtained some positive results, including most notably the establishment of the Center for Comparative Studies in Race and Ethnicity (CSRE).

What explains this unexpected outcome? Might Burciaga and Rice—two renowned women of color—have increased the strike's visibility, or could it have been Stanford's high-profile image? While both factors were crucial, so were the bodies of the female strikers. This strike became prominent partially on the basis of their gender. Media accounts consistently noted all four fasters were women, even though this framing left them uncomfortable, particularly since the strike also involved a fifth student, Felipé Barragan, who was often overlooked. Like the UCSB and UCLA hunger strikes, this action was a collective effort that involved female and male students as well as supportive faculty, parents, and community members. What was different about this strike was that it took place on a private, rather than public, university campus. Because Stanford receives no state funding, one might assume that it would be less concerned about its image than UCLA and UCSB, but that was not the case. In the 1990s, when "image was everything," private *and* public universities could not ignore popular opinion without tarnishing their hallowed reputations.[3]

Given the people that were involved and the setting (Stanford is arguably the nation's second most prestigious university after Harvard), this hunger strike merits closer attention. Surprisingly, with the exception of Rice (2010) and Casper's (2014) memoirs, one master's thesis (González-Clarke 2006), and many newspaper articles, the scholarly literature on it is extremely thin. This chapter seeks to fill that considerable gap with scores of interviews with all four hunger strikers, key student organizers, faculty, and campus officials, including Casper (but, unfortunately, not Rice, who never replied despite receiving multiple requests to be interviewed for this study). Through these interviews and other archival materials, I developed a substantive description and analysis of the three-day hunger strike, but before presenting that material, I briefly explore the long history of social justice activism that existed on campus before the protest began on May 4, 1994. Chicana/o and Latina/o students had been pressing for a Chicano studies department since the late 1960s, and some became very involved in the so-called canon wars and antiapartheid movement that shook the campus in the 1980s. These events, combined with a significant split within MEChA in the late 1980s, are critical for understanding the context behind the 1994 hunger strike.

"DOWN ON THE FARM": STANFORD, RACE, AND STUDENT ACTIVISM, 1884–1993

Stanford University emerged from tragedy. In 1884, Leland and Jane Stanford's only child (named Leland Stanford Junior) died unexpectedly—he was just fifteen years old. Gravely despondent, the former Republican California governor, U.S. senator, and railroad tycoon had a powerful and transformative dream about his son several days after he passed away. When he woke up the next morning, he said, "The children of California shall be our children" (Mirrielees 1959: 20). Shortly thereafter, he and his wife drew up plans for establishing a university, even though UC Berkeley was located just forty miles away from its future site in the Santa Clara Valley. After several unsuccessful attempts, Leland Stanford Junior University opened in October 1891 with David Starr Jordan serving as its inaugural president (Davis and Nilan 1989).

With his vast fortune (accumulated on the backs of Chinese labor, which he opposed and then favored), Stanford purchased eight thousand acres of land, mainly for horse ranching, breeding, and training, in the 1870s and 1880s (Saxton 1971). Before he bought what became known as the Palo Alto Stock Farm (or simply the Farm, as it is still called today), it was divided into several large ranchos by the Mexican government. Those landowners, including José Peña, Secundino Robles, Antonio Bulena, and Rafael Soto, helped establish what became known as Palo Alto in the 1830s and 1840s (McDonnell 2008; Vélez-Ibañez; 1996). However, long before that moment, Spanish "explorer" Gaspar de Portolà and his men landed in Northern California and reportedly slept under a large redwood tree ("El Palo Alto") in 1769 (McDonnell 2008). Redwood was critical for the Ohlone/Muwekma people who lived throughout the Bay Area for more than five thousand years before the Spanish arrived (Margolin 2003). Indeed, when Portolà landed, there were about ten thousand Ohlone/Muwekma people living in the Santa Clara Valley, including what became the city of East Palo Alto (EPA) in the early 1980s (Rigenhagen 1993). Reviled in the early 1990s as the "murder capital of the nation," EPA has been a site of struggle and resistance for decades that many Stanford Chicana/o and Latina/o students found compelling because of their desire to create not only a more just campus but also a more just community, state, nation, and world (Moraga 2002).

This hunger for justice can be traced back more than three decades, when African American Ravenswood High School students occupied their campus administration building in September 1968, demanding, among other things, more black history courses, contemporary black literature, and the principal's resignation (Levin 1996). Because of redlining and residential segregation that kept Palo Alto lily-white for many years, EPA was largely black and Ravenswood High School was nearly all black until the late 1960s (Camarillo 2009; Ruffin 2014). Pervasive racism prompted some black Civil Rights Movement and Black Power activists to unsuccessfully seek to rename the city "Nairobi" (Biondi 2012: 221).

Meanwhile, across the 101 freeway (which separates EPA from Palo Alto), a nonviolent uprising occurred on the Farm. Occurring just four days after Martin Luther King was assassinated, about seventy students associated with the Black Student Union (BSU) rose from their seats on April 8, 1968, and took the microphone from Stanford provost Richard Lyman during an event called Stanford's Response to White Racism (Lyman 2009: 72–74). Concerned about the gap between what King (1981: 40) might have called the university's "high blood pressure of creeds and [its] anemia of deeds," BSU chair Kenny Washington proclaimed, "Put your money and your action where your mouth is," while other black students read a list of ten demands, including "the hiring of minority group faculty members and curriculum relevant for minority group members" (Phillips 1990: 17). The BSU also called for greater recruitment of black, Mexican American, American Indian, and other minority group members from EPA, East Menlo Park, Santa Clara County, and San Mateo County, indicating overlap between campus-based and community struggles.[4]

Former provost and president Richard Lyman (2011: 6) claimed that the university administration "to varying degrees, enthusiastically supported" these goals, quickly agreeing to all the demands but one.[5] The university, for example, established the Program in African and Afro-American Studies in 1969. Renowned scholar St. Claire Drake served as the program's first chairperson (Phillips 1990: 18). Black freshman student enrollment, moreover, increased from *two* (less than 0.1 percent) in 1960 to 134 (6.0 percent) in 1970 (UCMI 1989: 55–61).[6] Focusing not only on recruitment but also retention, the Black Student Volunteer Center was created in 1969 and the first black-oriented residential hall or "theme dorm" (named Ujamaa) opened its doors in the early 1970s (Phillips 1990: 20, 24).

Regarding Chicana/o student enrollment and Chicana/o studies, Stanford admitted ninety-two Chicana/o freshmen in 1970, 5 percent of that year's incoming class (UCMI 1989: 61).[7] In 1972 there were 164 Chicana/o graduate students, and one year later (thanks partially to aggressive recruiting by the Ford Foundation) that number rose to 235 (UCMI 1989: 109). In 1971–1972, the Chicano Fellows Program, offering undergraduate courses taught mostly by advanced Chicana/o graduate students, was established (Camarillo 2012). Stanford environmental engineering professor James Leckie (2012) recalled that there were very few Chicana/o faculty in those days: "There were just three of us in the early 1970s—Renato Rosaldo, Arturo Islas, and myself."[8] In 1980, the Stanford Center for Chicano Research (SCCR) was created, with scholars publishing numerous studies and monographs on a wide variety of issues and topics (Camarillo 2013). While effective, the SCCR was not responsible for the Chicano studies undergraduate "program," which did not exist institutionally at Stanford in the 1970s and 80s. Students could major in Chicana/o studies, taking courses in several disciplines across campus, but the tiny Chicano Fellows Program was understaffed and resource-starved (Leckie 2012). Consequently, very few Stanford students graduated with a degree in Chicano studies from Stanford in the 1970s and 80s.

Despite these issues, the percentage of Chicana/o freshmen slowly increased during those two decades, rising to 10 percent in 1988. In contrast, the number of Chicana/o graduate students *dropped* sharply between 1973 and 1988, generating significant concern within the university administration and Chicana/o student community (UCMI 1989: 61, 109).[9] Like the black theme dorm, Ujamaa, a Chicana/o residential house, Casa Zapata, was opened in 1972, and El Centro Chicano de Estanford (known simply today as El Centro Chicano) was established in 1978 (González-Clarke 2012; Najarro 2012).[10] Located in the Nitery basement (in White Plaza, the center of campus) along with the Chicano Fellows Program, El Centro Chicano became an alternative "safe space," although it was poorly maintained and sometimes utilized by mostly white fraternities and sororities for their organizational events (A. Medina 2012).[11]

While less politicized and militant than perhaps their counterparts in the 1960s and 70s, college students in the 1980s remained politically active, especially around Central America, South Africa, and issues concerning people of color, women, working-class people, and queer people in the United States (Martin 2011). As they organized, they quickly discovered that they faced a familiar foe—Ronald Reagan, who had mocked and targeted student radicals and the UFW as California governor some two decades earlier.[12] After taking over the White House, Reagan assembled his cabinet, which included former U.S. labor secretary and Stanford University professor George Shultz, who became secretary of state in 1982. Shultz's ties with Stanford go back to the late 1960s, when he was a fellow at the Center for Advanced Study in the Behavioral Sciences. Aside from Shultz, twenty-nine officials within the Reagan administration had ties with Stanford's arch-conservative Hoover Institution in the early 1980s (Turner 1983). The nation's thirty-first president, Herbert Hoover was part of Stanford's first class in 1891, graduating in 1895 with a geology degree. Hoover later became a member of the Stanford University board of trustees in the early 1910s and left a lasting imprint on the campus through his close friendship with Stanford president Ray Wilbur (1916–43) (Lowen 1997). Hoover often put pressure on Wilbur to deny faculty promotions and raises on the basis of someone's liberal views, which he successfully resisted in the 1920s. President David Jordan had not been as effective, as Jane Stanford fired sociology professor Edward A. Ross in 1900 (Mohr 1970). Ross supported economic populism but also favored Chinese exclusion and racial eugenics.[13] Stanford University's close alliance with right-wing politicians and business leaders continued throughout the post–World War II period as it eventually became one of the nation's leading "Cold War universities" with extensive ties to the military-industrial complex (Lowen 1997).

In response to Reagan's harmful domestic and foreign policies and his close ties with Stanford's Hoover Institution, a militant, multiracial organization calling itself Students Against Reagan (STAR) emerged on campus in the 1980s (Hernández-Clarke 2012). STAR activists had multiple concerns, including the Reagan administration's support for the repugnant South African regime. Like many students all over the nation, STAR members became involved in the antiapartheid movement, building makeshift shantytowns and calling on the university to divest from South Africa (Ervin 2011; Soule 1997).[14] Georgina ("Gina") Hernández-Clarke (2012), a Chicana student from Whittier, California, remembered feeling initially inspired by primarily African American—and to a lesser degree, progressive white—students that were involved with STAR and the antiapartheid movement. She also recalled that she voted for the first time ever for Jesse Jackson in the Democratic presidential primary election in 1984, her freshman year on campus.[15] "This was a mind-blowing time period for me," she stated, "I first became active in STAR and later the whole debate around Western Culture blew up."

Called the canon or "culture wars," the nationwide controversy surrounding multiculturalism and the Western Culture course became especially intense at Stanford in the middle and late 1980s (Lindenberger 1990; Newfield 2008; Pratt 1990; Rosaldo 1989). Following Allan Bloom's best-selling *Closing of the American Mind* (1987), U.S. Education Secretary William Bennett (1988) and National Endowment for the Humanities chairperson Lynne Cheney (1988) blasted Stanford for replacing its Western Culture course with a class called Culture, Values, and Ideas (CIV) on the grounds that it would fragment and *disunite* the United States.[16] Concerns about what conservative commentator Pat Buchanan (2002) later called the "death of the West" permeated the culture wars at Stanford as texts written by white straight male authors were supplemented and sometimes replaced by ones authored by women, people of color, and queer people, including "third world people" such as Guatemalan indigenous activist Rigoberta Menchú (Newfield 2008: 70). Conservative icons like Dinesh D'Souza (former Hoover Institution fellow) thus were invited to campus, and significant resources were poured into the far right *Stanford Review*, the local version of William F. Buckley's conservative magazine *National Review*.

Often seen as a sinister, conspiratorial plot foisted on America's youth by a zealous group of "tenured radicals" from the 1960s (Kimball 1990), the impetus for curricular reform at Stanford actually came from below. In the mid-1980s, Gina Hernández-Clarke (2012) stated that a "rainbow coalition" of students emerged around Jesse Jackson's presidential campaign and the antiapartheid movement. A multiracial alliance of student organizations, including the Black Student Union (BSU), Movimiento Estudantil Chicano de Aztlán (MEChA), the Stanford American Indian Organization, the Asian American Student Organization, and the Students United for Democracy in Education, also pressed for the elimination of Western Culture, the freshman yearlong course, on the basis of BSU president Bill King's words that it "crushed people's psyche" and "hurt them mentally and emotionally in ways that are not even recognized" (Lindenberger 1990; Phillips 1990: 42; Pratt 1990: 16).[17] Speaking even more bluntly, BSU member Amanda Kemp said, "The implicit message of the current curriculum is nigger go home" (Rosovsky 1998: 130–31).[18] Chris González-Clarke (2012), Gina Hernández-Clarke's husband, who was an undergraduate student activist and later a musician in Dr. Loco's Rockin' Jalapeño Band during the 1980s and 90s,[19] recalled that turbulent era:

> The campus was much more polarized back then. There were two very articulate poles; the organized right-wing had ties with the *Stanford Review*, which was connected to the *National Review*. They were constantly attacking us, saying that ethnic centers like El Centro Chicano were bad and promoted self-segregation. Pay Pal founder Peter Thiel established the *Review* and ran articles attacking Casa Zapata's supposedly anti-white murals, questioning the need for ethnic theme dorms.[20] Meanwhile there was a strong progressive wing too at that time. There was STAR, Students for Jackson, the antiapartheid movement, and a huge rally, with ten thousand people, which our band played at, for Jackson, held in May 1988.[21] Then there was the Western Culture debate with Bill Bennett. There were so many things going back then; people were just willing to go at it.

On January 15, 1987, Martin Luther King's fifty-eighth birthday and BSU's twentieth anniversary, five hundred students marched with Jesse Jackson at Stanford, chanting, "Hey hey, ho ho, Western Culture's got to go" (Phillips

1990: 42–43). The main target of this protest was the Academic Senate, which was discussing plans for revising the Western Culture course. Organized by the campus-based Rainbow Coalition, the multiracial collective issued the "Rainbow Agenda" in May 1987, calling for, among other things, the elimination of the Western Culture course, along with an independent commission to study racism on campus, divestment from South Africa, and a ban on table grapes. During a ceremony commemorating Stanford's forthcoming centennial, "300 Rainbow Coalition student activists released black balloons in the air and stood with their fists in the air" just before Stanford president Donald Kennedy began to speak. Several minutes later, the students interrupted U.S. Secretary of State George Shultz, chanting, "'Just say no to the Contras, just say no to apartheid' [before] silently walk[ing] out and humming 'We Shall Overcome'" (46).[22]

After a lengthy two-year process that sparked nationwide attention, the Stanford Academic Senate voted to replace the Western Culture course with the CIV course in March 1988 (Lindenberger 1990: 156; Pratt 1990: 18–22).[23] Despite this progressive step, two months later eight white fraternity students, wearing hockey masks and holding candles, held a silent, nonviolent "vigil" in May 1988 to protest the eviction of a white freshman student from Otero House for harassing and verbally assaulting a gay resident assistant (Cole 1991: 214). This episode further inflamed the campus, with student activists organizing demonstrations and rallies (Phillips 1990).

The next racially charged incident took place in late September 1988 in Ujamaa, when two white students crudely defaced, with exaggerated stereotypical features, a Beethoven poster; two weeks later, a black fraternity flyer was found with the word "niggers" written on it (Cole 1991: 220). These events generated an emergency house meeting in Ujamaa that ended in "utter chaos" and "hysteria" (Bunzel 1992: 28–30). Anti-white flyers were soon found under some white students' dorm-room doors (Cole 1991: 226).

Responding to the Otero and Ujamaa events, the Rainbow Coalition held a rally against racism and released a new series of demands, called "The Mandate for Change," on October 26, 1988. The demands included "strengthen and fully institutionalize Ethnic Studies programs at Stanford (Afro-American Studies, Chicano Studies, Asian American Studies, Native American Studies); institute an ethnic studies graduation requirement; full institutional support for the Ethnic Centers (full-time deans, increased staffing and funding); strengthen the Fundamental Standard to state clearly that racist acts are a violation of the campus code of conduct; and commit to enforcing the University Commission on Minority Issues (UCMI) report" (Phillips 1990: 49). After holding a march, BSU chair Mary Dillard tacked the "Mandate for Change" on President Kennedy's office door (48).

The university then investigated the Otero and Ujamaa episodes, with President Kennedy stating that "freedom of speech" forbade Stanford from punishing the students responsible for these activities (Cole 1991: 227; Phillips 1990: 48).[24] Kennedy's remarks exacerbated racial tensions on campus, prompting the *Stanford Daily* to comment, "The decision [to not discipline the students in Otero and Ujamaa] sent a final, frightening message to the community: Racism does not threaten personal honor nor is it fundamentally opposed to this university's principles. . . . Until a standard that can be and will be upheld is established, *doubts and fears about the university's commitment to an education free from the horror of racism are justified*" (Phillips 1990: 49, emphasis added). Citing his relatively tepid, but still public, support for the CIV course and the UCMI report (which the Rainbow Coalition had called for back in May 1987), some student activists saw Kennedy as an ally, whereas others grew increasingly frustrated with him and the slow pace of change in 1988–1989 (Wu 2012).

Despite the release of the UCMI report in March 1989, many doubted that the university would actually implement its recommendations (Hernández-Clarke 2012). Therefore, planning commenced for a dramatic nonviolent demonstration in the hope that it might prod Stanford to bring about much-needed and long overdue reforms (Wu 2012). Inspired partially by a similar nine-day protest at the City University of New York in April 1989, nearly sixty Stanford student activists occupied President Kennedy's office on May 15 (Hernández-Clarke 2012; A. Medina 2012; Wu 2012). Demands included "hiring a tenure-track Asian American History professor; establishing a discrimination grievance board; conducting a search for a new Afro-American Studies Chair; including BSU in search for a new admissions officer; creating a full-time Dean for Chicano community; democratic functioning of El Centro Chicano; hiring a Native American Studies professor; rescinding 8% tuition hike; banning table grapes; increasing financial aid grants and funding for teaching assistants" (Phillips 1990: 52). Speaking about the protest's broader goals, Stanford student activist Judy Tzu-Chun Wu (2012) stated, "We wanted to create a different vision of the university, not just training the country's elite. We thought that knowledge should be reflective of the diversity of all Americans. With that knowledge, we thought that we could change the world for the better. From that action, I also realized people have power collectively. This event became a life-changing moment for me."

Wu's comments illustrate that the nonviolent occupation was a form of "spectacular speech" that had two key objectives. The student activists hoped that President Kennedy would concede and implement their demands, but they knew without "third-party supporters" (that is, the general student body) he would not do so. Because the action was organized clandestinely, very few students outside the Rainbow Coalition knew about it until some activists took over the president's fax machines and began disseminating their demands around 8 a.m. (Wu 2012). Through these tactics, some students rallied behind the occupiers, but when riot-clad Santa Clara County police officers showed up, the crowd swelled, as many physically blocked buses and cars from taking those who were arrested to jail. Gina Hernández-Clarke (2012), one of the protest's main organizers, remembered feeling exhilarated when she saw so many students rally behind their cause, taking high-risk actions and putting their bodies on the line. Sixty students, most of whom were not involved in the initial protest inside President Kennedy's office, were arrested. Some, like Hernández-Clarke, were threatened with expulsion (a significant threat given she was in her senior year), but all academic and criminal charges were eventually dropped.

The May 1989 occupation was important for several reasons. First, it was partially effective—an Asian American history professor was hired; democratic decision-making for El Centro was instituted; and BSU was given a slot on the search committee for a new black admissions officer (Phillips 1990: 52). Following the UCMI report's recommendations, Stanford planned to hire three new faculty of color annually over the next ten years. Table grapes were not banned, but students in the residence halls were allowed to vote on whether to eliminate them from their menus (A. Medina 2012). Second, the multiracial Rainbow Coalition that emerged in the mid-1980s around the antiapartheid movement spilled over into other issues (namely the Western Culture debate) and persisted into the late 1980s. Stanford students not only organized around identity-specific concerns (race, class, gender, sexuality), they collaborated across identity, pushing for social justice for all disenfranchised people. Third, as Wu stated, the Stanford occupation went beyond tangible concerns such as challenging canonical reading lists. This movement was not, in other words, only about the "great books." Like global justice activists in the 1990s and 2000s, Stanford students like Wu were calling for another world, *another university*; a world and university, in the words of the Zapatista National Liberation Army, where many worlds and universities fit. Seen from this perspective, the multiracial Stanford student movement in the 1980s had a "revolutionary edge," seeking empowerment for "third world peoples" in the United States and elsewhere through divestment, institutional transformation, and curricular reform (Wu 2012).

Despite these lofty aspirations, the Rainbow Coalition faltered postoccupation. While the organization itself survived into the 1990s, becoming the Student of Color Coalition in 1994, one of its key members, MEChA, experienced significant inner conflict that later affected the 1994 hunger strike. Shortly after the 1989 protest ended, allegations emerged that the League of Revolutionary Struggle (also known as the Liga) had infiltrated or taken over Stanford MEChA (A. Medina 2012).[25] The Liga's historical roots can be traced back to the August 29th Movement (ATM), a small Marxist-Leninist-Maoist (pro-China) organization that was created in the mid-1970s. Its rival, the Center for Autonomous Social Action, was also Marxist-Leninist (pro-Soviet Union) and fought with ATM for control of MEChA in the 1980s (Licón 2009: 79–87). In the late 1970s, ATM collaborated with the Asian American I Wor Kuen and the African American Revolutionary Communist League to establish the Liga.

Historian Gustavo Licón (2009: 91) contends that the Liga "became the dominant force within the California MEChA state-wide structure in the 1980s." Claiming that the Liga was insufficiently nationalist and did not fully support Chicanismo (it favored a multiracial coalition of all working-class people and other oppressed peoples to abolish capitalism), non-Liga MEChA campuses—particularly, but not exclusively, from Southern California and UC Berkeley—began attacking the Liga in 1985 (Licón 2009: 91). The split between the mostly Northern California, internationalist (read: multiracial) Liga MEChA chapters versus the Southern California, nationalist MEChA chapters came into full view during the 1986 MEChA statewide conference held at UC Berkeley (Licón 2009: 92; Muñoz 1989: 185–87). Stanford MEChA member Chris González-Clarke (2012) recalled that meeting: "The nationalists took over; they literally blocked the stage for four hours, linking arms, stopping the Liga people from speaking. They gave incoherent speeches about the Liga. I really didn't realize what they were talking about. The guys who took over the stage were pretty crazy. We said that the Liga is not really the issue and from that moment on, we were seen as a Liga campus."

Over the next three years, pro-Liga MEChA chapters consolidated their hegemonic position within the California MEChA statewide organization, writing a new constitution, El Plan de MEChA, which superseded El Plan de Santa Barbara, MEChA's foundational document, written and adopted in 1969.

El Plan de MEChA embraced Chicano self-determination for "our oppressed nation, Aztlán," but it also called for supporting "worker causes" and highlighted the gains that MEChA made through "alliances with African Americans and Asian Americans." El Plan de MEChA also criticized white-led radical organizations such as the Socialist Workers Party and the Revolutionary Communist Party (RCP) for infiltrating MEChA, and it condemned a "minority of ultranationalistic Mechistas" for "pushing their own agenda and ideology on MEChA through threats, red-baiting, and disruptive tactics" (Licón 2009: 93).

As these events unfolded, most Southern California MEChA chapters created an oppositional structure known as MEChA Summit (Licón 2009: 94). Pledging allegiance to El Plan de Santa Barbara, these chapters claimed they constituted the "real" MEChA and adopted what was eventually called the Philosophy of MEChA in 1992. Having done so, MEChA Summit chapters focused on removing the Liga from MEChA. As stated in chapter 3, on December 1, 1990, the same day that the UCLA MEChA members released their proposal for a Chicana and Chicano studies department, MEChA Summit chapters gained control of the Los Angeles County MEChA Central (96). MEChA Summit chapters soon took over other local and regional MEChA bodies. Around this same time, Liga fell apart, partially because of China's violent crackdown of the June 1989 pro-democracy movement and the fall of the Soviet Union. The Liga officially dissolved in September 1990 (98–99).

These internal machinations and divisions debilitated Stanford MEChA (Friedly 1990a, 1990b, 1990c). After the 1989 occupation, a vigorous debate took place within the Stanford chapter, as some members criticized the "radicals" (known as the Ligistas) for taking extreme measures and for not voting internally on whether to support the occupation. MEChA member and first-year student Alma Medina (2012) recalled that each organization within the Rainbow Coalition went through a similar soul-searching process post-occupation, with some claiming that a "core group within MEChA was promoting an outside agenda."

With key activists like Gina Hernández and Miguel Méndez having graduated, and with Alma Medina in Spain for two quarters on a study-abroad program, Stanford MEChA atrophied in the early 1990s.[26] In its place, a new more "social" (less political) organization known as the Latino Student Association emerged in 1991, which appealed to some but did not inspire first-year students such as Eva Silva, Martha ("Gabi") Cervantes, and Jorge Solis, all of whom would play key roles during the 1994 hunger strike (A. Medina 2012). Living in Casa Zapata during their freshman year in 1990–1991, Cervantes, Silva, and Solis found the Chicano theme dorm inspiring and empowering with its politically engaging murals and lively discussions. However, Silva (2012a) remembered attending a MEChA regional meeting during that year and being told to remain quiet. She stated, "We all started crying; they thought we were Ligistas, but we didn't know what they were talking about. We were not allowed to speak. They told us to focus on our local campus, not MEChA statewide."

Taking that advice, Silva and her colleagues established ties with local high school MEChA chapters, De Anza Community College, and CSU San Jose. Gradually, Stanford MEChA rejoined the California MEChA statewide organization. Several years later (May 1993), the Stanford and Berkeley MEChA chapters co-hosted the California statewide MEChA conference, which included a proposed march to a nearby Safeway grocery store to support the UFW grape boycott—but before doing so, the meeting devolved into bickering over identity-based issues. Frustrated with the endless debate while farm workers were being poisoned, Silva (2012a) said, "I took the microphone and said that we need to stop fighting over labels (such as Hispanic, Chicano, Latino) and stop wasting time. It was all pretty sad."

Stung by accusations that "outside forces" (Ligistas) hijacked the organization's mission and purpose, Stanford MEChAistas "turned inward" and experienced a "lull" in the early 1990s, but many members remained active around the UFW grape boycott and immigration-related issues (Cervantes 2012). Yet, given justifiable fears that they might be red-baited for being Ligistas, Stanford MEChAistas did not actively collaborate during that time with other student-of-color organizations or progressive white students like they did in the middle and late 1980s (A. Medina 2012). They also did not openly share their plans regarding the 1994 hunger strike with Chicana/o faculty, although SCCR director and political science professor Luis Fraga (2012, 2013) claimed that they did, with him offering strategic advice.[27] Nor did they receive much support from other MEChA chapters, who still distrusted them because of the Liga controversy (A. Medina 2012). Haunted and wounded, Stanford MEChA acted autonomously in April–May 1994, not actively seeking support from students of color and white students, making it appear as if they were "nationalist." Despite these dynamics, the Stanford hunger strikers and their allies cultivated support with students and faculty after the action got under way.

This overview indicates that the 1994 hunger strike did not occur in a vacuum. Fed up with "life on the Farm," students of color and progressive white students have long resisted and pushed for substantive change. Intense battles occurred in the 1960s and 1980s, both on and off campus. While crucial reforms were implemented over time, many Chicana/o students felt that they had been mistreated and rendered invisible in the early 1990s. The struggle was not over. Given the post-1989 occupation fallout, they set out mostly on their own, determined to change themselves, the campus, EPA, and even the entire world.

BEANERS, GO HOME: CECILIA BURCIAGA AND THE FLICKS "FIASCO," 1993–1994

The 1993–1994 academic year was a challenge for Stanford Chicana/o students like Elvira Prieto. Coming from a small farm-worker community (Reedley) in California's Central Valley, Prieto (2012) felt isolated from her freshman dorm roommate, who had a "car, allowance from her parents, and had not known any Mexicans besides the ones that worked as maids in her home." Becoming involved with MEChA and El Centro Chicano during her freshman year in 1992–1993 mitigated those feelings, although she was still uneasy because she wasn't working full-time to provide her family with much-needed financial support (Prieto 1998).[28] Prieto worked part-time at El Centro Chicano with federal program funding. Understaffed and underresourced for years, El Centro Chicano faced a new crisis in 1993–1994.

Stanford president Donald Kennedy stepped down in September 1992 because the university faced a $20 million deficit that year, largely stemming from allegations that Stanford overcharged the federal government $200 million in indirect costs for contracts and grants (Celis 1994; Rice 2010: 283).[29] A search committee for his successor was soon established, which included political science associate professor Condoleezza Rice, among others. University of Chicago provost and law professor Gerhard Casper, a German immigrant who was "known as a conservative with very traditional views of the academy," was chosen by the university's board of trustees as Stanford's new president (Rice 2010: 286). Shortly thereafter, Provost Jim Rosse resigned and Casper asked Rice (despite the fact that she had just been conveniently promoted to full professor and never served as department chair or dean before) if she would replace

Rosse and become the university's second-ranking official.[30] She accepted, stating that her primary task would be the budget deficit: "We cannot live beyond our means. Unlike the federal government, I can't print money" (290).

The ascension of Rice and Casper as provost and president illustrated that a conservative regime change had occurred at Stanford in the early 1990s. Therefore, the "political opportunity structure" for protest and dissent narrowed. Rice's "post-racial" financial plan (she called on *all* units, including academic departments, to cut their budgets by 5 to 10 percent in 1993–1994), however, morally outraged students like Prieto (1998) who worried that the Chicana/o community's convivial, counterhegemonic space or "home away from home," El Centro Chicano, would be cut back or consolidated with all the other ethnic student centers into one broad-based multicultural center. What galled Prieto most particularly was the fact that the university in fall 1993 had asked all ethnic student centers to prepare reports demonstrating how they fulfilled Stanford's academic mission. Prieto noted that despite the fact that the UCMI had earlier praised the centers for facilitating the recruitment and retention of students of color and recommended expanding their funding with more full-time staff positions, "[Rice and other top officials] were [now] asking us to 'prove' that what little we had should be allowed to continue to exist."[31]

Underscoring the Stanford Chicana/o and Latina/o community's precarious status, the campus student body (the Associated Students of Stanford University) voted in their general election in spring 1994 against a special fee that would have provided MEChA with additional funding and support in 1994–1995 (Berselli 1994; Prieto 2012). While special fees were approved for the Asian American Student Organization, funds for the BSU and the Stanford American Indian Organization were rejected (Prieto 1998). Before the election actually took place, MEChA's posters and flyers were defaced with racist comments such as "Beaners, go home!" These attacks were directed only toward MEChA and the Chicana/o and Latina/o community; no flyers from the other three organizations were vandalized.

The special-fee defeat and the specter of possible budget cuts to El Centro Chicano mirrored, in some respects, the broader anti-immigrant, anti-Latino backlash that emerged in the early 1990s, culminating in November 1994 with the landslide passage of the ballot measure Proposition 187 (Martinez HoSang 2010). While eventually ruled unconstitutional, Proposition 187's underlying message was essentially no different than the defaced MEChA flyers found on campus: "Beaners, go home!" Stanford effectively put those words into practice when it fired Stanford Associate Dean for Student Affairs and Development Officer for Student Resources Cecilia Burciaga on March 22, 1994—during Spring Break, when most students were on vacation and away from campus (Villagrán 1994).

Citing budgetary constraints, Stanford Vice-provost and Dean for Student Affairs Mary Edmonds (Burciaga's supervisor) stated, "When you have to cut over $1 million of the budget [in Student Affairs] it's very difficult. We have to look at who is in what position and how we can reduce" (Chandrasekaran 1994). Provost Rice took a slightly different approach, praising Burciaga ("She's done a terrific job") but also claiming, on the other hand, that fiscal constraints limited Stanford from offering her another high-ranking position within the university administration. Burciaga previously suggested that her position could be eliminated, with the assumption that she would be reassigned, not fired (Chandrasekaran 1994; Rae-Dupree 1994).[32] Seeing the matter much differently, MEChA co-chair and senior undergraduate student Gabi Cervantes said, "Cecilia has been here for 20 years. You just don't lay off someone like that without creating another position. It seems like they just wanted to get rid of her as soon as possible. It just seems like the new administration cannot account for diverse opinions. They don't want criticism. It really seems like a definite political move" (Chandrasekaran 1994). Burciaga's dismissal, therefore, generated a "frame battle" between the university (which relied on color-blind, apolitical discourse—"economic hard times left us no other choice") and Stanford MEChAistas (who saw this as yet another racist "slap in the face" to the Chicana/o and Latina/o community). Burciaga, incidentally and quite ironically, helped hire Rice in the early 1980s, a fact that Rice glosses over in her memoir (Rice 2010: 296).

Newspaper articles and interviews with students, faculty, and administration officials all agree—Burciaga's firing was the proverbial "last straw," as graduate student Ben Olguin stated in the *Stanford Daily* (Chandrasekaran 1994). Burciaga first came to Stanford in 1974 after working in Washington, DC, for the U.S. Information Agency, the Interagency Committee on Mexican-American Affairs, and the U.S. Commission on Civil Rights (Meier and Gutiérrez 2003: 323–24). Hired as the special assistant to the president for Chicano affairs, Burciaga held that position for two-and-half years before taking other slots, including associate dean of graduate studies, assistant provost for faculty affairs, affirmative action officer, associate dean for student affairs, and development officer for student resources (C. Burciaga 2013). In the late 1970s,

President Jimmy Carter appointed her to the National Advisory Commission on Women; then in 1994 (before her firing) President Clinton named her to the Commission on Educational Excellence for Hispanic Americans. She also served on the UCMI in the late 1980s. Finally, Burciaga and her husband, Tony, became resident fellows (RFs) at Casa Zapata in 1985, living and working there until August 31, 1994, their last day on campus.[33]

Burciaga's impressive résumé includes countless awards and accolades, many from undergraduate Stanford Chicana/o and Latina/o students who enthusiastically proclaimed that she changed or even "saved" their lives (González Luna 2013a). She left an indelible imprint on the lives of everyone she met because of her work ethic, outspoken views, and vigorous defense of women and people of color. In a paper written for a graduate seminar, hunger striker Elvira Prieto (1998) underscored these points:

> I still remember the *disbelief* with which I received the news. In addition to her work within student affairs, developing recruitment programs for graduate students of color, Cecilia played an integral role in the recruitment and retention of undergraduates as one of the Resident Fellows at Casa Zapata. Through her undying commitment to students and fearless integrity, Cecilia openly discussed her opinions about the way in which the university was conducting its business, even if it mean she was not following the "party line." It was evident to all who knew her that the well-being of students was her top priority and she served as a *role model* for students (particularly women) from all communities at Stanford. The university's decision to eliminate Cecilia's position, with another *budget cut excuse*, made students and community members feel even more insulted and alienated by the administration. *We felt Cecilia's forced departure was a thoughtless form of disrespect to our community.* (emphasis added)

Hunger striker Julia González Luna (2013a) echoed Prieto's comments. Recalling a pivotal life-changing discussion with Burciaga during her first year on campus, she said,

> It was shortly after my first quarter at Stanford and my freshman advisor scheduled an appointment for me to meet her. He knew something terrible was happening to me and knew that Cecilia would know what to do. When I walked into her office, she was sitting behind a large redwood desk. I had never seen a Latina with a desk that big before and so I knew that she must be someone important.

She greeted me, asked me to sit down, and then asked me questions about myself. Where was I from? Who was my family, etc.? I nervously answered her questions. And then for a moment, she became silent. Then, she reached across her desk, looked straight into my eyes and said, "You know for every one of you, there are a thousand of you who don't make it here. You are responsible for those thousand." I was immediately transformed.

Calling Burciaga "our mother, there's really no other word for it," González Luna (2013a) felt morally outraged and compelled to act because "if they could take Cecilia away in a blink of an eye, they could take anything." Hunger striker Tamara Alvarado (2012) expressed similar emotion and sentiments:

So we went on [spring] break and came back, only to find out that Cecilia had been budgeted out [fired]. We were already irritated and going through proper channels of communication [to address possible cuts to El Centro Chicano and other issues mentioned above] and we were like "Ya estuvo" [that's it]. We were like, "What the fuck?" We went on break and we come back and she is not on staff because of budget cuts? What do we look like, idiots? We were like, "Don't you know who you have here?" So we were very, very upset and had more and more meetings which got more and more intense. We said, "What are we going to do about this? We really need to do something. This proper channel stuff just is not working."

These comments indicate that Burciaga's firing was the match that lit the flames, but students were not the only ones that expressed their outrage. Sixteen Chicana/o and Latina/o faculty members criticized her dismissal in the "liberal" *Stanford Daily*.[34] "Not only do we believe that Cecilia's termination was ineptly executed," the professors wrote, "we reject the characterization that her dismissal was simply a budgetary decision. We judge the administration's actions in terms of their consequences. The administration has eliminated the most prominent Latina associated with Stanford without regard to its effects on Chicana/o students, faculty, and staff and thereby signaled to us the low priority that is given to Stanford's Chicanas/os and other communities of color." Moreover, the Stanford Chicano Graduate Student Association, Burciaga's resident fellow colleagues, and coworkers from across campus also published letters in the *Stanford Daily* lambasting the university while emphasizing her numerous contributions.

While most highlighted Cecilia Burciaga's numerous contributions, Humanities Center Associate Director and former Madera House Resident Fellow Charles Junkerman (1994) emphasized that the university was sending "away two of our best voices, two of our most imaginative minds, two of our most generous spirits—are we so rich or so poor that we can afford to do that?" This comment raises a critical issue: Casa Zapata was a crucial, convivial, and safe space on campus that politicized and raised the consciousness of all Stanford students, but most especially Chicanas/os and Latinas/os. Adorned with inspiring and controversial murals like Tony Burciaga's "The Last Supper of Chicano Heroes" and "The Spirit of Hoover Tower," Zapata was not a typical residence hall; many MEChAistas were also Zapatistas, perhaps explaining why Rice effectively fired Cecilia *and* Tony Burciaga—because they were caring, charismatic teachers that inspired so many and providing them with much-needed hope.

Burciaga's firing therefore rippled across campus, breaking some people's hearts, but not their spirits. Indeed, a small group of Chicana/o and Latina/o students, mostly MEChAistas, began meeting and holding strategizing sessions shortly after Burciaga was dismissed. Concerned about infiltration, deciding exactly where to hold these meetings became rather important. Tamara Alvarado (2012) remembered the process became "underground" as people gathered not at El Centro Chicano but in large outdoor spaces at ten o'clock in the evening. Prieto (2012) stated that the meetings were held in apartments, dorms, and classrooms, while González Luna (2013a) declared they were initially held in a "tiny underground room in the history [department] corner." Elaborating, González Luna said, "We had a secret knock that you had to use to enter the room. I didn't realize it at first, but later over time it became very secretive and exclusive, so only certain people could attend. Those that attended were told how to knock and when the meeting times were; other people were given the wrong meeting times so they couldn't attend. So a small group of people took it upon themselves to decide who was 'down' and should be part of this movement and who should not be. That took place from the very beginning." While somewhat unusual, it bears repeating here that one of the lingering legacies of the 1989 occupation was allegations that "outsiders" (Ligistas) had taken over Stanford MEChA. Alma Medina (2012), who took part in that sit-in, witnessed how post-occupation allegations fragmented and weakened MEChA in the early 1990s. After that challenging experience, it is not too surprising that key hunger-strike organizers may have followed a purportedly "narrow" organizing model focusing on the most politicized and "authentic" Chicanas/os. González Luna (2013a) recalled that some MEChA members like her were criticized for not saying their own names properly, while other Chicanas were looked down on for dating non-Chicanas/os or embracing "alternative" clothing and musical preferences.[35]

Despite these dynamics, organizing continued, with students debating what strategy and location they might embrace. Reflecting on conversations the 1994 MEChAistas had with Gina Hernández-Clarke and Chris González-Clarke about the 1989 occupation, hunger striker Eva Silva (2012b) said, "They helped us see things that we had not considered—like telling everyone at the protest, especially those that were not citizens, not to get arrested because they might be deported. They also helped us understand that El Centro Chicano and Casa Zapata would not have been established unless students had struggled in the past. They helped us appreciate that history and see more clearly what had been accomplished. They also gave us good advice about a possible site for the protest."

While the president's office was briefly considered, it was eventually ruled out because, as Silva (2012a) recalled,

> It had been done before and so we were not sure [about doing it again]. We also didn't want them to come right in and arrest us immediately, pretty much like they did in 1989. We wanted to do something that would generate attention. We needed to take drastic action to get the attention of the university. We knew that we were dealing with two tough people [Casper and Rice]; a takeover would have played into their hands. They would have taken a hard line and ended the occupation and nothing would have changed, but a fast [hunger strike] played back into our hands.

Alvarado (2012) expressed similar sentiments:

> We knew it [a sit-in or occupation] had been done before, and what did we get from it? Some change took place, but *things still weren't right*—there was no Chicano studies department, for example, on campus. We knew what we were doing. We wanted to take over this big space, in front of Memorial Church, where tourists and people often come by; it is a very public setting. (emphasis added)

Armed with a location, the students turned toward strategy. Silva (2012a, 2012b) and Prieto (1998), coming from immigrant farm-working families in Salinas and Reedley, respectively, and knowing that other Chicana/o and Latina/o students at UCSB and the University of Colorado, Boulder, were or recently had been on hunger strikes, both favored following César Chávez, endorsing what they pointedly called a "hunger strike" rather than a "fast."[36] Silva spoke about her early childhood experiences and admiration for Chávez:

> We were migratory workers, following the crops. We lived in our car and had no stable place to live. I crossed the border when I was seven years old and lived in Salinas. We lived in my dad's friends' house for two years. We moved around and switched schools several times before settling down by eighth grade. My parents were very supportive of César Chávez and the UFW. Chávez would come often to Salinas with the UFW, holding marches. I would run from house to house as they came by, going out to greet them with flags. The union was a big part of our community. (2012a)

> When the hunger strike began my mother started crying. She had a hard time with this, even though she supported me. Chávez was our hero; we had grown up in Salinas—everyone believed in him and the cause. We thought it was common sense, what he was fighting for. The short-handed versus long-handed hoe, having bathroom breaks and water—all these things were common sense. He risked his life for these issues. We realized that the only way we would be taken seriously was by doing this [going on hunger strike]. Students had been struggling for years for a Chicano studies department; they had done many petitions, but no one listened to them. We thought that what we were calling for made common sense, too. (2012b)

Having grown up in modest working-class homes in suburban locales (Escondido and Burbank, respectively), Alvarado (2012) and González Luna (2013a) also expressed how much Chávez inspired them, with the former stating, "We were hugely influenced by him and the UFW. Chávez died in 1993 and that was big for us. We knew that part of his work was peaceful and through hunger striking he had been effective. We knew that it had been used at other universities and that it had been effective on those campuses, too." Alvarado (2012) also spoke about the role of religion: "The majority of us were Catholic and understood that Catholicism is full of sacrifice, particularly self-sacrifice of the body. So that too was an influence, as was Chávez, who was also Catholic, of course. We understood it [self-sacrifice] was an effective and peaceful way to bring about social change."

Like many other MEChA chapters during that time, Stanford MEChA became involved in the UFW grape boycott in the early 1990s (activism around this issue on campus can be traced back to at least the late 1980s, if not earlier, with the Rainbow Coalition). Indeed, first-year MEChAistas Silva and Solis helped bring César Chávez to Stanford in 1990–1991, where he delivered a conference keynote speech and visited Casa Zapata to sign Tony Burciaga's "The Last Supper of Chicano Heroes." Stanford MEChA also organized a demonstration outside a local Safeway store, pulling grapes off the shelves and stomping on them in the parking lot (González Luna 2013a; Silva 2012a). Along with Stanford environmental engineering professor James Leckie (who was conducting research on the relationship between pesticide exposure and public health risks and was one of the few Chicana/o faculty in the "hard sciences"), some MEChAistas held educational workshops in the dorms about the UFW grape boycott. In 1989, President Donald Kennedy had agreed to let each residence hall vote on whether to ban grapes. Taking that opportunity, Stanford MEChA "Campaigned for eighteen months, but no one took us seriously," González Luna (2013a) said, "They literally just laughed at us."

After that response, Stanford MEChAistas scaled up their efforts, successfully requesting that the UFW ten-minute documentary film, *No Grapes*, be shown before the scheduled May 1, 1994, Flicks on Sunday film, *Mrs. Doubtfire* (Houston and Pulido 2002).[37] Traditionally popular and well-attended, Flicks movies often start at 10 p.m.; however, this particular evening, the lights did not dim inside the Memorial Auditorium (with its nearly two thousand seats) until 10:15. Almost immediately thereafter, the following events took place:

A group of students in the balcony section began chanting, "Fast forward." Laughter broke out in the nearly full auditorium as other students joined in the jeering. "Give grapes a chance," yelled one student. "Yes pesticides," others yelled as a screen depicted a helicopter spraying a field filled with farm workers. Others applauded at the sight of a deformed child. And still others yelled "Beaners go home!" It was a painful experience, said Nicole Sánchez, a Chicana senior at Stanford. "The video is only 10 minutes long, but with all the shouting, it seemed to be going on forever," Sánchez said. "It wasn't just a few students; there were hundreds of voices screaming cruel and awful things. I just wanted it to end. They seemed a short step away from hate words to violence. Many of the freshmen in particular were shocked. They ran to the lobby, some of them crying and saying that they wanted to leave the school for good. They couldn't believe that this was happening at their university." (Figueroa 1994)

Such remarks prompted a flurry of letters published in the *Stanford Daily* and *Stanford Campus Report*.[38] More than thirty Chicana/o and Latina/o students (Díaz et al. 1994), for example, wrote,

> We are repulsed and appalled by the racist reaction of our fellow students on Sunday evening, May 1, when in honor of Cinco de Mayo, we showed the United Farm Workers' video, "No Grapes" at the 10 p.m. Flicks. While we understand that Flicks is a time for fun, many of us feel that we have no other forum for informing students of the situation. Our petitions go unnoticed; programs are unattended, and administrative ears turn deaf to this grave matter. Ten minutes was all we asked for on a Sunday night. What we were subjected to was 10 minutes of intolerance and hate. We never thought at this institution, that an image of boy born with no legs and arms projected on the Memorial Auditorium video screen would be welcomed with shouts of vicious laughter.

Claiming to be "outraged," Associated Students of Stanford University senator and senior undergraduate biology major Peter Cousins (1994) maintained, in contrast, that he had been held "hostage" and compared MEChA to the Ku Klux Klan and the Communist Party.

Taking sides, the *Stanford Daily* mimicked Cousins's hyperbolic discourse. In an editorial titled "Fixing Flicks' Fiasco," the paper argued, "Short films should not be *forced* upon students not interested in viewing them" (emphasis added). Stanford English professor Lora Romero later observed that most *Daily* letter-writers (along with the *Daily* itself) claimed that those who acted inappropriately during Flicks were "rude, but not racist." She also noted that Chicana/o students were criticized for relying on "Nazi propaganda tactics [showing a film financed by the UFW to a 'captive' audience]." "The people who planned to show it were thinking of it as an opportunity to expose the campus to issues of importance to our community," she said, "But 10 minutes of power on the part of the Chicano community on this campus makes us comparable to Nazis in Germany" (O'Toole 1994).

While the so-called "Flicks fiasco" did not affect the hunger strike organizing plans already under way,[39] the incident certainly did not help matters.
Students continued organizing with renewed vigor, poring over the campus climate and other pressing issues, most critically Burciaga's firing. After a month-
long deliberative process, the students whittled down their demands from
twenty-six to four: finding a high-level position for Cecilia Burciaga; establishing a Chicano studies program; creating a community center in East Palo Alto
(where many low-paid, nonunionized Latina/o Stanford employees lived); and
banning grapes from campus (Alvarado 2012; Dworkin 1994).

The next step after devising their strategy, location, and demands was implementation. During organizing meetings after Flicks on May 1, the small group
of MEChAistas that began planning after Burciaga was fired decided who the
hunger strikers would be (A. Medina 2013). With their heads down, four students—Tamara Alvarado (junior), Julia González Luna (senior), Elvira Prieto
(sophomore), and Eva Silva (senior) (first-year student Felipé Barragan also
agreed to go on strike for three days)—volunteered, raising their hands. Shortly
after this secret ballot was taken, Alma Medina encouraged the strikers to call
and inform their families. Julia González Luna (2013a) remembered this conversation with her father:

> My dad threatened me. He said, "Why would you want to go hungry again after
> all the hunger that you have had in your life?" Let me back up here. We immi-
> grated to the United States when I was four years old. I remember that we slept
> in the car for a little while, and I remember my mom had a piece of plywood with
> contact paper and that was our table until we had enough money for furniture. I
> remember specifically not eating and saying I was not hungry so my two younger
> brothers could eat. I had been trained from birth to look after them, so I was not
> about to let them go hungry. I had real-life experience with hunger and that is
> why my father said what he did. And so I said, "This is what you taught me," then
> he got really quiet. I will never forget that. During the strike he drove up [from
> Burbank, California] and tried to convince me to stop, but once he saw the tents
> and all the people, he realized that I was not going to back down.

Finally, just days after the Flicks incident, the planning group publicly presented its proposals to be voted on to the MEChA general body at El Centro Chicano (Berselli 1994). During this meeting (which included more than

one hundred people and lasted several hours), committees (media, medical, security, etc.) were established, negotiators were selected, and logistical details were hammered out (Silva 2012b). Faculty were deliberately kept in the dark to protect them and mitigate accusations that they, rather than the students, organized the hunger strike (Alvarado 2012; A. Medina 2013; Silva 2012b). The students were also briefed on their legal rights. González Luna and Silva were permanent residents in 1994, not U.S. citizens, so they faced additional risks, as did other nonstriking students who faced possible arrest and even deportation because of their status.

Once word leaked out about the meeting at El Centro Chicano, student allies showed up, offering support and solidarity. Because of previous accusations about outside infiltrators and MEChA's preexisting plan for the hunger strike, such assistance was generally and politely turned aside. While such actions may give one the impression that this action was nationalist, it was not, as MEChA often collaborated with other student-of-color organizations during this period. Yet organizing the hunger strike and mediating relationships with other organizations was a recurring, logistical challenge for MEChA.

THE HUNGER STRIKE, MAY 4–MAY 7, 1994

Despite embracing, partially for historical and ideological reasons, an arguably confined organizing model (which some questioned), the strike began at 8 a.m. on May 4, 1994. Timed to coincide with Cinco de Mayo, Eva Silva said "everything"—El Centro Chicano's uncertain future; the special-fee election results; defaced flyers; Cecilia Burciaga's firing; and the Flicks incident—just "piled up" (Koh 1994). Anger and frustration were widespread, as forty-two students fasted for one day in solidarity with the other five hunger strikers. Just before pitching their tents in the quad, Tamara Alvarado (2012) called her mother:

> I said hello and she said, "Its five a.m., why are you up so early?" I talked with her and just said, "We're on hunger strike because things aren't right here." And she was like, "I am going to be there." I wasn't sure what that meant. Then she showed up that day—or maybe the next day. My mom got on a plane and came up here and stayed with us in the quad. She slept with us in the tents. There was no way for her not to be there. I was on hunger strike and she wanted to be there to support me, as a mother. That felt good to everyone; that a parent was there with us.

FIGURE 14. Students supporting hunger strikers (notice signs focused on Chicano Studies and Proposition 187), May 4, 1994. Stanford Daily Inc.

Hours into the strike, approximately fifty students "dressed in black shirts and red armbands" held a protest in the quad, holding picket signs stating, "Stop immigrant bashing," "Strike—Chicana/o Studies Now," and "No uvas! Boycott Grapes" (Dworkin 1994; see figure 14). Despite this pressure, Casper and Rice did not capitulate or offer concessions during the strike's first day. Indeed, far from adopting a conciliatory approach, Casper complained that the students were holding a "gun to his head" and that he did not possess "dictatorial powers" to create new academic programs such as a Chicano studies department. Casper also claimed that Buricaga's firing was a budgetary decision, adding that the hunger strike might "destroy the university" because it relies on "compulsion" rather than persuasion and academic discourse (Dworkin 1994; Koh 1994).

The strike, therefore, continued into the evening. While Casper relied on apocalyptic discourse, events soon unfolded that undermined his assertion that the university might "fall apart." Just before dusk some Stanford students rallied behind the hunger strikers, strengthening the "new" university that they and their allies were implicitly seeking to create. Prieto (1998) recalled this moment:

> We were exhausted from a full day of setting up, marching, chanting, and educating all the students who stopped by on their way to class to find out what we were doing. Surprisingly, no arrests were made and the negotiating had begun with the dean of students, provost, and president. They offered the creation of committees and we decided to continue to strike. It was getting dark and the majority of volunteers who were not staying out with us were gone. We were winding down for the evening and starting to realize how few of us were actually left when we heard marching coming down from a far corner of the quad. There was a large group of students from Ujamaa, the African American theme house. They came over after their house meeting where many students decided to come and support us by bringing blankets, jackets, and water. Many of the students stayed out with us that evening to keep up company. Also, the Native American community was hosting the annual Stanford powwow that weekend, and some of the host drum groups came out to the quad to join us.

The following day, on Cinco de Mayo (the day the UCSB hunger strike ended), MEChA held a press conference with local English- and Spanish-language media and organized a rally and class walkout held in the quad starting at 11 p.m. (*Stanford Campus Report* 1994). Two hundred students attended the event, and representatives from the BSU, the Stanford Women's Community Center, Hillel, and several other organizations, along with the hunger strikers, spoke. Later that same day, "the Asian American Student Association, the Gay/Lesbian/Bisexual Coalition, environmental student groups, and other ethnic student groups provided the striking students with water and needed supplies and passed out flyers all over campus" (Prieto 1998). These actions, along with ones from the previous night, indicate that a short-lived, multiracial, progressive student coalition was created during the action.

The same sixteen Chicana/o and Latina/o faculty members that condemned the university administration for firing Cecilia Burciaga in April, moreover, wrote a letter to Rice and Casper supporting all of the students' demands except Burciaga's rehiring (this letter was written on May 4 and published the next day in the *Stanford Daily*). When asked about this apparent omission, Stanford law professor Miguel Méndez (2012), who eventually became actively involved in the negotiation process, along with Professors Luis Fraga and James Leckie, said, "It wasn't an oversight, but a choice, a strategic one. We thought it was futile and counterproductive to focus on her position and her."[40]

The hunger strikers welcomed this support from the faculty and various student organizations (Alvarado 2012; González Luna 2013a; Prieto 1998, 2012; Silva 2012a). Meanwhile, Medina, Cervantes, and Solis attempted to meet directly with President Casper. Ironically, just moments after she left Casper's office, Medina accidentally bumped into Rice. She asked the provost to take more bold action to break the stalemate, but "she ignored me and said that she had to go to breakfast. She didn't care that there were students out there starving while she went to go eat" (A. Medina 2013). Rice's intransigence angered many MEChAistas. She acted as a buffer between Casper and the hunger strikers, keeping him isolated and almost completely uninformed about why these students took such dramatic action. Having lived in Germany until the mid-1960s when he became a UC Berkeley political science professor, Casper worked for more than twenty years as a professor, dean, and provost at the University of Chicago Law School (1966–92), publishing articles and books on constitutional law and legal theory. Race was definitely not his forte. He knew that the UFW had boycotted grapes in the 1960s but didn't realize that the union had resumed it the mid-1980s and thus wasn't clear why the students were focused on that issue (Koh 1994; A. Medina 2013).[41] While he might have been relatively unaware several key issues, Casper ultimately recognized the strike was about respect. He also strongly condemned those that were responsible for the Flicks incident (calling them "stupid at best and racist at worst") and generally seemed more open to negotiate, whereas Rice took a more hard-line approach (A. Medina 2013).

Indeed, later that day (after the press conference, rally, and seventy-five-minute bargaining session that Solis called "ineffective"), Rice attended a Faculty Senate meeting where some faculty members said, "Don't you feel bad that our children are sleeping on the quad and not eating?" Without skipping a beat, Rice (2010: 296) said, "I am sleeping and eating just fine. They can stay there until hell freezes over. My decisions stand." She also was quoted in the *Stanford Daily* as saying, "We have gone as far as we can go. We have done as much as we can. We have to preserve university processes and procedures" (Doyle 1994).

With both sides dug in, Stanford faculty and staff tried, through back-channel negotiations, to break the stalemate and end the strike. Fraga (2012), for example, spoke informally with Rice without notifying the hunger strikers or his fellow Chicana/o and Latina/o faculty colleagues that were affiliated or had ties with the SCCR. Fraga and Rice were colleagues in the Political Science Department in the early 1990s (the former was hired in 1991, the latter in 1981). Because of these professional ties, Fraga (2012) claimed that he had "credibility" with Rice, but Chicana/o and Latina/o faculty members told him to essentially "be quiet because I was the newest kid on the block. I had the least experience on campus; my colleagues were saying things like, 'Luis you just don't understand how we do things here.' I respected these older faculty members and tried to learn from them, but I believed that I was acting the best interests of the students."

Fraga (2012) also stated that he provided MEChA student activists with crucial strategic advice *before* the hunger strike started, telling them to go for "maximum impact" by selecting "secondary targets" (e.g., foundations, wealthy donors, key alumni, etc.), who might, in turn, put economic pressure on Stanford. Despite this assertion, the four Chicana student hunger strikers, along with Alma Medina, could not remember Fraga doing this, with González Luna (2013a) sharply adding, "He never stuck his neck out for us; he didn't have a record with us."

Given these dynamics, some Chicana/o and Latina/o faculty members requested a face-to-face meeting with Casper, and the students asked Professors Jerry Porras, James Leckie, and Miguel Méndez for advice (Leckie 2012; A. Medina 2013; Méndez 2012). Some MEChAistas also consulted with El Centro Chicano director Frances Morales, El Centro Chicano associate director Chris González-Clarke, and Native American Cultural Center director Jim Larimore (A. Medina 2013). González-Clarke attended all negotiating sessions with Rice, Casper, and the three student negotiators, conveying and "translating" occasionally technical discussions to the student hunger strikers who started to experience cognitive difficulties and physical problems as the strike wore on (González Luna 2013a). Morales, González-Clarke, and Larimore also met with Dean of Students Michael Jackson, Vice-provost and Dean of Student Affairs Mary Edmonds, and Director of the Office for Multicultural Development Sally Dickson to facilitate a possible settlement (A. Medina 2013).

These interactions illustrate that key unofficial discussions took place during the strike's first two days. The Stanford administration was thus no monolithic entity; it had multiple entry points that the students sought to leverage. Yet, because of Rice's steadfast opposition (and her belief that the hunger strike was unjustified in light of a forthcoming report from a student task force on El Centro Chicano),[42] most Stanford administrators supporting the hunger strikers offered their support while expressing concern for their health and physical well-being (A. Medina 2013).

With Rice and Casper steadfastly dug in, the strike continued into its third day. During the May 5 rally, students were encouraged to boycott their classes the following day and attend a creative teach-in called Aztlán University on Friday, May 6. Rain forced the alternative classes to take place under the plaza's arcades and archways (*Stanford Campus Report* 1994). Six Chicana/o faculty and staff, including Lora Romero (English), Guadalupe Valdés (education and Spanish and Portuguese), Renato Rosaldo (anthropology), Luis Fraga (political science), Yvonne Yarbro-Bejarano (Spanish and Portuguese), Rudy Busto (religious studies), and Frances Morales, along with José Cuellar ("Dr. Loco," raza studies) from San Francisco State University, participated after being recruited by graduate student Daniel Contreras, who stated "the students wanted to continue their education during the strike" (*Stanford Campus Report* 1994).

The *Stanford Campus Report* (1994) stated that "several hundred students" attended Aztlán University's classes, which were designed to raise consciousness about crucial issues facing the Chicana/o and Latina/o community, both on and off campus. However, many of the sessions also focused on the ongoing hunger strike and events surrounding it, such as the May 1 Flicks incident. For example, Professor Romero told her class, "There's a tendency in U.S. culture as a whole and on campuses to interpret political action as being juvenile, coming out of emotion rather than intellect, and as being extraneous to the university. What you are doing is an intellectual act and don't let anybody tell you otherwise." She later deconstructed discursive claims that MEChA's tactics were "fascist," emphasizing such victimization tropes were "part of a national backlash to gains made by ethnic minorities nationally and on the Stanford campus in recent years" (O'Toole 1994).

Two of the teach-in sessions also focused on one of the students' four demands: creating a community center in EPA. Professor Valdés spoke about how Stanford students could make positive interventions that would improve the lives of EPA's primarily Latina/o public school students. Visiting professor and SCCR Fellow Fernando Soriano (psychology) focused on participatory, rather than "imperial," scholarship that seeks to empower marginalized communities on the basis of their suggestions and agency. He also pointed out that some EPA residents viewed university-backed research projects with skepticism because they gained very little from previous ones and felt exploited. Finally, on a different matter altogether, when asked why the letter that the sixteen Chicana/o and Latina/o faculty sent to Casper and Rice did not include rehiring Cecilia Burciaga, Stanford anthropology professor Renato Rosaldo said, "We probably made a mistake. She made it clear that she didn't want to remain here. We felt this was a [mostly] symbolic issue. We mistakenly felt you were focusing on the other issues" (O'Toole 1994).

With pressure building on Rice and Casper, the university's top two officials blinked. But before doing so, Rice kept Casper from meeting directly with the hunger strike negotiators. A curious situation eventually unfolded, as the hunger strike negotiators and key Chicana/o faculty such as Jim Leckie and Miguel Mendez met separately in a conference room while Casper and Rice hunkered down in the president's office. Leckie (2012) recalled the unusual series of events:

> The students thought they were going to sit down and talk with Condi [Rice] and Casper directly, but they were not in the room. We wondered, "Where are they?" They left the room and Sally [Dickson] and Michael [Jackson] said, "They will not come inside this room; we'll go back and forth and do shuttle diplomacy." I was confused and so too were the student negotiators. The structure didn't make sense. I said "Jesus Christ, it's just a couple of freshmen that want to talk," why are they making this so convoluted? But then it started and quickly became a paper exercise and evolved into a document that would satisfy both sides. The students asked Miguel [Méndez] and I to go back over their drafts and wording. By that time it was nearly eleven or twelve in the evening and we were going back and forth editing and rewriting the document. It seemed like shuttle diplomacy in the Middle East, like between the Israelis and Palestinians. It was the most bizarre, Kafka-like set up. Why couldn't we just sit down and talk?

As the late-night maneuvering wore on, the student negotiators noticed that Casper was more congenial than Rice, who remained inflexible (A. Medina 2013). The provost's style did not escape Leckie, who quipped, "Condi is one tough nut. You would have thought she was negotiating with the Russians and not with students. She clearly received her management training in the Pentagon" (Katz 1994a). Medina recognized that progress was impossible with

Rice present, so she asked for her to be removed from the negotiating process. Casper surprisingly agreed, and an agreement on three of the students' four demands (excluding rehiring Burciaga) was soon reached.

While far from perfect, Medina (2013) understood the agreement would generate much-needed change. Reflecting on its provisions, she stated,

> After being reassured by all our sources that this was all that we were going to get—a committee on grapes, a promise on getting a Chicano studies major, something for the community in EPA—we thought about it and knew these things didn't exist before. There was just no way that Cecilia was going to be rehired. She wouldn't take a job a Stanford after the way that she was treated. The University also refused to offer a public apology about the way that she was fired. We took the victories that we could get. We also received assurances that students would be on the committees [on grapes, Chicano studies, and the EPA community center] that were established. We felt that we had made our voices heard and we would continue to fight for what we were asking for. Some felt that we should have done something more drastic, but things were getting really hard to manage at that point as hundreds of students joined our protest and brought their own issues to the table.

After finishing the late-night negotiations and armed with the agreement, the hunger strike negotiators took the text to the hunger strikers and other MEChA members for discussion and vote. Tensions soon emerged, however, as some (Medina, Prieto, Silva) understood that the decision to end the strike would be done "democratically," with everyone participating and voting. However, Alvarado (2012) and González Luna (2013a) had a different understanding; they assumed, on the basis of the meetings that they attended, that the hunger strikers themselves would determine when the strike would end.

Given such disparate views, conflict was inevitable. González Luna (2013a) described the scene when it started raining hard on the night of May 6:

> People started to come into the tents and said that they didn't want to do this anymore. Tamara and I said "Hell no. We're not stopping for rain; we're doing this until the end, until we get what we want." Some people were uncomfortable sitting there in the quad in the rain; they didn't want to negotiate in the rain. The organizers wanted it to stop; the negotiators wanted it to stop on the second day because there was no movement on the demands, and by the third day, they really

wanted it to stop. I don't remember who said what, but a vote was called with everyone [voting], and I said "You guys said that we [the strikers] would have the last word and so what is going on," and they said, "No, no, we just want to see where people are at and if we should stop." It was framed like, "let's just see where everyone is at." So when the vote came down and they said to stop, that's what happened. Tamara [Alvarado] and I broke down; people were hugging and congratulating us, but Tamara threw her hands out [telling them to back off] and started screaming "Get out!" Tamara and I had the biggest issue with it [the agreement]; Eva [Silva] went along with it and Elvira [Prieto] was sick, or starting to get sick. They actually called in a clinical psychologist because Tamara and I were crying so loud that they told other people that they had to leave. We were so angry. I will never forget that. Tamara's mom was there and put her body over us because we were so upset.

Prieto (2012) and Silva (2012a, 2012b) agreed with González Luna and Alvarado, even though Prieto blacked out earlier that morning from her diabetic condition and Silva lost a whopping fourteen pounds. During the strike, all four women drank nothing but water and Pedialyte (which contains electrolytes, potassium, and glucose), except Prieto, who did not care for the latter (González Luna 2013a). This decision may have facilitated her blackout because she was not getting sufficient glucose. Putting her health issues aside, Prieto (1998) wanted to continue, but she knew she could not make that decision unilaterally. In her words,

One of the most difficult moments of the strike happened at the end, on Friday evening. The negotiating team came back from the final meeting of the day, knowing that provost and president had left campus for the weekend—or so they said. They kept offering committees and so we had to decide, should we keep going for two more days? Would that bring about more progress? The majority of the negotiating team made it very clear that they believed the administration was not going to budge and they felt to continue the strike would only be harmful for the strikers. As strikers, we felt that we wanted to continue so it was *extremely difficult* to hear what our negotiating team was suggesting. *The formation of committees was not what we went out there for.* However, we had come to an agreement *before the strike began* that all decisions would be made democratically, so we put it to a vote. The vote was to stop, so that's what we did. The emotion, which erupted under the tent, was almost unbearable. In accepting the group's decision, I had to remind myself that just like I trusted this group with my physical well-being when I decided to go on strike, I also had to trust we were all making the right decision to end it. In the end, it was the community's decision. (emphasis added)

Prieto's narrative illustrates that Casper and Rice, while seemingly different, united around a tough, hard-line position: take the committees or risk greater bodily harm. That tactical maneuver helped fragment the hunger strikers, negotiators, and core organizing group. After discussing the administration's offer (which many found problematic because it did not include an outright ban on grapes) for more than one hour, and receiving assurances from Professor Fraga that the committees would produce substantive reforms, several secret votes were taken inside the tents (Silva 2012b). Because of an "unusually high number of abstentions and an unsure hand count," the first two results were cast aside. Finally, with Fraga counting, "The group of 35 voted by a slim margin to end the strike that night" (Katz 1994a). Remarking on its conclusion and despite her private reservations, Alvarado publicly stated, "The four of us were committed to do it until the community decided that we had done enough. We're going to put the community first" (Katz 1994a). Nearly twenty years later, she spoke more openly:

I felt a lot of clarity and very little pain. I was good to go. I remember Julia [González Luna] and I were like, "We just started, what is your problem?" Later I was like, "Why are you all trippin? We have shit to do here." I knew the other strikes [at UCLA and UCSB] had gone longer [fourteen and nine days, respectively] and knew that we could too. Remember, Cecilia's [Burciaga] firing was the spark for the strike. Why would we stop if that demand had not been addressed? I was concerned about Elvira [Prieto] and she was conscious of her situation, but I felt that I could continue and thought that those who could continue with the strike should do that because we had not got what we wanted. (Alvarado 2012)

Despite Alvarado and González Luna's cries, the hunger strike "ended" in the early morning hours of May 7, 1994. The agreement included the following provisions:

Grape Boycott

The issue of the boycott of grapes has been brought to our attention by students as an important issue. Professor Luis Fraga will form and head a committee that will assess and, if necessary, recommend changes to the university's present policy on grapes. Professor Fraga will consult with students, staff, and faculty on the membership of the committee. The committee will include members from all parts of the university. The committee should submit its recommendations no later than the end of Fall quarter 1994.

Flicks Incident

Sally Dickson is heading an effort to examine the university response to the Flicks incident. This effort may include recommendations to increase campus awareness of the grape issue via dorm viewings and discussions of the video shown at Flicks, as well as discussion of other views.

Burciaga Layoff

We recognize that the layoff of Cecilia Burciaga has been a source of distress for many in the Stanford community and that her role at Stanford went beyond her duties in the Vice Provost for Student Affairs area. We recognize that Cecilia contributed to the mentoring, recruitment and retention of Chicano students, particularly at the graduate level and women in particular. We are committed to the recruitment and retention of minority graduate students. The university recognizes that it is important to have a diverse staff to provide mentoring opportunities.

Relations to East Palo Alto Community

We recognize that there is interest on the part of students in enhancing the university's ongoing collaborations with East Palo Alto. Further, we will explore ways, including fundraising assistance, to support student initiatives to consolidate and better coordinate their service programs in East Palo Alto.

Chicano Studies

The provost will entertain a proposal from the dean of humanities and sciences to consider establishing a Chicano studies program. In constituting the committee to draft proposals and examine associated academic issues, the chair will consult with students, faculty, and H&S [Humanities and Sciences] deans. The school will report on a schedule that will allow consideration on the findings in the context of next planning and budget cycle.

Asian American Studies

The School of Humanities and Sciences will also examine the requests that have been pending concerning Asian American studies. (*Stanford Campus Report* 1994)

After the vote was taken to end the protest, the hunger strikers ate their first meal—ramen noodle soup—in seventy-two hours. The tents did not come down that night, however, because MEChA wanted Casper and Rice to speak with them and publicly sign the agreement the following morning (May 7). Standing in the rain, more than "one hundred people chanted 'Chicano Studies, sí! Uvas, no!' for five full minutes before allowing Casper to speak." Before the assembled crowd, including the hunger strikers, Casper said, "I know that your strike was importantly about respect—respect that the provost and I have always had for you even though some of you have felt otherwise." The students then assumed from their discussions from the previous night that Casper would sign the agreement (before the media that were present), but he refused, generating additional tension and confusion. Saying that the students misunderstood him, Casper stated, "I thought that you understood that trust had to be the basis [for moving forward with the agreement's provisions] rather than signatures" (Katz 1994a). Casper eventually relented, however, as did Rice, who also initially opposed publicly signing the agreement (Ratnesar 1994; see figure 15). Gabi Cervantes's wry smile illustrates the students had effectively outflanked the obdurate provost.

Alvarado (2012) recalled the controversial signing ceremony somewhat differently because of an exchange between her mother and Rice. "I remember my mother was there," she said, "and she spoke in Spanish. Condoleezza Rice tried to shake her hand afterward and I said, 'we don't do that (*no saludes*). This woman is not here to support us.' I said, 'we are not shaking hands with Condoleezza Rice, not after how she's treated us.'" Alvarado and her mother, Hilda, later warmly embraced each other (see figure 16). Coming on Mother's Day weekend, Medina (2013) claimed that Rice lacked "maternal instinct" when she went to breakfast instead of meeting with starving students in the quad on the strike's second day. Because their "mother," Cecilia Burciaga, had just been fired, many Chicana students viewed Rice, a fellow woman of color, with great contempt (Silva 2012a). Such animosity, combined with real ideological and political differences, made bargaining difficult, but a compromise was reached and the tents came down before noon (just in time for a wedding inside Memorial Church) on May 7, after *all* the parties signed the agreement.

FIGURE 15. Hunger strike signing ceremony, Martha ("Gabi") Cervantes and Condoleezza Rice, May 7, 1994. Stanford Daily Inc.

FIGURE 16. Hilda and Tamara Alvarado, May 7, 1994. Stanford Daily Inc.

THE IMMEDIATE AFTERMATH:
MAY 9, 1994–JUNE 1994

After Mother's Day, a celebratory rally, which included nearly one hundred people (including El Teatro Campesino founder Luis Valdez), took place outside El Centro Chicano on May 9. During the event, MEChA served lunch and Hilda Alvarado spoke before offering a prayer of thanksgiving. Just before the celebration ended, Cecilia Burciaga addressed the crowd: "Tony and I will always remember what you gave us. Know that your hunger has fed this community for at least the coming decade. Your passion will stand as a living monument" (Katz 1994b). Finally, Chicana/o students expressed their support for a letter that some Asian American students sent to Casper during the hunger strike backing MEChA's demands *and* the establishment of an Asian American studies major program (Katz 1994b; Wack 1994). This letter may have prompted Casper and Rice to include a provision on Asian American studies in the hunger strike agreement (Wack 1994). Asian American Student Association co-chair Lisa Lee participated in the May 9 rally, proclaiming, "We are here in solidarity, to see that the administration stays accountable" (Katz 1994b).

Later that afternoon, three *Stanford Review* staff members attempted to distribute the latest edition of the arch-conservative newspaper inside Casa Zapata (Herman 1994a). Stating that posting flyers violated the theme dorm's policies and procedures, Tony Burciaga picked up stacks of the *Review* and placed them inside the recycling bin, calling the publication "trash." What prompted that action was the *Review*'s May 9, 1994, lead editorial, titled "El Protesto Stupido." Relying on highly charged and provocative discourse, the paper charged,

Just as students were beginning to doubt the sanity of funding separatist ethnic enclaves, along comes MEChA to prove us right. At a protest in the Quad last week, the Chicano/Latino student organization took itself hostage by declaring a hunger strike. No doubt, the group envisions that its *fanaticism* will translate into dramatic front-page newspaper photos of emaciated protestors being carted out in front of President Casper's office. Personally, we don't think that these modern-day Gandhis will have sufficient will-power to fast very long. After all, they live among the comforts of an elite university. Until they bring scales into the Quad and weigh in at the beginning of each new day of protest, we'll assume that at least some are sneaking out for *midnight runs to Taco Bell*. (emphasis added)

Casting themselves as victims (a charge that the *Review* often leveled at MEChA), the paper filed a complaint with the campus Judicial Affairs Office against Tony Burciaga, stating that he violated their First Amendment rights (Herman 1994b).[43] Saying that their personnel had been "verbally assaulted," the *Review* launched a smear campaign against Tony Burciaga, claiming that he "hated America" and favored fascism and communism. *Stanford Review* managing editor Aman Verjee (1994), moreover, wrote, "How sad that the final media images of Mr. Burciaga's career at Stanford will not be pictures of a benevolent, thoughtful leader, but of a wan and pensive man, face ablaze with blind, neurotic fury, forcibly confiscating newspapers from a hapless *Review* staff member." Tony Burciaga (1994) responded:

> Like so many here at Stanford, I have been on the verge of tears, anger, and exasperation every day. Every time we turn around there is a fire of cruelty against Zapata, against MEChA, against undocumented immigrants. For these intolerant bigots to hide under the guise of freedom of expression is pathetic. Bigotry comes in many colors. We are tired; we are wounded; we are pained; but we will fight back and I will put my dear life on the line rather than have these beautiful hunger strikers insulted. Ya basta! Or to quote University President Gerhard Casper, "Too much is too much!" *The administration's actions in regard to the ethnic centers and my wife Cecilia's layoff have empowered the extreme right wing to express their bigotry.* (emphasis added)

The day after the *Stanford Review* incident (which ultimately resulted in no disciplinary action against Tony Burciaga), President Casper spoke at the Associated Students of Stanford University Senate meeting on May 10, 1994. While stating that he would support positive recommendations for Asian American studies and Chicano studies from the humanities and sciences dean, he also said, "How do we come out of the culture of niches?" (Luh 1994). This remark mirrored broader concerns about identity politics and the culture wars articulated by some conservative and liberal scholars in the 1980s and 90s (Newfield 2008).

Far from being niche, Stanford Asian American students saw themselves and their ancestors as integral to the broader university; indeed, without low-wage Chinese railroad workers who helped make Leland Stanford extremely wealthy, the "Farm" may have never been established.[44] Keeping up the pressure, a multiracial group of students confronted Casper during a May 12 Academic

Senate meeting (Krueger 1994). Thirty minutes into the session, twenty-five representatives from Concerned Students for Asian American Studies snuck inside, interrupting the proceedings before Senate Chair Pat Jones adjourned the meeting.

Shortly thereafter, Casper delivered his second annual "State of the University" speech in Kresge Auditorium. Channeling President Reagan, he criticized governmental "red tape" and warned that the Western Association of Schools and Colleges (WASC), which oversees and accredits universities, was becoming a Soviet-style "Ministry of Education" (Bartindale 1994). This was not the first time that Casper tangled with WASC. Calling the agency's regulatory power and push for greater faculty, student, and curricular diversity "disturbing," Casper sent WASC a letter stating, "Stanford will not endorse WASC's continuing attempts to intrude upon institutional autonomy and integrity. No institution should be required to demonstrate its commitment to diversity to the satisfaction of an external review board" (Will 1994).[45] Cecilia Burciaga publicly challenged Casper's views on WASC and diversity during a conference in San Francisco on Chicano/Latino higher education, leading some to speculate that those remarks contributed to her firing in March 1994 (A. Medina 2013; Rae-Dupree 1994).[46]

Aside from disparaging WASC, Casper condemned the racist remarks made during the May 1 Flicks incident and he criticized the "politics of ultimatum" (for example, the hunger strike) (Bartindale 1994; Krueger 1994). After the president finished his speech, Concerned Students for Asian American Studies member Kris Hayashi asked Casper, "Do we have to starve to be heard? Do we have to risk suspensions and expulsion to be heard?" (Bartindale 1994). Sophomore Jerry Chen echoed those comments before the Faculty Senate meeting, stating, "This struggle has been going on for 25 years, of course, we're frustrated. We keep being told to talk to someone else, but there comes a point when students' patience starts to fade and they want to take things into their own hands" (Krueger 1994).

Of course, this is precisely what the five Chicana/o hunger strikers (including Felipé Barragan) and their allies did—they effectively took matters into their hands, but that momentum and excitement was not sustained over time. Despite calling the hunger strike agreement a "real victory" during the May 9 celebration rally at El Centro Chicano (*Stanford Campus Report* 1994), Alvarado and Luna remained ambivalent, if not angry, about its outcome. Describing what took place after the strike ended, González Luna (2013a) said,

We had a bunch of meetings and we divided in an instant. I was with the media girls who were more "alternative" [lighter-skinned, nontraditional Mexican/ MEChA members] and talked a lot about being excluded from the final vote. There were some people in the room that backed up Alma [Medina] while others started attacking her for what happened. At one point someone stood up and said something and then others stood around her and protected her. There was a lot of yelling and then separate meetings came about, just like before the strike began, with similar dynamics—some were included and others—people that were critical, like me—were not.

Medina (2013) also recalled the tensions that emerged within MEChA post-strike:

Toward the end of the hunger strike, a lot of frustration and anger existed. Some thought that their voices had not been heard. There was just a lot of anger and some students had written "sell-outs" on MEChA signs after the vote to end the hunger strike occurred. Because so much conflict and tension existed after the strike, some of us said it would be helpful to heal those wounds afterward, so we went to El Centro Chicano (with Jim Larimore from the Native American Student Cultural Center guiding the discussion) and we sat in a huge talking circle and each of us took turns speaking our minds while holding a rock. We tried to let all our emotions and thoughts out. During the talking circle most of that anger was directed toward me. I took the brunt of it and was the speaker near the end of the circle, so I had to listen to all of the anger, criticism, and commentary before I took my turn. Community members that had never been involved in fighting for Chicano rights on campus or in the community and who were not involved in the strike complained about our course of action. People with other agendas complained about the decision to end the strike. Even people with personal concerns unrelated to the issues we were fighting for took a turn to speak against our leadership. Some issues got clarified during this session, but some resentment existed even after the meeting ended.

Regarding the strike's outcome, Medina (2013) took a slightly more optimistic but still critical approach:

We were willing to accept it. We had won as much as we could from that action. We brought attention to the issues, and while we didn't create an independent

Chicano Studies Department, a comparative ethnic studies program was established. The university later praised us for leading the strike and what we did to affect change in the university, but this is not what we wanted. We raised awareness of important issues in our community, forced the university to begin a dialogue with students about our responsibility in East Palo Alto, and created a catalyst for the development of ethnic studies. Our voices were finally heard. Those were our goals.

González Luna (2013a) expressed similar sentiments, but her comments were more revealing and self-reflexive about the entire strike as well as its outcome:

People come and praise me for the strike and I say "I don't know what you are talking about. I did nothing." I don't feel like we did anything. Thinking back now, I remember a Black Student Union member said before the strike, "You're not ready." He was right. We weren't ready, based on the final negotiations and what happened after the strike. . . . I remember that we were given an eagle feather.[47] It happened during Mother's Day weekend and the Stanford powwow; Native American students gave us an eagle feather to recognize what we did and they invited us to give a speech, thanked us, and gave us a feather and Alma [Medina] took it. After that I never saw it again. Where is our feather? I wanted something to show that I had done something. I hate that eagle feather [starts crying].

Asked whether or not she felt "proud" about her actions, she stated,

No. I am not sure that I will tell my daughter about it [the strike]. I don't think that I will. I will teach her how to walk into things with her eyes wide open; accept help from people who offer it and listen to people who say that you're not ready. . . . I left Stanford wounded; the first time that I had been back on campus was a few years ago. My daughter was eighteen months old. When I left back in 1994, I just had a horrible breakup with my boyfriend; it was very traumatic. My friend taught me that you should go back to the place where you suffered terrible trauma and leave flowers where you had good and bad memories. I didn't have any flowers, but I had my daughter—she was my flower—and I took her to all those places like Casa Zapata, the quad, and others, and I was fine. I took her to El Centro Chicano because I had picked out the floor there with Chris [González-Clarke] and I was like, "Look, it's still there!" Nothing else is still there. I just wanted something to point to for what happened and I don't feel that.

It took me a long time to take my high school kids to Stanford, because I told them about the strike, but not that I was one of the strikers. Stanford was a place where I had been beaten up and so it was hard to go back there and even speak about it now.

Later, after speaking with Alvarado, who pointedly told her to "be kind to yourself," González Luna (2013b) explained her views, recalling a pivotal discussion she had with Cecilia Burciaga during her freshman year when she told her, "You know for every one of you, there a thousand of you who don't make it here. You are responsible for those thousand":

> Through this interview, I now understand those words better than ever. I understand that the heartbreak I felt when the vote in the tent went down was not because we had been told the strikers would have the last word, but that it was the fear that I had not lived up to my responsibility to those thousand—why the committees felt like such a slap in the face. We owed it to them to do more—right? I felt that responsibility and spent the next fifteen years pouring everything into teaching high school students ethnic studies. I wish that I could stop crying. I really thought that I was carrying scars from the strike, not well-covered wounds.

González Luna's feeling that she had not done enough for those faceless thousand is common among activists who often unknowingly act like Sisyphus, taking the world's ills on their shoulders, unfortunately without much success (Wheatley 2012). While admirable, this enormous task can also be debilitating, sparking burnout and low self-esteem. It is true that besides establishing the three committees, very little was initially accomplished. Professor Fraga's committee did not recommend a ban on grapes, and funding for the EPA community center never materialized.[48] Cecilia Burciaga was not rehired. Tony Burciaga died two years after the hunger strike ended—he was just fifty-six years old. Such outcomes were humiliating. González Luna had higher aspirations; she wanted dignity for all, and when that wasn't achieved, she screamed, as did Alvarado when the strike ended.

Yet something tangible—which González Luna, Alvarado, and Medina all opposed—was achieved: the Center for Comparative Studies in Race and Ethnicity (CSRE) was established. While not a full-fledged Chicana/o studies department, the CSRE has changed people's lives, raising their consciousness about racial, gender, and class inequality thanks to students like González Luna, who helped "thousands" because of her self-sacrifice. Stanford became more dignified when she and her sisters and brothers stopped eating. New indignities have since surfaced, but the legacy of this action lives on, inspiring students in 2011, who occupied space and pressed for dignity and justice at Stanford and all across the nation.[49]

THE CCSRE AND THE LONG-TERM AFTERMATH: 1994–2013

As the hunger strike agreement stipulated, Humanities and Sciences Dean John Shoven established committees on Asian American studies and Chicano studies, headed by Daniel Okimoto (political science) and Ramón Saldívar (English and comparative literature), respectively. Saldívar also served on the Asian American studies committee and worked under Shoven as associate dean for undergraduate studies (González-Clarke 2006). The committees also included students, as well as history professor Albert Camarillo, who had worked with history professor George Fredrickson to create the Mellon Foundation–funded interdisciplinary faculty seminar in 1992 on comparative studies on race and ethnicity. That seminar helped lay the foundation for what would eventually emerge as the CSRE (Camarillo 2012). In February 1995, Shoven and the two committees delivered their reports to the Faculty Senate, recommending a new "cutting-edge program in comparative studies in race and ethnicity." Shoven stated that the new program would include majors in Asian American and Chicano studies and integrate the existing African and African American Studies (AAAS) program. That latter proposal generated opposition from African American faculty and students, who claimed it represented a "step backward" for AAAS. The BSU members pointedly rejected the future CSRE program while still supporting the call for Chicano, Native American, and Asian American studies (González-Clarke 2006).

These objections prompted revisions to the original proposal. The new version included a Native American studies major, as well as majors in Chicano and Asian American studies. The AAAS program was not included in this draft, but it was "mentioned as an affiliate, rather than core member of the CSRE program" (González-Clarke 2006). The Faculty Senate approved this proposal on

November 21, 1996. It then traveled to Provost Rice, who commented on its "rigor" and gave her assent. Had she opposed the proposal, Rice would have sparked even greater controversy around racial matters, something Stanford hoped to avoid (Saldívar 2013a).

Since its inception, the CSRE has grown steadily. Indeed, over the past six years, because of the Faculty Development Initiative led by Camarillo, twelve new faculty have been hired, including its newest director, Professor José David Saldívar.[50] The program has added twenty-two new courses to its curriculum and a new major in Jewish studies in August 2012. The CSRE graduated fifty-five to sixty students in June 2013, according to then-director José David Saldívar (Jue 2014). Center faculty are also considering establishing a PhD program in CSRE in the near future (Saldívar 2013a).

While these are all positive accomplishments, skepticism remains. The Chicana/o-Latina/o studies program within the CSRE includes very few majors, and the SCCR, which published more than fifty critical papers on Chicana/o issues from the 1970s to the 1990s, exists in name only. Previous SCCR director Luis Fraga (2012) suggested that while the CSRE emerged from the hunger strike, it came with a high price—the SCCR was gutted and Chicana/o and Latina/o faculty members became increasingly fragmented, which some disputed and rebutted (Camarillo 2012; Saldívar 2013b).

CONCLUSION

The 1994 Stanford hunger strike was relatively successful. While the students pressed for tangible reforms on and off campus, they had broader concerns that included obtaining dignity for all marginalized people (Holloway 2010). Most hunger strikes involving women are mocked, dismissed, and depoliticized because of patriarchal views; consequently, they generally are not very effective. The four Chicana students who went without food for three days largely escaped this fate. They received largely positive media attention, backing Casper and Rice—or "arroz con leche" (rice pudding) as some called them—into a corner. Given the anti-immigrant, anti-Latino sentiment that existed in California in the 1990s, such coverage was remarkable.

The fact that these women won such an improbable, but admittedly limited, victory merits greater analysis. While the majority of hunger strikers, negotiators, and key organizers were Chicana, it bears mentioning that some Chicanos like Felipé Barragan and Jorge Solis (among others) were also involved and played critical roles. That said, women led this struggle, successfully out-dueling a powerful woman of color who helped bring down the Soviet Union in the early 1990s. How did they do this? Simply put, they capitalized on Stanford's all-important public image. Like antisweatshop activists in the 1990s, Stanford Chicana/o and Latina/o students recognized the nation's second-most prestigious university had a vulnerable Achilles' heel that they skillfully exploited. Reeling from the indirect cost scandal and Cecilia Burciaga's firing, Casper and Rice were effectively trapped. They played "good cop, bad cop" and talked tough, but in the end, they capitulated. The students probably could have gotten more, but they took what they could get, much to Julia González Luna's chagrin.

Dignity for all was not achieved. That said, these students, combined with key faculty allies such as Professors Camarillo, Fraga, and Ramón Saldívar (sadly, Chicana faculty are not mentioned in the CSRE origin narrative), created something meaningful that African American, Asian American, Chicana/o, Native American, and progressive white students and faculty had wanted for nearly thirty years. Camarillo and Saldívar's social skills and academic/cultural capital were important in establishing the CSRE, but that would have never happened without the hunger strike (Fligstein 1997; Rojas 2007). That daring and risky act opened a closed political opportunity structure (with Casper and Rice at the helm), creating space and breathing room for reform and social change. The CSRE is thriving and growing, and its courses and events have made a lasting impact on the Stanford community.

Still, more could have been done. The 1994 Stanford hunger strike and the events surrounding it opened wounds that still have not properly healed. Tony Burciaga died tragically just two years after the hunger strike ended. In 2013, Cecilia Burciaga passed away (Trounson 2013). While Stanford ran a lengthy and largely effusive obituary on its website, her numerous positive contributions still have not been fully recognized on campus or in Chicana/o Studies for that matter.[51] Beyond the Burciaga family, hunger strikers like Tamara Alvarado and Julia González Luna lived for years with some bitterness and shame regarding the strike's final outcome. They wanted more, as *all* who were involved did. Despite their best efforts, their screams did not stop injustice, prompting them to scream even louder when the strike ended. The CSRE was a critical breakthrough, but it did not substantively change people's everyday lives for EPA residents, farm workers, immigrants, and other oppressed peoples. Speaking spectacularly temporarily slowed the "machine of destruction," but it still exists and appears to be picking up speed, as tuition rises, inequality widens, and the planet grows even hotter.[52] How can these trends be reversed? How can dignity for all be achieved? These questions are explored in the final chapter.

6

"TWO, THREE, OR MANY HUNGER STRIKES"

Screaming and Dreaming for a New World

INTRODUCTION

I
N HIS APRIL 1967 "MESSAGE TO THE TRICONTINENTAL," Che Guevara
called for "two, three or many Vietnams."[1] Like Trotsky (2010), he recognized that "permanent revolution" was critical for defeating imperialism. Capitalism could survive "socialism in one country," such as the Soviet
Union, Cuba, or Vietnam; however, should multiple revolutions emerge in
Africa, Asia, and Latin America—among "third world peoples"—the imperialist system might collapse, Guevara believed.[2] Such thinking sparked his
involvement in revolutionary struggles in Congo and Bolivia in the mid-
1960s, both of which ultimately failed (J. Anderson 1997; Guevara 1985, 1994,
2000; Harris 2000).

While unsuccessful, Guevara's call for multiple uprisings echoed in the
1990s as college students all over the country, but especially in California and
the Southwest, organized two, three, and indeed, many hunger strikes. Shortly
before the UCSB hunger strike, for example, students of color and white students created a multiracial organization known as the Alliance at the University of Colorado, Boulder (CU-Boulder) in April 1994. Calling for an ethnic
studies department, greater student and faculty diversity, and assistant professor of sociology Estevan Flores to receive tenure, more than thirty students
(mostly Chicana/o and Latina/o) went on an indefinite, water-only hunger

strike (Cohen and Raiford 2010; Stewart 2012). After six days, CU-Boulder President Judith Albino signed the "Declaration of Diversity," which stipulated that the university would, among other things, establish an ethnic studies department. On January 1, 1996, the department—which first emerged as a center that focused on comparative studies on race and ethnicity in 1988—opened its doors.[3]

The Alliance (which included the United Mexican American Students, MEChA, and the Student Coalition for the Advancement of Ethnic Plurality) did not disappear after obtaining this critical victory that student activists had been pushing for since the 1970s (Hu-Dehart 2012; Stewart 2012). Days after the CU-Boulder strike ended, the Alliance faxed UCSB Vice-chancellor for Student Affairs Michael Young a letter supporting the student hunger strikers on that campus, stating, "The demands that El Congreso makes coincide with and greatly amplify demands that are being made at universities across the country, including the University of Virginia at Charlottesville, Michigan State University, Harvard Law School, Yale University, and the University of Colorado, Colorado Springs."[4] The Alliance also placed these U.S.-based hunger strikes alongside "recent events in Chiapas, Paris, and South Africa," where significant social change, protest, and radical social movements were taking place. Although brief, mentioning these struggles for social justice indicated that Alliance activists had broader objectives and "freedom dreams" that extended beyond CU-Boulder. They too were decolonial hunger artists who longed for a world without misery and injustice.

That same ethos informed a small—some would say quixotic—hunger strike that occurred at UC Irvine in October 1995. Multiple concerns sparked this protest, including higher fees, Proposition 187, and Republican California governor Pete Wilson and UC Regent Ward Connerly's proposal to abolish affirmative action in the UC system (Cervantes 2012). Known as SP-1 and SP-2, those resolutions narrowly passed in July 1995 despite widespread opposition from students, faculty, and many UC chancellors, including Charles Young (UCLA) and Henry Yang (UCSB) (Ly. Chávez 1998).[5] Several months later, five Chicano students—Juan Cazarez, Angel Cervantes, César A. Cruz, Manuel Galvan, and Enrique Valencia—decided that they would go on a prolonged hunger strike to press the regents to reestablish affirmative action, lower student fees, increase financial aid, and expand recruitment and retention programs for students of color (Miller and Loar 1995). The hunger strikers also critiqued the Republican Party's so-called Contract with America, which would have balanced the federal budget through massive spending cuts and had a dis-proportionate effect on people of color, women, and workers (Miller 1995a).

Camped directly across from Aldrich Hall (UC Irvine's main administra-tion building), the hunger strikers and their allies, who included Danza Mexica Cuauhémtoc spiritual leader Arturo "Pastel" Mireles and several Aztlán Mex-ica Nation Harmony Keepers, initially attracted little media attention (Cer-vantes 2012; Miller 1995).[6] After riot-clad campus police officers violently tore down the strikers' encampment and arrested all five hunger strikers, plus two more UC Irvine students on the strike's twelfth day, the protest became much more widely covered (Miller 1995b). Citing "health and family considerations," Galvan reluctantly dropped out one day later, stating, "We don't know if they [the UC regents] will actually reconsider [their vote on affirmative action] or not. So we have to weigh our decisions . . . we don't want to die for noth-ing" (Miller 1995c). Facing an intractable and seemingly heartless series of foes (Wilson and Connerly, among others), Cervantes expressed age-old concerns about the efficacy of nonviolent actions, "We are trying to appeal to people's humanity. Of course, we worry. *What if people have no humanity?* (Miller 1995c, emphasis added)"[7]

With white middle- and working-class voters opposed to affirmative action, the UC Irvine hunger strikers never really had a chance. Wilson and Connerly mocked their actions, with the latter stating, "We're not going to be stampeded and blackmailed by a handful of students who resort to these sorts of methods when they don't get their way. If we were to be held hostage to this kind of behavior, we might as well disband the Board of Regents" (Bailey 1995). Given minimal support for a new vote on affirmative action from the UC regents, the remaining four hunger strikers ended their fast without any tangible gains (Miller and Hernandez 1995).[8]

Seen from this perspective, the 1995 UC Irvine hunger strike looks like a categorical failure, but it, along with other protests against Propositions 187 and 209 (which banned affirmative action in California in 1996), inspired students like Alison Harrington to become involved with the movement to "save" ethnic studies at UC Berkeley in April 1999. Having spent a year in Northern Ireland before taking her first classes at Berkeley in 1997, Harrington worked in West Belfast and became acquainted with the 1981 Irish Republican Army hunger strike and *troscad*, the ancient Irish tradition of fasting on the doorstep of the person who committed a transgression or exercised their power inappropriately (Beresford 1987). After those experiences, Harrington (2012) came back home to the Bay Area angry and outraged about the elimination of affirmative action and budget cuts that sharply affected the storied UC Berkeley Ethnic Studies Department that emerged from the Third World Liberation Front (twLF) in the late 1960s (Ferreira 2003).

In April 1999, just days after a conference commemorating the thirtieth anniversary of the twLF, a new twLF emerged. Its members, including Harrington, peacefully occupied Barrows Hall, where the Ethnic Studies Department is located, for ten hours (Shiekh 1999). The protest ended violently when campus police officers pulled students by their ears and placed them in choke holds as they dragged them from the building. Forty-six students were arrested, booked, and jailed (D. Hernández 1999a; Ng 1999). They were later suspended from the university for fourteen days (Shin 1999).

Like the UCLA Faculty Center occupation and excessive response by the LAPD in May 1993, these events were the emotional tipping point that sparked plans for a hunger strike that two Chicana undergraduate students first aired.[9] Six students, including Harrington, Luis Alarcón (father of three young children), Cynthia Gómez, Marío Maldonado, Rafael Solórzano, and Isabel Cristina Pulido (from nearby San Francisco State), went on a liquid-only hunger strike starting on April 29, 1999.[10] The twLF stated, in a press release, "Today Ethnic Studies is near extinction. The systematic decline of our programs is causing a slow and steady death of Chicano Studies, Asian American Studies, Native American Studies, and Ethnic Studies."[11]

Mimicking that process, the six hunger strikers slowly and steadily began dying. While initially symbolic, Harrington became dehydrated and her heart rate rapidly increased after she and eighty-two other students were arrested on the strike's sixth day (May 4, 1999) at 3:30 a.m. (Sheikh 1999). Given insufficient water behind bars, Harrington's body rapidly declined and she was later hospitalized after she was released from jail (D. Hernández 1999b). She eventually recovered, but recalled delivering her first "sermon" (she is currently a pastor at Southside Presbyterian Church in Tucson, Arizona) shortly before the police cleared the strikers' encampment.[12] Relying on biblical scripture, she inspired the strikers and their allies by stating, "We offered our starving bodies peacefully while they offered us riot police" (Harrington 2012). Later, while she was receiving medical treatment, Margot Kelly read Harrington's spoken-word piece before a large assembled crowd outside California Hall (where UC Berkeley chancellor Robert Berdahl's office was located):

This poem pleads for Ethnic Studies, Native American Studies, African American Studies, Asian American Studies, Chicano Studies. You cannot put pain holds on this poem without it getting louder. You cannot put handcuffs on this poem without it getting stronger. I wanted to give you a poem, but I offer my body instead. (Shiekh 1999)

Having offered their bodies and gained moral leverage through self-sacrifice, Chancellor Berdahl capitulated, meeting nearly all the hunger strikers' demands, including eight new faculty positions in the Ethnic Studies Department, a new research institute on race and gender studies, a student multicultural center, a mural inside Barrows Hall, more funding for recruiting students of color, and no punitive action for those arrested more than twice before and during the hunger strike (D. Hernández 1999c). Shortly after reaching this agreement, twLF negotiators joined hundreds of supporters outside California Hall, chanting, "What did we get? Ethnic Studies! When did we get it? Now!" Despite that celebratory discourse, UC Riverside Ethnic Studies Department chairperson and former Berkeley Ethnic Studies graduate student Dylan Rodríguez (2010: 18) claimed that the "possibility of a sustained, creative, and collective modality was rather quickly absorbed into the myopic pragmatism and transparent pseudo-radicalism of a few Bay Area nonprofit progressives and liberal 'revolutionaries' who tamed the budding twLF."

THE DREAM OF RIDICULOUS MEN AND WOMEN: A WORLD TURNED UPSIDE DOWN

While unduly harsh, Rodríguez's "cry" mirrors Julia González Luna's "scream" (Holloway 2010; Maldonado-Torres 2008).[13] After the Stanford hunger strike ended, González Luna sobbed inconsolably, hoping and dreaming for more than she and her comrades achieved. Not satisfied with a center on comparative racial and ethnic studies, she wanted a full-fledged Chicano studies department and justice for all farm workers, especially those who were picking grapes and being poisoned with dangerous pesticides. She also wanted justice for low-income, immigrant families in East Palo Alto who struggled financially and were often blamed for the nation's economic woes even though they typically performed back-breaking labor that took them away from their children.

Finally, she finally wanted justice for Cecilia Burciaga, who deserved a high-level position after pouring her heart, soul, and spirit into Stanford University for twenty years, counseling and mentoring numerous students, faculty, staff, and administrators, including Condoleezza Rice, the person whom she hired, but later fired *her*.

Taken collectively, González Luna and Rodríguez wanted something more than could be obtained in 1994 and 1999. It would have taken more than two, three, or many hunger strikes to create what they desired—a more dignified world. Because dignity cannot be achieved within a capitalist society that consistently blocks, limits, and frustrates dignity for all, those pushing for another world, a world where the "last shall be first and the first shall be last" will be constantly screaming, howling, wailing, and crying for more—more Chicana/o studies and ethnic studies classes and departments; more community centers that offer marginalized groups a space where they can organize and receive much-needed support for themselves and their children; more opportunities for social mobility and personal fulfillment; more freedom to achieve their dreams as people of color, women, workers, immigrants, queer people, and disabled people; more joy; more love; more of that which currently doesn't exist.

The UCLA, UCSB, UC Irvine, UC Berkeley, and CU-Boulder students that starved themselves in the 1990s all wanted this elusive "more." While they focused on tangible and concrete goals, such as establishing or expanding Chicana/o studies and ethnic studies departments, this was never the end goal. They had been repeatedly humiliated and felt constantly under siege. Like their comrades in Los Angeles, Chiapas, Seattle, and really anywhere someone was "struggling for a decent job or struggling to be free," they had had enough.[14] It was time to act, and by putting their bodies on the "wheels and levers of the machine," they slowed down its "destructive" nature.[15]

The fact that essentially sixty male and female starving bodies, mostly "brown," on six different campuses accomplished what they did is rather remarkable and merits praise. Given their race and gender, one might have thought that their "spectacular speech" would have fallen on deaf ears, but that didn't happen. People heard their screams and responded, creating much-needed change. Were those changes sufficient? Clearly, they were not, but they partially decolonized the colonial university that had excluded them for decades.

Fully decolonizing the university and the wider society will take a very long time. Coloniality is pervasive and obscure, although sometimes it becomes visible in egregious cases such as the recent deaths of Michael Brown, Eric Garner, Meagan Hockaday, and many other African American men and women.[16] Coloniality can also be clearly seen in Gaza, where thousands of Palestinians were killed in 2009 and 2014. Remarkably, Gazans provided activists and community residents in Ferguson, Missouri, with strategic advice about surviving police violence (Mackey 2014). State violence also claimed the lives of forty-three students in Ayotzinapa, Guerrero, Mexico, in September 2014, sparking tremendous outrage and resistance all over Mexico and the entire world (Goldman 2015). For more than twenty years, a femicide has been taking place in Mexico (six women were killed every day in 2014), and over the past decade, more than one hundred thousand people have died in a U.S.-backed "drug war" that has clearly failed (Matloff 2015; Robinson 2014).

These recent events may seem unrelated, but they are not. The hunger strikes that took place in the 1990s emerged from a similar *coyuntura*, or conjunctural moment.[17] As Frantz Fanon predicted, imperial rule could not be sustained forever; the "wretched of the earth" would eventually rise up and take what was rightfully theirs (Abbas 2011). Having repeatedly pushed people of color around since racial apartheid was abolished in the 1960s, some students unmasked the propaganda of a "post-racial" America by going without food. Their actions, while seemingly insignificant and tiny, were actually part of a much bigger, global movement for justice that started even before the Zapatistas emerged in Chiapas in 1994.[18] Through racial and gendered neoliberalism, the system reaped what it sowed, generating the seeds of rebellion and resistance. Fanon called this process "the year of the boomerang," and it persisted for several years, not just one.

Some have critiqued these hunger strikes (specifically the UCLA action) for being nationalist, patriarchal, homophobic, myopic, and pseudo-radical (E. Martínez 1998; Rodríguez 2010; Soldatenko 2005). These tendencies certainly existed, but they were also inclusive, feminist, transgressive, transnational, democratic, and expansive. They were not either-or, but both—reformist and revolutionary; sexist and nonsexist; exclusionary and inclusionary; nationalist and internationalist. Until now, these actions have been ignored or reduced to identity politics (Rhoads 1998). Identity was crucial, but so was justice for farm workers, immigrants, students, and working-class people. These hunger strikers were concerned about themselves and their own communities as Chicanas/os and Latinas/os, but they had broader aspirations that went beyond identity. They simply wanted to change the world and felt that through their starving bodies, they could do that.

What they did was brash, dangerous, and foolish, but couldn't the same thing be said about the Freedom Riders in the early 1960s, the DREAMers in the 2000s, workers sitting down in their factories in the 1930s, and Jesus feeding the five thousand with five loaves and two fish?[19] Given insurmountable odds, these actions, along with Óscar Romero shouting "stop the repression," must have seemed ridiculous—how could they ever defeat white supremacy, immigrant-bashing, capitalism, and imperialism—but as Che Guevara famously said, "let me say at the risk of sounding ridiculous, that a true revolutionary is guided by great feelings of love."[20]

These hunger strikes were acts of love, and love can be sometimes messy. Through self-sacrifice, these students thought that they could rouse their campuses and pierce people's hearts. They were "ridiculous" men and women (in the Dostoevskyan sense) living in a ridiculous, mad world that they desperately wanted to change. They succeeded and failed. What they needed were more ridiculous people—people willing to love and love fully, as the Good Samaritan did. The same thing could be said today. What's needed isn't two, three, or many Fergusons or two, three, or many hunger strikes, it is more compassionate, caring, and loving people. Becoming such people isn't easy, but through fasting and giving up one's fears, anxieties, and privileges, it is possible. Fasting is ultimately about personal and political transformation. It is about turning the world upside down through love. In the end, love is our best weapon since it "never ends" (1 Corinthians 13:7–8). With it, anything is possible—even dignity and justice for all.

NOTES

CHAPTER 1

Epigraphs: Russell's (2005) quote is found on pages 73–74 and 93. "Words" can be found on Missing Persons' *Spring Sessions M* album (Capitol 1982).

1. Savio delivered this speech, often called "Bodies Upon the Gears" or "The Machine," on December 2, 1964, on the steps of Sproul Hall, UC Berkeley's main administration building.

2. The Central American solidarity movement was broad-based and included many Central Americans who transmitted "signal flares," providing mostly white North Americans with morally outrageous information about human rights violations and massacres in the region in the 1980s (Perla Jr. 2008). While some North American activists traveled to Central America to act as "witnesses for peace" to protect communities under siege from U.S.-backed military regimes and death squads, others provided shelter in churches and homes for refugees who fled political and economic violence (Bibler-Coutin 1993; Peace 2012; C. Smith 1996; C. Weber 2006).

3. The project that I worked on was, by today's standards, archaic. I literally cut and pasted (with scissors and glue) information regarding human rights abuses on white sheets of paper. I marked down the victim's personal information (name, age, gender, date of birth, etc.) and when, where, and how the

person had been arrested, tortured, disappeared, or killed. It was gruesome, but critical work given that the Salvadoran government had routinely destroyed such "data," mitigating claims that it was responsible for gross human rights abuses.

4. For more on El Salvador's civil war, see Almeida (2008).

5. More than 85 percent of human rights violations were committed by the military or extralegal forces, commonly known as "death squads" (UN Truth Commission 1993).

6. Largely because of social movement activism, the SOA "closed" in December 2000 and reopened as WHINSEC in January 2001. Despite the shift, activists assert, WHINSEC is simply "new name, same shame" (Gill 2004: 229).

7. The anti-SOA movement actually began in Panama years before SOA Watch was founded in 1990. The full history of this movement, emphasizing the role of Latinas/os throughout the Americas, has not yet been written.

8. See School of the Americas Watch (www.soaw.org) for more on the legal ramifications for crossing the line.

9. "Ain't Gonna Let Nobody Turn Me Around" was one of the Civil Rights Movement's most inspiring songs. The anti-SOA movement has deep roots within this movement as well as many other social justice movements.

10. I could have been technically arrested for aiding and abetting this action. One person was actually arrested in 2005 for holding up the fence.

11. This line is taken from the HBO film *Walkout*, when lead character Paula Crisostomo (Alexa Vega) tells LAPD officer Robert Avila (Jeremy Valdez) "you know the schools may not have changed, but *we* did." For current information on the movement to close down the SOA, see School of the Americas Watch (www.soaw.org).

12. For more on the global justice movement, see Starhawk (2002).

13. To his credit, Maryknoll Father Roy Bourgeois, one of the original founders of the School of the Americas Watch, began pushing for women's ordination in the mid-1990s. After being repeatedly informed that he would be dismissed from his "sacred bonds," the Vatican removed him from the priesthood because of his support for women's ordination in November 2012, one day after the annual anti-SOA demonstration ended.

14. For a sustained critique of liberation theology, see Althaus-Reid (2000).

15. See Matthew 4:1–11 for Jesus's three temptations.

16. Jesus says "Father, if you are willing, remove this cup from me; yet, not my will but yours be done" (Luke 22:42). See Mark 14:36 for a similar passage. The Good Samaritan parable can be found in Luke 10:25–37.

17. Menchú is a Guatemalan Mayan Indian woman who opposed the country's military dictators in the 1970s and 80s and later won the Nobel Peace Prize in 1992.

18. Morrison shockingly brought along his one-year old daughter Emily to the Pentagon where he lit himself on fire. She somehow escaped injury. While many sympathized with his actions given the horror of the Vietnam War, others could not forgive him for taking Emily (see Morrison Welsh 2008).

19. Not all these movements failed. After facing prolonged protests, particularly from UC Berkeley students, the UC board of regents voted to divest from South Africa in 1986, while Stanford students pushed its board of trustees to partially follow suit that same year (Ervin 2011: 76; Masaover 2014).

20. These were not the only campuses where such actions took place during the decade. Hunger strikes also occurred at Columbia University, Northwestern University, and the University of Minnesota, to name but a few.

21. See chapter 3 for a full listing of citations on the UCLA hunger strike.

22. Many strikers on all three campuses were graduating seniors whose plans for attending commencement ceremonies were either delayed or postponed. Others saw their grades suffer, sometimes dramatically.

23. This point is crucial because, as many former hunger strikers astutely noted, these strikes were collective, not individual, efforts that involved nonstriking students who also made great sacrifices that have not been recognized.

24. As will be shown in chapters 3 through 5, these specific individuals (professors, staff, and activists) all indirectly or directly influenced these three hunger strikes along with many other people. It should be clearly noted that these well-known figures did not organize these actions nor did the students go on strike solely *for* them, as some have alleged or assumed.

25. This quote is included in the Zapatista National Liberation Army's Fourth Declaration, which was released from the Lacandon Jungle in Chiapas on January 1, 1996 (Zugman Dellacioppa 2009).

26. Holloway leaves out the qualifier "capitalist" in his chapter on the Zapatista movement and dignity. While he omits it because many dignities and forms of injustice exist, class is still crucial but by no means primary as many Marxists alleged for decades.

27. While the literature on these figures is not as extensive as it is for male hunger strikers, it is still vast. It is critical to note that the U.S. suffragist movement did not generally include African American women, even though many actively supported *universal* suffrage (Terborg-Penn 1998). Mexican women and

other women of color also pushed for the right to vote for *all* women in the United States in the early 1900s.

28. There are multiple Chicana feminisms (nationalist, socialist, anarchist, liberal, etc.). For more on Chicana feminisms, see Arrendondo et al. (2003).

29. When scholars suggest the movement ended in 1975, they are ignoring the fact that Chicana/o and Latina/o queer organizations emerged that very same year. Far from falling apart or "dying," the movement was just taking off in the mid-1970s. For more on these issues, see Roque Ramírez (2003).

30. Challenging Grant's argument, Lennon (2007) has claimed that the long traditions of hunger striking, hunger, and fasting in India and Ireland pre-1900 inspired Dunlop. Thus Lennon suggests that the hunger strike emanated from the "peripheral," colonized world, rather than from the imperial "center," as Grant and Vernon both imply.

31. U.S. suffragist activist Alice Paul also went on hunger strike and was force-fed in England (Walton 2010: 27). Paul later returned home and became a leader in the suffragist movement. She went on hunger strike during World War I to press for (white) women's suffrage, which was finally granted in 1920.

32. Despite their support for suffrage in England and Ireland, relations between the WSPU and IWFL were sometimes tense, as the latter felt the former had too much power over the wider movement (W. Murphy 2014: 17–22).

33. Although unsuccessful in the short-run, memories of the Rising and its leaders lived on, inspiring Irish republicans for decades; particularly IRA members like Bobby Sands who went on a sixty-six-day hunger strike before he died in May 1981 (Beresford 1987; O'Hearn 2006).

34. The Amritsar or Jallianwala Bagh massacre took place on April 13, 1919, when soldiers, under the command of British General Reginald Dyer, opened fire on nonviolent protestors, killing 370 and wounding 1,200. Some sources suggest that 1,000 died. Dyer did not express regret, and some British officials praised his actions. The massacre morally outraged twelve-year-old Bhagat Singh, who later became a revolutionary activist (Nair 2009).

35. When presented with a stark choice between "cowardice and violence," Gandhi supported the latter, implying he was not consistently nonviolent (Juergensmeyer 2005: 152).

36. Fasting can be found within Islam, Judaism, Hinduism, and Buddhism (Rogers 2004). Many Native Americans also practice fasting, as do many other indigenous peoples all over the world. Christianity was often imposed on Native Americans, and many converted under great duress and started fasting on

the basis of the Christian liturgical calendar. Despite these colonizing practices, some continued fasting in line with tribal customs for purification purposes and "vision quests." Because many Chicana/o and Latina/o university students in the 1990s were influenced by *indigenismo*, several hunger strikers on the three separate campuses attended sweat lodge ceremonies before they stopped eating; they saw their actions from an indigenous, rather than Christian, perspective.

37. See Exodus 34:28.

38. Jesus's racial and ethnic background has long been debated. Based on the region where he lived, it seems likely he was not phenotypically white. For a fascinating account of how Jesus became "white" in the United States, see Blum and Harvey (2012). On the issue of Jesus's sexism, see Matthew 15:21–28.

39. All Bible quotes in this book are taken from the New Revised Standard Version (NRSV).

40. The "devil" in this parable represents what Borg and Crossan (2006: 7–9) call the "domination system."

41. See Wink (1999) for more on historical and contemporary "powers and principalities."

42. For more on Mary Magdalene, see Bourgeault (2008).

43. Some scholars have questioned early Christian martyrdom, claiming it was invented to provide the mistaken impression that Christianity was a persecuted church. For more on this crucial issue, see Moss (2013).

44. See Matthew 19:21, Mark 10:21, and Luke 18:22 for more on this specific story. The Catholic Church for centuries stipulated that its followers (except for those with age and health considerations) should abstain from all food on Ash Wednesday and Good Friday and not eat any red meat during the forty-day Lenten season nor on any Friday during the calendar year (T. Ryan 2005: 52–54). More guidelines regarding fasting were implemented over the years, which many mocked and ignored, not recognizing that the practice had radical roots that were not food-related at all.

45. These actions are known collectively as the Corporal Works of Mercy (Matthew 25:31–46). Crucial for all Christians, they are the guiding philosophy of the radical, anarchist Catholic Worker organization. For Marx's quote on religion, see *A Contribution to the Critique of Hegel's Philosophy of Right* (1843).

46. The most influential women who focused on tireless charity were Mother Teresa and Dorothy Day, although the latter would have surely choked on the word "charity" given her revolutionary nature.

47. The organization's name is the Meira Paibis, or "women who carry torches." Manipuri women nonviolently rose up against British rule in 1904 and 1939 (Mehrotra 2009).

48. Regarding self-immolations, Alice Herz, an eighty-two-year-old pacifist, lit herself on fire and died protesting the Vietnam War in March 1965 in Detroit. Despite her action, Norman Morrison still receives far more attention than she does even though she acted first. For more on Herz, see C. Ryan (1994).

49. English prime minister Winston Churchill made that unfortunate remark in 1931, which Gandhi sarcastically endorsed years later just before India gained its independence.

50. This phrase is a play on the 1960s antiwar chant, "The whole world is watching."

51. This does not mean that the social-movements field has not been tilled at all. For one comprehensive study on hunger strikes from an empirical and theoretical perspective, see Scanlan, Stoll, and Lumm (2008). Several scholars have also examined the UFW relying on social movement nomenclature and discourse (Jenkins and Perrow 1977; Jenkins 1985; and Ganz 2009). Aside from these studies, very few scholars have examined other Chicana/o Movement organizations from a social movement perspective.

52. More than ten thousand California prisoners went on hunger strike in 2011 and Guantánamo Bay detainees first went on hunger strike in January 2002, holding many such actions over the next twelve years (Ahmad 2011; Kurnatz 2009). Haitian and Cuban prisoners also went on hunger strikes in the 1990s at Guantánamo Bay (Kaplan 2005).

53. Despite famously signing an executive order to shut down Guantánamo Bay just two days into his presidency, Barack Obama backed away from his pledge over the next four years until more than one hundred detainees began a hunger strike in February 2013 (Finn and Kornblut 2011). That action generated widespread media and global attention, prompting Obama to state that he would push to permanently close Guantánamo. It remains open, however.

54. This phrase plays on Goodwin and Jasper's (1999) influential article, titled "Caught in a Winding, Snarling Vine."

55. This incident was known as the "Sleepy Lagoon" case.

56. Thich Quang Duc was a Vietnamese Buddhist monk who immolated himself in September 1963, generating tremendous media attention. Mohamed Bouazizi was a Tunisian street vendor who lit himself on fire in December 2010, sparking the downfall of the long-standing dictatorial regime and igniting protests all over the world in 2011.

57. The *Hunger Artist* was first published in German in 1922. It first appeared in English in 1938.

58. US labor leader Nicholas Klein apparently made a statement like this one, not Gandhi, in 1914 (O'Carroll 2011).

59. Several hunger strikers stated that the Zapatistas, the North American Free Trade Agreement (NAFTA), and Proposition 187 all partially influenced them, fueling them with hope and rage (T. Gutiérrez 2011; E. López 2011a).

60. Long-time activist Tom Hayden made this remark at the 1999 "Battle in Seattle" (Friedberg and Rowley 2000).

61. Most studies on the UCLA hunger strike do not include quotes from interviews or archival materials, although there are some exceptions. Most previously published works on this protest are not theoretical or analytical. For more on these studies, see chapter 3.

CHAPTER 2

Epigraph: Time Zone's "World Destruction" can be found on their single of the same name (Virgin 1984). Time Zone included hip-hop artist Afrika Bambaataa and John "Johnny Rotten" Lydon, former lead singer from the seminal English punk band the Sex Pistols.

1. California's prison population expanded by 500 percent between 1982 and 2000 (Gilmore 2007: 7). Meanwhile, the only UC campus that opened between 1965 and 2005 was UC Merced.

2. Chicana writer and activist Elizabeth Martínez (2000) notes that the criminalization of youth of color in the early 1990s, which preceded Proposition 21, sparked the development of the "schools not jails" movement in Southern *and* Northern California.

3. For more on this historic and controversial address, see Smiley (2010).

4. These quotes are taken directly from "A Time to Break Silence."

5. Those recessions took place in 1973, 1981–1982, and 1990–1991.

6. For more on the Central Park jogger case, see S. Burns (2011).

7. This video was released just one month *before* the "uprising" took place in April 1992 (Acuña 1996: 183).

8. The phrase "make a way out of no way" is a popular expression within the African American community. It is based partially on Isaiah 43:16, when God parted the waters for the Israelites to flee Egyptian oppression (see also

Exodus 14:16–31). That story was foundational for the Civil Rights Movement, as African Americans "made a way out of no way" by relying on mass meetings, singing, boycotts, marches, and many other tactics to end segregation.

9. The subhead's "I'm living in the eighties" is the key line from Killing Joke's 1984 hit single "Eighties." It is on their *Night Time* album (EG Records 1985). The song's lyrics, "I have to push, I have to struggle," encapsulated the decade for many. "Mister Reagan" is repeated many times on Time Zone's "World Destruction" extended twelve-inch-single version (Virgin 1984).

10. Reagan had been a FBI informer since the 1940s, naming names and appearing before the House Un-American Activities Committee (HUAC) as a "friendly" witness (Rosenfeld 2012: 120–26). His actions helped bring about the infamous Hollywood blacklist, which he rhetorically opposed and even denied existed but facilitated with his testimony and decisions (Rogin 1988).

11. Reagan never admitted higher fees were linked, in a disciplinary manner, to the UC Berkeley Free Speech Movement. This decision was an ominous one, as tuition in the UC system has skyrocketed since the late 1960s, forcing more and more students to work and attend classes, leaving them with very little time to organize and demand social change. Given this trajectory, one might logically presume this was the intent all along.

12. Reagan was also SAG president in 1959.

13. See Yager (2006) for Reagan's transition from Democrat to Republican.

14. The International Monetary Fund (IMF) and World Bank started pushing for "structural adjustments" in developing countries in the 1970s because they assumed that deregulation, privatizing state-owned enterprises, and cutting back subsidies on basic goods and services would generate economic growth and facilitate debt repayment. Critics noted, however, these policies generated the "recolonization" of the third world (Danaher 1994).

15. "Dark night of the soul" is the title of a well-known poem written in the sixteenth century by Saint John of the Cross.

16. *Happy Days* was one of the highest-rated television shows in the 1970s. Its final episode aired in 1984.

17. The "Vietnam Syndrome" emerged after the United States lost the Vietnam War in 1975. It was believed that the intense conflict and deaths associated with that ten-year long war made the public skeptical about future armed conflicts. Because of that logic, the United States did not launch any major wars between 1975 and 1989, although it invaded Grenada in 1983. While the 1991 Persian Gulf War is seen as evidence that the U.S. public had finally

kicked the Vietnam Syndrome for good, President Bush laid the groundwork for doing so with the 1989 Panama invasion, labeled Operation Just Cause. For more on these issues, see Trent (1992).

18. Clinton campaign strategist James Carville is often credited with coining this phrase.

19. The Glass-Steagall Act was passed in 1933 to prevent bank runs, excessive risk-taking, and future depressions.

20. In an otherwise outstanding documentary film, *Inequality for All* (Kornbluth 2014), former Clinton labor secretary Robert Reich conveniently overlooks the fact that while employment grew in the 1990s, pay did not.

21. The CEO–average worker pay gap was 273 in 2012 and 331 in 2013 (www.epi .org/publication/the-ceo-to-worker-compensation-ratio-in-2012-of-273 and www .aflcio.org/Corporate-Watch/Paywatch-2014). The top 1 percent owned approximately 35 percent of all wealth in 2010 (C. Collins 2012: 3). For current information on income and wealth inequality, see http://inequality.org/author /chuck-collins and http://faireconomy.org/issue/growing-divide.

22. The subhead's "Fight the Power" is Public Enemy's perhaps most well-known song, released in 1989 on the *Do the Right Thing* soundtrack (Motown). It was later included on the group's *Fear of a Black Planet* (Def Jam 1990). The term "racial neoliberalism" was coined by David Theo Goldberg (2011) and the "New Jim Crow" by Michelle Alexander (2010).

23. The post–Civil Rights Movement era emerged after the Civil Rights and Voting Rights Acts were passed in 1964 and 1965, respectively. After segregation was eliminated, new—really old—issues emerged, namely poverty, which cut across race and gender, sparking the impetus for the PPC (1967–68). While quite radical, the PPC was still a largely masculine project that did not address gender inequality (Estes 2006).

24. Internal divisions were crucial in bringing down the PCC, but the FBI also applied pressure. McKnight's (1998) book on the PPC demonstrates that the FBI practiced extensive surveillance on it, illustrating that it fell apart not because of myriad divisions between peoples of color but because of state repression. For more on the FBI's long campaign against King, see Garrow (1981).

25. Nixon recognized that punitive approaches would generate only partial success; he therefore supported drug prevention and rehabilitation programs too (Jarecki 2012). Thus, while he declared drugs to be "public enemy number one," he did not favor mass incarceration as was done starting in the early 1980s.

26. Alexander (2010: 49–53) brilliantly demonstrates that Reagan declared the War on Drugs in October 1982, three years before crack became a national issue. She contends that this temporal gap illustrates this war was never really about stopping drugs, but controlling people of color (mainly black and brown men).

27. The subhead's "California Über Alles" refers to the single of the same name (Alternative Tentacles 1979) released by the Dead Kennedys (DKs), a Bay Area-based, multiracial punk band, during California governor Jerry Brown's second gubernatorial term. It was covered (and updated with new lyrics, discussed later in this chapter) by the Disposable Heroes of Hiphoprisy on their album *Hypocrisy is the Greatest Luxury* (4th and Broadway 1992).

28. César Chávez often blamed Deukmejian for the UFW's downfall the governor appointed pro-grower officials to the Agricultural Labor Relations Board (ALRB). Other scholars contend, however, that Chávez unwittingly weakened the board and hence the UFW (Bardacke 2011; Mt. García 2012; Pawel 2014). Whatever the case, the union's membership fell from 30,000 to fewer than 12,000 in the early and mid-1980s (Griswold del Castillo and Garcia 1995: 134). The union's woes led Chávez to call for a renewed grape boycott. That action did not produce tangible results, but it inspired Chicana/o and Latina/o college students, as will be seen in chapters 4 and 5. For more on César's "last fast," see Pérez and Parlee (2013).

29. Anand (2012) notes that state budget expenditures fell for higher education from 12.6 percent in 1991 to 11.3 percent in 1993 and increased for corrections from 5.9 percent in 1991 to 7.8 percent in 1993 (http://cacs.org/research/winners-and-losers-corrections-and-higher-education-in-california).

30. Disposable Heroes of Hiphoprisy, "California Über Alles."

31. UC tuition increased 300 percent from 2000 to 2010. The whopping 32 percent fee hike in November 2009 generated protests and arrests on many different campuses (Gordon and Khan 2009). UC undergraduate fees for 2014–2015 were $12,192.

32. The UC Student Association includes representatives from different UC campuses' student-government organizations, such as the Associated Students of UC Santa Barbara and Graduate Student Association of UCSB.

33. Gardner had actually been an assistant professor and assistant chancellor at UCSB during the turbulent late 1960s. He left the university in 1970 and became president of the University of Utah in 1973. He became UC president in 1983 and resigned in 1991. The ensuing controversy around his retirement package generated substantial news coverage, particularly in the *Los Angeles*

Times. UC officials denied the decision regarding Gardner was made secretly, stating it was a strictly "personnel matter," which are always held behind closed doors. For more on his controversial severance package, see L. Gordon (1992c).

34. Wilson's approval rating in mid-1993 was 15 percent. Shortly after he publicly announced his support for SOS, it rose to more than 50% (Maharidge 1995). Other sources suggest his approval ratings increased more modestly, rising from 30 percent in March 1993 to 39 percent in May 1994 (Wroe 2008: 43).

35. Wilson voted for the 1986 Immigration Reform and Control Act (IRCA), which provided citizenship to millions of unauthorized migrants, only after it was amended to include a guest worker provision that he sponsored and the agricultural industry favored (Wroe 2008: 22).

36. It should be noted that Democratic senator Dianne Feinstein embraced anti-immigration positions in June 1993, two months *before* Pete Wilson wrote his infamous letter to President Clinton in August 1993 calling for $3 billion in immigration-related costs and an end to birthright citizenship. Other Democratic politicians, including Senator Barbara Boxer, State Treasurer Kathleen Brown, President Clinton, and Attorney General Janet Reno also adopted a tougher stance on immigration in 1993–1994 (Martinez HoSang 2010: 172–76).

37. Barbara Coe, founder of the Orange County–based California Coalition for Immigration Reform (CCIR), was one of the key forces behind SOS and Proposition 187. Another key pro-187 group was Voices of Citizens Together (VCT), led by Glen Spencer. Coe once called Mexicans "savages" and said that undocumented immigrants were "illegal barbarians who cut off the heads and appendages of blind, white, disabled gringos" (Fernandes 2011: 203). Spencer routinely spoke about a covert reconquista and stated other white-supremacist views. Not surprisingly, the Southern Poverty Law Center categorized CCIR and VCT as "hate groups" (Fernandes 2011: 203).

38. Based on *Leticia A. v. Board of Regents* (1985), undocumented immigrant students attending UC and CSU campuses were classified (provided they met certain criteria) as state residents, significantly lowering their tuition costs. The *Regents of the University of California v. Superior Court of Los Angeles County* (1990)—also known as the Bradford decision for the student who successfully claimed that *Leticia A.* discriminated against legal immigrants and citizens—decision, however, limited the *Leticia A.* ruling, stating that any undocumented student enrolled after 1991 would not be categorized as a state resident. Proposition 187 would have banned *all* undocumented students from

attending public universities such as the UC, CSU, and community colleges. It wasn't until AB 540 passed in 2001 that undocumented students became eligible for paying in-state tuition again. Under the California Dream Act (AB 131), passed and signed into law by Governor Jerry Brown in 2011, undocumented students are now eligible for financial aid.

39. See the Arizona-based group No More Deaths (http://forms.nomoredeaths .org/en/) for current information on deaths along the U.S.-Mexico border related to Operation Gatekeeper.

40. The subhead's "The Year of the Boomerang" is a Rage Against the Machine song released in 1995 (Sony). Fanon initially coined the term in *Wretched of the Earth* (1961). Colonialism often generates boomerang effects like the guerrilla movement in French-occupied Algeria in the 1950s. Some might say that 1994 was the year of the boomerang, when the Zaptatistas emerged along with pro-immigrant marches, labor movement activism, and student hunger strikes. "The Year of the Boomerang" can ironically be found on the *Higher Learning* (Singleton 1995) movie soundtrack. For more on *coyuntura* analysis, see http://cril.mitotedigital.org/coyuntura. This website has extensive links on autonomous Marxism, the Zapatista movement, and many other topics.

41. See the following clip: https://www.youtube.com/watch?v=yıdQazDYgag.

42. The appellation "CIV" was confusing for many since it raised the specter that the new yearlong course would focus exclusively on Western civilization. A required freshman class on Western civilization actually existed at Stanford from 1935 until the late 1960s, when campus unrest emerged. The Western culture class was instituted in 1980 and lasted only eight years until the Stanford Faculty Senate approved CIV in 1988 (Lindenberger 1990).

43. Burns, a conservative Fresno Democrat, investigated claims that the 1948 DiGiorgio labor strike, organized by the National Farm Labor Union and Ernesto Galarza, was "communist-inspired" (Valdés 2011: 197–98).

44. Durazo had been active in the Center for Autonomous Social Action, a radical, Chicana/o Marxist organization that emerged in the late 1960s that focused on organizing Mexican workers on both sides of the U.S.-Mexico border. Its newspaper was called *Sin Fronteras*, underscoring its decolonial, transnational politics.

45. For more on business unionism, see Buhle (1999); for social movement unionism, see Voss and Sherman (2000).

46. Scenes from this attack are included in *Bread and Roses* (Loach 2000). Actual coverage of the beating can be viewed at http://www.youtube.com /watch?v=WKfQ_gUn7UNg.

47. See Early (2011) for a critical perspective on the decision to place Local 399 under trusteeship.

48. See chapter 3 for more on the organizations that were involved with UCLA.

49. See Cornel West's comments on *Democracy Now* about Bob Marley and the *Wailers*, not the "whiners": www.democracynow.org/blog/2011/9/29/cornel _west_on_occupy_wall_street_its_the_makings_of_a_us_autumn_respond ing_to_the_arab_spring.

50. Aztlán Underground's first album was titled *Decolonize* (1995), and in 1998 they released a song with the same title. Lyrics include this popular protest chant: "We didn't cross the border, the border crossed us."

51. See Collins (2004) for more on emotional energy.

CHAPTER 3

Chapter title: This quote comes from Balvina Collazo, who when asked "Are you hungry," replied, "Yes, I am hungry; hungry for justice" (Mabalon 1993h). Epigraph: This well-known poem by Nicaraguan poet and author Gioconda Belli (1978) was found while researching archival material on the 1993 hunger strike in the Chicano Studies Research Center (CSRC). It was apparently made into a flyer and passed out during the action.

1. Jasper (1997: 302–6) calls such decisions "blunders." In "strategic interactions" between social movements and targets, the latter often stumble, providing the former with considerable leverage that they may use for their own advantage (McAdam, Tarrow, and Tilly 2001).

2. The UCLA students that were involved in this struggle in the late 1980s and early 1990s deliberately used the words "Chicana" and "Chicano" in nearly all their press releases and public statements. Such language mirrored ongoing shifts with Chicana and Chicano studies during that era. The National Association for Chicano Studies, for example, changed its name to the National Association for Chicana and Chicano Studies just two years after the strike ended in 1995 (E. Martínez 1998). For clarity, some prefer the a/o ending, given its inclusivity, whereas others favor spelling out both names, Chicana and Chicano. The word "Chicano" has also been contested, with many activists and some scholars preferring "Xicana/o" in the 1990s because the fact that the "ch" sound is spelled with an *x* in Nahuatl (Moraga 2011: xxi). The feminist and indigenous "turns" in Chicana/o studies in the 1980s and 1990s helped transform the field. Today some prefer the term *Chicanx*, based on the notion that the *a/o* ending reinforces gender binaries.

3. Some UCSB and Stanford students involved with hunger strikes on their campuses in 1994 also attended Chávez's funeral (N. García 2011; Silva 2012a).

4. Chávez sent his letter to Chancellor Young on May 6, 1991 (John Fernández personal collection).

5. More than half of all those who were arrested were women (Gordo 2012a).

6. Because Aguilar did not agree to be interviewed for this study, I could not confirm this account. The Coalition for Chicana/o Studies (CCCS) complied a chronology of the entire struggle for Chicana/o Studies, going back to 1968 when the United Mexican American Students (UMAS) made its first proposal for a Chicano Studies Department. The CCCS states that the proposal for a hunger strike first emerged on May 17, 1993, just six days after the Faculty Center occupation (John Fernández personal collection). This document doesn't say where those plans were first aired.

7. Ferguson also declined to be interviewed for this study. She is married to Marcos Aguilar.

8. Martin Luther King, in a 1967 interview, stated "a riot is the language of the unheard" (D'Arcy 2014).

9. While the students involved with these hunger strikes were part of generation X (post–baby boomers), Jeff Chang (2005) frames them as belonging to the "hip-hop generation."

10. McWilliams (1946: 24) states the "minimum" was 130,000, with "estimates reaching as high as 700,000."

11. See W. Churchill (1997) for more on Lemkin and genocide.

12. See Anaya and Lomelí (1989) and Carrasco (1999) for more on the Aztecs and Aztlán.

13. The Aztecs were also known as the Mexica people. Both terms, like all racial and ethnic categories, are social constructions, of course.

14. The literature on "settler colonialism" is extensive. I mention the concept here because the Chicano hip-hop musical group, Aztlán Underground (AUG), in their song "Decolonize," state "We didn't cross the borders, the borders crossed us, yet the *settler nation* lives in disgust." AUG played at UCLA during the hunger strike (Alvarez 2014). See Francoso (2012) and R. Hernández (2012) for more on AUG.

15. Otis was also rabidly antiunion, as were most of Los Angeles' early power brokers. The term "white spot" thus is about racism *and* capitalism (Laslett 2012; Milkman 2006).

16. There is little empirical data, unfortunately, on how many students of color attended USC in the late nineteenth and early twentieth centuries. Because

of where the university was located, it can only be inferred that their numbers were infinitesimal.

17. The California State Normal School was first created on May 5, 1862 (six years before UC Berkeley was founded). It was located in San Francisco and moved to San Jose in 1870. After a fire destroyed the school in 1880, it was rebuilt and a new southern branch of the Normal School was opened in Los Angeles. Originally slated to be built in Boyle Heights, a "group of citizens living *west* of the Los Angeles River moved quickly to forestall this possibility" (Hamilton and Jackson 1969: 22–23, emphasis added).

18. Los Angeles City College is currently located on the site of the old Normal School. Its original buildings were razed in the 1960s based on seismic safety concerns (Dundjerski 2011: 25).

19. Rodolfo Acuña first conceptualized and popularized the notion that Chicanas/os were living in "occupied America" in his similarly titled classic book, first published in 1972.

20. Fees for UCLA students were $25 a semester in 1930 (Dundjerski 2011: 60).

21. See www.oac.cdlib.org/findaid/ark:/13030/tf029000tj for more on Strack's life.

22. During the Free Speech Movement, Hoover told his top aides that Kerr was "no good" (Rosenfeld 2012: 7).

23. As UC President, Sproul regularly cooperated with the FBI (Kerr 2001: 49–74).

24. Estrada (2008: 259) notes that this day is arbitrary, as the city was settled centuries earlier by indigenous peoples. The city's African ancestors were not officially recognized, however, until the early 1980s, culminating a decades-long struggle led by African American librarian Miriam Matthews.

25. For more on this controversy, see the HBO documentary film *Bastards of the Party* (Sloan 2012).

26. The Ford Foundation's role in funding black studies and Chicano studies programs and departments has generated some scholarly attention and controversy. See Acuña (2011a), Biondi (2012), and Rojas (2007) for more on these issues.

27. During the El Plan de Santa Barbara conference in April 1969, students agreed to fold UMAS and other Chicana/o student organizations into MEChA (Muñoz 1989).

28. See Caputo (2005) for more on the Kent State shootings.

29. Simón González, Rodolfo Alvarez, David Sanchez, and a Mesa Directiva preceded Gómez-Quiñones as CSRC directors before he took over in 1974 (www .chicano.ucla.edu/about). Gómez-Quiñones unfortunately did not agree to

be interviewed for this study. He noted his thoughts about the 1979 memo and related matters concerning the IDP and the struggle for Chicana/o studies in an unpublished memo titled "Between the Idea and the Reality . . . Falls the Shadow" (John Fernández personal collection).

30. The CUCC had been releasing reports critical of the IDP since 1980 (*La Gente* 1990).

31. "Lupe's Song" includes these horrific lines: "Now Lupe's dead and buried, and lies in her tomb. While maggots crawl out of her decomposed womb. The smile on her face is a sure cry for more. My hot fucking, cocksucking Mexican whore" (D. González 2003).

32. The phrase "benign neglect" has been widely condemned as a racial code word signaling the conscious or unconscious abandonment of African Americans, especially after the Civil Rights Movement. For more on racial code words and benign neglect, see Omi and Winant (1994) and Steinberg (1995).

33. On Waugh attending Davis's lectures, see Dundjerski (2011: 180).

34. Critical race theory is known for developing the concept of "majoritarian narratives." See Yosso (2006).

35. See Massey and Denton (1993) for a forceful rebuttal of the culture of poverty thesis.

36. To express solidarity with the South African antiapartheid movement and because of growing Pan-African sentiment, the UCLA Black Student Union changed its name to the Afrikan Student Union in 1989.

37. See also "MEChA position paper on Chicana/o Studies" (MEChA 1990). CSRC Library Hunger Strike Collection.

38. Ortiz became IDP chair in fall 1990 (Ortiz 2011).

39. Fees increased sharply in the early 1990s, starting with a 10 percent hike in 1990 (L. Gordon 1992a). Student fees increased 125 percent between 1990 and 1995, prompting major rallies and protests (see chapter 2). "Low-intensity warfare," as opposed to "high-intensity warfare," refers to more restrained operations, generating less violence and fewer deaths. The concept can be applied beyond those parameters, as low-intensity war sometimes slips into academia, minus overt violence, but with real consequences on people's minds, bodies, and spirits.

40. He later changed his name to El-Hajj Malik El-Shabazz. Like the indigenous "turn" in the Chicana/o, Latina/o community in the late 1980s and early 1990s, there was an "Afrocentric turn" in the African American community during that same period (Hill Collins 2006).

41. For more on these claims, see Soldatenko (2005).

42. The students that worked on this proposal received independent studies units through UCLA education professor Daniel Solórzano, who later served as MEChA Calmecác advisor for several years (Solórzano 2011). Calmecác was the recruiting and retention program that MEChA established after breaking ties with AAP in 1990.

43. Olvera Street had been whitewashed decades earlier, in the 1920s and 1930s, under Christine Sterling, the so-called Mother of Olvera Street, who ran the area for thirty-three years (W. Estrada 2008: 181–201). In the late 1980s, the street faced further "ethnic cleansing" and corporate development—raising alarms that the street might turn into the next "Taco Bell" (Acuña 1996: 27). Because of strenuous opposition, those plans did not go forward.

44. The alliance also included the Mexican American Legal and Defense Education Fund (MALDEF); the National Chicano Moratorium; the AFL-CIO LA County Federation of Labor; United Food and Commercial Workers (UFCW) Local 770; Congressional Representatives Edward Roybal and Esteban Torres; State Assemblypersons Lucille Roybal-Allard, Xavier Becerra, Richard Polanco, and Maxine Waters; LA County Supervisor Gloria Molina; LA City Councilpersons Richard Alatorre and Mike Hernández; LA School Board Member Leticia Quezada; and American Civil Liberties Union Representative Antonio Villaragosia.

45. "Bring the Noise" was released in 1988 on Public Enemy's *It Takes a Nation of Millions to Hold Us Back* album.

46. The motto of the global justice movement in the early 2000s was "another world is possible."

47. CSRC Hunger Strike Collection, folder 1.

48. Those professors were Raúl Hinojosa, José Monleon, Raymond Rocco, George Sánchez, Edward Telles, Clara Lomas, Vilma Ortiz, Sonia Saldivar-Hull, Daniel Solórzano, Juan Gómez-Quiñones, and Leobardo Estrada.

49. The author thanks Executive Vice-chancellor Scott Waugh for making these departmental memos available. The History Department vote was eighteen yes, eight no, four abstentions.

50. Memo from History Department Chairperson Scott Waugh to Dean of Social Sciences David Sears, June 15, 1992.

51. Memo from Matthew Malkan, Executive Committee of the College of Letters and Science, to Dean of Social Sciences Scott Waugh, November 3, 1992; memo from Waugh to Professors Estrada, Gómez-Quiñones, Hinojosa,

Monleon, Ortiz, Rocco, Saldivar-Hull, Sánchez, Solórzano, and Telles, November 19, 1992.

52. CSRC Hunger Strike Collection, folder 1.

53. MEChA flyer, CSRC Hunger Strike Collection, folder 1.

54. Memo from Dean Scott Waugh to Interim Provost Herbert Morris, January 19, 1993, EVC Waugh Collection.

55. Rhoads (1998: 77) claims that Aguilar was actually "kicked out" of MEChA for his single-minded focus on creating a Chicana/o Studies Department, while Alvarez (2011a) stated that a motion to remove him was introduced and failed by one vote. Because Aguilar declined to be interviewed, I could not corroborate either account. Rhoads's chapter, like Soldatenko's (2005), includes very few quotes from students, faculty, staff, and community members.

56. This conference also included Ramón Ruiz, Refugio Rochín, Ricardo Romo, Adaljiza Sosa-Riddell, Rodolfo Acuña, Yolanda Broyles-González, Alex Saragoza, Antonia Castañeda, Ramón Gutiérrez, and George Lipsitz. CSRC Hunger Strike Collection, folder 2.

57. CSC opposed López because it felt he didn't challenge the Chicano Studies Library cuts more forcefully.

58. The John Singleton–directed film *Higher Learning* (1995) was filmed at UCLA. It depicted a highly racially polarized environment, much like the one that existed on campus during that era. See chapter 2 for more on the film and its soundtrack.

59. Blanca Gordo (2012a) claimed that the LAPD actually broke down the doors that the students barred themselves behind during the demonstration.

60. "Why Asian Students Should Join the Chicana/o Studies Struggle," CSRC Hunger Strike Collection, folder 3.

61. See note 9 above. The CCCS claimed that the hunger strike was first publicly debated on May 17, 1993, at a meeting that included more than one hundred students at Campbell Hall. Mancillas (2011b) claimed that the idea was discussed before this meeting at Bonzo's restaurant on Olvera Street. Once vetted, it then went before the general assembly on May 17.

62. The sign beside Montañez pointedly says "United Chicanas/os, Latinas/os," indicating that the movement did not completely exclude non-Mexicans, as some have alleged (Soldatenko 2005).

63. See Carrasco (1999) for more on the Aztecs and violence before the Spanish Conquest.

64. Andrea L. Rich and Arthur Lee Smith, *Rhetoric of Revolution: Samuel Adams,*

Emma Goldman, Malcolm X (Durham: Moore, 1970); Andrea L. Rich, *Interracial Communication* (New York: Harper and Row, 1973).

65. Anonymous letter to Chancellor Young, June 2, 1993, CSRC Hunger Strike Collection, folder 3.

66. Flyer to save Nursing Program, n.d., CSRC Hunger Strike Collection, folder 3.

67. Letter from Los Angeles Association of White People to Chancellor Young, n.d., CSRC Hunger Strike Collection, folder 3.

68. Namely, the joint MEChA-UCLA proposal (December 1, 1990) and the Chicana/o, Latina/o faculty proposal (January 28, 1992).

69. Macías didn't become the Center's director until January 1, 1999 (Macías 2011).

70. The 1993 hunger strike agreement included language regarding future a MA/PhD program in Chicana/o studies. The program's first cohort started taking classes in 2012–2013.

71. The Native American D-Q University was established in 1971 in Northern California. It remained open until 2005 when it lost its accreditation.

CHAPTER 4

Chapter title: This quote comes from El Congreso, "Hunger Strike Declaration," April 27, 1994, El Congreso Hunger Strike Files, El Centro Arnulfo Casillas (Building 406).

Epigraph: This quote is taken from the Robert F. Kennedy Community School, located on the site of the former Ambassador Hotel on Wilshire Boulevard in Los Angeles. The Ambassador was the place where Senator Robert F. Kennedy was assassinated on June 3, 1968, after he won the California Democratic Party presidential primary. Chávez and the United Farm Workers (UFW) were among Kennedy's strongest supporters; indeed, UFW co-founder Dolores Huerta was at his side when he was killed (Bender 2008).

1. This quote is taken from Mario Savio's speech, called "Bodies upon the Gears and Wheels," at UC Berkeley on December 3, 1964. For more on Savio's life, see Cohen (2009, 2014).

2. The department changed its name to the Department of Chicana and Chicano Studies in 2009.

3. For more on the controversy surrounding Gardner's retirement package, see chapter 2.

4. The two professors were black studies professors Cedric Robinson and Gerard Pigeon. For more on this hunger strike, see UCSB Davidson Library, Department of Special Collections, California Ethnic and Multicultural Archives (CEMA), UCSB Ethnic Studies Protests Collection, box 3, folder 9.

5. See also Arnulfo Casillas, "Symposium: UCSB Chicano Political Development—The Roots of El Congreso," May 2, 1986 (unpublished paper), Alma Flores personal collection.

6. The title of this subheading comes from Rojas's 2007 book, *From Black Power to Black Studies*.

7. Asian Americans and African Americans have also faced discriminatory treatment in Santa Barbara for centuries.

8. All UC campuses were overseen by UC president Robert Sproul until he retired in 1958.

9. UMAS members Joel García, Cástulo de la Rocha, and Juan Arroyo were among the "handful of students invited by BSU to enter the occupied building in solidarity" (Moreno 2009: 178).

10. Chavarría "was a Latin American social and intellectual historian specializing in Peruvian Marxist ideology and revolutionary social movements" (Moreno 2009: 173). After not being granted tenure, Chavarría founded *Hispanic Business* magazine in 1979. Scruggs left UCSB in 1969. His work on the Bracero Program was influential. The Bracero Program was a temporary-work program that lasted from 1942 to 1964. Enacted as an emergency wartime stopgap measure to help supply agribusiness with farm workers, it was repeatedly prolonged long after World War II ended in 1945. Braceros were often mistreated and blocked from organizing labor unions. Nevertheless, many resisted and tried to improve their wages and working conditions.

11. USCB bought the Francisco Torres Residence Hall in 2003. Its name has since been changed to Santa Catalina.

12. The Black Studies Department proposal came soon thereafter (Moreno 2009: 201).

13. De Necochea was also quite familiar with Peruvian student politics, having written a paper on the topic during his senior year at Dartmouth College (Moreno 2009: 172).

14. There is some discrepancy between Yolanda Márquez and Marisol Moreno's dissertations regarding the number of FTE in the Chicano Studies Department. The former states that there were 3.5 FTE in the 1970–1971 academic year, while the latter declares there were 3.0 FTE. All appointments were

joint, meaning faculty members divided their time equally between the Chicano Studies Department and another academic department.

15. Moreno (2009: 220) notes that members of the campus Chicana/o community would "advise" the chancellor in selecting the department's chairperson and curriculum.

16. See Casillas (1986). Panetta later became a member of Congress, eventually serving as CIA director and defense secretary under President Obama.

17. Casillas (1986).

18. For more on El Congreso's founding, see Y. Márquez (2007: 228–34).

19. The CCS's first director, Jesús Chavarría, resigned in June 1972. The CCS had no director from 1972 to 1975, although Associate Dean of Letters and Science Henry W. Offen served as its acting director during those three years. Fernando de Necochea was the CCS's associate director from 1970 to 1980 (Y. Márquez 2007: 84). Professor Luis Leal replaced him as acting director in 1981.

20. Those faculty members were Jesús Chavarría, Amado Padilla, Reyes Ramos, and Carlos Zamora.

21. Sprecher was a mathematics professor while Rickborn was a chemistry professor. CCS acting director Henry Offen was the latter's colleague in the Chemistry Department. The fact that so many faculty from the natural sciences oversaw the new CCS and Chicano Studies Department, which were entirely composed of faculty from the humanities and social sciences, surely complicated matters for both units in the 1970s.

22. Chela Sandoval was the first full-time faculty member of the Chicano Studies Department. She was hired in fall 1993.

23. For more on this department's history, see www.religion.ucsb.edu. The Religious Studies Department today has more than twenty-five full-time faculty, whereas the Chicana/o Studies Department has ten.

24. Talamantez was the first woman ever hired in the Chicano Studies Department (Y. Márquez 2007: 302).

25. The CCS, the Colección Tloque Nahuaque, Chicano EOP, and El Congreso all remained in El Centro. The former two moved out in the 1990s. The EOP left in the 2000s, moving to the new Student Resource Building (SRB) located near the Pardall Road tunnel. Some EOP counselors still meet with students at El Centro, but the building's first floor is largely a shared space between different campus entities, including El Congreso, the Department of Chicana and Chicano Studies, the Chicano Studies Institute, La Mesa Directiva, Students for Justice in Palestine, and several other organizations.

26. García served as chair from 1984 to 1988 and in 1989–1990. Lomelí served as chair in 1988–1989 while García was on leave. UC regulations stipulate chairs can serve no longer than five years. His first book, *Desert Immigrants: The Mexicans of El Paso, 1880–1920*, was published in 1981, and his second book, *Mexican Americans: Leadership, Ideology, and Identity, 1930–1960*, was released in 1989. García has published numerous other works over the past twenty-five years.

27. García FTE memo to Michaelsen, December 23, 1987, pg. 11.

28. Lomelí (2011) claimed that the iconic scholar Luis Leal first suggested creating a doctoral program in Chicano studies in 1981, several years before the 1987 FTE memo was written. Leal worked at UCSB from 1976 until 2006. He was 102 years old when he died in 2010. For more on Leal's life, see M. García (2000).

29. The class was offered once a week in Isla Vista Theater. The lectures were videotaped, but they apparently have not yet been archived in any university library collection. The tapes are apparently missing and have not been located as of this writing.

30. Acuña (1998: 124) claimed that "El Congreso students and my wife" urged him to apply for the UCSB position.

31. After the first and second editions of *Occupied America* (1972, 1981) were published, the text changed, with Acuña focusing more on gender, especially in the third and fourth editions (1988, 2000). The book is currently in its eighth edition (2014).

32. García and San Miguel Jr. did not vote on Acuña's case as both were on leave in 1990–1991. Faculty votes are confidential; only in the rarest circumstances, such as the Acuña lawsuit, are they made public.

33. The committee members were Robert Kelley (history), Giles Gunn (English), and Wallace Chafe (linguistics). Kelley served as chair (Acuña 1998: 131–32).

34. For more on Sprecher's views, see Acuña (1998: 187–89).

35. Acuña was offered a Step VI Full Professor position. Step VI is a highly coveted and prestigious step that requires a career review and substantive scholarly accomplishments. Some campus officials and faculty felt that Acuña's record did not merit him being hired at this level. While debatable, it bears mentioning that Professor Acuña had been working at CSUN, where teaching loads are noticeably higher than they are for UC faculty. Such requirements undoubtedly affect one's research "production rate." Nevertheless, Acuña had published several key books outside *Occupied America* and was possibly the field's most cited author.

36. Acuña defeated the UC system in his lawsuit in October 1995, receiving $326,000 that he used to create the Friends of Rudy Chicana/Chicano Studies Foundation (FCCSF). Initially focused on providing resources for those who pursued employment discrimination cases, it currently provides scholarships for students regardless of their immigration status. For more on FCCSF, see https://forchicanachicanostudies.wikispaces.com.

37. Rosalina Fregoso to UCSB Provost Llad Phillips, August 13, 1991, Alma Flores personal collection. Fregoso obtained a position at UC Davis.

38. Guadalupe San Miguel Jr. to Chairperson, Chicana/o Studies/Education, April 24, 1992, Alma Flores personal collection. San Miguel Jr. secured a position at the University of Houston.

39. The 4.25 FTE included Lomelí, Segura, García, San Miguel Jr., Broyles-González, Fregoso, Castañeda, Favela, and Vargas (who had a quarter-time appointment).

40. Lomelí was in Costa Rica as the director of the UC Education Abroad Program Study Center, while Castañeda had received a Ford Foundation Post-doctoral Fellowship and was in residence at Trinity University in Texas.

41. Yolanda Broyles-González to Llad Phillips, via Don Zimmerman, February 7, 1994, Alma Flores personal collection. Emphasis in the original.

42. Castañeda 1993; Rosalinda Fregoso to UCSB Provost Llad Phillips, August 13, 1991. Alma Flores personal collection.

43. The terms *national reality* and *engaged university* come from Salvadoran philosopher, intellectual, and liberation theologian Ignacio Ellacuría. Ellacuría was rector of the University of Central America (UCA), a private, Catholic-based university in San Salvador, during the country's brutal decade-long civil war in the 1980s. Ellacuría and his colleagues thought that universities should be engaged; that is, their mission should be to address and transform the national reality, which was marked by widespread poverty and violence. In other words, the UCA would take a preferential option for the poor, with all faculty and students working for social change. Given this orientation, Ellacuría was targeted as a subversive and he was assassinated, along with five other UCA professors, their housekeeper, and her daughter, on November 16, 1989. In the early 1990s, sociologists such as Drexel University's Douglas Porpora (1991) wrote about the UCA and "participatory research," which would have made oppressed peoples subjects, not objects, of study. While seemingly tenuous, it seems as if most Chicana/o students wanted more engaged Chicano studies departments in the early 1990s, which would address labor exploitation, sexism, heterosexism, racism, and so on. In 2006, UCLA Chicano studies

professor (and later chair) Reynaldo Macías and Kathy O'Byrne wrote about "engaging departments," but their chapter did not focus on the UCA model.

44. I am deliberately using the term *sanctuary* here, as the Central American sanctuary movement was formative for many in the 1980s. For two decades, the Chicano Studies Department was perceived as cold and uninviting, much like the wider society. El Congreso members hoped that the hunger strike would change that orientation, providing them with affirmation, safety, and new knowledge as they struggled to create a more just world.

45. Indeed, many El Congreso members from that era went on and became professors, teachers, lawyers, social workers, high school counselors, community organizers, mentors, parents, and so on. They are still engaged.

46. El Congreso, "Hunger Strike Declaration," April 27, 1994, UC Santa Barbara El Congreso Hunger Strike Collection, El Centro Arnulfo Casillas.

47. Ibid.

48. *Racial battle fatigue* and *microaggression* were not commonly used terms in the early 1990s, although they can be traced back to the early 1970s (Sue 2010). As Paulo Freire argued in *Pedagogy of the Oppressed* (2000), naming the world with a specific word can be empowering.

49. El Congreso, "Hunger Strike Declaration."

50. Some key EOP staff members from the 1970s, 80s, and 90s include Jeanette Padilla, Ozzie Espinoza, Pete Villareal, Harold Kennedy, Yolanda García, and Charlie García.

51. El Congreso, "Hunger Strike Declaration," April 27, 1994.

52. This quote is from Arnulfo Casillas and is displayed on a plaque outside El Centro.

53. El Congreso, "Hunger Strike Declaration," April 27, 1994.

54. Ibid.

55. Ibid.

56. The person not retained was Antonia Castañeda.

57. For more on the Community Service Organization in Ventura, see F. Barajas (2014).

58. Mancíllas was a UCLA professor and hunger striker (see chapter 3), and Trujillo was a long-time Santa Barbara community activist who had a close friendship with César Chávez and extensive ties with Casa de la Raza.

59. Yang's term actually began on July 1, 1994.

60. El Congreso Hunger Strike Files, El Centro Arnulfo Casillas.

61. As was described in chapter three, some UCLA hunger strikers were involved

in negotiations with campus officials, creating additional complexity and possibly forestalling a speedier resolution. The UCSB hunger strikers and students learned from these events and elected to have nonstriking students negotiate on their behalf.

62. The Multicultural Center emerged from the 1989 hunger strike.

63. González and Limón were also the only two hunger strikers who were not members of El Congreso.

64. Dr. José G. Limón-Olivares is currently a practicing pediatrician in Modesto, California.

65. Half-size sheet flyers, which listed all six demands in bullet-point fashion, were passed out during the strike. Lisa Valencia Sherratt personal collection.

66. This account comes from Naomi García's audiotaped journal, dated April 28, 1994. Included on this tape are reflections from Heather González, Claudia Leiva, and Naomi García.

67. Naomi García audio journal, April 28, 1994.

68. University of California, Faculty Legislature, Santa Barbara Division of the Academic Senate, Minutes, April 28, 1994, pg. 2. UCSB Academic Senate executive director Deborah Karoff provided me with this document.

69. See Heesun Wee, "9 Students Begin Fast in Protest at UCSB," *Santa Barbara News-Press*, April 29, 1994. Huerta was UCSB's affirmative action coordinator from 1974 to 2003. He was a lecturer for many years in the Chicano Studies Department, teaching classes on legal issues and civil rights. He also supported a campuswide ethnicity requirement that was established after students and faculty went on a hunger strike in 1989 (UCSB, California Multicultural and Ethnic Archives, 1989 Hunger Strike, box 3, folder 5).

70. Naomi García audio journal, April 28, 1994.

71. The sweat lodge was held in Santa Ynez. Not all hunger strikers and El Congreso student organizers attended, as some were too busy or had reservations about indigeneity (Muñoz 2011).

72. Based on privacy concerns, the names of those involved have been omitted. I should mention here that what took place was not categorically "proven," although many strikers and nonstrikers mentioned this incident during their oral history interviews. While indigenous danza groups have been liberating for many, they are not immune from dangerous practices such as sexual harassment and assault. Such activities have left some women deeply wounded. It bears mentioning here that DMC was heavily involved with the UCLA hunger strike, as its members both fasted and provided security (see chapter 3).

73. Naomi García audio journal, April 30, 1994.
74. Barajas had developed ties with some UCLA hunger strikers and DMC members while attending Oxnard College in spring 1993. He transferred to UCSB in fall 1993.
75. As a feminist historian, Naomi García clearly emphasized this point during her interview.
76. Naomi García audio journal, April 30, 1994.
77. Associated Students Commission on the Status of Women. May 3, 1994. Alma Flores personal collection.
78. The Alliance to Michael Young, May 5, 1994, Naomi García personal collection.
79. Gladys de Necochea is the niece of Fernando de Necochea, associate director for the CCS from 1970 to 1980.
80. Letter from Parents and Friends to Chancellor Uehling and Vice-chancellor Young, May 1, 1994, Alma Flores personal collection.
81. UCSB Medical Coordinator (name not legible) letter, May 3, 1994, Alma Flores Personal Collection.
82. "Hunger Strike Ends with Agreement and Breaking of Bread," *Santa Barbara Independent*, May 12, 1994.
83. Barajas was indirectly referring to the University of Colorado, Boulder, hunger strike and similar actions all over the country in 1994.
84. Donald W. Crawford, Executive Vice-chancellor to Academic Department Chairs, "Resolution of Hunger Strike: USCB Response to Demands of El Congreso," May 6, 1994, pg. 1. This document will be called "Hunger Strike Resolution" hereafter. On file with author.
85. "Hunger Strike Resolution," 2, 7–8.
86. Ibid., 6–7.
87. Ibid., 3–4.
88. Ibid., 4–6, 8.
89. "Hunger Strike Ends with Agreement and Breaking of Bread," *Santa Barbara Independent*, May 12, 1994.
90. The title of this subheading comes from a banner that stated, "Occupied America, Occupied UCSB," held by UCSB students during the November 16, 1994, Take Back Chicano Studies rally.
91. Don H. Zimmerman, Dean of Division of Social Sciences, College of Letters and Science, to Yolanda Broyles-González, Chair, Department of Chicano Studies, "Term Transfer of Faculty into the Department of Chicano Studies," May 17, 1994, El Congreso hunger strike files, El Centro Arnulfo Casillas.

Those five faculty were Manny Casas, Carl Gutiérrez-Jones, Juan-Vicente Palerm, Inés Talamantez, and Denise Segura.

92. Juan-Vicente Palerm, Inés Talamantez, J. Manuel Casas, Denise Segura, and Carl Gutiérrez-Jones to the Hunger Strikers and their Representatives, "Coalition Plan," May 5, 1994. Alma Flores personal collection.

93. Yolanda Broyles-González et al., to Chancellor Barbara Uehling, Executive Vice-chancellor Donald Crawford, May 2, 1994, Alma Flores personal collection. This letter also stated, "We come together at this time to express our great concern for the health of the students and express our support for the spirit of their demands. We understand that the students felt compelled to respond to a long history of institutional neglect and broken promises by engaging in a life-threatening hunger strike."

94. Yolanda Broyles-González et al. "Chicano Studies Department Response to May 17 Memo," 3. May 30, 1994.

95. Ibid., 4.

96. Ibid.

97. "Minority Report," May 30, 1994, Alma Flores personal collection (memo in author's possession).

98. Don Zimmerman to Yolanda Broyles-González, "Non-Reappointment," June 7, 1994, Alma Flores personal collection.

99. "Hunger Strike Resolution," 6.

100. El Congreso (signed by Abel Gutiérrez) to Executive Vice-chancellor Donald W. Crawford, "The Possible Term Transfers into the Department of Chicano Studies," June 8, 1994; El Congreso (signed by Abel Gutiérrez) to Executive Vice-chancellor Donald Crawford, "Threatened Removal of Dr. Yolanda Broyles-González as Chair of the Department of Chicano Studies," June 9, 1994; El Congreso (signed by Alma Flores) to J. Manuel Casas et al., "Your Memo of 6/15/1994," June 24, 1994, Alma Flores personal collection.

101. Antonia Castañeda, Ramón Favela, and Chela Sandoval to Don Zimmerman, June 9, 1994, Alma Flores personal collection.

102. Antonia Castañeda to Chancellor-Elect Henry Yang and Executive Vice-Chancellor Donald H. Crawford. June 24, 1994, Alma Flores Personal Collection.

103. Ibid. Emphasis added.

104. Broyles-González later successfully sued the University of California, challenging the unequal pay of women and minority faculty. She received $100,000 in damages and attorney fees when the case was settled in October 1997. She

was later honored by President Clinton on the thirty-fifth anniversary of the signing of the Equal Pay Act in June 1998. Broyles-González left UCSB in 2004. She currently is Distinguished Professor of Ethnic Studies at Kansas State University (https://www.k-state.edu/ameth/faculty/core-faculty/broyle sgonzalez.html).

105. Castañeda to Yang and Crawford, June 24, 1994.

106. "Report from the Executive Vice-chancellor on Chicano Studies at UCSB," August 24, 1994, Alma Flores personal collection. The title of this document makes it appear as if the hunger strikers were concerned only about Chicano Studies when they had much broader objectives.

107. "Report from the Executive Vice-chancellor on Chicano Studies," August 24, 1994, pg. 1.

108. Ibid., 3.

109. Yolanda Broyles-González et al. to Henry T. Yang, Chancellor, and Donald Crawford, Executive Vice-Chancellor, "Chairship Options," July 5, 1994, Alma Flores personal collection. Castañeda sent a separate, longer letter to Yang and Crawford on this issue on July 19, 1994.

110. Yolanda Broyles-González et al. to Provost Gretchen Bataille, College of Letters and Sciences, "Department of Chicano Studies," October 17, 1994, pg. 5, Alma Flores personal collection. Sandoval was in her second year on campus in fall 1994; it was Pérez-Torres's first. Appointing such "young" faculty was not without precedent; Assistant Professor Jon Cruz was named acting chair of the Asian American Studies Department in the 1990s (ibid., 5).

111. I have been unable to locate this specific memo from Provost Bataille. The previous two administrative chairs of the department were Bruce Rickborn and David Sprecher (both served in the 1970s).

112. El Congreso, "Threatened Removal of Dr. Broyles-González as Chair."

113. These flyers appeared in two newspaper articles—Wallace (1994) and Valles (1994).

114. Héctor González's piece (undated, citation unclear, on file with author), "Latino Activist Honored at College," did emphasize that he was at UCSB to "attend a demonstration where students were protesting the hiring of a Caucasian professor to head that school's Chicano Studies Department."

115. Pepe Urquijo is currently working on a documentary film about Gómez Jr.'s life.

116. Don Zimmerman, Acting Chair, to Chicano Studies Faculty, "Department Chair," December 7, 1994, Alma Flores personal collection.

117. Don H. Zimmerman, Social Sciences Division Dean, to Chicano Studies Department Faculty, Memo on "Department Chair," n.d., El Congreso Hunger Strike files, El Centro Arnulfo Casillas.

118. Deena González to Yolanda Broyles-González, June 8, 1996, Alma Flores personal collection.

119. While faculty can offer suggestions for departmental chairpersons, social science deans (at UCSB) make the ultimate decision regarding who will be offered this position. Departmental autonomy, therefore, is limited, even though UC often emphasizes the fact that it operates on the basis of what is called "shared governance."

120. Donald Crawford, "Summary of UCSB Actions to Implement Hunger Strike Agreement," July 24, 1996, El Congreso files.

121. Ibid. El Centro was spared because of budget cuts, but El Congreso members worried that it could be destroyed when funding was secured for the library's expansion. Thus the fact that it remained standing was seen as a victory.

122. See www.chicst.ucsb.edu/graduate/student-community for more on the department's graduate program.

123. The UC Regents implemented the comprehensive review process in fall 2002. It has sparked considerable debate and controversy, with conservatives claiming that it constitutes disguised affirmative action.

124. For more on Hispanic Serving Institutions, see www.hacu.net/hacu/HSI_Fact _Sheet.asp.

125. See www.research.ucsb.edu/ccs/activity.htm#Grads for more on these activities.

126. For more on conviviality from a radical perspective, see Callahan (2012).

127. No faculty member in the Chicana/o Studies Department had risen from associate to full professor in more than twenty years until Professor Gerardo Aldana achieved that distinction in 2013.

128. It bears mentioning here that Michel, Palerm, and Segura were not full-time faculty in the Chicana and Chicano Studies Department. They worked in the Departments of Black Studies, Anthropology, and Sociology, respectively. Because departmental norms stipulate that department chairs should be full professors, it was nearly impossible between 1998 and 2013 to nominate someone from inside the department to fill that position. Sandoval served as department chair, however, as an associate professor in the mid-2000s for several years.

129. Of course, these views are not widely shared, but the department has been "branded" over time—sometimes rather unfairly—as troubled. These troubles

are long-standing, but it still is a space that consistently challenges the status quo and is invigorating and uplifting. It is a complicated and contested site that has transformed many people's lives, both on and off campus. After nearly fifty years, it is still not fully integrated into the university. Given its origins and ethos, perhaps it may never be.

CHAPTER 5

Chapter title: This quote comes from Stanford undergraduate student Tamara Alvarado (2012) who called her mother on May 4, 1994, at 5 a.m. to explain to her why she was going on hunger strike.

1. For more on this mural and other Casa Zapata murals, see www.stanforddaily .com/2012/05/02/murals-mirror-movements.

2. In the early 1990s, a whistle-blower working for the U.S. Navy (Paul Biddle) claimed that Stanford excessively billed the federal government for indirect costs on numerous research projects. Funds from Washington, DC, were reportedly spent on luxury items, such as expensive linen, silverware, and a yacht. Stanford disputed those assertions and settled with the government for $1.2 million, a far cry from the $200 million that the university over-billed the government for. Based on terms of the settlement, Stanford paid a fine, but accepted no responsibility for the scandal. These events forced Stanford president Donald Kennedy to resign in 1992 (Folkenflik 1994). Stanford's funds from government research grants were subsequently sharply cut back, giving rise to budget austerity and concerns that programs for students of color would be cut or eliminated in the early 1990s.

3. The phrase "image is everything" comes from tennis star Andre Agassi's Canon commercials from late 1980s and early 1990s.

4. Given residential segregation in EPA for decades, the city was predominantly white until the 1950s, when restrictions eased. As redlining receded, EPA became majority black in the 1960s. In 1990, 50 percent of EPA residents were African American, but today that number has dropped to less than 25 percent (Camarillo 2009). More than 60 percent of its population is currently Latina/o.

5. The only demand not met was the dismissal of Vice-provost of Minority Affairs Robert Rosenzweig, who the BSU wanted to be replaced with a full-time black administrator selected with its approval (Lyman 2011: 78).

6. Only two black students attended Stanford in the 1940s, and very few gradu-ated before that. The university's first black student, Ernest Johnson, gradu-ated with the inaugural class in 1895.

7. While data exist for black student enrollment between 1960 and 1967, it was not collected during that time for Mexican American, Native American, and Asian American students. It is not clear when the first students from these communities graduated from Stanford. Very few students of color attended Stanford before the 1960s.

8. Professor Rosaldo (anthropology) taught at Stanford from 1970 to 2003. He currently teaches at New York University. Professor Islas (English) was on the Stanford faculty from 1971 until he died in 1991.

9. Indeed, on April 1, 1994, shortly after learning that Cecilia Burciaga had been fired, approximately twenty-five protestors greeted prospective graduate stu-dents with signs saying, "There are fewer minority grad students now than in 1974," and "We need you now more than ever!" Burciaga played a crucial role in expanding the number of graduate students of color when she served as associate dean of graduate studies in the middle and late 1980s.

10. Casa Zapata and El Centro Chicano were established after Chicana/o stu-dent protests in the 1970s. For more on Casa Zapata and its history, see www .stanford.edu/dept/rde/cgi-bin/drupal/housing/node/675.

11. Alma Medina (2012) stated that El Centro Chicano was overrun with "cats and fleas" in the early 1990s.

12. See Mt. García (2012), Perlstein (2014), and Rosenfeld (2012) for more on Reagan.

13. For more on the Ross "affair," see Mohr (1970).

14. The Stanford antiapartheid movement actually emerged in the mid-1970s (Phillips 1990).

15. Jackson came in third place during that year's Democratic Party primaries, finishing behind Gary Hart (second) and Walter Mondale (first). Mondale lost to Reagan in a landslide in November 1984.

16. Pratt (1990: 8) notes that Columbia University was the first campus to intro-duce a class on Western civilization in 1919. Stanford adopted its own Western civilization course in 1935, and it was abolished in 1970. It was reintroduced as a yearlong course on Western culture, which was required of all new students, in 1980 (Pratt 1990: 11). Concerns about the fragmentation and dissolution of the United States were infamously articulated in Harvard University political science professor Samuel Huntington's controversial 2004 book *Who Are We?*

17. Students United for Democracy in Education mostly included progressive white students (male and female).
18. Kemp was BSU's chair in 1986–1987.
19. Dr. Loco is Professor José B. Cuellar, professor of Raza Studies at CSU San Francisco. For more on the band, see www.drloco.com.
20. Thiel co-founded the *Stanford Review* with Norman Book in 1987. He graduated from Stanford with a BA in philosophy in 1989 and received his JD from Stanford in 1992. Thiel coauthored (with David O. Sacks, who also worked at the *Review* and later PayPal) a book lambasting multiculturalism at Stanford titled *The Diversity Myth* (1996). He was also one of former Education Secretary William Bennett's speechwriters. Thiel gave Ron Paul's presidential campaign more than $2 million in 2012. The libertarian billionaire is a critical Republican Party funder, who supported Donald Trump's presidential campaign.
21. This protest took place during a statewide conference called Taking Action for Our Future held at White Plaza (Phillips 1990: 62). California Republican governor George Deukmejian called the protestors "whiners and complainers" for pressing for the restoration of budget cuts that he had proposed in education. The California legislature did, in fact, overturn those cuts. Michael Dukakis, incidentally, narrowly defeated Jesse Jackson for the 1988 Democratic Party presidential nomination. George Bush Sr. later edged Dukakis for president.
22. Shultz served as secretary of state in the Reagan administration from 1982 to 1989. He strongly championed U.S. support for the Contras, who received millions of dollars in assistance to topple the socialist Sandinista government in Nicaragua that came to power in 1979. "Just say no" was the motto of First Lady Nancy Reagan's antidrug campaign in the 1980s. Shultz is currently a distinguished fellow with the Hoover Institution at Stanford.
23. As Lindenberger (1990) notes, in 1980, because of previous opposition, Stanford changed the name of its Western Civilization course to Western Culture. Student groups opposed the adjective "Western" on the grounds that it excluded the majority of the world's peoples, especially people of color. After their criticisms and activism, the Western Culture course was scrapped and replaced with Cultures, Ideas, and Values (CIV). Some questioned this move on the grounds that it seemed to closely related to the old Western "Civ" class.
24. For more on freedom of speech and fighting words, see Matsuda (1993).
25. Medina (2012) claimed that the *Stanford Review* deliberately overemphasized

this controversy to weaken MEChA. It should be noted here that the *Stanford Daily* ran three articles on the Liga in May 1990, so the attacks were not just part of a vast "right-wing conspiracy." That said, the *Review* consistently criticized MEChA, especially after the 1994 hunger strike.

26. Upon returning to Stanford, Medina worked carefully with Eva Silva, Jorge Solis, Gabi Cervantes, and others to strengthen and rebuild MEChA.

27. Disagreement between the hunger strikers and student organizers exists on this point. Some remembered having discussions with several faculty before the strike, while others do not.

28. Elvira Prieto. 1998. "Project Proposal/Reflection." Class paper, Harvard Graduate School of Education Seminar, 1998 (unpublished, in author's possession).

29. When Stanford president Gerhard Casper and provost Condoleezza Rice came into office in 1992 they inherited a $45 million budget deficit. They cut $25 million in 1992–1993 and $20 million in 1993–1994 (Casper 2013). This shortfall came directly from the financial scandal involving indirect costs, which reduced Stanford's overall budget (see note 2).

30. Several people stated that Rice's rapid ascension up the Stanford administrative ladder was problematic, if not highly questionable, because of her thin publication record (she had only one single-authored book and one co-edited book under her belt when was she became the youngest provost in Stanford's history).

31. See UCMI (1989: 198–99, 206–7) for more on the Stanford ethnic student centers.

32. In an interview with the *San Jose Mercury News*, Cecilia Burciaga spoke about this matter: "I saw the budget situation coming and as a team player, I did send that message. I heard nothing more about it until they told me my job was being eliminated and they didn't see anything else for me to do" (Rae-Dupree 1994). Burciaga thought Stanford would find her another position within the administration should hers be terminated. Obviously, this did not happen.

33. The university never, technically speaking, hired Tony Burciaga as an RF, although he was hired to teach classes on muralism, which he routinely did in the 1980s and 90s.

34. The faculty were Rudy Busto, Albert Camarillo, Luis Fraga, James Leckie, Gerald López, Yvonne Maldonado, Miguel Méndez, Fernando Mendoza, Amado Padilla, Jerry Porras, William Rhine, Lora Romero, Renato Rosaldo,

Ramón Saldívar, Guadalupe Váldes, and Yvonne Yabaro-Bejarano. See Busto et al. (1994a).

35. As González Luna (2013a) said, "I didn't call myself *Julia* until I got to Stanford because in Burbank I was *Julie*—you know? I remember Eva yelling at me, saying, 'pronounce your name right!' I was like, 'You don't get to tell me how to say my name; it's my name.' So I started to develop my own way to protect myself from some white people and some Mexicans. I just didn't fit into the 'Mexican no matter what' or 'white-washed' camp."

36. Chávez stated, "A hunger strike is an act of protest directed against an opponent. A fast is first an internal spiritual act and is not intended as a weapon against anyone" (M. García 2007: 110). By this definition, the Stanford students were on a hunger strike since their action targeted two opponents, Rice and Casper.

37. The UFW released a similar film, titled *The Wrath of Grapes*, in 1986.

38. The *Stanford Campus Report* is the university's official news outlet. It was published once a week in the 1990s, but has since gone daily and is distributed only online. The *Stanford Daily* is the campus student newspaper.

39. MEChA co-chair Gabi Cervantes stated the decision to go on strike was "already made" before Flicks (Berselli 1994), whereas first-year law student and hunger strike negotiator Alma Medina (2013) said that the decision to hold the strike came after the movie incident. Conflicting accounts may stem from the fact that the situation was very fluid in late April and early May 1994.

40. See Busto et al. (1994b).

41. For more on the UFW's grape boycott in the 1980s, see Pérez and Parlee (2014) and Shaw (2008).

42. This task force had been established in February 1994, before Burciaga had been fired. During the strike's first day, when Rice said that she was surprised by the action, Medina said that the "task force is still meeting and preparing to meet with her and the strike is a separate process" (Dworkin 1994).

43. Conservative writers have long bemoaned what they call "the culture of victimhood." For two examples—twenty years apart—see Sykes (1992) and Bawer (2012).

44. Leland Stanford, of course, was the co-founder of the powerful Central Pacific Railroad Company, which made him incredibly wealthy in the late nineteenth century. The company relied on cheap, nonunionized Chinese (and later Japanese) workers to construct the transcontinental railroad that connected the

nation's east and west coasts (Takaki 1989: 84–85). Had it not been for Asian labor, Stanford University might not have ever been established; thus, from far being niche, Asian Americans are an integral part of the campus's past and present.

45. Fourteen universities, including USC, Caltech, and Stanford, opposed WASC's new guidelines, which 122 other colleges approved in February 1993. Conservative writers such as George Will (1994) praised Casper for his "heroic" stand against WASC, affirmative action, and excessive governmental intrusion.

46. Cecilia Burciaga participated in a Stanford University 1991 WASC Accreditation Self-Study. The entire report can be found at https://wascdev.stanford .edu/files/wasc1991Accreditation/1991WASC_intro.pdf.

47. Eagle feathers have long been considered sacred for many Native Americans. To be awarded an eagle feather is a rare honor, bestowed, some believe, from the Creator who made the eagle "master of the sky."

48. Because it could not be scientifically "proven" that pesticides were causing birth defects and other health-related issues, Fraga's committee did not recommend that Stanford completely eliminate grapes. I could not find any information regarding why the community center was never established. In her memoir, Rice (2010: 276–81) discusses, however, how she and others helped create the Center for a New Generation to improve local public schools and graduation rates in 1992 in EPA. Rice's account implies this center obviated the need for another community center, which the hunger strikers saw as an organizing or "radical" space (Alvarado 2012).

49. In 2012, the CSRE sponsored a series called #OccupyArt. It included a panel discussion on the history of Stanford occupations from the 1980s to 2010s. Hunger striker Elvira Prieto was one of the invited speakers.

50. See the Center's fall 2014 newsletter (http://ccsre.stanford.edu/sites/default /files/images/ccsre-2014-web-best.pdf) for more on these and other current developments. José David Saldívar and Ramón Saldívar are brothers. Sociology professor Tomás Jimenez is the Center's current director.

51. See Stanford's piece on Burciaga at http://news.stanford.edu/news/2013 /april/cecilia-burciaga-services-040213.html.

52. Long-time social justice activist Tom Hayden uttered the phrase "slowing down the machine of destruction" during the Battle in Seattle that shut down the World Trade Organization in November 1999.

CHAPTER 6

1. See https://www.marxists.org/archive/guevara/1967/04/16.htm for the complete speech. For more on the "Message" and its radical, anti-imperialist politics, see R. Young (2003).

2. A long debate has existed within Marxist theory around "permanent revolution" versus "socialism in one country." Trotsky has been credited with the former, while Stalin embraced the latter. Widespread disagreement exists over this neat distinction, with some claiming that Lenin, Marx, and Engels (along with other Marxist theorists in the late nineteenth and early twentieth centuries) sometimes embraced one position only to change their views over time.

3. For more on this strike, see Kriho (2014).

4. Letter from the Alliance to UCSB Vice-chancellor for Student Affairs Michael Young, May 5, 1994, Naomi García personal collection.

5. Both resolutions (banning affirmative action in admissions, contracting, and hiring) passed 14–10.

6. Before becoming involved in the UC Irvine hunger strike, Cervantes was an undergraduate student at Occidental College in Los Angeles. He became very involved in the movement against Proposition 187, along with César A. Cruz. Some activists within this movement, including Cervantes, later joined the Four Winds Movement. Four Winds was a "Marxist, internationalist, multiracial organization" that MEChA opposed, feeling that it might be another "Liga" (Cervantes 2012). Cervantes, Cruz, and five other students (some of whom were still in high school) went on a three-day fast on Olvera Street in February 1995 to protest Proposition 187 and Wilson's plans to abolish affirmative action (M. Martínez 1995). The UC Irvine hunger strike, therefore, can be traced back to racist attacks on immigration and the broader "war" on people of color that emerged in the 1980s and 90s. When the strike began, Cervantes was actually a history graduate student at the Claremont Colleges, located just outside Los Angeles.

7. Critiquing Martin Luther King's notion of "redemptive suffering," Stokley Carmichael famously stated, "He made one fallacious assumption: In order for nonviolence to work, your opponent has to have a conscience. The United States has no conscience" (cited in Olsson 2011). For nonviolence to be effective, your opponent must have a "heart."

8. The strike lasted fifteen days, from October 17 to November 1, 1995. Just three regents (Ralph Carmona, Judith Levin, and Student Regent Ed Gómez) favored a new vote on affirmative action.

9. One of those students is CSU Channel Islands Chicana/o Studies professor Jennie Luna. Luna was one of the main organizers of the Berkeley hunger strike and movement to "save" ethnic studies at Berkeley.

10. Harrington (2012) repeatedly recognized Professor Luna's critical role and her own as a white ally in a multiracial movement. On another note, much was made about Pulido (an openly identified Latina lesbian) since her involvement symbolically resurrected the alliance between the twLFs that existed at SF State and UC Berkeley in 1969 (Ferreira 2003).

11. 1999 UC Berkeley hunger strike files, box 10, folder 2.

12. Southside Presbyterian Church was one of the first churches to become involved in the Sanctuary Movement in the early 1980s (Bibler-Coutin 1993; Nepstad 2004). It is currently involved in the "new" Sanctuary Movement. For more on this movement, see http://thinkprogress.org/immigration/2014/08/06/3468449/new-sanctuary-movement/.

13. This subheading is a play on Fyodor Dostoevsky's 1877 short story, "The Dream of a Ridiculous Man" and Jack Johnson's song "Upside Down" (Bushfire 2006).

14. This line is partially lifted from the title track of Bruce Springsteen's 1995 album, *The Ghost of Tom Joad* (Columbia). Rage Against the Machine covered the song for their 1997 video, *Rage Against the Machine* (Sony), and album, *Renegades* (Epic).

15. This line is a reference to Mario Savio's December 2, 1964, speech at UC Berkeley and Tom Hayden's speech at the anti-World Trade Organization demonstrations in Seattle, Washington, in December 1999.

16. Hockaday is not as well known as Brown or Garner. For more on the circumstances surrounding her death at the hands of a Latino Oxnard police officer, see www.vcstar.com/news/local-news/oxnard/march-mourns-woman-shot-by-officer_63594860.

17. See http://cril.mitotedigital.org/coyuntura for more on conjunctural analysis. I am indebted to former UCSB Chicana/o Studies Department lecturer Manolo Callahan for making me aware of this perspective.

18. When this movement first emerged is an open question, but "third world countries" in Latin America, Asia, and Africa resisted globalization, structural adjustment policies, and neoliberalism as early as the 1970s (N. Klein 1999).

Thus, what happened in Chiapas in 1994 was critical, but it, too, was part of a larger and much longer movement for social justice that can be traced back five hundred years (Maldonado-Torres 2008).

19. DREAMers are undocumented students pushing for the passage of the federal DREAM (Development Relief and Education Act for Alien Minors) Act, which would provide them with citizenship. Since it was first introduced in 2001, students have organized numerous demonstrations, protests, and hunger strikes, but so far they have been unsuccessful. For more on this movement, see Nicholls (2013). See also Matthew 14:13–21 for more on Jesus and the feeding of the five thousand. The parable is also included in the Gospels of Luke, Mark, and John.

20. See "Socialism and Man" (Guevara 1987).

WORKS CITED

PUBLISHED WORKS (BOOKS, ARTICLES, FILMS)

Abbas, Fatin. 2011. "Year of the Boomerang? Frantz Fanon and the Arab Uprisings." *50.50*, April 11. https://www.opendemocracy.net/5050/fatin-abbas/year-of-boomerang-frantz-fanon-and-arab-uprisings.

Abdullah, Melina, and Regina Freer. 2010. "Bass to Bass: Relative Freedom and Womanist Leadership in Black Los Angeles." In *Black Los Angeles: American Dreams and Racial Realities*, edited by Darnell Hunt and Ana-Christina Ramón, 323–42. New York: New York University Press.

Acuña, Rodolfo F. 1972. *Occupied America*. San Francisco: Canfield Press.

———. 1996. *Anything But Mexican: Chicanos in Contemporary Los Angeles*. London: Verso.

———. 1998. *Sometimes There Is No Other Side*. Notre Dame, IN: University of Notre Dame Press.

———. 2011. *The Making of Chicana/o Studies: In the Trenches of Academe*. New Brunswick, NJ: Rutgers University Press.

Agamben, Giorgio. 1998. *Homo Sacer: Sovereign Power and Bare Life*. Stanford: Stanford University Press.

Ahmad, Muneer. 2011. "Resisting Guantánamo: Rights at the Brink of Dehumanization." *Northwestern University School of Law* 103 (4): 1684–762.

Alegría, Andres. 2011. *COINTELPRO 101*. Oakland: PM Press.

Alexander, Michelle. 2010. *The New Jim Crow: Mass Incarceration in the Age of Color-Blindness*. New York: New Press.

Almaguer, Tomás. 1984. "Racial Domination and Capitalist Agriculture: The Oxnard Sugar Beet Workers' Strike of 1903." *Labor History* 25 (3): 325–50.

Almeida, Paul. 2008. *Waves of Protest: Popular Struggle in El Salvador, 1925–2005*. Minneapolis: University of Minnesota Press.

Almeida, Paul, and Linda Brewster Stearns. 1998. "Political Opportunities and Local Grassroots Environmental Movements: The Case of Minamata." *Social Problems* 48 (1): 37–60.

Alter, Joseph S. 2000. *Gandhi's Body: Sex, Diet, and the Politics of Nationhood*. Philadelphia: University of Pennsylvania Press.

Althaus-Reid, Marcella. 2000. *Indecent Theology: Theological Perversions of Sex, Gender, and Politics*. New York: Routledge.

Alvarez, Luis. 2008. *The Power of the Zoot: Youth Culture and Resistance During World War II*. Berkeley: University of California Press.

Anand, Prerna. 2012. "Winners and Losers: Corrections and Higher Education in California." United States Common Sense. September 5. http://cacs.org/research/winners-and-losers-corrections-and-higher-education-in-california. Mountain View: California Common Sense.

Anaya, Rodolfo, and Francisco Lomelí, eds. 1989. *Aztlán: Essays on the Chicano Homeland*. Albuquerque: University of New Mexico Press.

Anderson, Jon. 1997. *Che Guevara: A Revolutionary Life*. New York: Grove.

Anderson, Patrick. 2004. "To Lie Down to Death for Days: The Turkish Hunger Strike, 2000–2003." *Cultural Studies* 18 (6): 816–46.

———. 2009. "There Will be No Bobby Sands in Guantanamo Bay." *MLA* 124 (5): 1729–36.

———. 2010. *So Much Wasted: Hunger, Performance, and the Morbidity of Resistance*. Durham, NC: Duke University Press.

Anima, Tina. 1990a. "Chicano Studies May Be in Danger." *Daily Bruin*, April 25.

———. 1990b. "Students Crowd Murphy Offices." *Daily Bruin*, April 26.

———. 1990c. "Young Against Establishment of Department." *Daily Bruin*, May 11.

———. 1990d. "Funding for L&S Major Granted by Committee." *Daily Bruin*, May 22.

———. 1990e. "MEChA Meeting with Vice Chancellor Called a 'Waste of Time.'" *Daily Bruin*, May 16.

———. 1990f. "Students Rally at Chancellor's House." *Daily Bruin*, June 1.

———. 1990g. "Committee Agrees Chicano Studies Needs a Department." *Daily Bruin*, June 7.

———. 1990h. "Conference Centers on Future of Chicano Studies." *Daily Bruin*, November 19.

Anzaldúa, Gloria. 1987. *Borderlands/La Frontera*. San Francisco: Aunt Lute.

———. 2009. *The Gloria Anzaldúa Reader*. Durham, NC: Duke University Press.

Aquino, María Pilar. 1993. *Our Cry for Life: Feminist Theology from Latin America*. Maryknoll, NY: Orbis.

Armbruster-Sandoval, Ralph. 2011. "The Life of the Party: Alice McGrath, Multiracial Coalitions, and the Struggle for Social Justice." *Aztlan* 36 (1): 69–98.

Arrendondo, Gabriela F., Aída Hurtado, Norma Klahn, Olga Najera-Ramirez, and Patricia Zavella, eds. 2003. *Chicana Femimisms: A Critical Reader*. Durham, NC: Duke University Press.

Avila, Eric. 2004. *Popular Culture in the Age of White Flight: Fear and Fantasy in Suburban Los Angeles*. Berkeley: University of California Press.

Bachman, Rebecca. 2009. "Fighting and Fasting at UCSB." *Santa Barbara Independent*, December 8. www.independent.com/news/2009/dec/08/fighting-and-fasting-ucsb.

Bacon, David. 2004. *Children of NAFTA: Labor Wars on the U.S.–Mexico Border*. Berkeley: University of California Press.

———. 2008. *Illegal People: How Globalization Creates Migration and Criminalizes Immigrants*. Boston: Beacon.

Bailey, Eric. 1995. "Hunger Strikers Rally in Capitol." *Los Angeles Times*, November 1.

Balderrama, Francisco, and Raymond Rodríguez. 2006. *Decade of Betrayal: Mexican Repatriation in the 1930s*. Albuquerque: University of New Mexico Press.

Banerjee, Sikata. 2012. *Muscular Nationalism: Gender, Violence, and Empire in India and Ireland, 1914–2004*. New York: New York University Press.

Barajas, Frank. 2006. "The Defense Committees of Sleepy Lagoon: A Convergent Struggle Against Fascism, 1942–1944." *Aztlan* 31 (1): 33–62.

———. 2014. "Community and Measured Militancy: The Ventura County Community Service Organization, 1958–1968." *Southern California Quarterly* 96 (3): 313–49.

Bardacke, Frank. 1993. "Cesar's Ghost: The Rise and Fall of the UFW." *The Nation*, July 26: 130–34.

———. 2011. *Trampling Out the Vintage: César Chávez and the Two Souls of the United Farm Workers*. London: Verso.

Barry, Tom. 1995. *Zapata's Revenge: Free Trade and the Farm Crisis in Mexico*. Boston: South End.

Bartindale, Becky. 1994. "Stanford President Blasts Red Tape." *San Jose Mercury News*, May 13.

Bawer, Bruce. 2012. *The Victims Revolution: The Rise of Identity Studies and the Closing of the Liberal Mind*. New York: Broadside.

Bell, Rudolph. 1987. *Holy Anorexia*. Chicago: University of Chicago Press.

Belli, Gioconda. 1978. *Linea de Fuego*. La Habana: Casa de las Américas.

Bello, Walden. 1994. *Dark Victory: The United States and Global Poverty*. San Francisco: Food First.

Bender, Steven W. 2008. *One Night in America: Robert Kennedy, Cesar Chavez, and the Dream of Dignity*. Boulder, CO: Paradigm.

Benford, Robert, and David Snow. 2000. "Framing Processes and Social Movements: An Overview and Assessment." *Annual Review of Sociology* 26: 611–39.

Bennett, William. 1988. "Why the West?" *National Review*, May 27.

Beresford, David. 1987. *Ten Men Dead: The Story of the 1981 Irish Hunger Strike*. New York: Atlantic Monthly.

Bernstein, Shana. 2011. *Bridges of Reform: Interracial Civil Rights Activism in Twentieth Century Los Angeles*. New York: Oxford University Press.

Berryman, Phillip. 1987. *Liberation Theology*. Philadelphia: Temple University Press.

Berselli, Beth. 1994. "Long History of Frustration Motivates Students to Strike." *Stanford Daily*, May 5.

Berta-Ávila, Margarita, Anita Tijerina Revilla, and Julie López Figueroa. 2011. *Marching Students: Chicana and Chicano Student Activism in Education, 1968 to the Present*. Reno: University of Nevada Press.

Bibler-Coutin, Susan. 1993. *The Cultures of Protest: Religious Activism and the U.S. Sanctuary Movement*. Boulder, CO: Westview.

Biggs, Michael. 2004a. "When Costs Are Beneficial: Protest as Communicative Suffering." Sociology Working Papers. Paper Number 2003-04. Department of Sociology, Oxford University. www.sociology.ox.ac.uk/materials/papers/2003-04 .pdf.

———. 2004b. "Hunger Strikes by Irish Republicans, 1916–1923." Paper Prepared for Workshop on Techniques of Violence in Civil War, Center for the Study of Civil War, Oslo.

———. 2005. "Dying Without Killing: Self-Immolations, 1963–2002." In *Making Sense of Suicide Missions*, edited by Diego Gambetta. Oxford: Oxford University Press.

————. 2013. "How Repertories Evolve: The Diffusion of Suicide Protest in the 20th Century." *Mobilization* 18 (4): 407–28.

Binford, Leigh. 1996. *The El Mozote Massacre: Anthropology and Human Rights.* Tucson: University of Arizona Press.

Biondi, Martha. 2012. *The Black Revolution on Campus.* Berkeley: University of California Press.

Biskind, Peter, Stephen Hornick, and John Manning. 1970. *Don't Bank on Amerika.* Cinecong Films. VHS tape.

Blackwell, Maylei. 2011. *Chicana Power! Contested Histories of Feminism in the Chicano Movement.* Austin: University of Texas Press.

Blake, Renee. 1994. "Kwong's Letter Lacks Knowledge, Awareness, Tolerance." *Stanford Daily,* May 11.

Block, Fred, Richard Cloward, Barbara Ehrenreich, and Frances Fox Piven. 1987. *The Mean Season: The Attack on the Welfare State.* New York: Pantheon.

Bloom, Alan. 1987. *The Closing of the American Mind.* New York: Simon and Schuster.

Bluestone, Barry, and Bennett Harrison. 1982. *Deindustrialization of America: Plant Closings, Community Abandonment, and the Dismantling of Basic Industry.* New York: Basic.

————. 1988. *The Great U-Turn: Corporate Restructuring and the Polarizing of America.* Boston: Basic.

Blum, Edward J., and Paul Harvey. 2012. *The Color of Christ: The Son of God and the Saga of Race in America.* Chapel Hill: University of North Carolina Press.

Bochner, Hart. 1994. *PCU.* Los Angeles: 20th Century Fox. DVD.

Bonacich, Edna, Lucie Cheng, Norma Chinchilla, Nora Hamilton, and Paul Ong. 1994. *Global Production: The Apparel Industry in the Pacific Rim.* Philadelphia: Temple University Press.

Bonilla-Silva, Eduardo. 2003. *Racism Without Racists: Color-Blind Racism and the Persistence of Racial Inequality in the United States.* Lanham, MD: Rowman and Littlefield.

Borg, Marcus, and John Dominic Crossan. 2006. *The Last Week: What the Gospels Really Teach About Jesus' Final Days in Jerusalem.* New York: Harper One.

Bourgeault, Cynthia. 2008. *Wisdom Jesus: Transforming Heart and Mind—A New Perspective on Christ and His Message.* Boston: Shambala.

Bourgeois, Roy. 2013. *My Journey from Silence to Solidarity.* Yellow Springs, OH: fxBear.

Boyarsky, Bill. 1993. "UCLA Strike Grew from Deep Historical Roots." *Los Angeles Times,* June 9.

Brockman, James. 2005. *Romero: A Life.* Maryknoll, NY: Orbis.

Brown, Elaine. 1993. *A Taste of Power: A Black Woman's Story*. New York: Anchor.

Brown, Michael, Martin Carnoy, Elliot Currie, Troy Duster, David Oppenheimer, Marjorie Schultz, and David Wellman, eds. 2003. *Whitewashing the Race: The Myth of a Color-Blind Society*. Berkeley: University of California Press.

Brown, Robert McAfee. 1984. *Unexpected News: Reading the Bible with Third World Eyes*. Louisville, KY: WJK.

Brown, Scott. 2003. *Fighting for Us: Maulana Karenga, the US Organization, and Black Cultural Nationalism*. New York: New York University Press.

Broyles-González, Yolanda. 1994. *El Teatro Campesino: Theater in the Chicano Movement*. Austin: University of Texas Press.

Brueggemann, Walter. 2001. *The Prophetic Imagination*. Philadelphia: Fortress.

Brumberg, Joan J. 2000. *Fasting Girls: The History of Anorexia Nervosa*. New York: Vintage.

Buchanan, Pat. 2002. *The Death of the West: How Dying Populations and Immigrant Invasions Imperil Our Country and Civilization*. New York: St. Martin's.

Buhle, Paul. 1999. *Taking Care of Business: Samuel Gompers, George Meany, Lane Kirkland and the Tragedy of American Labor*. New York: Monthly Review.

Bunzel, John H. 1992. *Race Relations on Campus: Stanford Students Speak Out*. Stanford, CA: Stanford Alumni Association.

Burciaga, José Antonio. 1994. "Burciaga Explains Zapata Incident, Is Unsure of Charges." *Stanford Daily*, May 12.

Burns, Melinda. 1994. "Chicano Studies Proposal Rejected." *Santa Barbara News Press*, June 17: B1.

Burns, Sarah. 2011. *The Central Park Five: A Chronicle of a City Wilding*. New York: Knopf.

Busto, Rudy, Al Camarillo, Luis Fraga, James Leckie, Gerald Lopez, Yvonne Maldonado, Miguel Méndez, Fernando Mendoza, Amado Padilla, Jerry Porras, William Rhine, Lora Romero, Renato Rosaldo, Ramón Saldívar, Guadalupe Valdés, and Yvonne Yabro-Bejararano. 1994a. "Chicano Faculty Members Criticize Firing of Burciaga." *Stanford Daily*, April 19.

———. 1994b. "Chicano Faculty Members Ask for Care for Protestors, Support Their Demands." *Stanford Campus Report*, May 11.

Butler, Judith. 1997. *Excitable Speech: A Politics of the Performative*. New York: Routledge.

Buxi, Arjun. 2011. "Fasting as Dissent: Examining the Body Discourses and Publicity of Mahatma Gandhi and Irom Sharmila." Master's thesis, California State University, Chico.

Bynum, Carole W. 1987. *Holy Feast and Holy Fast: The Religious Significance of Food to Medieval Women*. Berkeley: University of California Press.

Callahan, Manolo. 2004. "Zapatismo Beyond Chiapas." In *Globalize Liberation: How to Uproot the System and Build a Better World*, edited by David Solnit, 217–28. San Francisco: City Lights Books.

———. 2012. "In Defense of Conviviality and the Collective Subject." *Polis: Revista Latinoamericana* 33: 1–27, https://polis.revues.org/8432.

Camarillo, Alberto. 1979. *Chicanos in a Changing Society: From Mexico Pueblos to American Barrios in Santa Barbara and Southern California, 1848–1930*. Cambridge, MA: Harvard University Press.

———. 2009. "Blacks, Latinos, and the New Racial Frontier in American Cities of Color: California's Emerging Minority-Majority Cities." In *African American Urban History Since World War II*, edited by Kenneth Kusmer and Joe Trotter, 39–59. Chicago: University of Chicago Press.

Caputo, Philip. 2005. *13 Seconds: A Look Back at the Kent State Shootings*. New York: Chamberlin.

Carrasco, Davíd. 1999. *City of Sacrifice: The Aztec Empire and the Role of Violence in Civilization*. Boston: Beacon.

Carrigan, Ana. 2005. *Salvador Witness: The Life and Calling of Jean Donovan*. Maryknoll, NY: Orbis.

Casillas, Arnulfo. 1986. "Symposium: UCSB Chicano Political Development—The Roots of El Congreso," May 2 (unpublished paper). Alma Flores personal collection.

Casper, Gerhard. 2014. *The Winds of Freedom: Addressing Challenges to the University*. New Haven, CT: Yale University Press.

Castañeda, Antonia. 1993. "Sexual Violence in the Politics and Policies of Conquest: Amerindian Women and the Spanish Conquest of Alta California." In *Building with Our Hands: New Directions in Chicana Studies*, edited by Adela de la Torre and Beatríz Pasquera, 15–33. Berkeley: University of California.

Celis III, William. 1994. "Navy Settles a Fraud Case on Stanford Research Costs." *New York Times*, October 19. www.nytimes.com/1994/10/19/us/navy-settles-a-fraud-case-on-stanford-research-costs.html.

Ceniceros, Roberto. 1993. "Jubilant Strikers End Fast." *San Gabriel Valley Tribune*, June 8.

Cerna, Lucía, and Mary Jo Ignoffo. 2014. *La Verdad: A Witness to the Salvadoran Martyrs*. Maryknoll, NY: Orbis.

Chabrán, Richard. 1993. "Chicano Studies Trapped in UCLA's Ghetto." *Daily Bruin*, May 3.

Chandrasekaran, Rajiv. 1994. "Budget Cuts Force Burciaga from Job." *Stanford Daily*, April 1.

Chang, Jeff. 2005. *Can't Stop, Won't Stop: A History of the Hip-Hop Generation*. New York: Picador.

Chappell, Marisa. 2010. *The War on Welfare: Family, Poverty, and Politics in Modern America*. Philadelphia: University of Pennsylvania Press.

Chattarjee, Piya, and Sunaina Maira, eds. 2014. *The Imperial University: Academic Repression and Scholarly Dissent*. Minneapolis: University of Minnesota Press.

Chávez, Leo. 2013. *The Latino Threat Narrative: Constructing Immigrants, Citizens, and the Nation*. Stanford: Stanford University Press.

Chávez, Lydia. 1998. *The Color Bind: California's Battle to End Affirmative Action*. Berkeley: University of California Press.

Chávez-García, Miroslava. 2006. *Negotiating Conquest: Gender and Power in California, 1770s to 1880s*. Tucson: University of Arizona Press.

Cheney, Lynne. 1988. "The Stanford Reading List Debate." *Washington Post*, February 16: A19.

Chinchilla, Norma, Nora Hamilton, and James Loucky. 2009. "The Sanctuary Movement and Central American Activism in Los Angeles." *Latin American Perspectives* 36 (6): 101–26.

Chomsky, Noam. 1999. *The New Military Humanism*. Monroe, ME: Common Courage.

Chronicle of Higher Education. 1990. "Proposal to Revise Chicano Studies Divides UCLA." April.

Churchill, Lindsey. 2009. "Transnational Alliances: Radical U.S. Feminist Solidarity and Contention with Latin America, 1970–1989." *Latin American Perspectives* 36 (6): 10–26.

Churchill, Ward. 1997. *A Little Matter of Genocide: Holocaust and Denial in the Americas, 1492 to the Present*. San Francisco: City Lights.

Churchill, Ward, and Jim Vander Wall. 1990. *Agents of Repression: The FBI's Secret Wars Against the Black Panther Party and the American Indian Movement*. Boston: South End.

Clark, Paul. 2007. "No Fish Story: Sandwich Saved His McDonalds." *USA Today*, February 20. http://usatoday30.usatoday.com/money/industries/food/2007-02-20-fish2-usat_x.htm.

Cohen, Robert. 1993. *When the Old Left Was Young: Student Radicals and America's First Mass Student Movement, 1929–1941*. New York: Oxford University Press.

———. 2009. *Freedom's Orator: Mario Savio and the Radical Legacy of the 1960s.* New York: Oxford University Press.

———. 2014. *The Essential Mario Savio: Speeches and Writings That Changed America.* Berkeley: University of California Press.

Cole, Sally. 1991. "Beyond Recruitment and Retention: The Stanford Experience." In *The Racial Crisis in American Higher Education*, edited by Philip G. Altbach and Kofi Lomotey, 213–32. Albany: State University of New York Press.

Coleman, Monica. 2008. *Making a Way Out of No Way: A Womanist Theology.* Minneapolis: Fortress.

Collins, Chuck. 2012. *99 to 1: How Wealth Inequality Is Wrecking the World and What We Can Do About It.* San Francisco: Berrett-Koehler.

Collins, Chuck, and Felice Yeskel. 2005. *Economic Apartheid in America: A Primer on Economic Inequality in America.* New York: New Press.

Collins, Randall. 1979. *The Credential Society: An Historical Sociology of Education and Stratification.* New York: Academic Press.

———. 2004. *Interaction Ritual Chains.* Princeton, NJ: Princeton University Press.

Collisson, Craig. 2008. "The Fight to Legitimize Blackness: How Black Students Changed the University." PhD dissertation, University of Washington.

Comesaña Amado, Pablo. 1993a. "Otra marcha por un dpto. de estudios Chicanos." *La Opinion*, May 22.

———. 1993b. "Estudiantes y profesor de UCLA en huelga de hambre." *La Opinion*, May 26.

Cone, James. 2011. *The Cross and the Lynching Tree.* Maryknoll, NY: Orbis.

Cook, Sherburne. 1976. *The Population of California Indians, 1769–1970.* Berkeley: University of California Press.

Cornfield, Jerry. 1994a. "Viva La Huelga: UCSB Students Fast for Respect for Latinos, Chicanos, and Their Culture." *Santa Barbara Independent*, May 5–12: 29, 31.

———. 1994b. "Part-Time or Full-Time? Dispute Over UCSB Chicano Studies Professors Pits Department Chair and Students Against Administration and Faculty." *Santa Barbara Independent*, June 23–30.

Costello, Frank J. 1995. *Enduring the Most: The Life and Death of Terence MacSwiney.* Kerry, Ireland: Brandon.

Cousins, Peter. 1994. "Flicks Was Inappropriate Forum for Political Film." *Stanford Daily*, May 3.

Cranford, Cynthia. 1998. "Gender and Citizenship in the Restructuring of Janitorial Work in Los Angeles." *Gender Issues* 16 (4): 25–51.

———. 2001. "Labor, Gender, and the Politics of Citizenship: Organizing Justice for Janitors in Los Angeles." PhD dissertation, University of Southern California.

Crossan, John Dominic. 2008. *God and Empire: Jesus Against Rome, Then and Now.* New York: Harper One.

———. 2009. *Jesus: A Revolutionary Biography.* New York: Harper One.

Daily Bruin. 1992. "Chicano Studies Growing Pains." April, n.d.

———. 1993a. "Quote of the Day—Chancellor Charles Young." May 28.

———. 1993b. "They Feast, We Fast." June 1.

Daily Nexus. 1994. "Campus Group Threatens Hunger Strike Due to University Cutbacks." April 18: 1.

Dalton, John Frederick. 2003. *The Moral Vision of César Chávez.* Maryknoll, NY: Orbis.

Danaher, Kevin. 1994. *Fifty Years Is Enough: The Case Against the World Bank and International Monetary Fund.* Boston: South End.

Danner, Mark. 1993. *The Massacre at El Mozote.* New York: Vintage.

D'Arcy, Steven. 2014. *Languages of the Unheard: Why Militant Protest Is Good for Democracy.* London: Zed.

Davis, Angela Y. 2005. *Abolition Democracy: Beyond Empire, Prisons, and Torture.* New York: Seven Stories.

———. 2010. *Are Prisons Obsolete?* New York: Seven Stories.

Davis, Margaret. 2007. *The Culture Broker: Franklin Murphy and the Transformation of Los Angeles.* Berkeley: University of California Press.

Davis, Margo, and Roxanne Nilan. 1989. *The Stanford Album: A Photographic History, 1885–1945.* Stanford, CA: Stanford University Press.

Davis, Mike. 2002. "Burning Too Few Illusions." *Left Turn*, July 14. www.leftturn.org /burning-too-few-illusions.

de Alba, Gaspar. 1998. *Chicano Art Inside/Outside the Master's House: Cultural Politics and the CARA Exhibition.* Austin: University of Texas Press.

De Andreis, Yvette. 1990a. "Faculty, Students Call for Upgrading UCLA's Chicano Studies Program." *UCLA Today*, May 28–June 7: 1, 8.

———. 1990b. "New Support Pledged to Chicano Studies." *UCLA Today*, August 25–September 2.

Dear, Michael. 2000. *The Postmodern Urban Condition.* Oxford, UK: Blackwell.

Delgado Bernal, Dolores. 1998. "Grassroots Leadership Reconceptualized: Chicana Oral Histories and the 1968 East Los Angeles School Blowouts." *Frontiers: A Journal of Women's Studies* 19 (2): 113–42.

Deverell, William. 2004. *Whitewashed Adobe: The Rise of Los Angeles and the Remaking of Its Mexican Past.* Berkeley: University of California Press.

Díaz, Olivia, Yvette Espinoza, Ann-Marie Gallegos, Lisa Gallegos, Elsa Garcia, Leyda Garcia, Amanda Navar, Ben Olguín, Juan Antonio Puyol, Gloria Sánchez, Lubia Sánchez, Laura Uribarri (representing 21 other students). 1994. "Behavior During Screening Called 'Racist, Frightening.'" *Stanford Campus Report*, May 4.

Dickson, Edward. 1955. *University of California at Los Angeles: Its Origins and Formative Years*. Los Angeles: Friends of the UCLA Library.

Dinh, Thy. 1990. "Protestors Rally at Campbell Hall, Young's Office over AAP Move." *Daily Bruin*, June 7.

Dixon, W. C. 1999. "Hunger Strikes: Preventing Harm to Students." *Journal of American College Health* 48 (2): 87–90.

Doyle, Miranda. 1994. "Talks Reach Stalemate: Hunger Strike Continues." *Stanford Daily*, May 6.

D'Souza, Dinesh. 1991. *Illiberal Education: The Politics of Race and Sex on Campus*. New York: Free Press.

Du Bois, W. E. B. 1935. *Black Reconstruction*. New York: Russel and Russel.

Dundjerski, Marina. 2011. *UCLA: The First Century*. Los Angeles: Third Millennium.

Dunne, John Gregory. 2007. *Delano: The Story of the California Grape Strike*. Berkeley: University of California Press.

Dworkin, Andy. 1994. "Chicano Students Begin Fast." *Stanford Daily*, May 5.

Early, Steve. 2011. *The Civil Wars in U.S. Labor: Birth of a New Workers Movement or Death Throes of the Old?* Chicago: Haymarket.

Easwaran, Eknath. 2011. *Gandhi the Man: How One Man Changed Himself to Change the World*. Tomales, CA: Nilgiri Press.

Edsall, Thomas, and Mary Edsall. 1991. *Chain Reaction: The Impact of Race, Rights, and Taxes on American Politics*. New York: Norton.

Elbaum, Max. 2002. *Revolution in the Air: Sixties Radicals Turn to Lenin, Mao, and Che*. London: Verso.

Ellman, Deborah, Lorena Parlee, and Lenny Bourin. 1992. *No Grapes*. Keene, CA: United Farm Workers. VHS tape.

Ellmann, Maud. 1993. *The Hunger Artists: Writing, Starving, and Imprisonment*. Cambridge, MA: Harvard University Press.

Enriquez, Sam. 1992. "Member of CSUN Faculty Charges Bias in Suit Against UC." *Los Angeles Times*, September 26. http://articles.latimes.com/1992-09-26/local/me-1047_1_santa-barbara.

Epting, Charles. 2013. *University Park, Los Angeles: A Brief History*. Charleston, SC: The History Press.

Erikson, Erik H. 1993. *Gandhi's Truth: On the Origins of Militant Nonviolence*. New York: Norton.

Ervin, Donovan. 2011. "We Shall Overcome: The Anti-Apartheid Movement and Its Effects on the Stanford Community." Master's thesis, Stanford University.

Escobar, Edward J. 1999. *Race, Police, and the Making of a Political Identity: Mexican Americans and the Los Angeles Police Department, 1900–1945*. Berkeley: University of California Press.

Estes, Steve. 2006. *I Am a Man! Race, Manhood, and the Civil Rights Movement*. Chapel Hill: University of North Carolina Press.

Estrada, William David. 2008. *The Los Angeles Plaza: Sacred and Contested Space*. Austin: University of Texas Press.

Evans, Jeanne, ed. 2005. *"Here I Am Lord": The Letters and Writings of Ita Ford*. Maryknoll, NY: Orbis.

Fagan, Brian. 2006. *Fish on Friday: Feasting, Fasting, and the Discovery of the New World*. Boston: Basic.

Fanon, Frantz. 2004. *The Wretched of the Earth*. New York: Grove.

Farley, Giles. 1993. "Protestors Gain Legislative Allies." *Daily Bruin*, May 17.

Featherstone, Liza. 2002. *Students Against Sweatshops*. London: Verso.

Fernandes, Deepa. 2011. *Targeted: Homeland Security and the Business of Immigration*. New York: Seven Stories.

Ferreira, Jason Michael. 2003. "All Power to the People: A Comparative History of Third World Radicalism in San Francisco, 1968–1974." PhD dissertation, University of California, Berkeley.

Ferriss, Susan, and Richardo Sandoval. 1997. *The Fight in the Fields: Cesar Chavez and the Farmworkers Movement*. New York: Harcourt Brace.

Fierke, K. M. 2013. *Political Self-Sacrifice: Agency, Body, and Emotion in International Relations*. Cambridge: Cambridge University Press.

Figueroa, Angelo. 1994. "Free Speech? Or Just Plain Cruel Speech?" *San Jose Mercury News*, May 5.

Finn, Peter, and Anne Kornblut. 2011. "Guantanamo Bay: How the White House Lost the Fight to Close It." *Washington Post*, April 23. https://www.washingtonpost.com/world/guantanamo-bay-how-the-white-house-lost-the-fight-to-close-it/2011/04/14/AFtxR5XE_story.html.

Fischer, Louis. 1954. *Gandhi: His Life and Message for the World*. New York: Signet.

Flacks, Richard. 1976. "Making History vs. Making Life: Dilemmas of an American Left." *Sociological Inquiry* 46 (3–4): 263–80.

———. 1988. *Making History: The American Left and the American Mind.* New York: Columbia University Press.

Flamming, Douglas. 2005. *Bound for Freedom: Black Los Angeles in Jim Crow America.* Berkeley: University of California Press.

Fligstein, Neil. 1997. "Social Skill and Institutional Theory." *American Behavioral Scientist* 40 (4): 397–405.

———. 2001. "Social Skill and the Theory of Fields." *Sociological Theory* 19 (2): 105–25.

Folkenflik, David. 1994. "What Happened to Stanford's Expense Scandal?" *Baltimore Sun,* November 20. http://articles.baltimoresun.com/1994-11-20/news/1994 324051_1_stanford-incidental-expenses-auditors.

Frammolino, Ralph. 1993. "Report Rates UC Salaries Low." *Los Angeles Times,* September 23. http://articles.latimes.com/1993-09-23/news/mn-38202_1_executive-pay.

Francoso, Anthony. 2012. "We Have Been Silenced for Much Too Long: Music as Decolonial Resistance." PhD dissertation, University of California, Santa Barbara.

Freire, Paulo. 1994. *Pedagogy of Hope.* New York: Continuum.

———. 2000. *Pedagogy of the Oppressed.* New York: Continuum.

Fried, Sydnee. 2015. "UCSB Joins Million Student March." *Santa Barbara Independent,* November 13. www.independent.com/news/2015/nov/13/ucsb-joins -million-student-march.

Friedberg, Jill, and Rick Rowley. 2000. *This Is What Democracy Looks Like.* New York: Big Noise. VHS tape.

Friedly, Michael. 1990a. "Nationwide Organization Active Here, Students Say." *Stanford Daily,* May 18.

———. 1990b. "League Has Played Little-known Role in Campus Politics." *Stanford Daily,* May 23.

———. 1990c. "League Recruitment Deterred Many." *Stanford Daily,* May 30.

Fuentes Salinas, José. 1993. "Huelga de Hambre . . . la no violencia como arma política." *La Opinión,* July 4.

Galarza, Ernesto. 1964. *Merchants of Labor: The Mexican Bracero Story.* Charlotte: McNally and Loftin.

Galeano, Eduardo. 1997. *Open Veins of Latin America.* New York: Monthly Review.

Gamson, William, and David Meyer. 1996. "Framing Political Opportunity." In *Comparative Social Movements,* edited by Doug McAdam, John D. McCarthy, and Mayer Zald. Cambridge: Cambridge University Press.

Gandhi, Mohandas K. 1993. *An Autobiography: The Story of My Experiments with Truth*. Boston: Beacon.

———. 2001. *Non-Violent Resistance (Satyagraha)*. Mineola, NY: Dover.

Ganz, Marshall. 2009. *Why David Sometimes Wins: Leadership, Organization, and Strategy in the Farm Workers Movement*. New York: Oxford University Press.

García, Alma. 1997. *Chicana Feminist Thought: The Basic Historical Writings*. New York: Routledge.

García, Ignacio M. 1996. "Juncture in the Road: Chicano Studies Since 'El Plan de Santa Barbara,'" In *Chicanas/os at the Crossroads: Social, Economic, and Political Change*, edited by David R. Maciel and Isidro Ortiz, 181–204. Tuscon: University of Arizona Press.

García, Lena. 2015. "St. George Family Youth Center Opens," *Santa Barbara Independent*, October 17. www.independent.com/news/2015/oct/17/st-george-family-youth-center-opens-isla-vista.

García, Mario T. 2000. *Luis Leal: An Auto/Biography*. Austin: University of Texas Press.

———. 2007. *The Gospel of César Chávez: My Faith in Action*. Lanham, MD: Sheed and Ward.

García, Mario T., and Sal Castro. 2011. *Blowout! Sal Castro and the Chicano Struggle for Educational Justice*. Chapel Hill: University of North Carolina Press.

García, Matt. 2012. *From the Jaws of Victory: The Triumph and Tragedy of César Chávez and the Farm Workers Movement*. Berkeley: University of California Press.

Gardner, David. 2005. *Earning My Degree: Memoirs of an American University President*. Berkeley: University of California Press.

Garrow, David. 1981. *The FBI and Martin Luther King Jr.* New York: Penguin.

Gault-Williams, Malcolm. 2004. *Don't Bank on Amerika*. Santa Barbara, CA: M. Gault-Williams.

Geertz, Clifford. 1973. *Interpretation of Cultures*. New York: Basic.

George, Susan. 1991. *The Debt Boomerang*. London: Pluto.

George, Terry. 1996. *Some Mother's Son*. Burbank, CA: Warner Home Video. VHS tape.

Geron, Kim. 1997. "The Local/Global Context of the Los Angeles Hotel-Tourism Industry." *Social Justice* 24 (2): 4–14.

Gill, Lesley. 2004. *The School of the Americas: Military Training and Political Violence in the Americas*. Durham, NC: Duke University Press.

Gilly, Adolfo. 1983. *The Mexican Revolution*. New York: Random House.

Gilmore, Ruth. 2007. *Golden Gulag: Prisons, Surplus, Crisis, and Opposition in Globalizing California*. Berkeley: University of California Press.

Gitlin, Todd. 1980. *The Whole World Is Watching: Mass Media in the Making and Un-making of the New Left*. Berkeley: University of California Press.

Goldberg, David Theo. 2011. *The Threat of Race: Reflections on Racial Neoliberalism*. New York: Wiley.

Goldman, Francisco. 2015. "The Missing Forty-Three: The Government's Case Collapses." *New Yorker*, June 8. www.newyorker.com/news/news-desk/the-missing-forty-three-the-governments-case-collapses.

Golla, Victor. 2011. *California Indian Languages*. Berkeley: University of California Press.

González, Deena J. 2001. "Lupe's Song: On the Origins of Mexican/Woman-Hating in the United States." In *Race in the 21st Century*, edited by Curtis Stokes, Theresa Meléndez, and Genice Rhodes-Reed, 143–58. East Lansing: Michigan State University.

González, Gilbert G. 1990. *Chicano Education in the Era of Segregation*. Philadelphia: Balch.

González, Gilbert G., and Raul Hernández. 2003. *A Century of Chicano History: Empire, Nations, and Migration*. New York: Routledge.

González, Juan. 2000. *Harvest of Empire: A History of Latinos in America*. New York: Viking.

González-Clarke, Chris. 2006. "The Institutional Environment and Organizational Change: The Creation of Stanford's Program in Comparative Studies in Race and Ethnicity." Master's thesis, Stanford University.

Goodwin, Jeff, and James Jasper. 1999. "Caught in a Winding, Snarling Vine: The Structural Bias of Political Process Theory." *Sociological Forum* 14 (1): 27–54.

Gordon, Avery. 2008. *Ghostly Matters: Haunting and the Sociological Imagination*. Minneapolis: University of Minnesota Press.

Gordon, Larry. 1988. "Educator Will Be Inaugurated with Alcohol Charges Pending." *Los Angeles Times*, May 3. http://articles.latimes.com/1988-05-03/news/mn-2169_1_blood-alcohol.

———. 1992a. "UC Regents Raise Student Fees $550." *Los Angeles Times*, January 18. http://articles.latimes.com/1992-01-18/news/mn-301_1_student-fees.

———. 1992b. "Lawmakers Call for Probe of UC Bonuses to Executives." *Los Angeles Times*, April 17. http://articles.latimes.com/1992-04-17/news/mn-711_1_retirement-package.

———. 1992c. "Regents Vote to Reaffirm Gardner's Pension Package." *Los Angeles Times*, April 21. http://articles.latimes.com/1992-04-21/news/mn-578_1_speaker-support.

———. 1993a. "UCLA Plans to Cut, Combine Costly Programs." *Los Angeles Times*, June 4.

———. 1993b. "UCLA Strikers End Fast; Compromise Reached." *Los Angeles Times*, June 8.

———. 2015. "UCSB Overwhelmingly White? Not Anymore." *Los Angeles Times*, January 28. www.latimes.com/local/education/la-me-ln-ucsb-latino-20150127-story.html.

Gordon, Larry, and Marina Dundjerski. 1993a. "Protestors Attack Faculty Center." *Los Angeles Times*, May 12.

———. 1993b. "Budget Threats on Chicano Studies Fail to Budge UCLA." *Los Angeles Times*, May 15.

Gordon, Larry, and Amina Khan. 2009. "UC Regents Approve 32% Student Fee Hike." *Los Angeles Times*, November 20. http:// http://articles.latimes.com/2009/nov/20/local/la-me-uc-cuts20-2009nov20.

Gordon, Larry, and Sonia Nazario. 1993. "Fasters, UCLA Officials Meet to Defuse Protest." *Los Angeles Times*, June 6.

Gottlieb, Robert, Mark Vallanatos, Regina M. Freer, and Peter Dreier. 2005. *The Next Los Angeles: The Struggle for a Livable City*. Berkeley: University of California Press.

Grant, Kevin. 2006. "The Translocal World of Hunger Strikes and Political Fasts, c. 1909–1935." In *Decentering Empire: Britain, India, and the Transcolonial World*, edited by Durba Ghosh and Dane Kennedy. Andra Pradesh, India: Orient Longman.

———. 2011. "British Suffragettes and the Russian Method of Hunger Strike." *Comparative Studies in Society and History* 53 (1): 113–43.

Green, Barbara. 1997. *Spectacular Confessions: Autobiography, Performative Activism, and Sites of Suffrage*. New York: St. Martin's.

Griswold del Castillo, Richard. 1990. *The Treaty of Guadalupe Hidalgo*. Norman: University of Oklahoma Press.

Griswold del Castillo, Richard, and Richard A. García. 1995. *César Chávez: A Triumph of Spirit*. Norman: University of Oklahoma Press.

Gross, James. 1995. *Broken Promise: The Subversion of American Labor Policy, 1947–1994*. Philadelphia: Temple University Press.

Guerin-Gonzáles, Camille. 1994. *Mexican Workers and American Dreams: Immigration, Repatriation, and California Farm Labor, 1900–1939*. Brunswick, NJ: Rutgers University Press.

Guevara, Ernesto. 1985. *Guerrilla Warfare*. Lincoln: University of Nebraska Press.

———. 1987. *Che Guevara and the Cuban Revolution: Writings and Speeches of Ernesto Che Guevara*. Sydney, Australia: Pathfinder.

———. 1994. *The Bolivian Diary of Che Guevara*. New York: Pathfinder.

———. 2000. *The African Dream: The Diaries of the Revolutionary War in the Congo*. New York: Congo.

Gutiérrez, Gustavo. 1988. *A Theology of Liberation*. Maryknoll, NY: Orbis.

Hagstrom, Christine. 1990a. "UCLA Students Protest Threatened Suspension." *Daily Bruin*, April 25.

———. 1990b. "Students Rally for Chicano Studies Today." *Daily Bruin*, May 8.

———. 1990c. "Students Barred from Chicano Studies Meeting." *Daily Bruin*, July 2.

———. 1990d. "Professors Boycott Closed Meeting." *Daily Bruin*, July 15.

———. 1991. "MEChA Garners More Support for Chicano Studies." *Daily Bruin*, January 24.

Hall, Jacquelyn Dowd. 2005. "The Long Civil Rights Movement and the Political Uses of the Past." *Journal of American History* 91 (4): 1233–63.

Hamilton, Andrew, and John Jackson. 1969. *UCLA on the Move, During 50 Golden Years, 1919–1969*. Los Angeles: Ward Ritchie.

Hamilton, Nora, and Norma Chinchilla. 2001. *Seeking Community in a Global City: Guatemalans and Salvadorans in Los Angeles*. Philadelphia: Temple University Press.

Hannigan, Dave. 2010. *Terence MacSwiney: The Hunger Strike That Rocked an Empire*. Dublin: O'Brien.

Harding, Vincent. 2008. *Martin Luther King: The Inconvenient Hero*. Maryknoll, NY: Orbis.

Harris, Paul, Tracy McVeigh, and Mark Townsend. 2013. "How Guantánamo's Horror Forced Inmates to Hunger Strike." *Guardian*, May 4. www.theguardian.com/world/2013/may/04/guantanamo-hunger-strike.

Harris, Richard. 2000. *Death of a Revolutionary: Che's Last Mission*. New York: Norton.

Hartzog, Carol. 1993. "Reflections on Budget Cuts and a Hunger Strike."*ADE Bulletin* 106: 17–21.

Harvey, David. 2005. *A Brief History of Neoliberalism*. New York: Oxford University Press.

———. 2008. "The Right to the City." *New Left Review* 53 (September–October): 23–40.

———. 2012. *Rebel Cities: From the Right to the City to the Urban Revolution*. London: Verso.

Hassett, John and Hugh Lacey, eds. 1991. *Toward a Society That Serves Its People: The Intellectual Contributions of El Salvador's Murdered Jesuits*. Washington, DC: Georgetown University Press.

Hayes-Bautista, David. 2012. *El Cinco de Mayo: An American Tradition*. Berkeley: University of California Press.

Herman, Burt. 1994a. "Spat at Zapata." *Stanford Daily*, May 11.

———. 1994b. "Review Files Complaint Against RF." *Stanford Daily*, May 12.

Hernández, Daniel. 1999a. "Ethnic Studies Supporters Take Barrows Hall." *Daily Californian*, April 15.

———. 1999b. "Weakened Protestor Taken to Hospital." *Daily Californian*, May 7.

———. 1999c. "University, Ethnic Studies Protestors Negotiate Accord." *Daily Californian*, May 10.

Hernández, Roberto. 2012. "Sonic Geographies and Anti-Border Musics: 'We Didn't Cross the Border, the Border Crossed Us.'" In *Performing the US Latina and Latino Borderlands*, edited by Arturo Aldama, Chela Sandoval, and Peter García, 235–57. Bloomington: Indiana University Press.

Hernández, Sandra. 1990. "Students Rally in Support of Saving Major." *Daily Bruin*, April 26.

Herod, Andrew. 2001. *Labor Geographies: Workers and the Landscapes of Capitalism*. New York: Guilford.

Hill Collins, Patricia. 2006. *Black Power to Hip Hop: Racism, Nationalism, and Feminism*. Philadelphia: Temple University Press.

Hixson, Walter. 2013. *American Settler Colonialism: A History*. New York: Palgrave.

Hodge, James, and Linda Cooper. 2004. *Disturbing the Peace: The Story of Father Roy Bourgeois and the Movement to Close the School of the Americas*. Maryknoll, NY: Orbis.

Holloway, John. 1998. "Dignity's Revolt." In *Zapatista! Reinventing Revolution in Mexico*, edited by John Holloway and Eloina Perez, 159–98. London: Pluto.

———. 2010. *Change the World Without Taking Power*, 3rd ed. London: Pluto.

Holmes, Seth. 2013. *Fresh Fruit, Broken Bodies: Migrant Farmworkers in the United States*. Berkeley, University of California Press.

Honey, Michael. 2007. *Going Down Jericho Road: The Memphis Strike, Martin Luther King's Last Campaign*. New York: Norton.

Horne, Gerald. 1997. *The Fire This Time: The Watts Uprising and the 1960s*. New York: De Capo.

Hotel Employees and Restaurant Employees Union (HERE). 1992. *Los Angeles: City on the Edge*. Los Angeles: HERE. VHS Tape.

Houston, Donna, and Laura Pulido. 2002. "The Work of Performativity: Staging Social Justice at the University of Southern California." *Environment and Planning D: Society and Space* 20: 401–24.

Howard-Brook, Wes. 2010. *"Come Out My People!" God's Call Out of Empire in the Bible and Beyond*. Maryknoll, NY: Orbis.

Hughes, Langston. 2004. *Vintage Hughes*. New York: Vintage.

Huntington, Samuel. 2004. *Who Are We? The Challenges to America's National Identity*. New York: Simon and Schuster.

Inda, Jonathan. 2006. *Targeting Immigrants: Government, Technology, and Ethics*. Malden, MA: Blackwell.

Isasi-Diaz, Ada Marie. 1996. *Mujerista Theology*. Maryknoll, NY: Orbis.

Jarecki, Eugene. 2012. *The House I Live In*. New York: Virgil. DVD video.

Jasper, James. 1997. *The Art of Moral Protest: Culture, Biography, and Creativity in Social Movements*. Chicago: University of Chicago Press.

Jencks, Lynn. 2009. "Refusing the Syrophoenician Woman: The Disparate Perspectives of Jesus, Mark, and Feminist Critiques." In *Women in the Biblical World: A Survey of Old and New Testament Perspectives*, edited by Elizabeth McCabe, 71–86. Lanham, MD: University Press of America.

Jenkins, Craig J. 1985. *The Politics of Insurgency: The Farm Worker Movement in the 1960s*. New York: Columbia University Press.

Jenkins, Craig J., and Charles Perrow. 1977. "Insurgency of the Powerless: Farm Worker Movements (1946–1972)," *American Sociological Review* 42(2): 249–68.

Johnson, Gaye. 2013. *Spaces of Conflict, Sounds of Solidarity: Music, Race, and Spatial Entitlement in Los Angeles*. Berkeley: University of California Press.

Jue, Kylie. 2014. "Alberto Camarillo, Founding Director of the CCSRE, Discusses the Origins of the Program as Well as Hopes for the Future." *Stanford Daily*, May 23. www.stanforddaily.com/2014/05/23/albert-camarillo-founding-director -of-ccsre-discusses-the-origins-of-the-program-as-well-as-hopes-for-the -future.

Juergensmeyer, Mark. 2005. *Gandhi's Way: A Handbook of Conflict Resolution*. Berkeley: University of California Press.

Junkerman, Charles. 1994. "Does Burciaga Layoff Call Core Values into Question?" *Stanford Campus Report*, April 6.

Kafka, Franz. 1995. *Franz Kafka: The Complete Stories*. New York: Shocken.

Kaplan, Amy. 2005. "Where is Guantánamo?" *American Quarterly* 57(3): 831–58.

Katz, Sarah. 1994a. "Strike Ends After Three Days, Agreement Reached: Committees to possible Grape Boycott, Chicano Studies, and EPA Community Center." *Stanford Daily*, May 9.

———. 1994b. "Students Rally in Celebration of Strike's End." *Stanford Daily*, May 10.

Kay, Tamara. 2011. *NATA and the Politics of Labor Transnationalism*. Cambridge: Cambridge University Press.

Kelley, Robert. 1981. *Transformations: UC Santa Barbara, 1909–1979*. Santa Barbara, CA: Associated Students.

Kelley, Robin D. G. 2002. *Freedom Dreams: The Radical Black Imagination*. Boston: Beacon.

Kennedy, Donald. 1997. *Academic Duty*. Cambridge: Cambridge University Press.

Kerr, Clark. 2001. *The Gold and the Blue: A Personal Memoir of the University of California, 1949–1967. Volume 1: Academic Triumphs*. Berkeley: University of California Press.

———. 2003. *The Gold and the Blue: A Personal Memoir of the University of California, 1949–1967. Volume 2: Political Turmoil*. Berkeley: University of California Press.

Kettmann, Matt. 2010. "Regents Approve UCSB Expansion." *Santa Barbara Independent*, September 15. http://independent.com/news/2010/sep/16/regents-approve-ucsb-expansion.

Khasnasbish, Alex. 2006. "An Echo that Reechoes: Transnational Activism and the Resonance of Zapatismo." *Ameriquests*. http://dx.doi.org/10.15695/amqst.v2i1.36.

Kimball, Roger. 1990. *Tenured Radicals: How Politics Has Corrupted Our Higher Education*. New York: Harper Perennial.

King, Martin Luther. 1967. *Where Do We Go From Here: Chaos or Community?* Boston: Beacon.

———. 1981. *Strength to Love*. Philadelphia: Fortress.

Klein, Jeffrey. 1993. "Nativist Son." *Mother Jones*, November–December: 3.

Klein, Naomi. 1999. *No Logo*. New York: Picador.

———. 2007. *The Shock Doctrine: The Rise of Disaster Capitalism*. New York: Picador.

Koh, Barbara. 1994. "Chicanos Launch Hunger Strike." *San Jose Mercury News*, May 5.

Kong, Debbie. 1993. "Torres to Oppose Regents." *Daily Bruin*, May 21.

Koopman, Sara. 2008a. "Imperialism Within: Can the Master's Tools Bring Down Empire?" *ACME: An International E-Journal for Critical Geographers* 7 (2): 283–307.

———. 2008b. "Cutting Through Topologies: Crossing the Lines at the School of the Americas." *Antipode* 40 (5): 825–47.

Kornbluth, Jacob. 2014. *Inequality for All*. Beverly Hills, CA: Anchor Bay. DVD video.

Kriho, Laura. 2014. "Ethnic Studies Celebrates Key Milestone at CU-Boulder," *Colorado Arts and Sciences Magazine* (December 15). https://artsandsciences.colorado.edu/magazine/2014/12/ethnic-studies-celebrates-key-milestone-at-cu-boulder/.

Krueger, Colleen. 1994. "Asian American Studies Protest Disrupts Faculty Senate." *Stanford Daily*, May 13.

Kurashige, Scott. 2008. *The Shifting Grounds of Race: Black and Japanese Americans in the Making of Multiethnic Los Angeles*. Princeton, NJ: Princeton University Press.

Kurnatz, Murat. 2009. *Five Years of My Life: An Innocent Man in Guantánamo*. New York: Palgrave.

Kwon, Soo Ah. 2013. *Uncivil Youth: Race, Activism, and Affirmative Governmentality*. Durham, NC: Duke University Press.

LaBotz, Dan. 1992. *Mask of Democracy: Labor Suppression in Mexico Today*. Boston: South End.

LaFeber, Walter. 1993. *Inevitable Revolutions: The United States in Central America*. New York: Norton.

La Gente. 1990. "State of Aztlán." May 1990.

Laslett, John. 2012. *Sunshine Was Never Enough: Los Angeles Workers, 1880–2010*. Berkeley: University of California Press.

Lassalle-Klein, Robert. 2014. *Blood and Ink: Ignacio Ellacuria, Jon Sobrino, and the Jesuit Martyrs of El Salvador*. Maryknoll, NY: Orbis.

Lee, John. 1993. "UC Meets LA." *LA Weekly*, June 18–24.

Lennon, Joseph. 2007. "Fasting for the Public: Irish and Indian Sources of Marion Wallace Dunlop's 1909 Hunger Strike." In *Enemies of Empire: New Perspectives on Imperialism, Literature, and History*, edited by Eóin Flannery and Angus Mitchell, 19–39. Dublin: Four Courts.

Leonard, Kevin Allen. 2006. *The Battle for Los Angles: Racial Ideology and World War II*. Albuquerque: University of New Mexico Press.

Levin, Michael. 1996. *Dreams of a City: Creating East Palo Alto*. Berkeley: University of California, Berkeley Extension.

Levine, Bettijane. 1993. "Ultimate Sacrifice." *Los Angeles Times*, June 1.

Licón, Gustavo. 2009. "La Hace Unión la Fuerza: MEChA and Chicana/o Student Activism in California, 1967–1999." PhD dissertation, University of Southern California.

Lindenberger, Robert. 1990. *The History in Literature: On Value, Genre, Institutions*. New York: Columbia University Press.

Lipsitz, George. 1998. *The Possessive Investment in Whiteness: How White People Profit from Identity Politics*. Philadelphia: Temple University Press.

Lipsky, Michael. 1968. "Protest as a Political Resource." *American Political Science Review* 62: 1114–58.

Loach, Ken. 2000. *Bread and Roses*. Santa Monica, CA: Lionsgate. VHS tape.

Lodise, Carmen. 2008. *Isla Vista: A Citizen's History*. Create Space.

Loo, Chantal. 1993. "Justice for Janitors Joins UCLA Rally." *Daily Bruin*, May 13.

López, Ronald. 2009. "Community Resistance and Conditional Patriotism in Cold War Los Angeles." *Latino Studies* 7: 457–79.

Los Angeles Times. 1993. "Reassessment, Please." May 13.

Loughran, Christina. 1986. "Armagh and Feminist Strategy: Campaigns Around Republican Women Prisoners in Armagh Jail." *Feminist Review* 23: 59–79.

Loveman, Mara. 1998. "High-Risk Collective Action: Defending Human Rights in Chile, Uruguay, and Argentina." *American Journal of Sociology* 104 (2): 477–525.

Lowen, Rebecca S. 1997. *Creating the Cold War University: The Transformation of Stanford*. Berkeley: University of California Press.

Luh, Jim. 1994. "Casper Discusses Protest at Senate: ASSU Condemns Flicks." *Stanford Daily*, May 10.

Lustig, Jeffrey, and Richard Walker. 1995. "No Way Out: Immigrants and the New California." Occasional paper, Campus Coalitions for Human Rights and Social Justice, Oakland.

Lyman, Richard W. 2009. *Stanford in Turmoil: Campus Unrest, 1966–1972*. Stanford, CA: Stanford University Press.

———. 2011. "Stanford in Turmoil." *Sandstone and Tile* 35 (1): 5–14.

Lynch, Shola. 2013. *Free Angela and All Political Prisoners*. Santa Monica, CA: Lionsgate.

Mabalon, Dawn. 1993a. "Chicano Studies Department Denied." *Daily Bruin*, April 30.

———. 1993b. "Students Rally for Library, Programs." *Daily Bruin*, May 12.

———. 1993c. "Royce Quad Host to Second Rally." *Daily Bruin*, May 13.

———. 1993d. "Students March Silently to Chancellor's Office." *Daily Bruin*, May 14.

———. 1993e. "Protesters Hold Rally, Show Unity." *Daily Bruin*, May 24.

———. 1993f. "Protestors Begin Hunger Strike." *Daily Bruin*, May 26.

———. 1993g. "Students at Irvine, Riverside, Also on Hunger Strikes." *Daily Bruin*, May 27.

————. 1993h. "'Hungry for Justice,' Strikers Continue Fast." *Daily Bruin*, June 7.

Macías, Reynaldo, and Kathy O'Byrne. 2006. "The Engaging Department of Chicano Studies: UCLA in LA." In *Engaged Departments: Moving Faculty Culture from Private to Public, Individual to Collective Focus for the Common Good*, edited by Kevin Kecskes. Bolton, MA: Anker.

Mackey, Robert. 2014. "Advice for Ferguson's Protestors from the Middle East." *New York Times*, August 14. www.nytimes.com/2014/08/15/world/middleeast/advice-for-fergusons-protesters-from-the-middle-east.html?_r=0.

Magnier, Mark. 2011. "In India, Love Tests World's Longest Hunger Strike." *Los Angeles Times*, November 4. www.latimes.com/world/la-fg-india-hunger-striker-20111104-m-story.html.

Maharidge, Dale. 1995. "California Schemer: What You Need to Know About Pete Wilson." *Mother Jones*, November–December. www.motherjones.com/politics/1995/11/california-schemer-what-you-need-know-about-pete-wilson.

Maldonado, David Emiliano Zapata. 2010. "Toward a Student-Initiated Retention Organizing Methodology: A Political History of Retention at UCLA." PhD dissertation, University of California, Los Angeles.

Maldonado-Torres, Nelson. 2008. *Against War: Views from the Underside of Modernity*. Durham, NC: Duke University Press.

Mancillas, Jorge. 1993a. "Huelga de hambre en UCLA." *La Opinion*, May 27.

————. 1993b. "At UCLA, the Power of the Individual." *Los Angeles Times*, June 11.

Mantler, Gerald. 2013. *Power to the Poor: Black-Brown Coalition and the Fight for Economic Justice, 1960–1974*. Chapel Hill: University of North Carolina Press.

Marable, Manning. 1984. *Race, Reform, and Rebellion: The Second Reconstruction of Black America, 1954–1982*. Jackson: University Press of Mississippi.

Marcos. 1996. *Our Word Is Our Weapon: Selected Writings*. New York: Seven Stories.

Margolin, Malcolm. 2003. *The Ohlone Way: Indian Life in the San Francisco-Monterey Bay Area*. Berkeley, CA: Heyday.

Mariscal, George. 2005. *Brown-Eyed Children of the Sun: Lessons from the Chicano Movement, 1965–1975*. Albuquerque: University of New Mexico Press.

Márquez, Yolanda. 2007. "La Universidad con la Promesa del Futuro: A Case Study of the UCSB Chicano Studies Department, 1965–1980." PhD dissertation, University of California, Santa Barbara, Education Department.

Martin, Bradford. 2011. *The Other Eighties: A Secret History of America in the Age of Reagan*. New York: Hill and Wang.

Martínez, Elizabeth. 1998. *De Colores Means All of Us: Latina Views for a Multi-Colored Century*. Boston: South End.

————. 2000. "The New Youth Movement in California." *Z Magazine*, March 1. https://zcomm.org/zmagazine/the-new-youth-movement-in-california-by -elizabeth-martinez.

Martínez, Marilyn. 1995. "Students Begin Fast to Protest Immigration Policies." *Los Angeles Times*, February 1995. http://articles.latimes.com/1995–02–17/local /me-33066_1_illegal-immigrants.

Martínez, Rubén. 1993. *The Other Side*. New York: Vintage.

Martinez HoSang, Daniel. 2010. *Racial Propositions: Ballot Initiatives and the Making of Postwar California*. Berkeley: University of California Press.

Marx, Karl. 1970 [1843]. *A Contribution to the Critique of Hegel's Philosophy of Right*. Cambridge, UK: Cambridge University Press.

Masaover, Steve. 2014. "UC Berkeley's Anti-Apartheid Movement: Setting the Record Straight." *Daily Kos*, www.dailykos.com/story/2014/01/31/1273884/-UC -Berkeley-s-anti-apartheid-movement-setting-the-record-straight#.

Massey, Douglas, and Nancy Denton. 1993. *American Apartheid: Segregation and the Making of the Underclass*. Cambridge: Cambridge University Press.

Matloff, Judith. 2015. "Six Women Murdered Each Day as Femicide in Mexico Nears a Pandemic." *Al-Jazeera America*, January 4. http://america.aljazeera.com /multimedia/2015/1/ mexico-s-pandemicfemicides.html.

Matsuda, Mari, ed. 1993. *Words that Wound: Critical Race Theory, Assaultive Speech, and the First Amendment*. Boulder, CO: Westview.

Matthews, Ann. 2010. *Renegades: Irish Republican Women, 1900–1922*. Cork: Mercier.

Matthiessen, Peter. 2000. *Sal Si Puedes: Cesar Chavez and the New American Revolution*. Berkeley: University of California Press.

Mauer, Marc. 2006. *Race to Incarcerate*. New York: New Press.

Maurin, Peter. 2010. *Easy Essays (Catholic Worker Reprint)*. Eugene, OR: Wipf and Stock.

Mayhall, Laura. 2003. *The Militant Suffrage Movement: Citizenship and Resistance in Britain, 1860–1930*. Oxford, UK: Oxford University Press.

Mazón, Mauricio. 1984. *The Zoot Suit Riots: The Psychology of Symbolic Annihilation*. Austin: University of Texas Press.

McAdam, Doug. 1982. *Political Process and the Development of Black Insurgency, 1930–1970*. Chicago: University of Chicago Press.

————. 1983. "Tactical Interaction and the Pace of Insurgency." *American Sociological Review* 48 (6): 735–54.

————. 1986. "Recruitment to High-Risk Activism: The Case of Freedom Summer." *American Journal of Sociology* 92 (1): 64–90.

McAdam, Doug, John D. McCarthy, and Mayer Zald, eds. 1996. *Comparative Perspectives on Social Movements: Political Opportunities, Mobilizing Structures, and Cultural Framings.* Cambridge, UK: Cambridge University Press.

McAdam, Doug, Sidney Tarrow, and Charles Tilly. 2001. *Dynamics of Contention.* Cambridge, MA: Cambridge University Press.

McArthur, John. 2000. *The Selling of "Free Trade": NAFTA, Washington, and the Subversion of American Democracy.* Berkeley: University of California Press.

McCarthy, John D., and Mayer N. Zald. 1977. "Resource Mobilization and Social Movements—A Partial Theory." *American Journal of Sociology* 82 (6): 1212–41.

McDonnell, Jeanne. 2008. *Juana Briones: of Nineteenth Century California.* Tucson: University of Arizona Press.

McGarry, Fearghal. 2010. *The Rising: Ireland—Easter 1916.* Oxford, UK: Oxford University Press.

McKnight, Gerald. 1998. *The Last Crusade: Martin Luther King, the FBI, and the Poor People's Campaign.* New York: Basic.

McWilliams, Carey. 1939. *Factories in the Fields.* Boston: Little, Brown, and Company.

———. 1946. *Southern California: An Island on the Land.* New York: Duell, Sloan, and Pearce.

MEChA. 1990. "MEChA Position Paper on Chicana/o Studies." *Daily Bruin,* May 29. UCLA CSRC Library Hunger Strike Collection.

MEChA and United Community Labor Alliance (UCLA). 1990. "Proposal for the Establishment of a Chicana and Chicano Studies Department at UCLA." Unpublished document, December. UCLA CSRC Library Hunger Strike Collection.

Medina, Jennifer. 2012. "California Cuts Threaten Status of Universities." *New York Times,* June 1. www.nytimes.com/2012/06/02/us/california-cuts-threaten-the -status-of-universities.

Meeropol, Michael. 1998. *Surrender: How the Clinton Administration Completed the Reagan Revolution.* Ann Arbor: University of Michigan Press.

Mehrotra, Deepti Priya. 2009. *Burning Bright: Irom Sharmila and the Struggle for Peace in Manipur.* New York: Penguin.

Meier, Matt, and Margo Gutiérrez. 2003. *Encyclopedia of the Mexican American Civil Rights Movement.* Westport, CT: Greenwood.

Merl, Jean. 1991. "Stanford President, Beset By Controversies, Will Quit." *Los Angeles Times,* July 30. http://articles.latimes.com/1991-07-30/news/mn-131_1_donald -kennedy.

————. 1992. "UC Chief's Severance Package Under Fire." *Los Angeles Times*, April 3. http://articles.latimes.com/1992–04–03/news/mn-265_1_retirement-package.

Meyer, David, and Nancy Whittier. 1994. "Social Movement Spillover." *Social Problems* 41 (2): 277–98.

Meyer, Josh. 1993. "A Young Believer." *Los Angeles Times*, June 3.

Mieder, Wolfgang. 2010. *Making a Way Out of No Way: Martin Luther King's Sermonic Proverbial Rhetoric.* New York: Peter Lang.

Mignolo, Walter. 2000. *Local Histories/Global Designs: Coloniality, Subaltern Knowledges, and Border Thinking.* Princeton, NJ: Princeton University Press.

Milkman, Ruth. 2006. *L.A. Story: Immigrant Workers and the Future of the U.S. Labor Movement.* New York: Russell Sage Foundation.

Miller, Martin. 1995a. "UCI Police Close Camp, Arrest Hunger Strikers." *Los Angeles Times*, October 30.

————. 1995b. "7 Arrested at UC Irvine Hunger Strike." *Los Angeles Times*, October 30.

————. 1995c. "Vowing to Press Their Demands for Affirmative Action Despite Arrests and Decision of One to Drop Out . . . Strikers Endure." *Los Angeles Times*, November 1.

Miller, Martin, and Greg Hernandez. 1995. "Protesters End Fast, Declare Victory: UCI Hunger Strikers Cite Health Reasons and Pledge by 3 Regents to Seek New Vote on Affirmative Action." *Los Angeles Times*, November 2.

Miller, Martin, and Russ Loar. 1995. "Hunger Strikers at UCI Protest Regents' Policies." *Los Angeles Times*, October 18.

Mirrielees, Edith. 1959. *Stanford: The Story of a University.* New York: G. P. Putnam's Sons.

Mishel, Lawrence, Jared Bernstein, and John Schmitt. 1999. *The State of Working America, 1998–99.* Ithaca, NY: Cornell University Press.

Mitchell, John L. 1991. "Coalition Backs Call for Chicano Studies Dept." *Los Angeles Times*, February 7: B1, 4.

Mitchell, Josh, and Maya Jackson-Randall. 2012. "Student-Loan Debt Tops $1 Trillion." *Wall Street Journal*, March 22. http://wsj.com/article/ SB10001424052702303812904577295930004 7604846.html.

Mizner, David. 2013. "Starving for Justice: From California to Israel, Hunger Strikes Are Breaking Out All Over the World, Because They Work." *The Nation*, December 4. www.thenation.com/article/starving-justice.

Mohr, James C. 1970. "Academic Turmoil and Public Opinion: The Ross Case at Stanford." *Pacific Historical Review* 39 (1): 39–61.

Moore, Ernest Carroll. 1952. *I Helped Make a University*. Los Angeles: Dawson's Book Shop.

Mora, Carlos. 2007. *Latinos in the West: The Student Labor Movement and Academic Labor in Los Angeles*. Lanham, MD: Rowman and Littlefield.

Moraga, Cherríe. 2002. *Watsonville/Circle in the Dirt*. Albuquerque, NM: West End.

———. 2011. *A Xicana Codex of Changing Consciousness: Writings, 2000–2010*. Durham, NC: Duke University Press.

Morales, Sylvia. 2009. *A Crushing Love*. New York: Women Make Movies. DVD.

Moran, Julio. 1991. "UCLA Faculty Panel Split on Chicano Studies Department." *Los Angeles Times*, April 19.

Mora-Ninci, Carlos. 1999. "The Chicano/a Student Movement in Southern California in the 1990s." PhD dissertation, University of California, Los Angeles, Education Department.

Moreno, Marisol. 2009. "Of the Community, for the Community: The Chicana/o Student Movement in California's Higher Public Education, 1967–1973." PhD dissertation, Univeristy of California, Santa Barbara.

Morrison, Danny. 2006. *Hunger Strike: Reflections on the 1981 Hunger Strike*. Dingle, Ireland: Brandon.

Morrison Welsh, Anne. 2008. *Held in the Light: Norman Morrison's Sacrifice for Peace and His Family's Journey of Healing*. Maryknoll, NY: Orbis.

Moss, Candida. 2013. *The Myth of Persecution: How Early Christians Invented a Story of Martyrdom*. New York: Harper One.

Muñoz, Carlos. 1989. *Youth, Identity, and Power: The Chicano Movement*. London: Verso.

Murphy, Cliona. 1989. *The Women's Suffrage Movement and Irish Society in the Early Twentieth Century*. Philadelphia: Temple University Press.

Murphy, William. 2014. *Political Imprisonment and the Irish, 1912–1921*. Oxford: Oxford University Press.

Nair, Neeti. 2009. "Bhagat Singh as 'Satyagrahi': The Limits to Nonviolence in Late Colonial India." *Modern Asian Studies* 43 (3): 649–81.

Najarro, Ilenana. 2012. "What's in a Name: The Founding of El Centro Chicano." *El Aguíla*, September 23. http://stanfordelaguila.com/whats-in-a-name-the-founding-of-el-centro-chicano.

Nazario, Sonia. 1995. "Hunger Strike Marks Union's Split." *Los Angeles Times*, August 8. http://articles.latimes.com/1995-08-08/local/me-32737_1_hunger-strike.

Nelson-Pallmeyer, Jack. 2001. *School of Assassins: Guns, Greed, and Globalization*. Maryknoll, NY: Orbis.

Nepstad, Sharon Erickson. 2004. *Convictions of the Soul: Religion, Culture, and Agency in the Central American Solidarity Movement*. New York: Oxford University Press.

Nepstad, Sharon Erickson, and Christian Smith. 1999. "Rethinking Recruitment to High Risk/Cost Activism: The Case of Nicaragua Exchange." *Mobilization* 4 (1): 25–40.

Nevin, Donal. 2006. *James Connolly: A Full Life*. Dublin: Gill and MacMillan.

Nevins, Joseph. 2002. *Operation Gatekeeper: The Rise of the "Illegal Alien" and the Remaking of the U.S.-Mexico Boundary*. New York: Routledge.

Newfield, Chris. 2008. *Unmaking the Public University: The 40-Year Assault on the Middle Class*. Cambridge: Harvard University Press.

Ng, Bernice. 1999. "Support, Opposition for Protest." *Daily Californian*, April 15.

Nicholas, Jane. 2008. "Hunger Politics: Toward Seeing Voluntary Self-Starvation as an Act of Resistance." *Third Space: A Journal of Feminist Theory and Culture* 8(1). http://journals.sfu.ca/thirdspace/index.php/journal/article/viewArticle/nicholas.

Nicholls, Walter. 2013. *The DREAMers: How the Undocumented Youth Movement Transformed the Immigrant Rights Debate*. Stanford, CA: Stanford University Press.

Noone, Judith M. 1995. *The Same Fate as the Poor*. Maryknoll, NY: Orbis.

Noorani, A. G. 2001. *The Trial of Bhagat Singh: Politics of Justice*. New York: Oxford.

Normark, Don. 1999. *Chávez Ravine, 1949: A Los Angeles Story*. San Francisco: Chronicle.

O'Carroll, Eoin. 2011. "Political Misquotes: The 10 Most Famous Things Never Said." *Christian Science Monitor*, June 3. www.csmonitor.com/USA/Politics/2011/0603 /Political-misquotes-The-10-most-famous-things-never-actually-said/First -they-ignore-you.-Then-they-laugh-at-you.-Then-they-attack-you.-Then-you -win.-Mohandas-Gandhi.

Ó Gráda, Cormac. 2009. *Famine: A Short History*. Princeton, NJ: Princeton University Press.

O'Hearn, Denis. 2006. *Nothing but an Unfinished Song: Bobby Sands, the Irish Hunger Striker Who Ignited a Generation*. New York: Nation.

Olsson, Goran Hugo. 2011. *The Black Power Mixtape, 1967–1975*. Stockholm: Sveriges Television. DVD video.

Omi, Michael, and Howard Winant. 1994. *Racial Formation in the United States*, 2nd ed. New York: Routledge.

Ono, Kent, and John Sloop. 2002. *Shifting Borders: Rhetoric, Immigration, and California's Proposition 187*. Philadelphia: Temple University Press.

Orlanski, Brett. 1994. "To Die For." *Daily Nexus*, May 4: 10.

Orosco, José Antonio. 2008. *Cesar Chavez and the Common Sense of Nonviolence*. Albuquerque: University of New Mexico Press.

Orozco, Cynthia. 1997. "Sexism in Chicano Studies and the Community," in *Chicana Feminist Writings: The Basic Historical Writings*, edited by Alma García, 265–69. New York: Routledge.

O'Toole, Kathleen. 1994. "Faculty, Students Dissect Strike Issues at Teach-in." *Stanford Campus Report*.

Owens, Rosemary Cullen. 1984. *Smashing Times: A History of the Irish Suffragist Movement, 1889–1922*. Dublin: Attic.

Pagán, Eduardo. 2003. *Murder at the Sleepy Lagoon: Zoot Suits, Race, and Riot in Wartime L.A.* Chapel Hill: University of North Carolina Press.

Pardo, Mary. 1984. "A Selective Evaluation of El Plan de Santa Barbara." *La Gente*, March–April: 14–15.

Parlee, Lorena. 1986. *The Wrath of Grapes*. Keene, CA: United Farm Workers. VHS tape.

Parson, Don. 2005. *Making a Better World: Public Housing, the Red Scare, and the Direction of Modern Los Angeles*. Minneapolis: University of Minnesota Press.

Passmore, Leith. 2009. "The Art of Hunger: Self-Starvation in the Red Army Faction." *German History* 27 (1): 32–59.

Pawel, Miriam. 2009. *Union of Their Dreams: Power, Hope, and Struggle in Cesar Chavez's Farm Worker Movement*. New York: Bloomsbury.

———. 2014. *The Crusades of Cesar Chavez: A Biography*. New York: Bloomsbury.

Peace, Roger. 2012. *A Call to Conscience: The Anti-Contra War Campaign*. Boston: University of Massachusetts Press.

Peer, Basarat. 2014. "The Longest Fast." *Al-Jazeera*, March 8. http://america.aljazeera.com/ features/2014/3/the-longest-fast.html.

Pelfrey, Patricia. 2012. *Entrepreneurial President: Richard Atkinson and the University of California, 1995–2003*. Berkeley: University of California Press.

Pérez, Emma. 1999. *The Decolonial Imaginary*. Bloomington: Indiana University Press.

Perez, Mary Anne. 1993. "A Hunger for Change." *Los Angeles Times*, June 6.

Pérez, Richard, and Lorena Parlee. 2014. *César's Last Fast*. Los Angeles: Monkey Mind Media. DVD video.

Perla Jr., Héctor. 2008. "Si Nicaragua Venció, El Salvador Vencerá: Central American Agency in the Creation of the U.S.–Central American Peace and Solidarity Movement." *Latin American Research Review* 43 (2): 136–58.

———. 2009. "Heirs of Sandino: The Nicaraguan Revolution and the U.S.-Nicaraguan Solidarity Movement." *Latin American Perspectives* 36 (6): 80–100.

Perlstein, Rick. 2014. *The Invisible Bridge: The Fall of Nixon and the Rise of Reagan.* New York: Simon and Schuster.

Phillips, Steven C. 1990. *Justice and Hope: Past Reflections and Future Visions of the Stanford Black Student Union, 1967–1989.* Palo Alto, CA: Stanford Black Student Union.

Polletta, Francesca. 2006. *It Was Like a Fever: Storytelling in Protest and Politics.* Chicago: University of Chicago Press.

Porpora, Douglas. 1991. "The Engaged University: How North American Universities Are Following the Example of the University of Central America in San Salvador." Paper presented at August Meetings of the Society for the Study of Social Problems. Cincinnati, Ohio.

Pratt, Mary Louise. 1990. "Humanities for the Future: Reflections on the Western Culture Debate at Stanford." *South Atlantic Quarterly* 89 (1): 7–26.

Pratt, Tim, and James Vernon. 2005. "'Appeal from This Fiery Bed . . . ': The Colonial Politics of Gandhi's Fast and Their Metropolitan Response in Britain." *Journal of British Studies* 44 (1): 92–114.

Prieto, Elvira. 1998. "Education for Social and Political Change." Unpublished paper submitted for Harvard Graduate School of Education, November 27.

Prins, Nomi. 2009. *It Takes a Pillage: An Epic Tale of Power, Deceit, and Untold Trillions.* New York: Wiley.

Pulido, Laura, Laura Barraclough, and Wendy Cheng. 2012. *A People's Guide to Los Angeles.* Berkeley: University of California Press.

Quijano, Anibal. 2000. "Coloniality of Power, Eurocentrism, and Latin America." *Nepantla: Views from the South* 1 (3): 553–80.

Raab, Kelley. 2000. *When Women Became Priests: The Catholic Women's Ordination Debate.* New York: Columbia University Press.

Rae-Dupree, Janet. 1994. "Grad Students Protest Over Lack of Diversity." *San Jose Mercury News*, April 2.

Ramírez, Catherine S. 2009. *The Woman in the Zoot Suit: Gender, Nationalism, and the Cultural Politics of Memory.* Durham, NC: Duke University Press.

Ramírez, Jerry. 1993. "Young's Timing Very Insensitive to Chicana/os." *Daily Bruin*, May 10.

Ramírez, Sarah. 2002. "Borders, Feminism, and Spirituality: Movements in Chicana Aesthetic Revising." In Decolonial Voices: Chicana and Chicano Studies in the 21st Century, edited by Arturo J. Aldama and Naomi H. Quinonez, 223–44. Bloomington: University of Indiana Press.

Ramón, Ana-Christina, and Darnell Hunt. 2010. "Reclaiming UCLA: The Education Crisis in Black Los Angeles." In *Black Los Angeles: American Dreams and Racial Realities*, edited by Darnell Hunt and Ana-Christina Ramón, 382–406. New York: New York University Press.

Ramos, George. 1992. "Plan Unveiled for UCLA Chicano Studies Department." *Los Angeles Times*, January 29: B1.

———. 1993. "Echoes of '60s Ring Through UCLA Protests." *Los Angeles Times*, May 17.

Ramos, Lydia. 1990. "Imperiled Chicano Studies Major to be Saved." *Los Angeles Times*, July 3: B1.

Rana, Bhawan Singh. 2005. *Bhagat Singh: An Immortal Revolutionary of India*. New Dehli: Diamond Pocket.

Ratnesar, Romesh. 1994. "After the Strike, a Clear Winner?" *Stanford Daily*, May 10.

Redmon, Michael. 2010. "Ednah Rich Morse." *Santa Barbara Independent*, November 29. www.independent.com/news/2010/nov/29/ednah-rich-morse.

Rhoads, Robert A. 1998. *Freedom's Web: Student Activism in an Age of Cultural Diversity*. Baltimore: Johns Hopkins University Press.

Rice, Condoleezza. 2010. *Extraordinary, Ordinary People: A Memoir of Family*. New York: Crown.

Riegle, Rosalie. 2013. *Crossing the Line: Nonviolent Resisters Speak Out*. Eugene, OR: Cascade.

Rigenhagen, Rhonda. 1993. *A History of East Palo Alto*. East Palo Alto, CA: Romic Chemical.

Robinson, William I. 2014. "In the Wake of Ayoztinapa, Adonde va Mexico?" *Truthout*, December 8. www.truth-out.org/opinion/item/27862-in-the-wake-of-ayotzinapa-adonde-va-mexico.

Rodney, Walter. 1981. *How Europe Underdeveloped Africa*. Washington, DC: Howard University Press.

Rodríguez, Dylan. 2010. *Suspended Apocalypse: White Supremacy, Genocide, and the Filipino Condition*. Minneapolis: University of Minnesota Press.

———. 2012. "De-provincialising Police Violence: On the Recent Events at UC Davis." *Race and Class* 54 (1): 99–109.

Rogers, Carole G. 2004. *Fasting: Exploring a Great Spiritual Practice*. Notre Dame, IN: Sorin.

Rogin, Michael. 1988. *Ronald Reagan, the Movie*. Berkeley: University of California Press.

Rojas, Fabio. 2007. *From Black Power to Black Studies: How a Radical Social Movement Became an Academic Discipline*. Baltimore: Johns Hopkins University.

Ronfeldt, David, John Arquilla, Graham Fuller, and Melissa Fuller, eds. 1999. *The Zapatista Netwar in Mexico*. Santa Monica, CA: RAND.

Roque Ramírez, Horacio. 2003. "That's My Place! Negotiating Racial, Sexual, and Gender Politics in San Francisco's Gay Latino Alliance, 1975–1983." *Journal of the History of Sexuality* 12 (2): 224–58.

Rosaldo, Renato. 1989. *Culture and Truth*. Boston: Beacon.

Rosenfeld, Seth. 2012. *Subversives: The FBI's War on Student Radicals and Reagan's Rise to Power*. New York: Farrar.

Rosovsky, Henry. 1998. "A Neglected Topic: Professional Conduct of College and University Teachers." In *Universities and Their Leadership*, edited by William Bowen and Harold Shapiro. Princeton, NJ: Princeton University Press.

Roulston, Carmel. 1989. "Women on the Margin: The Women's Movement in Northern Ireland, 1973–1988." *Science and Society* 53 (2): 219–36.

Roy, Arundhati. 2011. "I'd Rather not be Anna." *The Hindu*, October 2. www.the hindu.com/opinion/lead/id-rather-not-be-anna/article2379704.ece.

Ruffin, Herbert. 2014. *Uninvited Neighbors: African Americans in Silicon Valley, 1769–1990*. Norman: University of Oklahoma Press.

Ruiz, Vicki. 1998. *From Out of the Shadows: Mexican Women in Twentieth-Century America*. New York: Oxford University Press.

Russell, Sharman Apt. 2005. *Hunger: An Unnatural History*. New York: Basic.

Ryan, Cheyney. 1994. "The One Who Burns Herself for Peace." *Hypatia* 9 (2): 21–39.

Ryan, Thomas. 2005. *The Sacred Art of Fasting*. Woodstock, VT: Skylight Paths.

Sacks, David, and Peter Thiel. 1996. *The Diversity Myth*. Oakland: Independent Institute.

Sánchez, George. 1993. *Becoming Mexican American: Ethnicity, Culture, and Identity in Chicano Los Angeles, 1900–1945*. New York: Oxford University Press.

Sandos, James. 1985. "Levantamiento! The 1824 Chumash Revolt Reconsidered." *Southern California Quarterly* 67 (2): 109–33.

———. 1991. "Christianization Among the Chumash: An Ethnohistoric Approach." *American Indian Quarterly* 15: 65–89.

Santa Ana, Otto. 2002. *Brown Tide Rising*. Austin: University of Texas Press.

Santa Barbara Independent. 1994. "Hunger Strike Ends with Agreement and Breaking of Bread." May 12.

Santa Barbara News-Press. 1994. "Chicano Studies: UCSB Students Themselves Show Intolerance in Demonstration." November 18.

Sarabia, Saúl. 1993. "Chicano Studies Fight Involves Bigger Issue." *Los Angeles Times*, May 30.

Saxton, Alexander. 1971. *The Indispensable Enemy: Labor and the Anti-Chinese Movement in California*. Berkeley: University of California Press.

Scanlan, Stephen J., Laurie Cooper Stoll, and Kimberly Lumm. 2008. "Starving for Change: The Hunger Strike and Nonviolent Action, 1906–2004." *Research in Social Movements*, edited by Patrick Coy. New York: Emerald. 28: 275–323.

Scharlin, Craig, and Lilia V. Villanueva. 1992. *Phillip Vera Cruz: A Personal History of Filipino Immigrants and the Farmworkers Movement*. Los Angeles: UCLA Labor Center, Institute of Industrial Relations and UCLA Asian American Studies Center.

Schmidt, Randy. 2011. *Little Blue Girl: The Life of Karen Carpenter*. Chicago: University of Chicago Press.

Schrag, Peter. 2004. *Paradise Lost: California's Experience, America's Future*. Berkeley: University of California Press.

Scott, Allen, and Edward Soja. 1996. *The City: Los Angeles and Urban Theory at the End of the Twentieth Century*. Berkeley: University of California Press.

Scott, James. 1985. *Weapons of the Weak: Everyday Forms of Peasant Revolution*. New Haven, CT: Yale University Press.

Segura, Denise. 1999. *Latinos in Isla Vista: A Report on the Quality of Life Among Latino Immigrants*. Santa Barbara, CA: Center for Chicano Studies, UC Santa Barbara.

Sharp, Gene. 1973. *The Politics of Nonviolent Action*. 3 vols. Boston: P. Sargent.

Shaw, Randy. 2008. *Beyond the Fields: Cesar Chavez, the UFW, and the Struggle for Justice in the 21st Century*. Berkeley: University of California Press.

Shiekh, Irum. 1999. *On Strike: Ethnic Studies, 1969–1999*. San Francisco: Fifth Floor. VHS tape.

Shin, Linda. 1999. "Protestors Seize Campbell Hall." *Daily Californian*, April 16.

Sides, Josh. 2003. *L.A. City Limits: African American Los Angeles from the Great Depression to the Present*. Berkeley: University of California Press.

Simmons, William S. 1998. "Indian Peoples of California." In *Contested Eden: California Before the Gold Rush*, edited by Ramón A. Gutiérrez, 48–77. Berkeley: University of California Press.

Singleton, John. 1995. *Higher Learning*. Culver City, CA: Columbia TriStar. VHS tape.

Sirota, David. 2011. *Back to Our Future: How the 1980s Explain the World We Live in Now—Our Culture, Our Politics, Our Everything*. New York: Ballantine.

Sklar, Holly. 1995. *Chaos or Community? Seeking Solutions Not Scapegoats for Bad Economics*. Boston: South End.

Sloan, Cle. 2012. *Bastards of the Party*. New York: Black Power. DVD video.

Smiley, Tavis. 2010. *MLK: A Call to Conscience*. New York: PBS. DVD video.

———. 2014. *Death of a King: The Real Story of Martin Luther King's Final Year*. Boston: Little, Brown.

Smith, Andrea. 2005. *Conquest: Sexual Violence and American Indian Genocide*. Boston: South End.

Smith, Christian. 1996. *Resisting Reagan: The U.S.-Central America Peace Movement*. Chicago: Chicago University Press.

Smith, R. J. 2006. *The Great Black Way: L.A. in the 1940s and the Lost African American Renaissance*. New York: Public Affairs.

Smith, William A. 2004. "Black Faculty Coping with Racial Battle Fatigue: The Campus Racial Climate in a Post-Racial Era." In *A Long Way To Go: Conversations About Race by African American Faculty and Graduate Students*, edited by Darrell Cleveland, 171–90. New York: Peter Lang.

Snow, David, E. Burke Rochford Jr., Steven K. Worden, and Robert D. Benford. 1986. "Frame Alignment Processes, Micromobilization, and Movement Participation." *American Sociological Review* 51: 464–81.

Snyder, James. 1993a. "Silence Strengthens Groups' Demand." *Daily Bruin*, May 17.

———. 1993b. "Hunger Striker Collapses After Four Days of Fasting." *Daily Bruin*, June 1.

Sobrino, Jon. 1990. *Companions of Jesus: The Jesuit Martyrs of El Salvador*. Maryknoll, NY: Orbis.

———. 2003. *Witnesses to the Kingdom: The Martyrs of El Salvador and the Crucified Peoples*. Maryknoll, NY: Orbis.

Soldatenko, Michael. 2005. "Constructing Chicana and Chicano Studies: 1993 UCLA Conscious Students of Color Protest." In *Latino Los Angeles: Transformations, Communities, and Activism*, edited by Enrique C. Ochoa and Gilda L. Ochoa, 246–77. Tucson: University of Arizona Press.

———. 2009. *Chicano Studies: Genesis of a Discipline*. Tucson: University of Arizona Press.

Sotomayor, Frank. 1993. "UCLA Strikers Kept Alive César Chávez's Flame." *Los Angeles Times*, July 1.

Soule, Sarah. 1997. "The Student Divestment Movement in the United States and Tactical Diffusion: The Shantytown Protest." *Social Forces* 75 (3): 855–82.

Spellers, Stephanie. 2006. *Radical Welcome: Embracing God, the Other, and the Spirit of Transformation*. New York: Church.

Spivak, Gayatri. 1988. "Can the Subaltern Speak?" In *Marxism and the Interpretation of Culture*, edited by Cary Nelson and Lawrence Grossberg, 271–313. Urbana: University of Illinois Press.

Stanford Campus Report. 1994. "Chicano Students End 3-Day Fast, Protest, After Accepting Promise to Study Issues." May 11.

Stannard, David. 1992. *American Holocaust: The Conquest of the New World.* New York: Oxford.

Starhawk. 2002. *Webs of Power: Notes from the Global Uprising.* Gabriola, British Columbia, Canada: New Society.

Starr, Kevin. 1990. *Material Dreams: Southern California Through the 1920s.* New York: Oxford University Press.

Stegemann, Ekkehard, and Wolfgang Stegemann. 1999. *The Jesus Movement: A Social History of Its First Century.* Minneapolis: Fortress.

Steinberg, Stephen. 1995. *Turning Back: The Retreat from Racial Justice in American Thought and Policy.* Boston: Beacon.

Stiglitz, Joseph. 2004. *The Roaring Nineties: A New History of the World's Most Prosperous Decade.* New York: Norton.

Stites, Richard. 1978. *The Women's Liberation Movement in Russia: Feminism, Nihilism, and Bolshevism, 1860–1930.* Princeton, NJ: Princeton University Press.

Sue, Derald Wing. 2010. *Microaggressions in Everyday Life: Race, Gender, and Sexual Orientation.* Hoboken, NJ: Wiley.

Suk, Sarah. 1990. "Troubled Major's Future Debated." *Daily Bruin*, April 30.

———. 1992. "Ralliers Call for Chicana/o Studies." *Daily Bruin*, October 5.

Sykes, Charles. 1992. *A Nation of Victims.* New York: St. Martin's.

Takaki, Ronald. 1989. *Strangers from a Different Shore: A History of Asian Americans.* New York: Penguin.

Tarrow, Sidney. 1994. *Power in Movement.* Cambridge, UK: Cambridge University Press.

Tasch, Jacqueline. 2010. *40 Years of Ethnic Studies at UCLA, 1969–2009.* Berkeley: University of California Regents.

Taylor, Charles. 1994. *Multiculturalism: Examining the Politics of Recognition.* Princeton, NJ: Princeton University Press.

Taylor, Verta. 2010. "John D. McCarthy Lifetime Achievement Award: Culture, Identity, and Social Movements: Studying Social Movements as if People Really Mattered." *Mobilization* 15 (2): 113–34.

Taylor, Verta, and Nicole Raeburn. 1995. "Identity Politics as High-Risk Activism: Career Consequences for Lesbian, Gay, and Bisexual Sociologists." *Social Problems* 42 (2): 252–73.

Terborg-Penn, Rosalyn. 1998. *African American Women in the Struggle for the Vote, 1850–1920*. Bloomington: University of Indiana Press.

Tickner, Lisa. 1988. *The Spectacle of Women: Imagery of the Suffrage Campaign, 1907–1914*. Chicago: University of Chicago Press.

Tilly, Charles. 1978. *From Mobilization to Revolution*. Reading, MA: Addison-Wesley.

Tilton, Jennifer. 2010. *Dangerous or Endangered? Race and the Politics of Youth in Urban America*. New York: New York University Press.

Trent, Barbara. 1992. *The Panama Deception*. Los Angeles: Rhino. VHS tape.

Trotsky, Leon. 2010. *The Permanent Revolution: Results and Prospects*. Seattle: Red Letter.

Trounson, Rebecca. 2013. "Cecilia Preciado Burciaga Dies at 67; Longtime Stanford Administrator." *Los Angeles Times*, March 27.

Troy, Gil. 2007. *Morning in America: How Ronald Reagan Invented the 1980s*. Princeton: Princeton University Press.

Turner, Wallace. 1983. "Stanford Liberals Question School's Tie to Hoover Institution." *New York Times*, May 24. www.nytimes.com/1983/05/24/us/stanford-liberals-question-school-s-tie-to-hoover-institution.html.

Tutt, Louise. 1994. "Chair Urged to Resign by Officials." *Santa Barbara News Press*, June 20.

UCLA. 1970. "Violence at UCLA: May 5, 1970—A Report." Chancellor's Commission on the Events of May 5, 1970.

United Nations. 1993. *From Madness to Hope: The 12-Year War in El Salvador—Report of the Commission on Truth for El Salvador*. New York City: United Nations.

University Commission on Minority Issues (UCMI). 1989. *Final Report of the University Commission on Minority Issues*. Stanford, CA: Stanford University Press.

Urrea, Luis Alberto. 2004. *The Devil's Highway*. New York: Little, Brown.

Valadez, Verónica. 2012. "Dancing Amoxtli: Danza Azteca and Indigenous Body Art as Forms of Resistance." Master's thesis, California State University, Northridge.

Valdata, Patricia. 2006. "The Rebirth of D-Q University." *Diverse Issues in Higher Education*, April 20. http://diverseeducation.com/article/5766.

Valdés, Dennis. 2011. *Organized Agriculture and the Labor Movement Before the UFW: Puerto Rico, Hawaii, and California*. Austin: University of Texas Press.

Valles, Colleen. 1994. "Chicano Studies Students, Staff Demand Justice in the Department." *Santa Barbara News Press*.

———. 1995. "Father Accuses County of Racism, Faulty Investigation of Son's Death." *Santa Barbara-News Press*.

———. 1996. "Student Activists Say University Has Not Yet Met Hunger Strike Demands." *Santa Barbara News Press*, May 6.

Vandereycken, Walter, and Ron Van Deth. 1994. *From Fasting Saints to Anorexic Girls: The History of Self-Starvation*. Washington Square, NY: New York University Press.

Vargas, Zaragosa. 2005. *Labor Rights Are Civil Rights: Mexican American Workers in Twentieth-Century America*. Princeton, NJ: Princeton University Press.

Vélez-Ibañez, Carlos. 1996. *Border Visions: Mexican Cultures of the Southwest United States*. Tucson: University of Arizona Press.

Verjee, Aman. 1994. "Burciaga's Last Stand." *Stanford Review*, May 16.

Vernon, James. 2007. *Hunger: A Modern History*. Berkeley: University of California Press.

Villagrán, Elizabeth. 1994. "Woman of Diversity." *San Jose Mercury News*, May 13.

Voss, Kim, and Rachel Sherman. 2000. "Breaking the Iron Law of Oligarchy: Union Revitalization in the American Labor Movement." *American Journal of Sociology* 106 (2): 325.

Wack, Kevin. 1994. "Casper Approached About Asian American Studies." *Stanford Daily*, May 10.

Walker, Richard. 1995. "California Rages Against the Dying of the Light." *New Left Review* 209: 42–74.

Wallace, Nora. 1994. "UCSB Marchers Call for Changes in Chicano Studies Department." *Santa Barbara News-Press*, November 17.

———. 1995. "Father Seeks Clues to Death of Activist Son." *Santa Barbara News-Press*.

Walton, Mary. 2010. *A Woman's Crusade: Alice Paul and the Battle for the Ballot*. New York: Palgrave Macmillan.

Wanamaker, Marc. 2010. *Westwood*. Charleston, SC: Arcadia.

Weber, Clare. 2006. *Visions of Solidarity: U.S. Peace Activists in Nicaragua from War to Women's Activism and Globalization*. Lanham, MD: Lexington.

Weber, Devra. 1994. *Dark Sweat, White Gold: California Farm Workers, Cotton, and the New Deal*. Berkeley: University of California Press.

Wee, Heesun. 1991. "Latino Community Celebrates Chicano Studies Vote." *Daily Bruin*, April 9.

Wenzke, Marissa. 2013. "UCSB Graffiti Targets Undocumented Students." *Santa Barbara Independent*, August 8. www.independent.com/news/2013/aug/08/ucsb-graffiti-targets-undocumented-students.

West, Cornel. 1982. *Prophesy Deliverance: An Afro-American Revolutionary Christianity*. Philadelphia: Westminster.

———. 2004. *Democracy Matters: Winning the War Against Imperialism*. New York: Penguin.

Whalen, Jack, and Richard Flacks. 1989. *Beyond the Barricades: The Sixties Genera-tion Grows Up*. Philadelphia: Temple University Press.

Wheatley, Margaret. 2012. *So Far From Home: Lost and Found in Our Brave New World*. San Francisco: Berrett-Koehler.

Whitfield, Teresa. 1994. *Paying the Price: Ignacio Ellacuría and the Murdered Jesuits of El Salvador*. Philadelphia: Temple University Press.

Will, George. 1994. "'Diversity Police' on Campus." *Baltimore Sun*, February 21. http://articles.baltimoresun.com/1994-02-21/news/1994052027_1_wasc-academics -religious-colleges.

Wilson, John. 1995. *The Myth of Political Correctness: The Conservative Attack on Higher Education*. Durham, NC: Duke University Press.

Wilson, Leila. 1913. *Santa Barbara, California*. Santa Barbara, CA: Pacific Coast.

Wink, Walter. 1999. *The Powers That Be: Theology for a New Millennium*. New York: Doubleday.

Wolff, Edward. 1996. *Top Heavy: The Increasing Inequality of Wealth in America and What Can Be Done About It*. New York: New Press.

Wright, Scott. 2009. *Oscar Romero and the Communion of Saints*. Maryknoll, NY: Orbis.

Wroe, Andrew. 2008. *The Republican Party and Immigration Politics: From Proposi-tion 187 to George W. Bush*. New York: Palgrave.

Xu, Kaibin. 2013. "Framing Occupy Wall Street: A Content Analysis of *The New York Times* and *USA Today*." *International Journal of Communication* 7: 2412–32.

Yager, Edward. 2006. *Ronald Reagan's Journey: From Democrat to Republican*. Lan-ham, MD: Rowman and Littlefield.

Yelles, William. 1994. Letter to editor. *Daily Nexus*, May 5: 4.

Yosso, Tara J. 2006. *Critical Race Counterstories Along the Chicana/Chicano Educa-tional Pipeline*. New York: Routledge.

Yosso, Tara J., and David G. García. 2007. "This Is No Slum! A Critical Race Theory Analysis of Community Cultural Wealth in Culture Clash's *Chavez Ravine*." *Aztlan* 26 (1): 201–20.

Young, Robert. 2003. *Postcolonialism: A Very Short Introduction*. Oxford: Oxford University Press.

Zesch, Scott. 2012. *The Chinatown War: Chinese Los Angeles and the Massacre of 1871*. New York: Oxford University Press.

Zugman Dellacioppa, Kara. 2009. *This Bridge Called Zapatismo: Building Alternative Political Cultures in Mexico, Los Angeles, and Beyond*. Lanham, MD: Lexington.

INTERVIEWS

Alvarado, Tamara. 2012. In-person interview. October 11. San Jose, California.

Alvarez, Milo. 2011a. In-person interview. July 13. Los Angeles.

———. 2011b. Phone interview. August 4.

———. 2014. Personal communication.

Barajas, Salvador. 2011. Phone interview. April 29.

Bernal, Santiago. 2011. In-person interview. November 17. Los Angeles.

Broyles-González, Yolanda. 2011. E-mail communication. May 18.

Camarillo, Alberto. 2012. Phone interview. September 28.

———. 2013. E-mail communication. February 21.

Casper, Gerhard. 2013. Phone interview. February 12.

Cervantes, Angel. 2012. Phone interview. October 14.

Chávez, Bonnie. 2012. Phone interview. January 15.

Cohen, Michael, and Leigh Raiford. 2010. Interview with Michael Frye Jacobsen. October 17. http://hopedespair.yctl.org/michael-cohen-and-leigh-raiford-interview-transcript.

de Necochea, Gladys. 2011. Phone interview. February 28.

Estrada, Leobardo. 2011. In-person interview. November 15. Los Angeles.

Fernández, John. 2011. In-person interview. September 27, 2011. Montebello, California.

Flacks, Dick. 2011. In-person interview. May 3. Santa Barbara, California.

Flores, Alma. 2011a. In-person interview. April 7. Los Angeles.

———. 2011b. In-person interview. April 11. Los Angeles.

Fraga, Luis. 2012. Phone interview. October 23.

———. 2013. Phone interview. January 18.

García, Naomi. 2011. In-person interview. January 13. Delano, California.

Gómez, Ed. 2012. Phone interview. October 15.

González-Clarke, Chris. 2012. In-person interview. October 10. Palo Alto, California.

González Luna, Julia. 2013a. In-person interview. January 31. San Jose, California.

———. 2013b. E-mail communication. February 15.

Gordo, Blanca. 2012a. Phone interview. January 16.

———. 2012b. E-mail communication. March 15.

Green, Geoff. 2011a. In-person interview. January 24. Santa Barbara, California.

———. 2011b. In-person interview. February 7. Santa Barbara, California.

Gutiérrez, Abel. 2011. In-person interview. April 11. Los Angeles.

Gutiérrez, Gabriel. 2011. E-mail communication. June 20.

Gutiérrez, Tino. 2011. In-person interview. January 20, 2011. Long Beach, California.

Harrington, Alison. 2012. Phone interview. October 8.

Hayden, Tom. 2011. In-person interview. October 19. Brentwood, California.

Hernández-Clarke, Gina. 2012. In-person interview. October 11. Palo Alto, California.

Hu-Dehart, Evelyn. 2012. Phone interview.

Kurashige, Scott. 2011. E-mail communication. October 5.

Leckie, James. 2012. In-person interview. October 7. Palo Alto, California.

Leiva, Claudia. 2011. In-person interview. February 18. Ventura, California.

Lomelí, Francisco. 2011. In-person interview. March 1. Santa Barbara, California.

López, Edwin. 2011a. In-person interview. January 10. Santa Barbara, California.

———. 2011b. In-person interview. January 30. Santa Barbara, California.

Macías, Reynaldo. 2011. In-person interview. September 28. Los Angeles.

Mancillas, Jorge. 2011a. Phone interview. November 15.

———. 2011b. Phone interview. November 18.

———. 2011c. Phone interview. November 23.

Márquez, Marisela. 2011. In-person interview. Santa Barbara, California.

Medina, Alma. 2012. Phone interview. October 25.

———. 2013. Phone interview. February 5.

Méndez, Miguel. 2012. Phone interview. October 18.

Mendoza, Jackie. 2011. Phone interview.

Mitchell-Kernan, Claudia. 2011. In-person interview. November 17. Los Angeles.

Montañez, Cindy. 2011. In-person interview. October 4. Los Angeles.

Muñoz, Mike. 2011. In-person interview. February 8. Los Angeles.

Ochoa, Joaquín. 2011. Phone interview. November 10.

Ornelas, Carlos. 2000. In-person interview. Santa Barbara, California.

Ortiz, Vilma. 2011. In-person interview. July 19. Los Angeles.

Prieto, Elvira. 2012. In-person interview. September 23. Palo Alto, California.

Reyes, Leonor. 2013. E-mail communication. May 25.

Rich, Andrea. 2011. In-person interview. November 17. Los Angeles.

Roque Ramírez, Horacio. 2012. In-person interview. October 15. Santa Barbara, California.

Saldívar, Ramón. 2013a. Phone interview. February 5.

———. 2013b. Phone interview. February 13.

Segura, Denise. 2011. In-person interview. May 2. Santa Barbara, California.

Silva, Eva. 2012a. In-person interview. September 25, 2012. Salinas, California.

———. 2012b. In-person interview. October 11, 2012. Salinas, California.

Solórzano, Daniel. 2011. In-person interview. October 24. Los Angeles.

Stewart, Bernadette. 2012. Phone interview. December 19.

Tabrizi, Ali. 2011. In-person interview. October 20. Los Angeles.

Téllez, Michelle. 2011. Phone interview. October 16.

Torres, Benjamin. 2011. In-person interview. February 16. Los Angeles.

Valencia Sherratt, Lisa. 2011. In-person interview. April 28. Santa Barbara, California.

Valenzuela, Abel. 2011. In-person interview. November 17. Los Angeles.

Vásquez, André. 2011. In-person interview. April 28. Santa Barbara, California.

Waugh, Scott. 2011. In-person interview. December 15. Los Angeles.

Wu, Judy Tzu-Chun. 2012. Phone interview. October 12.

Young, Charles. 2011. Phone interview. November 14.

Young, Michael. 2011. In-person interview. February 16. Santa Barbara, California.

Zimmerman, Don. 2011. In-person interview. February 27. Santa Barbara, California.

ARCHIVES AND COLLECTIONS

Alma Flores personal collection

Naomi García personal collection

John Fernández personal collection

Edwin López personal collection

Eva Silva personal collection

Lisa Valencia Sherratt personal collection

UC Santa Barbara El Congreso Hunger Strike Collection, El Centro Arnulfo Casillas

UC Santa Barbara California Ethnic and Multicultural Archives (CEMA)

UCLA Chicano Studies Research Center

INDEX

109, 111, 234n9; Black studies at, 40; Center for Chicano Studies (CCS), 33, 105, 110–113, 116, 121, 147, 235n19, 235n21, 235n25; Chicana/o and Latina/o students at, 103; history of, 107–109; Long-Range Development Plan (LRDP), 121, 153; United Front, 109–110. *See also* Chicano Educational Opportunity Program; El Centro Arnulfo Casillas; El Congreso
University of California, Santa Barbara (UCSB) Chicana and Chicano Studies Department, 32, 104, 110
University of California, Santa Barbara (UCSB) hunger strike, 8–9, 22, 24, 32–35, 45, 104–106, 114–15, 117–56; criticism of, 135–37
University of Colorado, Boulder, 82, 207–208
University of Colorado, Boulder hunger strike, 8–9, 135, 180, 240n83

Valdés, Guadalupe, 189, 248n34
Valencia Sherratt, Lisa, 32, 104*f*, 119, 125–26, 133
Vargas, Zaragosa, 10, 106, 113, 117, 237n39
Vásquez, André, 124–25, 128–29, 140, 143*f*, 150
Vernon, James, 11, 218n30
Vietnam, 41, 207

Vietnam War, 7, 37, 65, 217n18, 220n48, 222n17

War on Drugs, 43, 224n26
Waugh, Scott, 53, 68, 79–81, 93, 95–98, 100–101
Western Association of Schools and Colleges (WASC), 199, 249n45
Western Hemisphere Institute for Security Cooperation (WHINSEC), 5, 216n6
white supremacy, 42–4, 48–49, 60, 108, 214, 225n37
Wilson, Pete, 43–44, 46, 79, 83, 98, 121, 136, 208–209, 225nn34–36, 250n6
Women's Social and Political Union (WSPU), 11–12, 16, 218n32
women's studies, 25, 79, 82, 88

Yang, Henry, 108, 126, 153, 208, 238n59
Young, Charles, 27, 33, 40, 61, 64–67, 86, 93, 96–98, 135, 208, 228n4; UCLA Chicana/o Studies and, 53, 55–56, 70–72, 78–79, 81, 83–85, 98, 158
Young, Michael, 138, 142–43, 153, 208

Zamora, Carlos, 111, 235n20
Zapatista National Liberation Army, 30–31, 47, 78, 99, 125, 169, 213, 217nn25–26, 221n59, 226n40
Zimmerman, Donald, 32, 117, 131, 138, 142, 144–48, 150, 153

ABOUT THE AUTHOR

Ralph Armbruster-Sandoval is an associate professor in the Chicana and Chicano Studies Department at the University of California, Santa Barbara. His work focuses on social movements, racial studies, urban studies, labor studies, and liberation theology. Professor Armbruster-Sandoval's first book, *Globalization and Cross-Border Labor Solidarity in the Americas: The Anti-Sweatshop Movement and the Struggle for Social Justice*, was published by Routledge in 2005. He has been actively involved in struggles for human rights, labor rights, and social justice on a national, statewide, and local level. Professor Armbruster-Sandoval's next project is on brown-black relations and tensions in Los Angeles and Santa Barbara County. He is interested in the Black Lives Matter movement and anti-black racism within the Latina/o community.

ABOUT THE AUTHOR

Missy Sheldrake lives in Northern Virginia with her amazingly supportive husband, brilliant son, and very energetic dog. Aside from filling the role of mom and wife, Missy is a mural painter, sculptor, and illustrator. She has always had a fascination with fairies and a great love of fairy tales and fantasy stories. Call of Sunteri is her second novel. You can see more of her work on her website:
www.missysheldrake.com

Call of Brindelier

KEEPERS OF THE WELLSPRINGS BOOK 3
Coming in 2016